Instructor's Resource
for Coon's
Essentials of Psychology
Ninth Edition

Saundra K. Ciccarelli
Gulf Coast Community College

THOMSON
WADSWORTH

Australia • Canada • Mexico • Singapore • Spain • United Kingdom • United States

0-534-59793-9

For more information about our products, contact us at:
Thomson Learning Academic Resource Center
1-800-423-0563

For permission to use material from this text, contact us by:
Phone: 1-800-730-2214
Fax: 1-800-731-2215
Web: www.thomsonrights.com

Asia
Thomson Learning
5 Shenton Way #01-01
UIC Building
Singapore 068808

Australia
Nelson Thomson Learning
102 Dodds Street
South Street
South Melbourne, Victoria 3205
Australia

Canada
Nelson Thomson Learning
1120 Birchmount Road
Toronto, Ontario M1K 5G4
Canada

Europe/Middle East/South Africa
Thomson Learning
High Holborn House
50-51 Bedford Row
London WC1R 4LR
United Kingdom

Latin America
Thomson Learning
Seneca, 53
Colonia Polanco
11560 Mexico D.F.
Mexico

Spain
Paraninfo Thomson Learning
Calle/Magallanes, 25
28015 Madrid, Spain

CONTENTS

INTRODUCTION TO THE INSTRUCTOR'S MANUAL

The purpose of this manual is to support the unique features of **Essentials of Psychology (9e)** and to facilitate its use. Provided in the manual are behavioral objectives, discussion questions, demonstrations, classroom exercises, role-playing scenarios, journal questions, suggested readings, video and multimedia suggestions, CD-ROM topics, Internet references, InfoTrac keywords, and references for teaching psychology. The brief comments that follow will acquaint you with the text, its ancillaries, and the contents of this manual.

THE TEXT

The content and format of the text reflect a combination of goals. First and foremost, the text is written for students, not for instructors. It attempts to make the reader a **voluntary participant in learning**, rather than a passive and inattentive captive. To achieve this goal, chapters are structured around a unique study/reading format. Also, each chapter includes a section on **practical applications of psychological principles**. It is our hope that the extra effort taken to show students how to apply psychology gives the text an unusual degree of relevancy and impact.

ORGANIZATION

The text consists of 17 topical chapters, a statistics appendix, a glossary, references, and an index. In an introduction that precedes the first chapter, various study skills are presented to students, including the **SQ4R method**. This section is a key to the rest of the text and should be assigned. In addition to giving students a good start and some helpful suggestions, it explains the chapter format and shows how it is designed to foster active learning.

Overall, the ordering of chapters and units was dictated by two concerns. Generally the organization reflects an underlying relationship among topics. But additionally, topics are ordered to balance high interest subjects with drier material. The chapters are quite independent and can be rearranged to suit the needs of various course outlines.

In a typical semester course the pace would be one chapter per week; in a quarter course, two per week. Either arrangement will produce a complete and well-paced course. Instructors who would like more rigor or breadth may want to assign an ancillary selection of readings (see list of references in the Appendix to this manual). However, the **Highlights** that are placed throughout each chapter are intended to serve as in-text "readings" to round out coverage. In most instances, no outside assignments will be necessary for a complete introductory course.

FORMAT

Perhaps the most distinctive aspect of the text is the chapter format, which guides students through an **active reading and information-processing experience**. Each chapter begins with an attention-arousing **Preview** of very high-interest material. Each Preview is accompanied by **Survey Questions,** key questions that guide the student through the topics in the chapter. Both of these features are designed to augment the survey portion of an SQ4R reading approach, but they are no substitute for an actual chapter survey. Students should, therefore, be encouraged to study all topic headings in a chapter and to read the **Chapter in Review** before they begin reading.

Throughout each chapter, the **Survey Questions** are repeated at appropriate places in the text to establish a feeling of dialogue and anticipate student questions. Following each major section of the chapter is a section called **Knowledge Builder**. Each of these sections includes subsections: **Essential Concepts**, key ideas from the previous reading; **Relate**, a short question or questions helping the student relate the material of the previous section to their own lives and experiences; and **Learning Checks** (brief self-quizzes). Learning Checks offer immediate feedback and a chance to do some recitation while reading. Most students will find them helpful enough to use them voluntarily. However, students might be further encouraged if you include some Learning Check questions on quizzes or tests and announce in class that you plan to do so. Included as part of each Learning Check are **Critical Thinking** questions. These questions challenge students to sharpen their thinking skills while pondering various conundrums related to the concepts they are studying. Answers to the Learning Check material, including the Critical Thinking questions, are at the end of each of these sections. The **running glossary** contains precise definitions of closely related concepts.

Highlights provide interesting sidelights to the core discussion. Each Highlight has been carefully placed where it will best mesh with the main body of the text. This placement is reflected in instructions ("see Highlight") that tell readers when to shift to a Highlight. Students should be encouraged to read Highlights when they are directed to—not simply when a box appears in the text. Reading Highlights at the specified points will ensure a smooth and coherent flow of ideas.

After core topics have been covered, each chapter has a **Psychology in Action** section that discusses explicit applications of psychological principles. Alternatively, the Psychology in Action sections offer added information of high personal relevance or practicality. The information presented in Psychology in Action is designed to meet the real needs of students and to bring psychology to life.

Exploring Psychology articles are included in each chapter. Many of these articles in this edition are entirely new, while others include topics from the previous edition presented in a new, more salient way. These articles should not only be informative, but thought-provoking as well.

A detailed, point-by-point **Chapter in Review** follows all of the preceding sections. As mentioned earlier, this summary should be read first, as part of each student's chapter survey. After reading the entire chapter, students should read the summary again to increase comprehension and to consolidate what they have learned.

STUDY GUIDE AND OTHER STUDENT AIDS

STUDY GUIDE

The Study Guide, revised for this edition by Dennis Coon, is designed to help students learn information presented in the text. Students using the Study Guide will find it easy to review in great detail--something many find difficult to do without guidance. Students can also use the Study Guide to test themselves prior to taking in-class quizzes or tests. By using the Study Guide to review and quiz themselves, students can greatly improve the quality of their studying and their classroom performance. Each Study Guide chapter includes the following sections:

☞ **Chapter Overview**—This section is a concise chapter summary, easily incorporated into the SQ4R method of study.

☞ **Learning Objectives**—A list of specific objectives provides a clear, point-by-point statement of learning goals for each chapter. Space is provided with each objective so that students can assess their mastery of each goal. (These same learning objectives appear in this Instructor's Manual, and are also keyed to the questions in the test bank that accompanies the text.)

☞ **Recite and Review**—This is a survey of major terms and concepts. It allows students to assess text reading comprehension and recall of important ideas.

☞ **Connections**—This section consists of matching items Through it and the following sections, students will learn whether or not they really understand the concepts they have read about.

☞ **Check Your Memory**—This section consists of true-false items

☞ **Final Survey and Review**—This section consists of fill-in-the-blank items and provides a final detailed review of the text chapter.

☞ **Mastery Test**—This section contains multiple-choice questions similar to those used in the classroom testing.

Like the text, the study guide is designed to structure learning and to reinforce study skills. Instructors who assign the Study Guide, or who arrange for the campus book store to carry optional copies, will find it is a valuable aid to students.

CHAPTER QUIZZES

Included with this edition is a supplement called *Chapter Quizzes*. This is a collection of quizzes, one quiz per chapter, containing multiple choice questions similar to those found on in-class tests. Each quiz is thirty questions covering the range of topics in the textbook chapter. Students can use the quizzes to practice for tests, to assess their mastery of chapter material, or to identify topics needing more study.

LANGUAGE DEVELOPMENT GUIDE

For many students, differences in language and culture prove to be a barrier to full comprehension. The new *Language Development Guide,* prepared by Robert Moore, helps clarify idioms and special phrases, historical and cultural allusions, and challenging vocabulary found in the text. All terms and phrases in the **Guide** are page-referenced and clearly defined.

COLLEGE SURVIVAL GUIDE: HINTS AND REFERENCES TO AID COLLEGE STUDENTS

The College Survival Guide, Fourth Edition has been revised by Bruce Rowe. This relatively little book provides big help to students in the areas of effective time-management, study tips, test-taking skills, and managing anxiety. This edition includes information on such programs as credit by examination and cooperative education programs, and should be especially useful to first-time college students, students reentering college, and non-native students.

WRITING PAPERS IN PSYCHOLOGY: A STUDENT GUIDE

Ralph and Mimi Rosnow have prepared the Fifth Edition of *Writing Papers in Psychology: A Student Guide*, a very valuable manual that tells students how to write a term paper or research report. This manual includes the new American Psychological Association reference guidelines, a discussion of citation ethics, how to find information, and the use of new research technologies.

CHALLENGING YOUR PRECONCEPTIONS: THINKING CRITICALLY ABOUT PSYCHOLOGY

The second edition of this paperbound book, written by Randolph Smith, helps students strengthen their critical thinking skills. Classic and current issues, such as hypnosis and repressed memory syndrome, are used to illustrate the basic principles of critical thinking.

SUPPLEMENTARY BOOKS, VIDEOS, AND READINGS

CROSS-CULTURAL PERSPECTIVES IN PSYCHOLOGY, Fourth Edition

This is a collection of original articles written by William Price and Rich Crapo. Designed to raise your students' awareness, understanding, and tolerance of other cultures, these readings begin with a question about behavior which is then explored through cross-cultural research.

READINGS IN INTRODUCTORY PSYCHOLOGY

Kathleen McDermott and Henry L. Roediger III have brought together a collection of articles, drawn from newspapers and popular magazines. These articles are highly readable and informative, and should be an ideal way to stimulate discussion.

PSYCHOLOGY: CAREERS FOR THE 21ST CENTURY VIDEO

Wadsworth offers this 5-minute video to adopters by exclusive agreement with the American Psychological Association. It contains a description of the field of psychology and the preparation needed for such a career.

CULTURE AND PSYCHOLOGY: PEOPLE AROUND THE WORLD, Second Edition

Written by David Matsumoto, this book discusses cross-cultural research findings, allowing students to become more culturally aware.

PSYCHOLOGY RESOURCES ON THE WORLD WIDE WEB

This is a concise guide to psychology-related resources on the World Wide Web by Edward Kardas.

MULTIMEDIA ANCILLARIES AND INTERNET RESOURCES

PSYCHNOW! CD-ROM

PSYCHNOW! is an exciting new CD-based multimedia presentation. Created by Joel Morgovsky, Lonnie Yandell, Elizabeth Lynch, and project consultant Dennis Coon, this software makes it possible for students to interactively explore psychology. *PSYCHNOW!* has an easy-to-use graphical interface, with on-screen menus and instructions.

The core of *PSYCHNOW!* is a collection of 39 learning modules (listed at the end of Appendix A of this manual) in eight subject areas of psychology. Each module includes: an interactive exploration of a topic, demonstrations, games, experiments, and full audio and video presentations. A glossary of over 500 terms is also included. The modules that relate to each of the eighteen chapters of the Eighth Edition are listed at the end of each chapter of this manual.

PSYCLIT AND CLINPSYC

PsycLIT and ClinPSYC are CD-ROM databases produced by the American Psychological Association. PsycLIT is a two-disc set with references to journal articles from 1974 to the present, with an additional database of book chapters and books published since 1987. ClinPSYC is a similar collection of information related to abnormal and clinical psychology.

WEB STUDY CENTER FOR ESSENTIALS OF PSYCHOLOGY, Ninth Edition

Wadsworth Publishing Company has a website established for this text. It can be located at the following address on the Internet: http://info.wadsworth.com/coonessentials9

The Study Center address for each chapter in the text will be listed at the end of each chapter in this instructor's manual. The Study Center has a link to *InfoTrac*, as well as online quizzes for each chapter, a faculty lounge virtual gathering place, hot topics for each month, a research and teaching showcase featuring abstracts of key presentations at meetings, abridged journal articles, and other teaching/research related material.

INFOTRAC COLLEGE EDITION

InfoTrac College Edition is an online library that is available with each new copy of a Wadsworth Psychology text. InfoTrac gives access to full articles (not abstracts) from more than 500,000 scholarly and popular periodicals from the last four years. See Appendix B for a guide to using InfoTrac. Subject guides or key words for this online service are listed at the end of each chapter of this instructor's manual. These terms are by no means the only terms useful in a search of this library, but should give the instructor or student a good start in finding articles relevant to each chapter.

PSYCINFO

The American Psychological Association maintains this site, which contains summaries of scientific literature in psychology. It is similar to *Psychological Abstracts*, the journal of abstracts in the field.

VIDEOS

THE BRAIN

Available with the Ninth Edition is a video from the PBS series, **The Brain**. This collection of thirty modules (2-11 minutes each) is edited from the original eight-hour presentation. This Peabody Award-winning series artfully blends **interviews with researchers and dramatic reenactments of landmark cases in medical history**. Programs explain and illustrate the brain's basic operating principles, its major structural and functional systems, and the biological foundations of emotion, memory, and consciousness. Celebrity case studies add human interest.

Programs from which the teaching modules are drawn include:
1. The Enlightened Machine
2. Vision and Movement
3. Rhythms and Drives
4. Stress and Emotion
5. Learning and Memory
6. The Two Brains
7. Madness
8. States of Mind

The modules will be sent to adopters on two 2-hour cassettes (VHS or Beta). An **Instructor's Manual** provides suggestions for classroom use. The original series was prepared by WNET/New York for Annenberg CPB.

THE MIND

This valuable collection consists of 38 video teaching modules from the PBS series *The Mind*. The modules range from about 3 minutes to 12 minutes in length and they address topics spanning the entire introductory course. A **Faculty Guide**, prepared by Frank J. Vattano, matches video segments with appropriate text chapters. Although they are brief, the modules are highly interesting and informative. They offer a convenient way for students to see examples of the behavioral phenomena they are studying. For more information, please contact your Wadsworth Publishing representative.

THE DISCOVERING PSYCHOLOGY VIDEO SERIES

This series contains 26 half-hour programs designed to encourage personal development and stimulate curiosity and creative thinking. New developments are measured against historical breakthroughs, and theories are tested by the recent findings of leading researchers. Superior computer animation and documentary footage of classic experiments help the viewer better understand psychological concepts and relate them to today's complex world. For more information, please contact your Wadsworth Publishing representative.

PCR: FILMS AND VIDEOS IN THE BEHAVIORAL SCIENCES

Pennsylvania State University has accumulated the world's largest collection of films and videos on human behavior. See the Appendix for the address to order materials.

Other videotapes may be obtained from the **Wadsworth Film and Video Library** for Introductory Psychology. Contact Wadsworth (800-354-0092) for information.

TRANSPARENCIES

Transparencies are among the most useful of all visual aids for the classroom. Tables, graphs, charts, and drawings can provide a wealth of information that otherwise would be difficult to present in class. An excellent set of **150 transparencies** to accompany this edition of **Essentials of Psychology** is available. These colorful transparencies are already on acetate so they are ready to use and will allow you to present, discuss, and review important concepts with greater visual impact and without laborious use of the chalkboard. An index of these transparencies is provided in Appendix A of this manual.

TEST BANK

The **Ninth Edition Test Bank,** published under separate cover and revised by Karen Wolford, contains more than four thousand multiple-choice questions. Items are organized to correspond to the learning objectives contained in this **Instructor's Manual**. In addition, items are page-referenced and classified according to type (factual, conceptual, applied). **All test items are incorporated into ExamView®, a test-generation program that is available on request.**

COMPUTERIZED TESTING

The computerized testing software, ExamView®, is free to qualified adopters of the Ninth Edition. This is an easy-to-use test generation program with complete documentation. It allows you to preview and edit existing test questions, select or randomly generate questions, and add new ones. For test security, you can scramble test items and print up to 99 versions of a test. *ExamView* offers both a Quick Test Wizard and an Online Test Wizard that guide you step-by-step through the process of creating tests. *ExamView* shows the test your are creating on the screen exactly as it will print or display online. Using a database, you can build tests of up to 250 questions using up to 12 question types. *ExamView's* complete word processing capabilities also allow you to enter an unlimited number of new questions or edit existing questions.

THE INSTRUCTOR'S MANUAL

This instructor's manual provides resources that can enrich the experiences of the student and make it easier for the instructor to provide the variety that successful teaching requires. Since students come to psychology with varied backgrounds and learning styles, a single mode of presentation cannot adequately meet their needs. This manual provides, for each chapter, ideas for fruitful discussion, classroom exercises, role-playing suggestions, journal questions, and more. There are also suggestions for films and readings. The learning objectives provide the instructor and students with a detailed outline of each chapter.

Another goal of this manual is to foster interactive dialogue with and among students, rather than continuous professorial monologues. This engages the part of teaching that is an art. Interactive instruction can make teaching an emotional dialogue between you and your students. That is, instructors can be facilitators of change and insight, as well as disseminators of knowledge. When a course is maximally effective, students change cognitively, affectively, and behaviorally. The way that you teach will be affected by your goals for the class, by your skills, and by your students. Each chapter of this manual provides you with the following ten categories of ideas: **Learning Objectives, Discussion Questions, Lecture Enhancements, Role-playing Scenarios, Value Clarification Statements, One-Minute Motivators, Broadening Our Cultural Horizons, Supplemental Activities, Journal Questions, Suggestions for Further Reading, Media Suggestions, and Computer and Internet Resources**. An overview of each category follows, along with suggestions for using the information you will find there.

INSTRUCTIONAL MATERIALS

LEARNING OBJECTIVES

Objectives follow the organization of the chapters and state in concrete terms what students should know when they have learned the material presented in the textbook. The objectives not only communicate to the students what they should learn from reading the text, but also serve as a way to review for tests since they clearly identify the important points in each chapter. **It is worth mentioning again that items in the Student Study Guide and the Test Bank are now organized according to these learning objectives.** An instructor should provide students with a copy of the objectives for each assigned chapter.

DISCUSSION QUESTIONS

These questions ask your students to go beyond a description of the concepts covered in each chapter. Whether your class consists of hundreds of students in a large lecture hall or a dozen students in a small, cozy seminar lounge, these questions can be discussed by the class as a whole, in small groups, or by pairs of students. Select a few Discussion Questions that fit your goals, or duplicate all of the questions for students as "food for thought." You may also want to consult the general discussions of critical thinking listed in the Appendix of this manual. (I certainly understand that not every instructor has the luxury of time enough for many of these discussions. They are included in this manual as a potential source for those who are lucky enough to have the time, or who are clever enough to find ways to insert discussion into a busy course.)

Students can learn from one another through discussion. Also, their thinking may be stimulated in an exchange with their peers. Planning and leading productive discussions requires skill; it doesn't just happen by itself. Some guidelines for planning and leading a discussion follow:

Leading Productive Discussions

1.   **One essential ingredient of productive discussion (over which instructors have little control) is the degree of preparation students bring to class.** If students have not read the material to be discussed, no amount of skill on the instructor's part is likely to produce an effective interchange. If a sizable portion of the students in a particular class do not seem to be keeping up with reading assignments, it might be wise to schedule a short quiz on days when you plan to devote class time to

discussion. If the quiz is brief and "painless", students will then be ready and eager to discuss what they have learned.

2. **It is frequently useful to set the stage for discussion with an overview of the topics to be addressed.** In the case of an enthusiastic and usually well-prepared class, this can serve as an alternative to the quiz strategy described above.

3. **Numerous specific questions are often essential to maintain high content quality and to keep a discussion moving.** It is usually best to begin an extended discussion with a long list of questions or issues in hand. The Behavioral Objectives can be useful for generating questions.

4. **If at all possible, try to phrase questions so that they cannot be answered "yes" or "no."** Also avoid questions that call for a straight factual answer. Remember that the goal is discussion, not rote recall of the text. Even if the question or issue at hand is fairly factual, questions should be stated in a way that encourages elaboration.

    If students feel that what they say must be "right," they are often very hesitant to say anything at all. Try to use phrases like, "How did you feel about," "Do you agree with," "What do you find attractive or unattractive about," "Do you see any problems with," "What might happen if," "Who has had an experience that relates to," and so forth. Once discussion is underway, it is relatively easy to shift to more challenging questions or issues, but at first it is important not to intimidate students.

5. **Don't worry about getting to another question or topic if the group is interested, and the discussion is informative.** However, as soon as the quality of contributions begins to decline (i.e. they become redundant or irrelevant), change immediately to a new question or issue. This type of movement is what distinguishes a sparkling classroom discussion from the sort of session that students and instructors may perceive as a waste of time. It also makes clear to the students that the instructor is providing structure and leadership.

6. **It is wise to avoid revealing your own position early in the discussion of a particular topic or issue.** This allows you to play devil's advocate, and it avoids closing off expression of divergent viewpoints. Eventually students will want to know what you think, but save this for a summary statement and then move on to the next question. Specific misinformation can and should be corrected immediately. Beyond this, however, be sure to make a clear distinction between your opinions and more factual information.

7. **Try to make your interest in students visible and liberally compliment interesting and informative contributions.** If the initial participants in a discussion are treated in a reinforcing manner, others are more likely to join in. Try to make it "safe" to participate. If you strongly disagree, say so, but try to do it in a non-threatening way. Often you need only say, "I'm not sure I agree with that. Who can think of a reason why?" Then another student will correct the first. In this way you can avoid being the sole dispenser of disagreement or disapproval.

8. **Don't allow one or two individuals to monopolize the discussion—even if they are articulate and what they say is interesting.** Strive to involve as many students as possible. This can often be done by simply saying, "(S)he says...Let's get another viewpoint." If no one volunteers, ask another

student, "What do you think?" Or say, "Who agrees (or disagrees) with (student's name)?" or, "Has anyone had a similar (or different) experience?" It is not unreasonable, of course, to return to particularly articulate students after others have had a chance to participate.

9. **Try to ensure that the entire group can hear questions and responses.** Whenever possible, try to prevent comments from becoming a conversation between you and an individual student. In larger classes a student who cannot be heard can be handled in several ways: **(a) Restate** for the class what the student has asked or said and call for a response. **(b) Compliment** the student on an interesting contribution and ask her or him to face the class and repeat it for others to hear. **(c) Walk** to the far side of the class as the student speaks so that his or her voice must be raised and directed at the class.

10. **It is generally a good idea to move around the classroom during a discussion.** Also make a point of establishing eye contact with students in each section of the classroom once every few minutes. Sometimes, looking expectantly at students in a particular area can be as effective as a direct question for prompting a response. Remember, too, that posture and gestures can influence classroom atmosphere. If you approach students, sit or lean on front desks, etc., a casual tone is set. Standing at a greater distance or behind a lectern or desk imparts a more formal quality. By effectively manipulating such cues, you can communicate your intentions (lecture or discussion) to students. This can be more effective than saying, "Now let's discuss...," (which is often as ineffective as saying, "Be spontaneous"). If you simply begin, students will follow your lead.

11. **When working with large classes, or when performing demonstrations that preclude participation by the entire class** choose one or two students and have them come to the front of the class. In this way, other students will identify with the participants and will feel involved. Also, your interaction with the surrogate participants will add a dimension of spontaneity that will make the class more interesting for you as well as for the students.

LECTURE ENHANCEMENTS

Involving the students in the classroom activity increases motivation and enhances learning. The activities presented in this section are intended to promote learning and enthusiasm for the course. They can provide the substance for a change of pace in the classroom routine and serve as demonstrations of how psychologists observe behavior. **Most are simple demonstrations or discussions, requiring little preparation or equipment.** In every instance, it is important to tie in the activity with the material being studied in the course, and the relevance of conclusions arrived at should be underlined for maximum benefit to the students. It should never be assumed that the students will make the connections on their own or that they are self-evident.

ROLE-PLAYING SCENARIOS

The exercises in this section are designed to **facilitate perspective-taking**. These scenes can be used as lecture examples in a large lecture course. Students can be asked to think about ways of handling a specific situation. Talking about an issue often mainly changes how we think. Role-playing can change thoughts, feelings, and behaviors. For example, students may say that it is "terrible that some parents physically abuse their children." But if the student has to articulate the feelings of the abusive parent, usually there is an increase in sensitivity to the parent's frustration and anger.

It is wise to gradually introduce students to role-playing. The first few "scenarios" may be clumsy and filled with refusals and giggles. However, even when students hesitate to act out the roles, they will talk about the issues and learn a great deal. You will soon know which students want to be coaxed and which students do not want to participate. Each time you use this technique you will find students protesting less and volunteering more. Additional sources of information on role-playing can be found in sources listed in the Appendix for this manual.

VALUE CLARIFICATION STATEMENTS

Controversial Value Clarification statements are included for each chapter. Ideally, the statements will prompt strong and diverse reactions from students. For example, the statement could be, "Children should be removed from the home of abusive parents." Four 8 X 20" signs are prepared. One sign says "Strongly agree," another "Agree," another "Disagree," and finally "Strongly disagree." In a large lecture hall, students can simply raise their hands and express why they support any given position. After arguments are made for all views, students can vote again. A student can be appointed "teller" to record the number of votes for each view. Often it will only take a few votes before public opinion on the issue will shift.

A "silent" value clarification can take place in a large lecture hall. A controversial statement can be written on a 5 X 8" filing card. The card is passed down each row and students write whether they agree or disagree and why. The cards are collected and are read to the student audience.

In smaller classes, the four position signs are placed around the four sides of the room. Students are asked to stand in the center of the room. A statement is read and students literally move to the sign describing their viewpoint. Students are reminded that:

☞ Feelings about issues are not right or wrong; they just are.
☞ Reactions to each statement depend on how the words are defined. Once all students have moved to a sign, a person from each side of the room will be asked to define terms and support his or her position.
☞ We can reject a person's views on an issue without rejecting that person in general.
☞ Feelings toward issues change when we receive new information or process old information in a new way. Listen to each other. If someone convinces you to change your mind, move to that side of the room.
☞ There is no sign for "neutral" because a lack of a stance usually becomes a position in support of the more vocal majority. It will be difficult, but students must take a stand on all issues.

The instructor's role is to reinforce short responses, to encourage people to change their views and move to another side of the room, and to move on to another statement when the key points of one issue have been covered. After about 20-30 minutes, students are asked to complete the following pre-prepared anonymous form. They are also told that they will be reading each other's anonymous sheets.

"I was pleased to learn that..."
"I was surprised to learn that..."
"I felt uncomfortable when someone said that..."
"I wish I would have said that..."
"I learned from this exercise that..."

Completed forms are passed to the right and each person silently reads the previous person's form. This continues until each student silently has read five or six forms. The instructor says, "Stop," and each student reads aloud one or two lines from the form in his or her hand. This feedback sheet has a powerful impact on both small and large classes.

Value clarification can be used with any topic. Usually students will be very open and direct about their feelings. The instructor may need to help students reword ideas so people disagree sensitively, and the instructor may need to support less "popular" views. Invariably, the most frequent student response at the end of this exercise is, "I was surprised to learn that we could still be friends after disagreeing so strongly." **Value clarification can help open up future class dialogues because students learn to feel that it is safe to disagree.**

ONE-MINUTE MOTIVATORS

Often it takes only a moment to motivate students to think about a topic, to feel the implications of an issue, or to make a commitment to change their behavior. One-minute Motivators are **quick demonstrations, examples, analogies, props, or challenges**. They need to flow into and out of your presentation; they should not seem contrived or artificial. These devices should be used as a way to change the pace of the class, not as ends in themselves. While they can diversify your presentation, they shouldn't serve as a substitute for meaningful analysis of the issues. A wealth of additional teaching ideas can be found in the sources listed under the heading Tactics, Resources, Demonstrations, in the Appendix.

BROADENING OUR CULTURAL HORIZONS

Ideas from this section can be used to analyze bias in psychological research, to update lecture materials, to role-play diverse cultural values, or to change how we respond to individuals different from ourselves. Students seem to be fascinated by intercultural information and would enjoy bringing to their instructors articles that discuss their own roots or the backgrounds of others. If you would like to add to your own cultural knowledge, you will find a list of helpful journals in the Appendix of this manual.

CLASSROOM EXERCISES

There are two or more classroom exercises developed for each chapter in the text. These exercises are more elaborate than those described in the previous sections. **Each of the exercises has a rationale, an explanation of the purpose and procedure, a specific set of directions for carrying out the exercise, data sheets and worksheets for collecting information, and some points for discussion after the exercise is completed.**

The data sheets and worksheets should be copied for distribution to the class. Where appropriate, directions and supplementary information are provided for students and may be duplicated as well. Some of the exercises can be done in one session in the classroom. Others may take more than one class period and may require some work outside the classroom. Most of the exercises require students to work in groups, which should help to promote student interaction. It is important to change the groupings for each activity so that students will get to know each other and will not get into a rut.

JOURNAL QUESTIONS

Questions from this section can be used to trigger a large class discussion, sharing in a small group or a pair, or a private dialogue between you and your student. Even if time is not available for answering all of the questions, making the questions available to students can help them reflect on parts of their life relevant to chapter content. Answers to these questions should always be handled sensitively, respectfully, and confidentially.

SUGGESTIONS FOR FURTHER READING

A list of additional readings is provided for each chapter in the text. While a few of these references are older, those references are considered classics in the field and are included for that reason. All other references have been updated. Some care has been taken to find reading material that is accessible to students and interesting to read. Some of these could be assigned as enrichment for the class. Assignments to review articles or books for credit or extra credit could be made from this list. Some of the items are classic and should be introduced to serious students of psychology. Other readings are simply informative and/or entertaining.

MEDIA SUGGESTIONS

Videos are suggested for each chapter. No attempt has been made to provide a complete list. These are simply some suggestions of videos or CD-ROMs that have been found by instructors to be helpful in class. Every teacher of introductory psychology will have personal favorites and could add to the list provided.

In Appendix A is an up-to-date listing of video sources. You can write for catalogs or have students send for them as a class assignment. Students who are writing major papers should be required to list some audio-visual materials as resources that they consulted.

COMPUTER AND INTERNET RESOURCES

In this section are several sources of CD-ROM and Internet materials pertaining to the chapter. References for *PsychNow!*, *InfoTrac* Subject Guide/Key Words, The Study Center address for the chapter, as well as other pertinent web addresses will be listed here. Although the web addresses listed in this manual were current at the time of preparation, web addresses have a tendency to change frequently, so no guarantee is made that these web addresses will be continue to be current. If you find a web address that is no longer active, simply type the name of the site into your web browser and the current URL should come up. (Dennis Coon has also listed several web addresses at the end of each chapter of the text, some of which may be duplicated in the instructor's manual.)

HELPFUL RESOURCES FOR TEACHING INTRODUCTORY PSYCHOLOGY

An introductory course in psychology does not address only students who are interested in majoring in this area, but a wide variety of persons who have many and varying needs, interests, and abilities. Therefore, teaching this kind of heterogeneous student body is a special challenge. In addition, the subject matter is constantly changing, and the number of topics and subfields to which students must be introduced is very large. It is difficult to put it all together so that the content is coherent and so the students can have a fulfilling experience. **The Helpful Resources section in Appendix A provides the instructor with a variety of references to material that can be of assistance.** The references include teaching tips, innovative ideas, experiments and activities, discussion methods, controversial issues, and more.

USER'S GUIDE TO USING INFOTRAC

Appendix B contains an easy-to-follow flow-chart for navigating in the InfoTrac "universe."

ACKNOWLEDGMENTS

The real credit for this manual, as always, goes to those who came before me: Kendra Jeffcoat, Carole Woodward, the late Michael C. Sosulski, and of course, Dennis Coon. I am grateful to these people for the tremendous amount of work they put into this manual before my own efforts to make the material more accessible and current. I would also like to thank my students and colleagues for their advice and for putting up with my somewhat reduced attention. Finally, my heartfelt thanks to my editor, Kristin Milotich. Kristin had the delightful task of coming into this project near the middle and picking up the pieces, so to speak. She has done an excellent job and provided me with much needed moral support throughout the process. Thank you, Kristin.

A few final words to you, the instructor using this manual: In any undertaking this huge, there are bound to be some mistakes. While proofreaders have caught almost all of the errors, you may find a few on your own. If you do, please feel free to write or to contact me at my email address listed below. I would like to make this manual as error-free as possible. Also, if you have found more recent addresses for the videos, or have suggestions for articles, books, or other materials you feel should be included or updated, fire away! I look forward to hearing from you. Thank you.

Saundra K. Ciccarelli
Gulf Coast Community College
5230 West Highway 98
Panama City, FL 32401
sciccarelli@gulfcoast.edu

CHAPTER 1

Psychology: The Search for Understanding

■ LEARNING OBJECTIVES

To demonstrate mastery of this chapter the student should be able to:

1.   List two reasons for studying psychology.
2.   Define psychology.
3.   Define the term "behavior" and differentiate overt from covert behavior.
4.   Explain the term "empirical evidence" and give an example of it.
5.   Explain the term "scientific observation."
6.   Give two reasons why the study of some topics in psychology is difficult.
7.   Write a brief summary of each of the following areas of specialization in psychology:
     a.   developmental   f.   biopsychology
     b.   learning   g.   psychology of gender
     c.   personality   h.   social
     d.   sensation and perception   i.   cultural
     e.   comparative   j.   evolutionary
8.   Explain why animals are used in research and define the term "animal model" in your discussion.
9.   Explain the four goals of psychology.
10.   Describe the field known as positive psychology.
11.   Explain the sentence "Psychology has a long past but a short history."
12.   Describe the school of psychology known as structuralism, including:
     a.   where and when it was established
     b.   who established it (the "father" of psychology)
     c.   the focus of its study
     d.   research method and its drawback
     e.   goal
     f.   who took structuralism to the United States
13.   Describe the functionalist school of psychology, including:
     a.   its founder
     b.   its goal
     c.   major interests
     d.   impact on modern psychology

14. Describe behaviorism, including:
    a. its founder
    b. why its founder could not accept structuralism or functionalism
    c. its emphasis
    d. Skinner's contribution and his concept of a "designed culture"
    e. its application in therapy
15. Describe the view of cognitive behaviorism.
16. Describe the Gestalt school of psychology, including:
    a. who founded it
    b. its goal
    c. its slogan
    d. areas of interest
17. Describe the contribution of women in the early history of psychology, and contrast the representation of women in psychology then and now. Name the first woman to receive her doctorate in psychology.
18. Describe the psychoanalytic school of psychology, including:
    a. who founded it
    b. its major emphasis
    c. the concept of repression
    d. its method of psychotherapy
19. Describe the humanistic school of psychology, including:
    a. how its approach differs from psychoanalytic and behavioristic thought
    b. who its major representatives are
    c. its position on "free will" (as contrasted with determinism)
    d. its focus on psychological needs
    e. its stress of subjective factors rather than a scientific approach
    f. the concept of self-actualization
20. Describe the eclectic approach.
21. List and briefly describe the five major perspectives in modern psychology.
22. Briefly describe biopsychology and cognitive psychology.
23. Describe how an appreciation of cultural relativity and human diversity might enrich the understanding of psychology.
24. Characterize the differences in training, emphasis, and/or expertise among psychologists, psychiatrists, psychoanalysts, counselors, and psychiatric social workers. Describe the roles of clinical and counseling psychologists, and define the term "scientist-practitioner model."
25. List the three points in the professional ethics code for psychologists established by the APA.
26. Identify the largest areas of specialization among psychologists. Name the major sources of employment for psychologists.
27. Differentiate basic from applied research.
28. Explain the problem with using common sense as a source of information.
29. List the six steps of the scientific method.

30. Define the term "hypothesis" and be able to identify one. Explain what an operational definition is.

31. Explain the purpose of theory building and the importance of publication.

32. Describe the technique of naturalistic observation including both the advantages and limitations of this method. Explain what the anthropomorphic fallacy is, and how it can lead to problems in psychological research.

33. Describe what a correlational study is, and list any advantages and disadvantages of this method. Explain what a correlation coefficient is, how it is expressed, what it means, and how it is related to causation.

34. List and describe the three essential variables of the experimental method.

35. Explain the nature and the purpose for the control group and the experimental group in an experiment.

36. Explain the purpose of randomly assigning subjects to either the control or the experimental group.

37. Identify the advantages and disadvantages of the experimental method.

38. Explain what a placebo is, how effective it is, how it probably works, and what its purpose in an experiment is.

39. Explain what single-blind and double-blind experimental arrangements are.

40. Explain the nature of the experimenter effect and how it is related to the self-fulfilling prophecy.

41. List and describe the three areas of ethical concern in psychological experiments, and explain the position of the APA in terms of ethical guidelines.

42. Briefly describe the clinical method of research, including advantages and disadvantages. Give an example of a case in which the clinical method would be used.

43. Briefly describe the survey method of investigation including the importance of a representative sample, and an advantage and a disadvantage of the method. Define the term "courtesy bias."

44. Define the term "critical thinking." Describe each of the four principles that form the foundation of critical thinking.

The following objectives are related to the material in the "Exploring Psychology" section of the text.

45. Briefly describe each of the following pseudo-psychologies:
    a. palmistry
    b. phrenology
    c. graphology
    d. astrology

46. List and explain the three reasons why pseudo-psychologies continue to thrive even though they have no scientific basis.

The following objective is related to the material in the "Psychology in Action" section of the text.

47.   List seven suggestions that your author gives to help you become a more critical reader of psychological information in the popular press.

■ DISCUSSION QUESTIONS

1.   How did you picture psychology and psychologists before reading Chapter 1? Has your image changed? How accurate are television and movie portrayals of psychologists? What psychological specialty do you consider most interesting at this point?

2.   Are there any possible disadvantages of studying psychology? Are there ever times when "ignorance is bliss?"

3.   What are the advantages and disadvantages of animal research? Under what conditions should animals be used instead of people? Most people anthropomorphize pets. How could this be a problem in the objective study of animals? What ethical guidelines do you feel should be followed in animal research?

4.   What are the ethical limitations of the goal of "control?" When should the results of psychological studies be used to intervene in individual lives? When is intervention inappropriate?

5.   What do you see as the strengths and weaknesses of each of the schools of psychology? What specific human problems do you think that psychologists should study? Which school of psychology would be most appropriate for the study of the problem you have identified?

6.   In what ways is your behavior controlled by the environment? Do you believe that you have free will? Is there any way to tell if an apparent "free choice" is really determined by your past?

7.   During the Victorian era (a time of marked sexual repression), Freud treated a large number of women with sexual problems. What kinds of psychological problems do you feel will be most common at the beginning of the twenty-first century? Why?

8.   Presently, a number of non-physicians can prescribe certain medications under certain conditions. Examples include optometrists, nurse practitioners, and physician assistants. In your opinion, should psychologists be trained to prescribe mood-altering drugs?

9.   What are the advantages and disadvantages of both basic and applied research? How should these two forms of research work together?

10. Is the value of common sense limited because of the kind of information collected? Or the process used to gather information? Explain.

11. What human problem or behavior do you think could most effectively be studied using naturalistic observation? For what behaviors would this approach be the least appropriate? Why?

12. What type of correlation would you expect to find between noise levels and productivity in an office? Between income and education? Between physical attractiveness and frequency of dating? Between class attendance and grades? Between use of alcohol by parents and their children? How would you demonstrate a causal link in any of these cases?

13. Give an example of a research hypothesis that you would like to investigate. What would you use as the independent variable? The dependent variable? What extraneous variables could distort your results? How would you try to control or eliminate these extraneous variables?

14. How should subjects be assigned to a control group and an experimental group in order to guarantee random selection?

15. Regarding self-fulfilling prophecies, how have the expectations of teachers, parents, or friends affected your expectations for yourself? If you have attended a school with slow, normal, and accelerated classes, what advantages and disadvantages do you see in such a system?

16. In your opinion, is it dishonest or unethical for a physician to administer placebos to patients? Why or why not?

17. Clinical cases are often described in the popular press. What could be the positive and negative effects of this kind of publicity?

18. Have you ever taken part in a survey? On the basis of your participation, how accurate do you think surveys are? What are the flaws of typical "person on the street" surveys often done by local newspapers? What can be done to make survey data as accurate as possible?

19. Could the courtesy bias ever take place within a lab experiment? What do you suggest could be done to reduce the experimenter effect and the impact of self-fulfilling prophecy?

20. Can you name additional systems of thought that you suspect are pseudo-psychologies? What are their claims? Can you use the points made in the Applications section to explain their attraction for believers?

■ LECTURE ENHANCEMENTS

1. **You may want to invite a spokesperson from a local animal rights organization to come to class.** Also ask someone to attend who is engaged in animal research (a local research hospital or college animal laboratory are good sources). This person should be prepared to discuss the care that research animals are given and the rationale for animal research. Rather than force your visitors to debate, it is probably best to have each state his or her position, after which students can discuss or debate the issues. This can be a risky activity, so be certain that the spokesperson for each position is articulate and well-informed.

2. **The history of psychology comes alive when you and your colleagues dress, talk, and act like key figures in psychology's past.** Students can ask each character basic questions about his or her theories. A presentation of this type can be videotaped so that the most lively segments can be shown during subsequent terms. Students enjoy trying to predict the future of psychology and they have strong feelings about the ethics and conditions of research, especially animal research.

3. **The limits of introspection as a method of observation can be demonstrated by a simple exercise.** Ask students to identify the most basic taste sensations. With some help from you, they will come up with the four basic taste qualities: sweet, sour, salty, bitter. Now ask students to introspect by analyzing the taste of water (from memory or from samples provided by you). They should identify which of the four basic tastes best describes the taste of water. Or if they prefer, a combination of two or more tastes may be listed. Students will arrive at a variety of answers, but mostly they will feel consternation because the task is nearly impossible. The difficulty of using introspection as a research method should be apparent.

4. **The day before talking about Gestalt psychology, ask everyone to wear a solid-color shirt or t-shirt to class.** Assign the role of "artist" to one student. Have that person "arrange" members of the class as if they were splotches of paint. Of course, have your camera ready to create snapshots. Then ask another "artist" to rearrange students to create a different design. Obviously, the arrangement of the parts affects the whole picture that is created. Exhibit these pictures somewhere in the classroom.

5. **One ability that separates humans from other species is the ability to think about our own behavior.** Students may better appreciate the importance of the cognitive perspective by completing the following examples. In each example, students should write a positive statement and a negative statement that the person in the described situations could be thinking. What are the implications of such thoughts for the person's behavior?

    a. Mark does poorly on a test in spite of studying for many hours. He has another test in a week. He is probably thinking that . . .

b. Shannon just bought a lottery ticket. She is probably thinking that . . .

c. Rashana is newly married and is finding it difficult to adjust to being sexually active. She is probably thinking that . . .

6. **A major theme of the second half of Chapter 1 is summarized by Bertrand Russell, who said "It is not what the man of science believes that distinguishes him, but how and why he believes it. His beliefs are tentative, not dogmatic; they are based on evidence, not on authority."** (In the interest of using non-sexist language, it might be best to paraphrase this quotation, substituting "scientists" for "man of science" and using the plural pronoun "they.") This can be the start of a good discussion on what science is and how it differs from philosophy, mathematics, values, religion, magic, art, and so forth.

7. **Individually, have students operationally define the following: hunger, love, aggression, frustration, commitment, jealousy.** Explain that for an experiment to be repeated (replicated) by another experimenter, the same definition must be used. To expand on the text, you may want to point out, however, that a conceptual replication occurs when different operational definitions of the same concepts or variables are used.

8. **Allow students to practice naturalistic observation, by showing an excerpt from the commercial film, "Gorillas in the Mist."** (Available at most videotape rental stores.) Ask each student to describe what the chimps do. Have students compare their descriptions. Point out disparities in these descriptions to underscore the importance of systematic observation, where the experimenter decides in advance exactly what is to be observed and how it will be quantified.

9. **As another exercise in naturalistic observation, students can observe other students in natural habitats, such as a cafeteria, library, gym, or parking lot.** Working in groups, they can decide in advance what they want to observe and how it will be quantified. Then they can present their "findings" to the class, including the frequency of certain behaviors and the theory or hypothesis they feel could explain those behaviors.

10. **Assign students to small groups. Ask them to think of a human or an animal behavior they would like to study experimentally.** Ask them to develop a hypothesis, describe the variables they want to study, explain how they would assign subjects to the various groups, manipulate the independent variable or variables, control extraneous variables, and minimized various forms of bias. Present the proposed study to the class as a whole for discussion and evaluation.

11.   **Many students find it difficult to recognize dependent and independent variables in situations other than those provided in the text.** To generalize these concepts, present the following descriptions and ask students to identify the independent and dependent variables in each.

    a. A biopsychologist injects several monkeys with male hormones and notes that by comparison to control animals, they display more aggressive acts in a testing situation.

    b. After being deprived of food for varying amounts of time, participants show a progressive decline in hand dexterity and steadiness.

    c. An educational psychologist finds no differences in the math achievement scores of elementary school students who have, or have not, been assigned to a special math-education program.

    d. A social psychologist observes that participants tested in crowded rooms have slower reaction times than those tested individually.

    e. A psychologist decides to test the idea that you "can't teach an old dog new tricks." What would the dependent and independent variables be?

12.   **To clarify the various elements of a carefully controlled experiment, and to review problems such as the placebo effect and experimenter expectancies, describe the following experiment to students and have them identify the mistakes that have been made:**

Let's say that I am interested in the effects of caffeine on memory. In order to test the effects of caffeine, I divide the class in half. All the students on the right are given five cups of coffee to drink, and one hour later they are given a test of memory. The students on the left are dismissed. After the first group has been tested, the second group returns and is given the same memory test as the first group. The average scores are compared, and they show that the first group remembered more than the second group.

Major errors that students should note are: The experimental and control groups were not formed by random assignment; subjects were not tested at the same time of day; no placebo was used; subjects were probably aware of the experimenter's hypothesis; the experimenter was not blind with respect to subject assignment. Extraneous variables were not identified or controlled. Pre-tests and post-tests were not given.

13. **Ask students to create a list of the conditions under which they would feel comfortable participating in an experiment.** Develop a list of conditions that would best protect the subject without making the research impossible or inaccurate.

14. **One way to illustrate the limitations of casual observation is to ask students to describe things in their environment that they "see" on a regular basis.** The following questions regarding items that people observe all the time can serve as a starting point. Answers are indicated in parentheses. You may be surprised at how poor most students are at identifying things they have seen many times.

   a. Everyone knows that it's red with white letters, but what is the shape of a stop sign? (Octagon)

   b. Which way does Abe Lincoln face on a penny? (To his left, which means the viewer's right.)

   c. In which hand does the Statue of Liberty hold her torch? (Her right hand)

   d. How many tines are on a standard dinner fork? (Four)

   e. Which two letters are missing on a standard telephone? (Q and Z)

   f. If a common pencil isn't cylindrical, how many sides does it usually have? (Six)

   g. On which side of their uniforms do police officers wear their badges? (On their left side)

   h. On the back of a $5.00 bill is the Lincoln Memorial, and on the back of a $10.00 bill is the U.S. Treasury Building. What is on the reverse side of a $1.00 bill? (The word ONE in large letters)

15. **At some point in coverage of the first chapter, you might want to bring up the subject of pop psychology, especially as it is represented in self-help books and commercial therapies.** As the New York Times News Service observed a few years ago:

   If you were to believe the current dogma, happiness is getting rid of your erroneous zones, looking out for No. 1, asserting yourself, taking charge of your life, and learning to love every minute of it. It is clearing your psyche by screaming, esting, rolfing, encountering, hallucinating, meditating, and levitating, tuning into your biorhythms, following your stars, getting in touch with your feelings, letting it all hang out, and teleporting yourself into an extrasensory universe.

16.   **In addition to providing a good contrast to academic psychology, pop psychology can lead into a discussion of empirical and non-empirical approaches.** At the very least, the self-help books pale in comparison to Maslow's work on self-actualization. As Jonathan Freedman of Columbia University points out in the same article, "most of the advice in the pop psych books and therapies is dangerously egocentric. It teaches people just to look out for themselves. Yet, to be happy, you have to care, to take responsibility. Egocentric, narcissistic types don't form relationships very easily or maintain them very well."

17.   **Countering widespread student belief in astrology can be worth the class time and effort.** The inaccuracy of the system can be illustrated by use of the adjective check-list that follows. In class, have students check all of the adjectives that apply to their personalities (interpretation follows).

1) pioneering	*13) extroverted*	*25) honest*
2) enthusiastic	*14) generous*	*26) impulsive*
3) courageous	*15) authoritative*	*27) optimistic*
4) stable	*16) critical*	*28) ambitious*
5) stubborn	*17) exacting*	*29) hard-working*
6) organized	*18) intelligent*	*30) cautious*
7) intellectual	*19) harmonizing*	*31) original*
8) adaptable	*20) just*	*32) open-minded*
9) clever	*21) sociable*	*33) independent*
10) sensitive	*22) secretive*	*34) kind*
11) nurturing	*23) strong*	*35) sensitive*
12) sympathetic	*24) passionate*	*36) creative*

The adjectives in this list were compiled by William Balch from eleven astrology books. They represent the most frequently mentioned characteristics for each astrological "sign." After students have made their responses, identify the signs corresponding to each group of three adjectives. **They are: 1-3, Aries; 4-6, Taurus; 7-9, Gemini; 10-12, Cancer; 13-15, Leo; 16-18, Virgo; 19-21, Libra; 22-24, Scorpio; 25-27, Sagittarius; 28-30, Capricorn; 31-33, Aquarius; 34-36, Pisces.** Next, call for a show of hands from those students who checked all three adjectives listed for "their sign." Follow this with a show of hands by students who checked all three adjectives for any other sign. You should, of course, get a roughly equal number of hands raised each time–showing that there is no compelling association between astrological signs and personality traits. (Adapted from Balch, W. R. 1980. "Testing the validity of astrology in class." *Teaching of Psychology, 7(4)*, pp. 247-250.)

18. **Ask students to watch three or four television commercials and to take notes on the "evidence" used to support the claims made in the commercials.** Should these claims be believed? Why or why not?

ROLE-PLAYING SCENARIOS

1. **Divide the class into small groups.** Assign each group a "school of psychology." Ask students to discuss their assigned theory in detail and to select a representative who will voice their viewpoint. At the front of the room, form a panel made up of each of the representatives. Ask each representative to discuss his or her approach. Field questions from the class.

2. **Divide the class into small groups of five or six students.** Give each group the handout, "Differing Views of Animal Research" reproduced below. Ask students to enact each role described in the handout. Students should attempt to express in detail their thoughts and feelings as they assume each view. What evidence would each person probably use to support his/her view? Students may also want to role-play the different views as they try to persuade the "politician" to vote a certain way on impending legislation. This could be done in small groups or in front of the class.

Differing Views of Animal Research

   a. Brenda is opposed to all animal research. She is active in animal rights organizations supporting legislation to limit animal research.

   b. Terri is a veterinarian who is in favor of some forms of research, as long as animals are prevented as much as possible from experiencing excessive pain.

   c. Ruth is a diabetic who depends on animal research for the production of improved forms of insulin. She understands the importance of preventing unnecessary pain, but she also knows that the lives of many diabetics have been saved because of research on dogs.

   d. Patrick is a university researcher whose work on the visual system of cats has brought him worldwide recognition. He feels that the blindness that often must take place in cats is a small price to pay for the human sight that has been restored by his research.

   e. Frank is an AIDS victim who has volunteered to receive a highly controversial medication because protests over animal research have stopped research in this area.

   f. Mary is an accountant who hates dogs, cats, and rats. She is more concerned about the effect of costly animal research on her taxes than she is about the effect on animals.

  g. Geraldine is a politician who is reviewing legislation to limit animal research. She has mixed feelings and wants more information on this issue.

■ VALUE-CLARIFICATION STATEMENTS

1. Lab experiments are too expensive, artificial, and time-consuming to be very useful to our understanding of human behavior.

2. It is an invasion of privacy to observe public behavior systematically without first receiving the permission of people being observed.

3. Students in introductory psychology courses should be required to participate in psychological research.

4. Any research that causes pain for animals should be banned, regardless of its value to humans.

5. A survivor of incest, alcoholism, or spousal abuse will always have emotional scars that will often affect his or her behavior.

6. Cloning of human body parts should be banned, regardless of the possible benefits for transplant patients.

■ ONE-MINUTE MOTIVATORS

1. **Ask one student to describe all of the things that he or she did, thought, and felt during the last five minutes.** Point out that human behavior is exceedingly complex.

2. **Quickly collect demographic data from the class by a raising of hands.** What kind of generalizations can be made about the "kind of people" in that specific class?

3. **Add examples of the way humans talk to public telephones, vending machines, automatic bank tellers, automobiles, and computers when the machines are "moody."** Is there anything wrong with this kind of anthropomorphizing?

4. **To demonstrate "diffusion of responsibility," as it relates to prosocial behavior, drop something and count the number of students who rush to help.** Do the same thing on the way to class when only a few students are present and bring that data to class for discussion.

5. **If your classroom is fairly soundproof, scream once to demonstrate a potent stimulus and point out the responses made by members of the class.**

6.   **Add a slide or transparency to your lecture to show closure or figure/ground shifts to demonstrate the premise of Gestalt psychology.**

7.   **Intentionally slip some malapropisms into the lecture.** See how many students notice–or did they unconsciously deny the presence of the errors to avoid embarrassing the instructor? How much human behavior is unconsciously motivated?

8.   **To demonstrate the tenor of cognitive psychology, say to students, "Imagine that I am going to give you a pop quiz. What thoughts would you have? What thoughts could help you do well?"** Put these on the chalkboard. Suggest that writing similar coping statements on file cards could affirm that students are going to do well in this course.

9.   **After describing the academic preparation of psychology professionals, ask, "What education and experience should a psychology professor have? Why?"**

10.   **Have students develop a continuing list of common sense statements based on overgeneralization and related thinking errors ("Absence makes the heart grow fonder," versus "Out of sight, out of mind").** Post these on the wall. As you progress through each chapter, point out under what conditions each statement is true or false.

11.   **Bring a still camera to class the first day to take photos of students in order to better remember their names.** After a posed shot, take a series of "natural" shots or use a video camera while the class is doing a small group activity. Develop the photos and show that people act differently when they know they are being observed.

12.   **Early in the first few weeks of class, ask students what they would like to know about each other.** Develop a questionnaire to be answered anonymously. Make the reply sheets available for students to thumb through. Then put the data through a simple statistical analysis to identify interesting means and correlations.

13.   **To demonstrate the experimenter effect and self-fulfilling prophecies, ask for a female volunteer.** Explain that you want to show that the reaction time of females is faster than that of males. You will drop a piece of paper. Her job is to catch it as quickly as possible. Ask another student to serve as timer. Before you start, say things like, "Are you relaxed? Do you understand what I want you to do? Are you ready?" Of course, she will catch the paper. Then ask for a male volunteer. Quickly say, "Ready, go." He invariably misses the paper. Conclude, "Thus you can see that female reaction time is faster than male reaction time." Ideally, as you start to move on, someone will say, "But that wasn't fair . . ."

14.   **To demonstrate a representative sample, bring in two boxes of candy, one filled only with nut chocolates and the other with a blend.** (Plain M&Ms and peanut M&Ms would also work for larger classes.) Ask students to sample one piece from each box and then draw

a conclusion about the whole box. While we need more than a piece or two to gain confidence in our conclusions, we really don't have to eat the entire box to be fairly accurate.

15.   **Ask the students if any of them have ever participated in an Internet survey.** Ask them to think about what kind of sample population is available to this type of survey, and what kind of biases might exist within that sample.

16.   **To quickly illustrate the fallacies of astrology, buy a bag of fortune cookies.** Have each student read his or her fortune and then explain how it is "true" or "accurate" in some way. Remind students that they received fortunes on a random basis and that the fallacy of positive instances is a likely explanation for any "accurate" fortunes.

17.   **A nice exercise in critical thinking involves asking students to think about the psychic hotlines advertised on television.** Ask them to think about how common "psychic" abilities must be if all of those agencies employ enough psychics to operate the telephone lines. Why would the "psychic" take some basic information and then promise to call the person back in several minutes?

■ BROADENING OUR CULTURAL HORIZONS

1.   **Ask students to read a short selection from an encyclopedia on the culture of the former Soviet Union.** Which school of psychology would a Russian most easily accept? Ask students to read about the Japanese culture. Which school of psychology would you guess would be most interesting to a person from Japan? Is it possible to have one valid psychology for all cultures?

2.   **Many people within the American culture highly value domesticated dogs and cats.** There are other cultures where dogs are not treated as "family." How would research in psychology be different if dogs and cats were not valued as they are in our culture?

3.   **Psychology is a system for explaining behavior.** In western cultures psychology is approached as if it were a natural science, with great emphasis placed on empiricism and scientific methods. Is this a cultural preference? Or is it the most defensible approach to psychology, regardless of cultural values?

■ SUPPLEMENTAL ACTIVITIES

TO THE INSTRUCTOR:

The four exercises that follow should help to get students more involved in the subject matter of Chapter 1. **The first** is a take-home exercise intended to help students understand what the subject matter of psychology is. **The second** is an in-class activity that should impress students with the difficulty of gathering objective data, especially by the method of introspection. Although students may deny relying on introspection, they do, in fact, treat their own sensory experiences as infallible. **The third** exercise is an in-class activity which will make the concept of correlation more relevant to students. **The fourth** is an exercise that requires students to look for reports of scientific "marvels" found in the supermarket tabloids. These often purport to be the astounding results of new research.

Exercise #1: What is Psychology?

The purpose of this exercise is to help students to learn what psychology is about and to impress on them that what psychologists are doing is different from the popular notions held by persons who are not familiar with what psychologists study. This exercise is set up on the following pages in such a way that it can be duplicated and distributed. Students may record responses and write their analysis directly on the form provided.

Exercise #2 Introspection

This exercise is a classroom activity that should generate discussion on methodology, particularly on the validity of self-reporting personal experiences as a method of understanding behavior. With a few simple materials you can involve students in this project. You can follow the directions, using three pairs, with the rest of the class as observers, or you can divide the whole class in pairs of "experimenters" and "introspectionists."

Exercise #3: Positive and Negative Correlation

In this exercise students are asked to respond to a questionnaire which will provide the class with raw data to be plotted on a scattergram. The students are more likely to give correct responses to the questions if they do not have to identify themselves, so keep the responses anonymous. Collect the questionnaires. They will provide you with plenty of data. You can read the data and have the students plot a scattergram. After plotting several pairs of variables, they will soon see that relationships are not all the same. You will find that some of the relationships will be positive and some negative. Other variables will show little or no relationship. (You and the class may wish to add other variables.)

Once the students see the relationships on the graph it is important to discuss cause and effect. Does it exist? How can you tell?

Copy and distribute the prepared data sheets and the diagrams provided for this exercise.

Exercise #4: "Scientific Marvels" in the News

Students should be able to evaluate reports of research using the principles of the scientific method discussed in this chapter. Students may find it fun to review some of the sensational reports found in the periodicals which are displayed in the grocery store checkout lines. This exercise should provide a clear demonstration of the absurdity of these reports when examined using scientific criteria.

WHAT IS PSYCHOLOGY?

TO THE STUDENT:

The purpose of this exercise is to help you understand what psychology is and how it differs from popular ideas that many people have about it. You probably had some of the same misconceptions before beginning this course. Begin by reading Chapter 1 of the text. Look for the definition of psychology given on page 2 and write it down so that you can complete this assignment. Then follow the directions, record responses and discuss what you find.

1.   Ask five people what they think psychology is. Ask each to give a brief statement about what it is or what psychologists study. Select a variety of people. They should be persons of various ages, sexes, and educational levels.

2.   Record pertinent data about each subject (sex, approximate age, and educational level) and the verbatim response to your question. Do not add to the response or try to clarify it.

3.   After you have collected all your responses, do an analysis, comparing what you were told by the respondents with the definition in the text. The questions which follow the data sheet should help you in your analysis.

WHAT IS PSYCHOLOGY?   DATA SHEET:

Subject #1   Sex_____   Age (approx.)_____   Education_____

Subject #2   Sex_____   Age (approx.)_____   Education_____

Subject #3   Sex_____   Age (approx.)_____   Education_____

Subject #4   Sex_____   Age (approx.)_____   Education_____

Subject #5   Sex_____   Age (approx.)_____   Education_____

WHAT IS PSYCHOLOGY?   ANALYSIS OF RESPONSES:

A.   What are some of the common elements in the statements made by your subjects?

B.   How do the popular notions about psychology differ from the definition given in the text?

C.   What are some of the misconceptions that your subjects had about psychology?

INTROSPECTION

TO THE INSTRUCTOR:

The concept of structuralism as a philosophical underpinning to early psychological inquiry is sometimes difficult for students to comprehend. This is partly attributable to the difficulty students have with introspection, the methodology of structuralism. Many students perceive introspection to be a valid source of information and find it difficult to question findings from this methodology. (How many people doubt the truthfulness of their own sensory experiences?) The purpose of the following demonstration is to assist students in understanding the methodology of introspection, the inherent difficulties of relying on data generated with introspection, and what structuralists were trying to accomplish through the use of this method.

Equipment: Data Sheets and several simple objects (e.g., apple, pencil, cup, an aromatic liquid)

Demonstration: Begin by exploring with the class what structuralists attempted to discover about the "mind." Be sure it is understood that structuralists were attempting to discover the "building blocks" of conscious experience. Next, discuss the methodology of introspection and its attendant language (reporting on a "pure" immediate sensory experience). Once this discussion is complete, you can begin the demonstration.

Have six students from the class volunteer to participate in the demonstration. Randomly assign three persons to be experimenters and three to be introspectionists. Divide them into three pairs, each with an experimenter and an introspectionist. Conduct the demonstration in the following manner:

1.   Give one of the objects to each of the experimenters. The experimenter should present the object to the introspectionist briefly (about two seconds), then remove it from sight.

2.   During the time the object is being presented, the introspectionist should say whatever comes to mind about the qualities of the object being considered. Allow students to determine for themselves what constitutes a basic quality or irreducible conscious element. Be sure the students do not report on emotional experiences, but on their sensory experiences as objectively as possible. The experimenter should record the responses on the data sheet.

3.   Have the experimenters repeat this procedure three to five times for the same object.

4.   Rotate the objects among the pairs so that each pair introspects with each object.

5.   After all of the objects have been "introspected," collect the data sheets and note the similarities and differences among the reports given to the experimenters. These should be listed on the chalkboard in the form of a table.

6.   The instructor should, at the conclusion of the above demonstration, have the students respond to one or more of the questions on the data sheet. These may be used in small group discussions in class or as a take-home exercise.

(Adapted from a demonstration by Dr. William C. Titus, Arkansas Tech University.)

INTROSPECTION–DATA SHEET

OBJECT	TRIALS				
	1	2	3	4	5
1.					
2.					
3.					
4.					

DISCUSSION QUESTIONS

A.   Should we rely on this methodology as a way of obtaining consistent and unbiased data? Why or why not?

B.   What problems exist with interpreting data based on this methodology?

C.   What problems exist with regard to studying certain types of psychological phenomena using the method of introspection (e.g., altruism, aggression, psychopathology)?

D.   To what degree (or how) does this methodology violate the basic tenets of empiricism?

POSITIVE AND NEGATIVE CORRELATION

TO THE STUDENT:

Complete this questionnaire giving information about yourself. You do not need to put your name on this sheet, so your information will be confidential. If you are not sure, estimate what you think the response should be. Your responses will be collected, and the class will use the information to study correlation.

Age_____   Height_____

Weight_____   Shoe size_____

Grade-point average_____

Number of members in your family_____

Number of hours of study per week_____

Number of hours of part-time or full-time work per week_____

Number of credit hours being taken by you this term_____

Number of courses from which you withdrew last term_____

Number of courses which you completed last term_____

Number of movies attended per month_____

Number of parties attended per month_____

Number of sports in which you regularly participate_____

Number of books that you read for pleasure per month_____

POSITIVE AND NEGATIVE CORRELATION

SCATTERGRAMS:

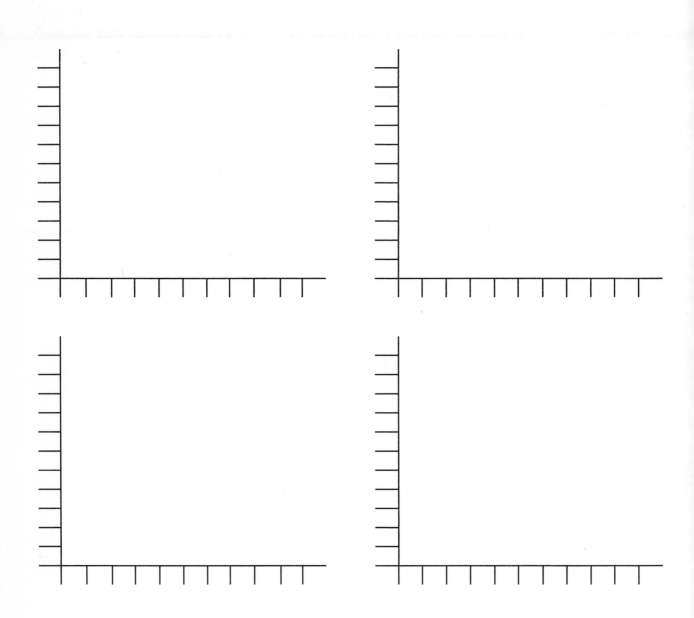

POSITIVE AND NEGATIVE CORRELATION

SCATTERGRAMS:

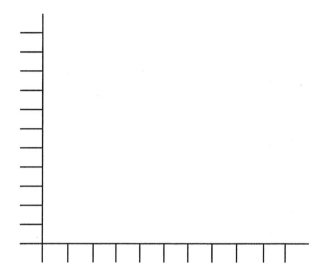
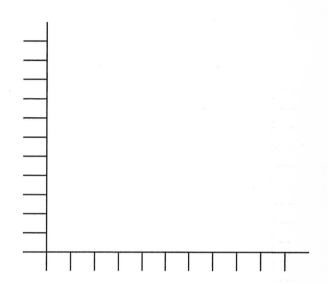

"SCIENTIFIC MARVELS" IN THE NEWS

TO THE STUDENT:

One can often read about marvelous and strange experimental results in the grocery store tabloids. They carry an air of credibility that may convince many people that what is reported is really scientifically sound or true.

Collect some of these findings by visiting your local supermarket. Select one of these reports that appears to be scientific and analyze it. Try to answer the following questions. Be prepared to discuss this in class.

1.   Is there a clear statement of a problem?

2.   What is the hypothesis?

3.   Was the population clearly identified?

4.   How was the sample selected, and was it adequate?

5.   What was the independent variable?

6.   What was the dependent variable?

7.   Were all important extraneous variables identified?

8.   How were extraneous variables controlled?

9.   Was there a control group?

10.   How were subjects selected for the experimental and control groups?

11.   Was the method of observation adequate to test the hypothesis?

12.   Was there any evidence of bias in the procedure?

13.   Are the conclusions based on accurate measuring and reporting of data?

14.   Are the conclusions warranted?

■ JOURNAL QUESTIONS

1. Which goal in psychology is most important to you? What are your goals in taking this course? What part of your life or behavior would you like to describe, understand, or control better?

2. Which area of specialization in psychology sounds the most interesting to you? Why? Which area sounds the least interesting? Why?

3. Which topic of research sounds the most interesting to you? Why? Which topic sounds the least interesting?

4. What theories do you have about human behavior? Do you feel people are basically good or bad? Strong or weak? Controlled by genetics or molded by their childhood? Totally free to select their own lifestyle and behavior, or controlled by unseen forces? What evidence can you cite to support your views?

■ SUGGESTIONS FOR FURTHER READING

History:

Atkinson, R. C. "Reflections of Psychology's Past and Concerns About Its Future." *American Psychologist.* 1977, 32, 205-210.

Hothersall, D. *History of Psychology*, 3rd ed. McGraw-Hill, 1995.

Mueller, C. G. "Some Origins of Psychology as a Science." *Annual Review of Psychology*, 1979, 30, 9-29.

Definition:

Hebb, D. O. "What Psychology Is About." *American Psychologist*, 1974, 29, 71-79.

Jerome, L. E. "Astrology–Magic or Science?" in *Objections to Astrology*. Prometheus Books, 1975.

Kelly, I. "Modern Astrology: A Critique." *Psychological Reports,* 1997, (81), p. 1035.

Koch, S. "The Nature and Limits of Psychological Knowledge: Lessons of a Century qua 'Science.'" *American Psychologist*, 1981, 36, 257-269.

Applications:

Career Associates. *Career Choices for Students of Psychology.* Walker and Company, 1990. DeGalan, J., and Lambert, S. *Great Jobs for Psychology Majors.* Lincolnwood, IL:VGM Career Horizons, 1995.

Grasha, A. *Practical Applications of Psychology,* 4th ed. HarperCollins, 1997.

Holland, M and G. Tarlow. *Using Psychology: Principles of Behavior in Your Life,* 2nd ed. Little, Brown & Co., 1980.

Super, Charles, and Donald Super. *Opportunities in Psychology Careers.* Lincolnwood IL.: VGM Career Horizons, 1994.

Methods:

Anderson, B. D. *The Psychological Experiment,* 3rd ed. Brooks/Cole, 1977.

Barber, T. *Pitfalls in Human Research: Ten Pivotal Points.* Pergamon Press, 1976.

Edwards, A. L. *Experimental Design in Psychological Research.* Harper & Row, 1985.

Goldstein, M. and I. Goldstein. *How We Know: An Exploration of the Scientific Process.* Plenum, 1981.

Goodwin, C. J. *Research In Psychology: Methods And Design*, 3rd ed. New York: John Wiley & Sons, 2001.

Kantowitz, B., H. L. Roediger, and D. Elmes. *Experimental Psychology: Understanding Psychological Research*, 7th ed. West Publishing Co., 2000.

Koocher, G. P. *Ethics in Psychology: Professional Standards and Cases.* Oxford University Press, 1998.

Miller, A. G. *The Obedience Experiments: A Case Study of Controversy in Social Science.* New York: Praeger, 1986.

Monte, C. F. *Psychology's Scientific Endeavor.* Praeger, 1975.

Shaughnessy, J. J. and E. B. Zechmeister. *Research Methods in Psychology.* McGraw-Hill, 1997.

Stanovich, K. E. *How To Think Straight About Psychology*, 6th ed. Allyn & Bacon, 2001.

■ MEDIA SUGGESTIONS

ISSUES IN PSYCHOLOGY (2002, Coast Community College District Telecourses, 30 min.)
Part of the *Psychology - The Study of Human Behavior Series*, this video presents a discussion with leading psychologists and teachers of important topics in psychology.

PAST, PRESENT, AND PROMISE (2001, from *Discovering Psychology,* Annenberg/CPB, 30 min.)
An introduction to psychology as a science at the crossroads of many fields of knowledge, from philosophy and anthropology to biochemistry and artificial intelligence.

RESEARCH METHODS (2002, Coast Community College District Telecourses, 30 min.)
Part of the *Psychology - The Study of Human Behavior Series*, this video shows footage of lobotomy, autism, and police investigators employing cognitive interview techniques.

RESEARCH METHODS IN PSYCHOLOGY (2001, Insight Media, 30 min.)
This program provides an overview of the processes of observational and descriptive research.

UNDERSTANDING RESEARCH (2001, from *Discovering Psychology,* Annenberg/CPB, 30 min.)
An examination of the scientific method and the ways in which data are collected and analyzed, with an emphasis on critical thinking skills.

WHAT IS PSYCHOLOGY (2002, Coast Community College District Telecourses, 30 min.)
Part of the *Psychology - The Study of Human Behavior Series*, this video describes the nature of psychology and what its practitioners do.

■ COMPUTER AND INTERNET RESOURCES

PSYCHNOW!

Accessing Psychology:
Psychology and its History
Critical Thinking in Psychology
Research Methods

PSYK.TREK

Unit 1: History & Methods
1a: Psychology's timeline
1b: The experimental method
1c: Statistics: Central tendency and variability
1d: Statistics: Correlation
1e: How to do library research

INFOTRAC

Subject Guide/Key Words: William James, Wilhelm Wundt, Behaviorism, Gestalt Psychology, Science and Psychology, Critical Thinking, Psychological Research, Psychoanalysis, Sigmund Freud, History of Psychology

WEB SITES

Wadsworth Online Psychology Study Center:
http://info.wadsworth.com/cooessentials9

APA's PsychNet and PsychInfo:
http://www.apa.org/

Fields of Psychology:
http://www.msubillings.edu/psychology/fields.htm

People and Discoveries:
http://www.pbs.org/wgbh/aso/databank/humbeh.html

SOSIG: Psychology Section:
http://sosig.ac.uk/roads/subject-listing/World-cat/psych.html

The Skeptical Inquirer Online:
http://www.csicop.org/si/

CHAPTER 2
The Brain, Biology, and Behavior

■ LEARNING OBJECTIVES

To demonstrate mastery of this chapter the student should be able to:

1. Name the basic unit of the nervous system, state what it is specifically designed to do, and list and describe its four parts.
2. Explain how a nerve impulse (action potential) occurs, how it is an all-or-nothing event, and how the cell returns to its resting state after the nerve impulse passes.
3. Describe the difference between the nature of a nerve impulse and the nature of the communication between neurons.
4. Explain how nerve impulses are carried from one neuron to another at the synapse.
5. Explain what determines whether a neuron will have an action potential triggered.
6. Explain the function of neuropeptides.
7. Differentiate a nerve from a neuron.
8. Describe the process of neurogenesis and its connection to brain repair.
9. Describe the effect of myelin on the speed of the nerve impulse.
10. Explain what determines whether or not a neuron or a nerve will regenerate. Briefly describe the progress in generating regrowth of brain and spinal cord neurons.
11. Chart the various subparts of the human nervous system and generally explain their functions.
12. Differentiate between the two branches of the autonomic nervous system.
13. Explain the mechanism of the reflex arc.

The following objectives are related to the material in the "Exploring Psychology" section of the text.
14. List and describe five techniques for studying the brain. Briefly describe how EEG works. Describe each of the four scanning techniques for studying the entire brain as it functions.

15. Describe the main difference between the brains of lower and higher animals. Name what appears to be the foundation of human intellectual superiority.
16. Describe the main difference between the brains of people who score high versus low on mental tests.
17. Define the term "hemispheres" and explain the function of the corpus callosum. Describe the problem known as spatial neglect.
18. Explain how and why a brain is "split" and describe what the resulting effects are.

19. Differentiate the abilities of the two hemispheres of the cerebral cortex. Describe what is known about their working together as well as how they process information.
20. Describe the function(s) of each of the following:
    a. occipital lobes
    b. parietal lobes (include the somatosensory areas)
    c. temporal lobes
    d. frontal lobes (include the motor cortex)
    e. associative areas (include Broca's and Wernicke's areas)
21. Explain the relationship between the size of the various parts of the somatosensory and motor areas of the cortex and the degree of sensitivity or importance of the corresponding body parts.
22. Describe the cause and effect of the disorder aphasia. Explain why there may be gender differences in aphasia.
23. List and be able to recognize the three areas of the subcortex.
24. Explain the function of each of the following parts of two of the three areas of the subcortex:
    a. Hindbrain (brainstem)
        i. pons
        ii. medulla
        iii. cerebellum
        iv. reticular formation
    b. Forebrain
        i. thalamus
        ii. hypothalamus
25. Name the structures that comprise the limbic system and explain its function (include a description of the function of the amygdala and the hippocampus).
26. Briefly describe the significance of "pleasure" and "aversive" areas in the limbic system.
27. List six basic functions of the brain.
28. Briefly describe the research of Bakay and Kennedy with cortical stimulation in paralyzed persons.
29. Briefly explain the purpose of the endocrine system. Describe the action of hormones in the body.
30. Describe the effect that the following glands have on the body and behavior:
    a. pituitary (include a description of giantism, hypopituitary dwarfism, and acromegaly)
    b. pineal
    c. thyroid (include a description of hyperthyroidism and hypothyroidism)
    d. adrenal medulla
    e. adrenal cortex (include a description of virilism, premature puberty, and the problems of anabolic steroids)

The following objectives are related to the material in the "Psychology in Action" section of the text.

31.   Describe the relationship among handedness, brain dominance, and speech. Describe the element of handedness that appears to be inherited.

32.   Explain how a person can determine which hemisphere is dominant.

33.   State the incidence of left-handedness and discuss the relative advantages and/or disadvantages of being right-handed versus left-handed.

■ DISCUSSION QUESTIONS

1.   If you could change the brain or nervous system in any way to improve them, how would you do it, and why?

2.   What effect would you expect a drug to have if it raised the firing threshold for neurons? If it mimicked the effect of a neurotransmitter? If it stimulated the RF? If it suppressed activity in the medulla?

3.   Neurons in the central nervous system do not have the capacity to regenerate. Develop your own hypothesis about why, based on your understanding of the structure and function of the neuron. Why do you think that neurons in the peripheral nervous system are able, at times, to repair damage to themselves?

4.   Have you known someone who has had a stroke or other brain injury? What were the effects? How did the person cope with the injury?

5.   A member of your family has been having outbursts of hostile and aggressive behavior. In the past year, they have become virtually uncontrollable. Brain surgery has been recommended as a way to alter the person's behavior. Would you condone its use?

6.   Do you think a sharp distinction between right and left hemisphere function is valid? For example, are there verbal skills involved in music, dance, or art?

7.   Robert Ornstein has urged us to recognize that full use of human potential should take advantage of the specialized skills of both cerebral hemispheres. Roger Sperry has charged that "our educational system tends to neglect the nonverbal form of intellect. What it comes down to is that modern society discriminates against the right hemisphere." Do you agree? What changes would you make in educational systems if you do?

8.   Many psychologists suggest that the split-brain person does not show deficits except in the lab because one hemisphere is able to learn from the other. How could this take place?

9.   If a person were kept alive with only the spinal cord intact, what kinds of responses would be possible? What if both the spinal cord and medulla were functioning? The spinal cord, medulla, and cerebellum? The spinal cord, medulla, and subcortex? All brain areas except the association cortex?

10.   A marathon runner completes a race but discovers that she has severely torn major ligaments in her calves. Why didn't she notice this during the race? Explain the series of events that you think probably took place.

11.   Can the brain ever expect to understand itself completely? Or, is the brain studying the brain like trying to lift yourself by your bootstraps?

12.   If the parents of a normal-sized child wanted to give the child growth hormone to make him or her taller, would you consider it ethical? Why or why not?

13.   Brain transplants done on lab animals typically make use of fetal brain tissue. It is possible that cells for transplants will eventually be grown in laboratory dishes. If this does not prove possible, and fetal cells are the only source for transplants, would you consider transplants ethical? If so, under what conditions?

14.   You have taken your superb understanding of psychology and physiology to the corporate world. You have decided to reorganize your new company according to the general plan of the human brain. What corporate activities would be most similar to the function of the different lobes of the cerebral cortex? To the function of the thalamus, the hypothalamus, and the hindbrain?

15.   The neurological system is very specific: a specific pathway will trigger a specific behavioral response. The endocrine system is very global: a specific hormone will trigger very general changes throughout the body. Why do we possess both systems? What is the adaptive value of this combination?

■ LECTURE ENHANCEMENTS

Students often describe this chapter as one of their favorites. The ideas are novel and exciting, yet the processes are potentially confusing and abstract. **It is typically useful to spend class time clarifying processes and encouraging students to articulate the processes in their own words.** It may help some students to think of this as a travel adventure into an intriguing foreign land. Transparencies can become their map and travel brochure.

Unless you have access to sophisticated lab equipment, only rudimentary demonstrations can be done to illustrate concepts from Chapter 2. In many cases the most effective recourse will be to obtain one of the films listed at the end of this section. **If your department owns either of the videotapes, "The Mind" or the "The Brain," you will find many segments to enhance your presentations.** Other visual aids can also be very helpful in clarifying difficult concepts. A model brain which can be disassembled to show its components is particularly effective. These can often be obtained from college or university biology or physiology departments.

1.   If you would like to try some **simple class demonstrations**, the following can be interesting:

> This demonstration is a sure-fire illustration of cortical localization and interference. Begin by asking the entire class to simultaneously move the right hand and right foot in a clockwise direction for a few seconds. This should be quite easy for everyone. Next ask that the right hand and left foot be moved in a clockwise direction. This is also easy. Next have students make circular movements in opposite directions with the right hand and the left foot. This is more difficult, but most students will master it. Finally, have students attempt to move the right hand and right foot in opposite directions. This is extremely difficult for most people. After making these observations, students should be challenged to explain them. If they need a hint, ask them to think in terms of probable activity in the motor areas of the cortex.

2.   **A national news service once reported the case of a child born without a brain.** According to the doctors interviewed at the time, such cases occur about once a year. In this instance the defect was not discovered until the child was several months old. The baby, who appears outwardly normal and healthy, began to cry excessively, and tests were performed to determine the cause. These tests revealed that the child had no brain. Doctors speculate that a cyst formed during prenatal development at the stem where the brain should have been and prevented further growth. The child survived because that portion of the brainstem which controls vital functions had already developed before the cyst formed. After students have read Chapter 2, they should be able to predict the kinds of abilities one might expect from such a child. You could ask them to describe the likelihood of this child having a personality, motivation, awareness, intelligence, and so forth.

3.   **Students are usually very interested in addressing the subject of the relationship between the brain and the mind.** You might begin a discussion of this topic by pointing out that many philosophical speculations regarding this issue have lost their relevance in light of new and innovative techniques (e.g., PET scans) for studying the human brain. The subject is, nevertheless, still very complex, and a lively class discussion can be generated by describing the following hypothetical experiment:

> You are looking at a PET scan of a brain while the radiologist taking the scan is sitting with you. You are discussing the activity depicted on the screen. Assume that the PET scanner is slightly advanced over what is presently available and depicts

glucose utilization immediately. (State-of-the-art scans require a 30- to 45-minute lead time.) As you are staring at the PET scan, the radiologist points out that the most active areas seen on the screen are in the left hemisphere, particularly the language area and the visual areas toward the back of the brain. At this moment you hear some music, and almost immediately the activity pattern of the scan changes. Now there is activity in the right hemisphere as well, and you call the radiologist's attention to that change. "That's in a region associated with the perception of music," she responds. Then a few minutes later she asks, "Do you have any comments on the PET scan?" "What do you mean?" you reply, and, at this point, you notice another change. The auditory areas, as well as the frontal lobes, light up. You look toward the radiologist and see that she is smiling, and you finally realize that the PET scan is depicting your own brain activity! It is showing a shift as you change from one thinking activity to another.

Now ask the students to consider the following questions: Is this an example of their minds studying their brains, or can they adequately explain it as the brain studying itself? For more speculation on this topic see R. Restak's *The Brain,* Bantam Books, 1984.

4.	**Watch the segment of "The Brain" series that shows a person walking with a computerized prosthesis.** Clarify that Delgado's research has not been replicated (Who would want to?); but that the concept of controlling behavior through stimulating different parts of the brain is a mainstream part of the new technology.

5.	**It is possible to give a sense of what it would be like to have a split brain by dividing students into groups of four.** One person serves as the split-brain subject; another serves as the experimenter; the other two as the two hemispheres. Ask each "hemisphere" to say something into the split-brain subject's ear at the same time. Prepare a script of questions for the experimenter to ask. If the experimenter says, "Tell me," the subject gives the answer the left hemisphere processed; if the experimenter says, "point to the right answer" the subject gives the answer the right hemisphere processed. Students should have to pause at first to think carefully about which response to give. Quickly, they will learn the cues.

6.	**Demonstrate the sensitivity of body areas by using two pencils on the back and the cheek of a student who has his or her eyes closed.** The student tells you whether there is one point or two. Gradually make the points closer and closer until they are perceived as one. The student will usually perceive one point even when there is about an inch of distance on the back between the two pencil points. On the face, the two pencils almost always seem like two points. Have the class "map" the body of their partner, making a sketch and indicating which areas are most and least sensitive. Compare this map to the sensory homunculus depicted in Chapter 2.

7.   **Give small groups of students a pile of wooden blocks in various shapes and colors.** Have them put together a model of a neuron, the brain, or of the nervous system. Have them explain their model to the class. Is it a structural or a functional model of the brain?

8.   **To demonstrate selective attention, have two students simultaneously read different passages into the ears of a third student.** Can the third student screen out irrelevant information and focus on only one message or the other? Can the student alternate from one ear to the other? Discuss the role of the reticular formation in selecting and routing incoming information.

9.   **Ask students to spend one day doing everything they can with their non-dominant hand--such as using scissors, opening jars, turning doorknobs, and the like.** (Students should exercise great caution to avoid accidents or injuries.) Have students share their feelings about this exercise and their insights into the relationship between brain and behavior.

10.   **Ask sports enthusiasts in your class to identify the handedness of prominent professional athletes in various sports.** Is there value in being right handed? Left-handed? Ambidextrous? In what ways are sports skills based on the body? On the brain? Why is it unlikely that a person could learn to be ambidextrous?

■ ROLE-PLAYING SCENARIOS

1.   **What would it be like to have facial agnosia?** What problems would you experience? What reaction do you think you would encounter from others? How would you feel? Enact this role as you attempt to interact with members of the class.

2.   **Try to behave as if you possessed only the abilities of the left hemisphere.** Then try to limit your behavior to that based on the specialized functions of the right hemisphere. (Other students can question the person enacting these roles. They should also note when behavior inappropriate to each role occurs.)

3.   **Try getting through an entire day while using your non-dominant hand.** What kind of problems do you run into? What is the most frustrating problem? How would you feel if someone (say, a teacher) told you that you must use this hand from now on?

■ VALUE-CLARIFICATION STATEMENTS

1.   Brain surgery should be required for individuals convicted of serial murders.

2.   A person could be a better athlete if he/she were ambidextrous.

3.   A parent has the right to decide whether medical treatment is given to his/her child, even if the child's life may be endangered by the decision.

4.   A person should be able to write a "living will" and prevent hospitals from using extreme measures to keep his or her body alive.

5.   Transplantation of brain tissue to cure human diseases and to reverse paralysis should be done even if fetal brains remain the only source of tissue.

■ ONE-MINUTE MOTIVATORS

1.   **Perhaps the model you have of the brain does in fact weigh about three pounds.** If not, develop one with clay. Pass it around the class. Students can best appreciate the size of the brain if you could also find an object weighing about 30 pounds.

2.   **Tinker-toys can be used to create a model of a neuron.** These can be placed on the eraser-ledge of a chalkboard. A few nerve pathways could extend onto a desk. Use one color for the excitatory pathways and another color for inhibitory pathways.

3.   **In order to conceptualize the firing of the neuron, students often need analogies to concrete objects.** Possible analogies include: a radio, a telephone, a fax machine, a stereo system, the process of sending mail, etc. The analogy must be developed carefully: it must clarify, not mystify or confuse. A cap pistol can be used to dramatize the all-or-none quality of the action potential. Since the text refers to a "domino effect" of sorts, set one up on a tabletop.

4.   **The power of neurotransmitters can be demonstrated using a squirt gun filled with laundry bleach.** Squirt a colorful fabric; then squirt a glass or porcelain plate. The point made is that neurotransmitters must adhere to appropriate receptor sites before an action potential can be triggered.

5.   **Without warning, suggest that it would be helpful to know something more about the interests of students.** Explain, "In five minutes I will pick a number from the roster and ask you to stand up and give a brief speech." After one student briefly talks, discuss

the sympathetic nervous system. Then guide students through a few minutes of deep breathing and relaxation to demonstrate the parasympathetic system. The transition from one to the other may be signaled by asking students when they have sufficient saliva to actually swallow a cracker.

6.   **To illustrate the enhanced surface area of the cortex,** wad up a piece of foil or aluminum foil to create a convoluted brain surface.

7.   **To contrast sequential and holistic processing,** play some music. Ask half of the class to tell you what mood it puts them in; ask the other half to learn the lyrics or the melody.

8.   **Read aloud a short example from the book,** *Phantoms in the Brain* **(V. S. Ramachandran and Sandra Blakeslee, William Morrow and Company, 1998).** For example, beginning on page 118 there is an interesting account of a person with spatial neglect. This, and other poignant examples from the book, can help make students aware of how totally we depend on a properly functioning brain.

9.   **Pass around a sugar cube, which is about the size of the hypothalamus in humans.** Remind students that the very small hypothalamus monitors and triggers a myriad of very complex processes.

10.   **Ask left-handers to meet outside of class and make a list of all of the inconveniences of living in a right-handed world.** Ask them to share any horror stories from their childhood about having their left hand tied to their back, etc.

■ BROADENING OUR CULTURAL HORIZONS

1.   **Different religions have diverse attitudes concerning the rights of humans to intervene medically so as to save a life and concerning the disposition of a person's body after death.** Compare and contrast the following views.

       a. Blood transfusions should not take place.
       b. The body should not be violated after death.
       c. Parts of the dead body should be immediately used for transplants.
       d. A person's body should be cremated at death.

2.   **A 25-year-old woman is dying of cancer.** She has asked that "no extreme procedures be used to prolong life." She is now comatose and can only be kept alive with machines. How would you decide whether her will should be respected?

A 25-year-old man is dying of cancer. He has asked that "no extreme procedures be used to prolong life." He is now comatose and can only be kept alive with machines. How would you decide whether his will should be respected?

Would the answers be different if each dying person's cultural background or religion were known?

3.   In what ways might different cultures make greater or lesser use of the various strengths of the right and left cerebral hemispheres?

4.   In many Middle Eastern cultures, using the left hand for eating or touching another person is forbidden. What kind of difficulties might a naturally left-handed person encounter in such a culture? How might children be trained to be right-handed, and what effect might that have on the growing child?

■ SUPPLEMENTAL ACTIVITIES

TO THE INSTRUCTOR:

Exercise #1: Lateral Eye Movement

An in-class activity that will demonstrate the functioning of the left and right hemispheres of the brain and which many show dominance of one hemisphere over the other involves observing lateral eye movement. A study by Schwartz, Davidson, and Maer serves as a model for this exercise. They were able to show that spontaneous lateral eye movement reflects activity in one or other of the hemispheres of the brain. Eye movement to the left seemed to indicate involvement of the right hemisphere, and movement to the right appeared to involve the left side. It has been observed that some people shift their eyes to the left more often than to the right. These are called left-movers. Others typically shift to the right and are called right-movers.

A conclusion drawn by researchers in this area is that left-movers have a right hemisphere dominance and tend to be more artistic, creative, and intuitive thinkers. Right movers have left hemisphere dominance and tend to be more logical, analytical, verbal, and numerical. These conclusions are considered to be general tendencies and therefore should be viewed with a skeptical eye. More study and research is needed to support these conclusions.

Lateral Eye Movement (or, Look Left and You'll Be Right)

1.   Select five students to be the subjects of the demonstration. Ask them to leave the room while preparations are made.

2.   Explain to the rest of the class that you will ask the subjects a list of questions. The students are to observe and record the eye movements of each subject when the questions are asked. Caution them that the eye movements may be slight and will be to the left or right. They will have to observe with care (and they will not have the benefit of slow motion or instant replays).

3.   Provide each student with a copy of the record sheet which contains the questions and a space to record the subject's responses.

4.   Admit the subjects, one at a time, and have each one stand in front of the class in full view of the students.

5.   You should ask each question and give the subject time to respond. The students will record their observation for each question. You should accept whatever answer is given and move on.

6.   After all subjects have been questioned, tally the number of observed left and right eye movements for each question and each subject.

7.   An analysis of the results should attempt to see:
        a.   which items tended to elicit a left eye shift, indicating right hemisphere activity and which elicited a shift to the right, pointing to a left hemisphere involvement.
        b.   if any subject had a tendency to shift more in one direction than the other, indicating a left or right hemisphere dominance.

8.   The record sheet has a series of questions which follow a pattern. All odd-numbered items should elicit left hemisphere activity (eye shift to the right), and even-numbered items should elicit right hemisphere activity (eye shift to the left).

Exercise #2: How Many Reflexes Can You Find?

Although reflexes are among the "simplest" behaviors, they can help students appreciate the extent to which much of their behavior traces back to the "wiring" of the nervous system. The following exercise will help students observe a number of reflexes beyond those with which they are already familiar. Students should work in pairs.

LATERAL EYE MOVEMENT RECORD SHEET:

TO THE STUDENT:

Record your observations on this sheet. Mark an L for left and an R for right. Remember that you are recording the subject's eye movement to HIS or HER right, not to yours. Do not do anything to distract the subjects, or yourself, since the eye movement may be slight.

	SUBJECT				
	1	2	3	4	5
1. How many weeks are there in a year?					
2. On what coin is John F. Kennedy pictured?					
3. What is the last line of "The Star-Spangled Banner"?					
4. Without looking at me, what is the color of my shirt (tie, skirt)?					
5. Define the term "psychology."					
6. On which side is the steering wheel of a car in England?					
7. Why do people pay taxes?					
8. Who is pictured on the front of a five-dollar bill?					
9. What do the letters in "NASA" stand for?					
10. About how far is it to the moon?					

HOW MANY REFLEXES CAN YOU FIND?

TO THE STUDENT:

Work with your partner to develop a list of reflexes that can be observed in humans. Expand your list with the following reflexes. Decide who will be the experimenter and who will be the subject. The experimenter will use the following instructions to try to demonstrate some additional reflexes.

1. **Using either a piece of thread or a strand of hair, tickle the inside of the nostril of your partner.** What is the response?

2. **Gently touch the center area of the eye (the cornea) with the thread or hair. Try not to touch the eyelashes.** What is the response?

3. **Ask your partner to close his/her eyes.** Cover the eyes with your hands. Then ask your partner to turn toward the brightest corner of the classroom and to open his/her eyes. What changes take place in the size of the pupils?

4. **Ask your partner to open one eye and close the other.** What changes take place in the size of the pupil of the open eye?

5. **Ask your partner to gaze at a distant object in the room.** Then ask him/her to look at a pencil that you hold six inches from the eye. What changes take place in the size of the pupil?

6. **Suddenly clap your hands in front of the eyes of your partner.** Record whether the blink is typical (T), partial (P), or if there is no blink (N). Clap for twenty trials, recording the type of blink each time. Then ask your partner to try to inhibit the blink for the next twenty trials. What pattern did you notice? Can reflexes be modified by conscious control? What else might explain any changes in the pattern of response?

7. **Take your partner's pulse.** Record the rate per minute three times to find an average. Ask your partner to close his or her eyes and use a hand to put moderate pressure on one eyeball. While this is done, measure the pulse rate again. Record that number. Then ask your partner to remove the pressure. How long does it take for the heart rate to return to normal? (This is the ocular-cardiac reflex).

Share your reactions to this demonstration with the class.

■ JOURNAL QUESTIONS

1.   Describe a time in your life when you were so involved in what you were doing that you didn't realize you were hungry, thirsty, or in pain.

2.   Which hemisphere of your brain do you think you rely on most as you process information? Under what conditions is such reliance most effective? When is it least effective?

3.   Describe your relationship to your brain: Do you think of your "self" as residing in your brain? Do you feel that you exist in some way that is apart from the brain? Do you make a distinction between your mind and your body? Do you regard your brain as part of your body? How can your brain be aware of its own existence?

■ SUGGESTIONS FOR FURTHER READING

Annett, M., and Manning, M. "Arithmetic and laterality." *Neuropsychologia, (28)*, 61-69, 1990.

Bakan, P. "Handedness and maternal smoking during pregnancy." *International Journal of Neuroscience, (56),* 161-168, 1991.

Bryden, M. P. "Perhaps not so sinister." *Contemporary Psychology, (38),* 71-72, 1993.

Congdon, P. J. *Lefty: a story of left-handedness.* London, England: Gifted Children's Information Centre Publications, 1994.

Corballis, M. C. "Laterality and Myth." *American Psychologist,* March 1980: 284-295.

Damasio, A. R. *The Scientific American Book of the Brain,* The Lyons Press, 1999.

DeKay, J. T. *The Left-hander's Handbook.* New York: Book-of-the-Month Club, Inc., 1994.

Elias, L. J., and Bryden, M. P. "Footedness is a better predictor of language lateralization than handedness." *Laterality, 3(1),* 41-51, 1998.

Gazzaniga, M. S. *The Social Brain: Discovering the Networks of the Mind.* Basic Books, 1985.

Levy, Jerre. "Right Brain, Left Brain: Fact or Fiction." *Psychology Today,* May 1985.

Ramachandran, V. S. and Blakeslee, S. *Phantoms in the Brain: Probing the Mysteries of the Human Mind.* William Morrow & Company, 1998.

Rosenzweig, M. R. and A. L. Leiman. *Biological Psychology.* Sinauer, 1996.

Sacks, O. *Awakenings.* HarperCollins Publishers, Inc., 1990.

Sacks, O. *The Man Who Mistook His Wife for a Hat and Other Clinical Tales.* HarperCollins Publishers, Inc., 1985.

Springer, S. P. and G. Deutsch. *Left Brain, Right Brain,* 4th ed. W. H. Freeman, 1993.

■ MEDIA SUGGESTIONS

THE ANIMATED BRAIN (2002, Insight Media, Mac/Windows CD-ROM)
This CD-ROM provides an understanding of the workings of the brain, covering neurocytology, neuronal communication, development, the gross brain, sensory systems, motor functions, the thalamus, cortex, cognition, learning and memory, and the biological bases of mental disorders. Included are illustrations, animation, narration, and exercises.

THE BIOLOGY OF BEHAVIOR (2002, from *Psychology- The Study of Human Behavior Series*, Coast Community College District, 30 min.)
Focuses on the human nervous systems and neurotransmission.

BRAIN STORY: NEW FRONTIERS IN BRAIN RESEARCH (2002, Films for the Humanities and Sciences, 6-part series, 50 min. each)
Enhanced by 3-D graphics and intimate case studies, this series explores the grand themes emerging from the latest brain research.

THE BRAIN: AN INSIDE LOOK (2002, Films for the Humanities and Sciences, 20 minutes)
Includes CT scans, MRI scans, and advanced surgical techniques to look at brain structure and function.

DEVELOPMENT OF THE HUMAN BRAIN (1990, Films for the Humanities and Sciences, 40 min.)
This film shows physiological development of the brain from conception through age eight, including motor and cognitive development.

DOPAMINE SEDUCTION: THE LIMBIC SYSTEM (2002, Films for the Humanities and Sciences, 25 min.) This Discovery Channel production contains extraordinary 3-D computer animations of hormonal and neurotransmitter activity, illustrating the function of the limbic system.

THE NERVOUS SYSTEM (2002, from *Psychology- The Human Experience Telecourse,* Coast Community College District, 30 min.)
This video looks at the components of the nervous system and the methods used for studying the brain through the story of a split-brain patient.

THE NEURON AND NEURAL TRANSMISSION (2002, from *Psychology- The Human Experience Telecourse,* Coast Community College District, 30 min.)
This video looks at how the brain communicates with the body by explaining what the neuron is, how it functions, and what happens to that communication when neurological disorders occur.

A number of videos are available from Thomson. Videos appropriate for this chapter include the following films from the CNN TODAY Introductory Psychology Video Series:

Volume 1, Section 2: The Brain
     Addicted Brain (2:50)
     Shrinking Brains (3:30)
     Memory Drugs (1:59)
     Warrior Mentality (2:54)
     Dyslexia Study (2:45)
     Brain Conference (2:41)

Volume 2, Section 1: The Brain
     Hyperactive Brains (2:11)
     Brain Mapping (2:29)
     Smell Memory (2:21)
     The Brain and ADD (1:51)

Volume 3, Section 1: The Biological Bases of Behavior
     Mood Chemicals (1:10)
     Stroke Brain Repair (1:54)
     Human Gene Repair (1:46)

Volume 4, Section 1: Substance Abuse
     Parents' Teen Smoking (1:31)
     Celebrity Addiction (2:57)
     Heroin Kids (1:55)
     Binge Drinking (2:07)

■ COMPUTER AND INTERNET RESOURCES

PSYCHNOW!

The Brain & Consciousness:
Neurons and Synaptic Transmission
Brain and Behavior

PSYK.TREK

Unit 2: Biological Bases of Behavior
     2a: The neuron and the neural impulse
     2b: Synaptic transmission
     2c: Looking inside the brain: Research methods
     2d: The hindbrain and the midbrain
     2e: The forebrain: Subcortical structures
     2f: The cerebral cortex
     2g: Right brain/Left brain

INFOTRAC

Subject Guide/Key Words: Neuron, Neuroanatomy, Structure of the Brain, Human Nervous System, Endocrine System, Hormones, Neuroscience, Neurotransmitter, Brain Scans, MRI, PET scan, Split Brain

WEB SITES

Wadsworth Online Psychology Study Center:
http://info.wadsworth.com/cooessentials9

Society for Neuroscience:
http://www.sfn.org/

Neuroscience-Net:
http://www.neuroscience.com/

Neurology Related Web sites:
http://www.herring.org/neuro.html

Brain and Cognitive Sciences:
http://www.bcs.rochester.edu/bcs/web_sites.html

Global Neurological Web sites:
http://www.neuro.onnet.co.kr/links.html

Neuroanatomy and Neuropathology on the Internet:
http://www.dote.hu/%7Ehegedus/index.html#Anatomy

Cognitive Neuroscience Society:
http://www.cogneurosociety.org/

External View of the Brain:
http://rpiwww.mdacc.tmc.edu:80/se/anatomy/brain

The Whole Brain Atlas:
http://www.med.harvard.edu:80/AANLIB

CHAPTER 3
Child Development

■ LEARNING OBJECTIVES

To demonstrate mastery of this chapter, the student should be able to:

1. Define developmental psychology and name its principal focus.
2. Define the terms "nature" and "nurture" as they relate to human development. Define the terms "heredity" and "conception."
3. Define or describe each of the following terms:
    a. chromosome
    b. gene
    c. polygenic
    d. dominant gene
    e. recessive gene
4. Describe genetic counseling and genetic screening. Differentiate amniocentesis from chorionic villi sampling.
5. Characterize the three types of children according to temperament and explain how these temperamental differences influence development.
6. Discuss the concept of sensitive periods.
7. Distinguish between congenital and genetic disorders.
8. Describe the relationship between the blood supplies of the mother and her developing child. Discuss the effect of teratogens on the unborn child, including the effects of drugs, alcohol (include a description of fetal alcohol syndrome), and tobacco.
9. Briefly differentiate conventional deliveries from prepared childbirth in terms of methods and effects.
10. Briefly describe the two most important differences in the brain of a newborn and brain of an adult.
11. Briefly discuss the impact of poverty on children's IQ and behavior.
12. Review the research demonstrating the benefits of enriched environments.
13. Briefly discuss the "Mozart effect" and the problems surrounding the original research.
14. Describe the apparent outcome of the nature-nurture debate. List the three factors that combine to determine a person's developmental level.
15. Name and describe four adaptive reflexes of a neonate.
16. Describe the intellectual capabilities and the sensory preferences of a neonate.
17. Discuss the concept of maturation and define the terms "cephalocaudal" and "proximodistal."

18.   Discuss the concept of readiness. Include in your answer the outcome of forcing a child to learn skills too early.

19.   With respect to maturation, describe the course of emotional development.

20.   Explain how there is an interplay between the emotions of infants and adults. Include the concept of the social smile.

21.   Explain the concepts of self-awareness and social referencing.

22.   Discuss the importance of emotional attachment, including the concept of separation anxiety. Include in your answer a differentiation of Ainsworth's attachment types as well as the key to secure attachments.

23.   Define "contact comfort," and explain the importance of breastfeeding and meeting a child's affectional needs.

24.   Discuss the effects of daycare on attachment.

25.   Discuss the importance of children's play, including the concepts of solitary play and cooperative play.

26.   Describe the extremes of the maternal caregiving styles and their results.

27.   Discuss the importance of paternal influences in child development. Compare these influences to maternal ones.

28.   Compare and contrast the following three parenting styles and their effects on children:
      a.   authoritarian
      b.   overly permissive
      c.   authoritative

The following objective is related to the material in the "Exploring Psychology" section of the text.

29.   Briefly describe some of the differences in child-rearing practices of the four ethnic groups listed in this section, and the conclusion that can be drawn from these differences.

30.   Give a brief description of each of the following childrearing techniques and describe their effects on children:
      a. power assertion
      b. withdrawal of love
      c. management techniques (include the concept of self-esteem)

31.   List and briefly describe the five stages of language acquisition.

32.   Briefly discuss the concept of the "terrible twos."

33.   Describe what the "language dance" is and explain why children probably do it.

34.   Define the term psycholinguist. Describe the role of learning in the acquisition of language.

35.   Explain how parents communicate with infants before infants can talk. Include the ideas of signals, turn taking, and parentese.

36.   Explain how a child's intelligence and thinking differ from an adult's. Explain the concept of transformations.

37.   List (in order) and briefly describe Piaget's four stages of cognitive development. Include an explanation of assimilation and accommodation.

38.   Briefly describe the research concerning a child's theory of mind.

39.   Describe the methods of encouraging intellectual development in children in each of Piaget's cognitive stages.

40.   Briefly describe the dangers of forced teaching.

41.   Describe the research that indicates that Piaget may have underestimated infant cognitive abilities.

42.   Describe the sociocultural theory of Lev Vygotsky, including a comparison to Piaget and the terms "zone of proximal development" and "scaffolding."

The following objectives are related to the material in the "Psychology in Action" section of the text.

43.   Name the two most important areas of effective parent-child relationships.

44.   Discuss the importance of using consistent discipline in childrearing.

45.   List seven guidelines that should be followed if physical punishment is used in disciplining children.

46.   List the four basic ingredients (Dinkmeyer & McKay) of a positive parent-child relationship.

47.   Describe four important aspects of communication between parents and children, including what Dr. Thomas Gordon calls an "I" message.

48.   Describe the use of natural and logical consequences to correct children's misbehavior.

■ DISCUSSION QUESTIONS

1.   A friend of yours has a child whose grasping reflex was absolutely phenomenal during the first year of life. Your friend was sure that her daughter would become a Hall of Fame quarterback. Now the child is one year old and the power of the grasp seems to be waning. Why?

2.   Why do babies seem to prefer complex visual patterns? Why would an infant progress from preferring familiar stimuli to a preference for the unfamiliar? What adaptive value is there in these tendencies?

3.   How would you go about doing an experiment to test whether basic emotional reactions are universal?

4.   How should a caregiver respond to a crying baby? Can't a baby become spoiled? Why or why not?

5.   How can a parent or caregiver know when a child is ready to learn a new skill?

6. Should humans try to control their own heredity? Who would decide what characteristics should be developed? Who would get them? For what purpose? Would you endorse use of genetic engineering to delay or prevent aging?

7. Which do you think would produce a better decision by prospective parents receiving genetic counseling: to be told that "There is a 1 percent chance of having a child with a chromosome abnormality" or to be given the same information this way: "You must realize that either it will or it will not happen"?

8. What are your thoughts on the practical and ethical questions that follow? Should children conceived by donor artificial insemination or by donor egg be told about their parentage? Should records be kept that would allow them to find their donor fathers or mothers if some extraordinary need were to arise? What would be the psychological impact of knowing that you were conceived *in vitro*?

9. In view of the importance of infant attachment and the participation of fathers in child care, what changes would you recommend in maternity and paternity leaves from work? Would you change the traditional division of labor in maternal and paternal roles? Why or why not?

10. Traditionally, mothers and fathers played a different role in the development of the baby. What effect would these different styles have on sex role development? Many girls are now raised only by their father; many boys are now raised only by their mother. How could that affect their social and interpersonal development?

11. What kind of a national infant care leave policy do you think would be appropriate? What impact would such a policy have on the child's development? On the parents' ability to be responsive to the child's needs? On businesses? If you were a politician, would you support such legislation? Why or why not?

12. You have asked your five-year-old to select a birthday gift for his 12-year-old sister. What will he probably select? Why? What does this tell us about his cognitive development?

13. What is your reaction to the following statement, made by anthropologist Margaret Mead? "Fathers are a biological necessity but a social accident."

14. In what ways is it accurate to treat children as "little adults"? In what ways is it inaccurate? What is the value of children in society?

15. How many ways can you think of for an infant to reward its mother and for the mother to reward the infant?

16.   What types of toys would you select for an infant or young child? Do you think simple toys or elaborate toys would be best? Why? Would your choice change for an older child? Why?

17.   Why is parental responsiveness to and interaction with the infant so very important? Can a parent be too responsive? What does this seem to be saying about the basic needs of humans? What consequences would you predict for the person who did not experience close interaction with parents?

18.   What, if anything, can a parent do to increase the rate at which a child learns a language or a sport? Why would a parent want to do this? Would this be to the child's advantage or detriment?

19.   How has heredity affected your development? How has environment affected you? How would child rearing be different if parents had to teach children to walk or to talk?

■ LECTURE ENHANCEMENTS

Since all of us were once children, students begin this chapter with considerable knowledge. We learn best about children by being with children. If only a few children are available to be brought to class, you can conduct all demonstrations and conversations in front of the class, or small groups of students can plan and carry out an activity with a child. If a large number of children are available, each student could be assigned a child partner. In the next class session, students can discuss their feelings about spending time with a child they didn't know. Interviews, role-playing, value clarification, and journals are all effective ways to talk about childhood and feelings about what is best for children.

1.   **Given that Chapter 3 is concerned with development in childhood, observing children at various ages makes a good outside assignment.** Children may be observed at home, in a college preschool or day-care center, or at private nursery schools. Students should write a detailed description of a half-hour sample of a child's behavior, giving special attention to cognitive skills such as those described by Piaget. Such observations provide many examples of chapter concepts for class discussion. Prior to the observation, discuss with the class appropriate guidelines for behavior during objective observation.

2.   **If you have willing parents in class, arrange for an infant and a pre-operational (four- or five-year-old) child to visit the class.** With the infant you can demonstrate a lack of object permanence (or its presence, depending on the age of the child), by holding a toy in the child's view and then behind your back. Simple sensory-motor coordination and purposeful behavior will be apparent in the child's attempts to touch a desirable toy. Separation anxiety can be illustrated by having the parent briefly leave the room. Bring

some props for the pre-operational child so that you can demonstrate a lack of conservation of length, volume, or area. Conversations with pre-operational children can be entertaining and instructive. Videotape the demonstration if possible. During the next class session, discuss not only the child's behavior but the reaction of your students to children of different ages.

3. **Although few psychologists would deny the pervasive effects of heredity on development, the general public often tends to over-emphasize hereditary effects.** To illustrate, you may want to approximate a technique originated by David Rosenhan of Stanford University. Professor Rosenhan shows a slide of his two children and encourages students to note the ways in which the children resemble each other and him. Once students are thoroughly drawn in, he tells the class that his children are adopted! To make the same point you could show a slide of two unrelated persons and tell the class they are siblings; then, after discussion, reveal that they have no hereditary connection. Follow with a discussion of hereditary/environmental interactions.

4. **While deciding whether or not to become a parent is one of the most important decisions anyone will ever make, it is surprising how little thought students have given to this subject.** It is particularly surprising since the overwhelming majority of them will, in fact, one day become parents. As a way to explore their motives for producing children, you could have students fold a sheet of paper down the center and on the left side list all the advantages of parenting and on the right side all the disadvantages. After they are finished, put some of their responses on the board and use them to generate a class discussion.

5. **Raise the question that is a burning issue today: When is the developing organism a human being?** The abortion issue has focused intense debate on this question. At what point between conception and birth is the organism human? Opinions will vary from the point of conception to the time when the fetus is viable. You should not try to convince students about your personal opinion. Rather, try to keep the discussion focused on the issue using as much scientific data as possible. One way to get students to step back from their positions, which may be somewhat hardened, is to ask them what scientific evidence they would require to change their opinions.

6. **The "Doughboy demonstration" is brief but powerful.** Bring to class the ingredients to make dough. The elements of the dough symbolize heredity, with yeast or chocolate serving as unique genes. The cooking procedure (baking of bread, frying of a tortilla) symbolizes the environment. Before class, bake some of the dough so that samples reflecting various combinations can be observed. For example, you can add excessive salt to exemplify genetic problems; burnt bread can symbolize congenital defects. Students should learn about nature-nurture interactions from these examples. They can also have fun eating some of the samples if you include some simple cookies.

7. **Ask students to interview a parenting couple and a pair of single parents.** The student can ask: What do you find most exciting about your life? What do you find most difficult? How are the two couples lives similar and different? This can also be done in class, with couples visiting and answering questions posed by the students.

■ ROLE-PLAYING SCENARIOS

1. **What might a fetus experience during the last trimester of prenatal development?** What does he/she feel when alcohol or smoke is ingested?

2. **Spend ten minutes acting unsocialized.** The behaviors will probably be "anti-socialized" but not inevitably anti-social behaviors. Once a person is socialized, is it possible to put aside that prior learning? (If you participate, be sure to remember which sections received this assignment. It could be embarrassing to begin class sitting on the floor or lapping food off a plate if students have no idea what you are doing.)

3. **Ask students to respond on paper, in pairs or in small groups, to a series of hypothetical situations:**

    a. You are taking care of a three-month-old nephew. Suddenly he begins to cry hysterically. What should you do? Why? (Change the wording on part of the forms to "niece." Do students respond differently?)

    b. You are a physician working with a mother who cannot decide what kind of infant delivery would be best. What guidance would you give her? Under what conditions is natural childbirth most desirable?

    c. You are a father who has been excluded from the delivery room and the birth of your child. How do you feel? How do you behave?

    d. You are a father who does not want to become involved in your child's delivery because you are afraid. Explain your feelings and your behavior.

    e. You are a mother whose husband has decided to become very involved in the delivery process. You are not pleased or grateful. What are your feeling and thinking? Why?

    f. You are a husband whose wife is going through post-partum depression. What should you say? What should you do? What should you not do? Why?

g.   You just inherited a children's toy manufacturing company. You want to extend the product line to include toys that would increase cognitive development. What toys would you manufacture for various age ranges?

h.   You are a preschool teacher. What should you do to foster the cognitive development of your students?

i.   You are a third-grade teacher and you want to create an enriched intellectual environment. What would you do? Why?

■ VALUE-CLARIFICATION STATEMENTS

1.   A mother convicted of abusing drugs during pregnancy should be required to prove abstinence for the entire first year of the child's life or give up the baby for foster care.

2.   All employers should be required to provide for (or pay for) preschool childcare for the children of their employees.

3.   Basic parenting skills should be taught in the public schools sometime before students reach child-bearing age.

■ ONE-MINUTE MOTIVATORS

1.   **Collect photographs of students taken during their childhood years.** Ask students to try to guess which classmate matches which childhood picture.

2.   **Pass a lump of clay around the room.** Ask each student to note what it looks like when they first touch it and to mold it in some way. Continue lecturing during this process. At the end, point out that the lump's "genetic material" never changed, that its form often changed, and that each student made an imprint on the clay. Have the class explain how this demonstrates our own development.

3.   **Ask two students before class to develop persuasive speeches on why a person should not smoke or drink during pregnancy.** Suddenly in the middle of lecture, say, "Jaime, tell me why you think smoking and drinking should be avoided." Later in the semester, this activity may be useful for illustrating attitude change related to cognitive dissonance: If the students you selected were not opposed to these behaviors prior to giving their speech, they probably will be after.

4.   **Conservation of volume can be easily demonstrated with two glasses of unequal size.** Ask students how to handle the following situation: Your four-year-old wants the same

amount of milk as your eight-year-old receives. You only have two glasses of different sizes. How could you resolve this situation to the satisfaction of both children?

5.   **Ask students to generalize the "Monopoly a la Piaget" example to sports.** How do children at the different stages play soccer or baseball? What techniques should a coach of a team of five-year-olds use to teach the game? What techniques should be used with a team of ten-year-olds?

6.   **Show the class four slides, 8 X 10 photos, or a short home video of a family composed of two unrelated parents and two unrelated children.** Ask the class to describe ways the children resemble each other and their parents. Students will try to be "helpful" and will find many similarities among the family members. Then explain that the children are not related to either each other or the adults. Discuss issues of heredity and environment. (This is a variation of the Rosenhan demonstration, described earlier.)

■ BROADENING OUR CULTURAL HORIZONS

1.   **Ask students to collect information on the Israeli kibbutz system of child-rearing.** What are the advantages and disadvantages of this system?

2.   **Different cultures "see" children in different ways.** How do you view children? Circle the number that is closest to your views:

I see children (age 5 to 12) as:

big babies	1	2	3	4	5	*little adults*
helpless	1	2	3	4	5	*responsible*
dependent	1	2	3	4	5	*independent*
fragile	1	2	3	4	5	*sturdy*
not smart	1	2	3	4	5	*very smart*
self-centered	1	2	3	4	5	*other-directed*

Share your views with others in class. In what ways are your views similar and different?

3.   **Often step-families blend two very different "cultures" in terms of rules and expectations of behavior.** What would you suggest that step-families do to minimize the cultural shock as the families merge?

4.   **Research suggests that certain facial expressions are universally expressed.** What does this suggest about the possibility of effective international communication?

5.   **If any of your students are bilingual, ask them to discuss the advantages and disadvantages they have encountered.** If any of your students are visiting from other countries, or if they are recent immigrants, ask them to tell how child-rearing practices different in their home culture.

■ SUPPLEMENTAL ACTIVITIES

TO THE INSTRUCTOR:

There are **two exercises** that focus attention on some aspects of development. **The first** is a way to demonstrate conservation, or the lack of it. This exercise usually illustrates a difference in cognitive functioning between preoperational and concrete operational children. This one takes some preparation and planning. Children of appropriate ages need to be found and brought to class. It may be difficult to get a natural and normal response from young children when they are being observed by a large number of adults.

The second exercise demonstrates some hereditary characteristics. No props or preplanning are needed. This exercise will provide a natural opportunity to discuss dominant, recessive, and sex-linked traits and characteristics.

Exercise #1: Conservation

These demonstrations of conservation are certain to impress the students with the idea that there is a qualitative difference in the cognitive functioning of a preoperational and a concrete operational child. They will see, furthermore, that this change does, in fact, occur at about seven years of age, as Piaget theorized.

This exercise can be done individually by each student if she/he can find enough subjects of the right ages. However, it is often easier to import a group of children for the class period. Students will probably have enough brothers, sisters, cousins, or neighbors of the right ages to do the project. Ask members of the class to volunteer to bring a child. This will take some planning since students will have to get the child's consent, the agreement of the parents, and permission from their schools to be absent on that day.

I.   **Preparation**

        A.   Get students to volunteer to bring the subjects. You will need ten altogether, a boy and a girl at each of the following ages: 5, 6, 7, 8, and 9. Set up a day and a time for the children to be at the school. The student or parent should bring them.

B. Prepare a set of materials ahead of time. You will need two short, fat beakers filled with colored liquid (use food coloring); and one tall, thin beaker; two large balls of modeling clay; and ten square cubes (these can be small toy blocks).

C. On the day of the exercise seat the students and the children in a way that will be non-threatening and make the children comfortable. Have the class and the children talk a bit, perhaps even mingle so they get used to each other. The students should have been prepared ahead of time to observe these children to see how they behave. Does their behavior square with the theories about what is appropriate for their ages?

D. Select a student to be the experimenter ahead of time. Be sure she/he has run through the experiment a few times to be ready for whatever happens. You can play the child's role for the practice session.

II. Demonstration

A. Remove the children from the room and set up the three exercises. They will be presented to each child one at a time. The experimenter should be trained so that she/he knows what to expect. Provide each student with a Data Sheet.

B. Bring the children in one at a time, starting with the youngest, and have them do each of the three exercises. The students in the class are observers, and they should be recording on the Data Sheet what they observe in an unobtrusive way so that they do not disturb the subject.

C. When all subjects have been tested, they should be assembled again, given a treat (the whole class should give themselves a treat), and sent on their way home. The students should look over their results and, on the next class day, discuss the observations.

III. The Three Demonstrations

A. Place the two short, fat beakers, filled almost full of liquid in front of the subject. Ask the subject, "Are they both the same, or does one have more than the other?" The child will reply that they are both the same. If she/he says one has more and one less, then pour a little from one to the other until the child says they are the same.

    Now pour the liquid from one of the beakers into the tall, thin one. Ask the child, "Are they both the same, or does one have more than the other?" If the child says the tall one has more, do not argue or question the child further, but, instead, simply pour the liquid back into the short, fat beaker. Again ask if they are now the same. After an affirmative answer, pour the liquid into the tall, thin glass and ask the question again. See if you get the same response.

B.   Place the two round balls of modeling clay in front of the subject. Ask the child, "Are the two balls of clay the same size, or is one bigger than the other?" When you have an affirmative answer, take one ball and, in full view of the subject, roll out one into a long, thin shape, like a sausage. Now ask the child, "Are they the same, or is one bigger than the other?" This one need not be repeated regardless of the answer.

C.   Place the ten blocks in two rows of five each in front of the child. Ask the child, "Do the two rows have the same number of blocks, or does one have more than the other?" After you get an affirmative answer, spread out the blocks in one row so the five blocks make a row about twice as long as the other five-block row. Now ask the child, "Do both rows have the same number of blocks, or does one have more than the other?" This one need not be repeated.

IV.   Discussion

A.   All observations should have been recorded by the students on their data sheets. It should have been evident at what age the change took place on each of the three tasks. You can also see if there were any differences between the boys and the girls.

B.   What can you conclude about conservation in children?

C.   Would the results obtained here be the same for all children of the same ages?

CONSERVATION: DATA SHEET

TO THE STUDENT:

Record your observations on the chart. Indicate the responses for females (F) and males (M) separately for each age. Enter an S if the subject says the two are the same and a D if she/he says they are different.

AGE	LIQUID M	LIQUID F	CLAY M	CLAY F	BLOCKS M	BLOCKS F
5						
6						
7						
8						
9						

Exercise #2: It's In The Genes

You can generate some interest in the genetic influences on behavior by a few simple exercises in the classroom. The purpose is to show the direct relationship between genes and behavior. Be sure to emphasize the point that practice does not improve one's ability to do any of the tasks. It's in the genes.

Try any or all of the following exercises:

1.   **Tasting:** This activity requires the use of paper soaked in phenylthiocarbromide (PTC). You can obtain this from the chemistry department.

        Ask the students to place the treated paper on their tongues and report the taste. Although a variety of tastes may be reported, a significant number in the class will report a bitter taste. Those who do are called "tasters" because they have a dominant gene for this trait. Those who experience anything else are "non-tasters." They have a pair of recessive genes for this "taste" trait.

        It has been estimated that about 70-75% of a typical class will be tasters. See how your class compares with this standard.

2.   **Color blindness:** Figure 5-14 in Chapter 5 of the text is a replica of the Ishihara test for color blindness. This is not a true test since the real color plates are of a different size and may differ in color quality. However, students can get some idea whether or not they are color blind. No doubt color blind persons will already know it, so this test will hold no surprises for them.

        Ask the students to look at each of the sixteen plates and note what they see. When finished, have them check their responses with the information printed at the bottom of Figure 5-14.

        If the class is big enough, you will almost certainly find one or more color blind persons. Students will likely know someone among family or friends who is.

        Ask students who are color blind to talk about their experiences. What were some amusing things that have happened to them? How do they handle traffic signals, clothing styles, color coding on forms and documents, etc.? They can recount many more such circumstances that could be problems. Color blindness is recessive and sex-linked. This means that it appears oftener in males than in females.

3.   **Tongue curling:** There are two ways a person can curl the tongue. The first is known as tongue rolling. The second is tongue folding. In **tongue rolling** the person sticks the

tongue straight out and turns the sides of the tongue up to form a U-shape. In **tongue folding** the person folds the tip of the tongue back to touch the back of the tongue. Some can roll and fold their tongues; others cannot. Those who can have a dominant gene, and those who cannot have the double recessive.

4.   **Attached earlobes:** A quick check of the students will verify the statement that not all earlobes are alike. They take on various shapes and sizes, some being very small and others large. However, a few people have what are called "attached" earlobes. This means the lobes are nonexistent, and the bottom of the ear slopes gently down to meet the neck.

Determine the proportion of persons in the class with attached earlobes. The number will be small. It is a recessive trait so it will appear in about 20-25% of the population.

Students could trace one of these traits in their family. As an additional exercise ask them to check among their relatives and try to draw up a family tree identifying those who had the trait. Tracing attached earlobes can be amusing and instructive.

(Based on a demonstration by Dr. William C. Titus, Arkansas Tech University)

■ JOURNAL QUESTIONS

1.   What forms of deprivation and enrichment have you experienced in your life? What impact did these experiences have on you? When you have children, what kinds of perceptual and intellectual stimulation are you going to encourage?

2.   Have you ever spent time with a crying baby? How did you react? How did you feel? What advice would you give to a new mother?

3.   What were your parents like when you were a baby? Did your father and mother nurture you in different ways?

4.   Did you attend child care or take your child to a preschool or a baby-sitter? What feelings did you have?

5.   Interview family members about the pregnancy that preceded your birth, your delivery, your neonatal temperament, and your behavior as an infant. How much touching did you receive as a child? What feelings have you developed as an adult about touch?

6.   How did you feel when you learned that the Tooth Fairy or Santa Claus are not real? Should parents tell their kids the truth? If so, when? How?

7.   Describe an event that stands out in your memory as a positive influence on your personal
        development. What made this event important or helpful?

■ SUGGESTIONS FOR FURTHER READING

Berk, L. *Landscapes of Development: An Anthology of Readings*. Wadsworth, 1999.

Brazelton, T. B., and J. Sparrow. *Touchpoints: Three to Six*. Perseus Books, 2001.

Bloom, P. How children learn the meanings of words. Cambridge, MA, US: The MIT Press, 2000.

Curtiss, S. *Genie: A Psycholinguistic Study of a Modern-Day Wild Child*. Academic Press, 1977.

Dorris, Michael (1990). *The Broken Cord: A Family's Ongoing Struggle with "Fetal Alcohol
Syndrome"*. Harper and Row.

Flavell, J. Cognitive Development: Children's Knowledge about the Mind. *Annual Review of Psychology*,
50, 21-45, 1999.

Ginsberg, H., and S. Opper. *Piaget's Theory of Intellectual Development, 3rd ed*. Prentice-Hall, 1997.

Hall, E., M. Perlmutter, and M. Lamb. *Child Psychology Today*. Random House, 1982.

Harlow, H. F. and M. K. Harlow. "The Effect of Rearing Conditions on Behavior." *Bulletin of the
Menninger Clinic*, September 1962: 213-224.

Hoff, E. *Language Development, 2nd, ed*. Wadsworth, 2001.

Kagan, J. *Galen's Prophecy: Temperament in Human Nature*. Basic Books, 1994.

Shaffer, D. *Developmental Psychology: Childhood and Adolescence, 6th ed*. Wadsworth, 2002.

Singer, Dorothy G. and T. Revenson. *A Piaget Primer: How a Child Thinks*. NAL, 1990.

Stern, Daniel N. *Diary of a Baby. (What the infant experiences from six weeks to four years)*. Basic
Books, 1990.

■ MEDIA SUGGESTIONS

ADOLESCENT DEVELOPMENT (2002, from *Psychology- The Study of Human Behavior Series*,
Coast Community College District, 30 minutes)
This video identifies the principal features of adolescent intellectual development. Experts define the
field and discuss development in puberty.

CHILDHOOD DEVELOPMENT (2002, Films for the Humanities and Sciences, 24 minutes each)
This six-part series examines various research methods, theories, and concepts of developmental psychology in early childhood.

COGNITIVE DEVELOPMENT (2002, from *Psychology- The Study of Human Behavior Series*, Coast Community College District, 30 minutes)
This video focuses on the theories of Jean Piaget and his contributions to the field of child psychology.

THE PSYCHOLOGICAL DEVELOPMENT OF THE CHILD (2002, Films for the Humanities and Sciences, 22-28 minutes each)
This eight-part series is devoted to the general psychological development of the young child, from conception until the end of the first year.

THEORIES OF DEVELOPMENT (1997, Insight Media, 29 minutes.
This video introduces the cognitive, psychosexual, behaviorist, social-learning, and sociocultural theories of child development, including the work of Piaget, Freud, Erikson, Gesell, Skinner, and Vygotsky.

TIME TO GROW (2002, from *Psychology- The Study of Human Behavior Series*, Coast Community College District, 30 minutes each)
This twenty-six part series covers the entire gamut of child development, from birth to adolescence, including physical, cognitive, and psychosocial growth and development.

UNDERSTANDING PARENTING STYLES: AUTHORITARIAN-DEMOCRATIC-PERMISSIVE
(2002, Films for the Humanities and Sciences, 27 minutes.
Using three vignettes, this program shows teens interacting with their parents in situations that demonstrate the traits of each parenting style.

VYGOTSKY'S DEVELOPMENTAL THEORY: AN INTRODUCTION (1994, Insight Media, 28 minutes)
Filmed in classrooms, this video illustrates the four basic concepts of Vygotsky's sociocultural theory.

A number of videos are available from Thomson. Videos appropriate for this chapter include the following films from the CNN TODAY Introductory Psychology Video Series:

Volume 3, Section 7: Human Development Across the Lifespan
     The Age Wave (9:04)

■ COMPUTER AND INTERNET RESOURCES

PSYCHNOW!

Human Development:
Infant Development
Child Development

PSYK.TREK

Unit 9: Human Development
   9a: Prenatal development
   9b: Erikson's theory of personality development
   9c: Piaget's theory of cognitive development

INFOTRAC

Subject Guide/Key Words: Adolescent Development, Jean Piaget, Vygotsky, Freud, Parenting Styles, Infant Development, Teratogen, Child Discipline, Child Development, Infant Attachment, Developmental Psychology, Infant Temperament, Prenatal Influences, Postpartum Depression, Separation Anxiety, Mozart Effect, Fetal Alcohol Syndrome

WEB SITES

Wadsworth Online Psychology Study Center:
http://info.wadsworth.com/cooessentials9

CH.A.D.D. Attention Deficit Disorder Information:
http://www.chadd.org/

Crack Babies:
http://www.TheLastPlanet.com/bbcrack.htm#HOMEPAGETITLE

Temperament.com:
http://www.temperament.com

Autism/PDD Resources:
http://www.autism-pdd.net/

Child Development Institute:
http://idealist.com/children/cdw.html

CHAPTER 4

From Birth to Death: Life-span Development

■ LEARNING OBJECTIVES

To demonstrate mastery of this chapter, the student should be able to:

1.   Define the terms "developmental milestones" and "life-span perspective."
2.   Describe the term "psychosocial dilemma" and explain, according to Erikson, how the resolution of the psychosocial dilemmas affects a person's adjustment to life.
3.   State the nature of the psychosocial crisis and the nature of an adequate or inadequate outcome for each of Erikson's eight life stages. Match each crisis with the corresponding age.
4.   Discuss the positive and negative aspects of stress on a developing child.
5.   List and describe (where applicable) nine "normal" childhood problems.
6.   Give a brief description of the following childhood disorders and their possible causes:
     a.   enuresis
     b.   encopresis
     c.   overeating
     d.   anorexia nervosa
     e.   pica
     f.   delayed speech
     g.   stuttering
7.   Describe what the label "learning disorder" includes. Briefly describe dyslexia, including its possible cause.
8.   Describe the following disorders in terms of symptoms, causes, and treatments:
     a.   ADHD (also explain what relationship sugar has to ADHD and the controversy surrounding the use of Ritalin for treatment of ADHD)
     b.   autism (include a definition of echolalia)

The following objectives are related to the material in the "Exploring Psychology" section of the text.
9.   Describe the characteristics of abusive parents and the conditions likely to foster abusive behavior.
10.   Describe what can be done to prevent child abuse.

11.   Define and differentiate the terms adolescence and puberty, and list the three most widely accepted criteria for adult status in North America.
12.   Discuss the advantages and disadvantages of early and late puberty for males and females.

13. Explain why Elkind believes that our society is rushing adolescents and what he feels the net effect will be.

14. Briefly discuss the impact of ethnic heritage on identity formation. Describe the interactions between an adolescent and his/her parents as identity formation occurs.

15. Discuss the importance of imaginary audiences to adolescents.

16. Describe the importance of the peer group in identity formation, including the danger of foreclosure.

17. Briefly describe each of Kohlberg's three levels or moral development as well as their respective stages.

18. Describe how Kohlberg's moral development levels are distributed among the population.

19. Explain Gilligan's argument against Kohlberg's system of moral development. Describe the current status of the argument.

20. Generally describe the pattern of adult life stages proposed by Roger Gould.

21. Describe what a midlife crisis is and how it can be both a danger and an opportunity. Explain how the midlife transition is different for women as opposed to men.

22. Distinguish menopause from the male climacteric and describe the typical reactions to each.

23. Briefly discuss the empty nest syndrome and the different effects of this syndrome on mothers who work at home versus mothers who work outside the home.

24. List six elements of well-being during adulthood.

25. Describe what is meant by the term "biological aging." Include the concepts of fluid and crystallized abilities in your answer.

26. Differentiate the concepts maximum life span and life expectancy. List seven suggestions for increasing life expectancy.

27. Describe the disengagement theory and the activity theory of aging.

28. Describe Baltes's view of selective optimization with compensation.

29. Outline the characteristics of ageism. List four significant myths of aging, and relate them to the concept of ageism.

30. Explain how fears about death might be expressed as a denial of death.

31. Explain the purpose or intent of a living will.

32. List and briefly characterize the five emotional reactions typically experienced by people facing death.

33. Explain how knowledge of the reactions to coping with death is important.

34. Describe what generally happens during a near-death experience (NDE), how it can be explained in two different ways, and how an NDE can change a person's life.

35. Describe the purpose of a hospice.

36. Discuss the general characteristics of the process of bereavement. Explain how suppression of the grieving process is related to later problems.

The following objectives are related to the material in the "Psychology in Action" section of the text.

37. Define the term "subjective well-being."

38. List five characteristics of a satisfied life.

39.   Briefly discuss the relationship of positive and negative emotional experiences to happiness.

40.   Briefly discuss the way in which perception, interpretation, and management of events is related to happiness.

41.   List and briefly discuss eight personal factors related to overall happiness.

42.   Discuss the connection between one's goals in life and happiness. Include a discussion of the findings of McGregor and Little.

■ DISCUSSION QUESTIONS

1.   Describe an incident from your own childhood that you consider growth-promoting. Describe an incident that set you back or had a negative effect on you. How do these incidents differ?

2.   Perhaps you remember being grouped in elementary school according to your skills in reading, writing, or math. Could such groupings (as well as competitive sports) contribute to feelings of inferiority? Why or why not?

3.   What factors do you think would make adolescence especially turbulent for an individual? How is it that some teens seem to thrive in the terrible physical and emotional conditions?

4.   Many children are now part of "blended" step-families. How would this affect the development of a child's sense of identity?

5.   In what ways do parents add to the conflicts of young adults who are seeking independence?

6.   Which of Erikson's crises do you think is most difficult to deal with? Which is most enjoyable or trouble-free? Why?

7.   Do you know a person who seems to have "flunked" one or more of Erikson's developmental stages? What effect has this had on the person's development?

8.   How did you answer Kohlberg's moral dilemma about the husband who stole a drug for his sick wife? Do you think your answer reflects the role of moral reasoning in your personality?

9.   You have been asked to complete a "moral development" inventory for a job. You really want this job; you can select a "test" based on Kohlberg's or Gilligan's theories. Which test would you take? Why? If asked how you resolve these two approaches, what would you say?

10.   Do you think the "draft dodgers," antiwar activists, or conscientious objectors of the 1960s were acting in self-interest or at higher levels of morality? What level of moral reasoning is most frequently displayed by the characters in TV dramas, comedies, or commercials? What level of moral reasoning would you say fits the actions of Dr. Jack Kevorkian?

11.   Anthropologist Margaret Mead once charged, "We have become a society of people who neglect our children, are afraid of our children." Do you agree? Why or why not?

12.   Do we need a "children's liberation movement" to establish the civil rights of children? (Keep in mind that few parents show their children the courtesy they show strangers.)

13.   While it is clear that parents shouldn't overfeed a child, is it wrong to force a child to diet? Explain.

14.   What reasons might there be for the shootings that have taken place in schools over the past few years, such as those at Columbine High School in Littleton, Colorado on April 20, 1999?

15.   What cultural factors do you think would affect the length of adolescence? The onset of puberty? The social effects of early and late maturation for males and females?

16.   How common do you think it is to experience a "midlife crisis"? Would you expect people of other cultures to experience a similar crisis? People born in various decades have very different life experiences. How much do you think this affects patterns of development and the likelihood of problems at midlife?

17.   Will the patterns of adult development in the year 2020 be the same as the patterns suggested by Gould? If not, what patterns do you hypothesize? Why?

18.   When and how would you prefer to die? If you had a terminal illness would you want to be told? Do you think sudden death or death with forewarning would be better?

19.   Should passive euthanasia be allowed? Should active euthanasia be allowed? What are the arguments for and against each? Do you think a "living will" is a good idea? Why or why not?

20.   If you could choose to remain a particular age which would you choose? Why? What are your attitudes toward aging and death?

21.   How general are the emotional stages of death described by Kubler-Ross? Do they describe the reactions (before death) of people you know who have died?

22. Why do you think dying individuals so often feel isolated? How could the emotional needs of dying persons be better served than they are now in hospitals and nursing homes?

■ LECTURE ENHANCEMENTS

Students often hunger to talk about their own development and to try to sort out the many challenges of adulthood. Journals, role-playing, interviews, and discussions can all aid the process. Many contemporary books also expand on the issues of this chapter. Students can be asked to analyze one of these books. As you present this chapter its breadth requires that you move the discussion at a rapid pace. Try to challenge students with such questions as: What are the elements of optimal development in childhood? What can we do to make our adult years productive and happy? Is it possible to stay married to the same person for 50 years? How can we deal with our own death if we rarely mention that process when we are alive?

1. **Challenge students working in small groups to develop a series of analogies about child development.** Is it like the growing of a plant? The development of a business? The planning of a special meal? The evolution of a pearl? Ask students to share their analogies with the class.

2. **The topics of alternative birthing practices and maternal-infant bonding are approached by many students with vehemence and polarization.** Given that feelings are strong, a debate or panel discussion can be quite interesting. Try to involve students who have had experience with alternative birth procedures, who work in medical settings, or who have a strong interest in the topics (e.g., prospective parents). Ask each to do research and find evidence for his or her position before the discussion is held.

3. **To stir up a rousing discussion on parenthood, read these news excerpts in class:**

BOULDER, COLO. (UPI)--Tom Hansen doesn't like the way his life has turned out and says it's because he was reared improperly. Hansen, 25, has filed suit against his mother and father, seeking $350,000 in damages because they reared him improperly and he will need psychiatric care the remainder of his life.

BOULDER, COLO. (AP)--A mother sued for "parental malpractice" by her son is going to court herself--to sue her son's psychiatrist who encouraged her son to sue her "for therapeutic reasons."

What would the class consider evidence of "parental malpractice?" Should or could parents be held responsible for the way their children turn out? If placed in the position of the judge, would students hear the case? (It was thrown out of court.)

4. **Within a decade suicide has moved from fourth to second place as the leading cause of death among American teenagers.** Of the approximately 25,000 Americans who commit suicide every year, 7 percent are between the ages of 15 and 19. (It is estimated that there are 20 times that number of suicide attempts.) A class discussion could revolve around these sad statistics and perhaps focus on the unique problems of adolescents. What are the problems? How do the students feel parents and schools contribute to them? How might the pressures on young people be reduced?

5. **Have students help you make a list of interesting topics that bear on generational differences.** Give students four forms. Ask them to describe their attitudes (positive to negative) on a 5-point scale and the attitudes of a person who is two decades older or younger. Topics could include: *institutionalized religion, premarital sex, dual-career marriages, punk hair styles, rap music, donating money for the poor,* and so on. Then ask the student to give two forms to the person whose attitudes they rated. Ask that person to rate their own views as well as the views they think your student holds. Ask your student to sit down with this person and compare their views, acknowledging differences but focusing on areas of similarity. Students should be prepared to discuss their observations in class.

6. **If your community has an Adopt-a-Grandparent program, a Gray Panthers group, Council on Aging,** or similar organization, invite a speaker to discuss the problems of the aged and misconceptions about aging.

7. **For an interesting outside assignment or project on aging and changes over a lifetime, ask students to interview one or more people from each of the following age brackets: 15-25, 35-55, 65 or up.** Questions can deal with issues such as, "What is middle age?", "When does a person become old?", "Do you (or did you) look forward to retiring some day?", and "Did you experience a 'midlife crisis'?" and "What has been the best period of your life so far?"

8. **Ask students to interview three people over 75 who live in different settings: a condominium, a senior citizen development, and a convalescent hospital.** Either prepare questions for the entire class or have each student (or group) develop a set of questions. Hopefully, students will conclude that while health can impact aging, there is tremendous diversity in the way people experience being 75.

9. **If you have a personal contact at a convalescent hospital, ask if your students could do some volunteer work.** Ask each student to donate one hour (perhaps, instead of class as an "individualized field trip"). Students could work in the kitchen, provide entertainment, talk to residents, or even (depending on legal parameters) take a resident for an outing. The purpose of the assignment is not to interview the senior; instead it is for the student to become more aware of his/her feelings about aging.

10.   **Act out aging by bringing to class: ear plugs, nose plugs, mittens, shirts with buttons, many pairs of socks, and ace bandages.** One wears the ear plugs, nose plugs and mittens. That person is given 5-10 minutes to put on the layers of clothing, in order to "get to a bus on time." This person's job is to dress him/herself and not accept help. The other person's job is to try to help. Hopefully, in a very short time, both parties will get frustrated. Then have them switch roles. At the end, have students discuss the thoughts and feelings they had about acting like a senior citizen or caring for an older person.

11.   **While society may be insensitive to the needs of senior citizens, we occasionally assume their needs are different from the needs of all citizens.** Develop (or have the class develop) a questionnaire asking what legislation citizens would want to pass. For example, "I would vote for legislation to:"

   a. *Increase social security*
   b. *Increase Medicare coverage*
   c. *Decrease property taxes*
   d. *Provide money for the homeless*
   e. *Provide money for elementary education*
   f. *Provide money for research on garbage disposing and recycling techniques*
   g. *Increase police protection*

Distribute the questionnaire to people of many different ages. Tally the frequencies for each age group. Remind students that senior citizens are a powerful political force with both specific interests and interests similar to people of other ages.

12.   **Have students fill out a behavioral contract that will contribute to the quality of their "young age"** (for example, passing a weekend without smoking, overdrinking, overeating, overspending, under-socializing, or under-exercising). Remind students that the person they are now may in many ways predict the senior citizen they will become.

13.   **Check with local hospitals or physicians for the name of a person who has had a near-death experience** and who might be willing to come to class and talk about what he or she saw or heard. Students should be cautioned in advance to be sensitive to the seriousness with which many people who have had an NDE take the experience, as well as the religious beliefs that such an experience may support.

14.   **All of us make decisions that reflect various levels of moral development.** Ask students to complete the following inventory.

When you make a decision about the following issues, what kind of moral analysis do you usually engage in? To the right of the following decisions, write PRE, CON, or POST: Kohlberg's preconventional, conventional, and postconventional levels.

Driving speed _____

Following parents' rules, directions, or wishes _____

Donating time or money to charities _____

Involvement in institutionalized religion _____

Eating behavior _____

Sexual behavior _____

Reasons for attending college _____

Use of alcohol and/or other drugs _____

Honesty on classroom tests _____

Action taken after finding lost money or valuables _____

Decision to vote or not to vote _____

How you would spend a million-dollar lottery prize _____

After collecting the anonymous responses, ask students to role-play post-conventional and caring explanations for choosing to engage in (or not engage in) various behaviors in the listed categories. Mention studies showing that our moral development is greatly influenced by modeling and the kinds of interaction we have with others.

15.   **Give students the Kohlberg and Gilligan hypothetical situations before they read this chapter.** Ask them how they would resolve the described dilemmas. Save these individual explanations for discussion when the concept of moral development is presented in class.

■ ROLE-PLAYING SCENARIOS

1.   **You are the parent of a two-month-old child who still does not sleep through the night.** When he cries you usually get angry, wait 20 minutes, and if he doesn't go back to sleep, you pick him up. Are you handling this situation effectively? What other options do you have? Which option could best teach your new son to trust the world (while giving you a chance to sleep)?

2.   **While you were in the bathroom, your two-year-old climbed out of the playpen, onto the kitchen counter, and in the process of grabbing a cookie knocked the jar to the floor.** What should you do?

3.   **Your son is not a skilled athlete yet he says he wants to play competitive team soccer.** Should you encourage him? Why or why not?

4.   **You are 40 years old.** You have been working for a supermarket chain for 20 years and have received every promotion possible. Now you manage a large store. But you have no college background and know this is the highest level you will be able to achieve. You are feeling bored and trapped. What else are you feeling? How are these feelings

being translated into behavior? Is there anything you can do to change the feelings and/or the behaviors?

5. **Your child has horrible dreams and gets in bed with you each night.** The bed is too small and you usually sleep poorly. What is your child feeling? How are you feeling? What should you do?

6. **Your 10-year-old child is very negative and unpleasant to be around.** She has no real friends and clings to you constantly. You are becoming increasingly annoyed. How is she feeling? What should you do?

7. **Your 7-year-old son refuses to eat any green vegetables and to drink any milk.** How is he feeling? What should you do?

8. **You have a 14-year-old son who wets his bed.** He says he just doesn't awaken in time to get to the bathroom. What is he feeling? What should you do?

9. **You are parent of an autistic child.** You feel frustrated, angry, and sad that your child is not "normal." Describe your feelings in detail. How do you try to cope with those feelings? What could you do to better cope?

10. **Your 30-year-old single son has moved back into the house.** He has completed his education and has a good job. While at first you enjoyed his presence, you now think that he is taking advantage of you. What is he feeling? What are you feeling? What should you do?

11. **You just received news of a death in the family.** What are you feeling? What should be said to you? What should not be said?

12. **Your mother has developed serious memory problems and can no longer live alone safely.** How do you discuss the possibility of changing her living arrangements? Should you take her into your home? Should you force her into an assisted living facility or nursing home? How does she feel about her loss of independence? How might you feel about having her live with you and your family? How will your spouse feel? Your children?

■ VALUE-CLARIFICATION STATEMENTS

1. Infants should be allowed to cry themselves to sleep.

2. Teens should be able to make most of their own rules.

3. The disadvantages of marrying before age 25 outweigh the advantages.

4.   It is normal for all children to run away from home at least once in their childhood.

5.   Stimulants should be used to help control hyperactivity.

6.   Movies now rated PG-13 should be rated PG-18.

7.   Adults should not try to dress like teens.

8.   It is the responsibility of people over 65 to disengage in order to allow younger people into professional and social roles.

9.   A person should be convicted of murder if the person intentionally ends the life of another, regardless of the circumstances.

10.   Government funds should be spent on providing more hospice facilities.

■ ONE-MINUTE MOTIVATORS

1.   **Bring a box of household items to class.** Put them on the front desk. Divide the class quickly into groups. Give each group 3 minutes to devise ways that the objects in front could be transformed into exciting toys for preschool children.

2.   **If your hair is not yet gray, gradually add a bit of gray paint (washable) to your hair.** During the week of the unit, begin walking slower, wear earplugs so you talk louder, and squint at the chalkboard. During this time, have one or two students watch the reactions of your other students to your rapid "aging." Probably they won't notice anything at first: Remind students that aging is a gradual process that affects all of us.

3.   **Give students a paragraph written so that many of the letters are backward, as the dyslexic person might see them.** Point out how difficult it would be to rapidly read chapters in a college text if one were afflicted by dyslexia.

4.   **Have a "T-shirt" day where everyone wears a shirt that has a specific message on it.** Briefly ask students to explain why their message is important to them and how it helps to communicate their "identity" to others.

5.   **Make a sign that says, "You are getting older and older minute by minute."** Place it near the classroom clock. A few times during the class ask students their age (to the minute). At the end of class, remind students that "None of us will ever get these minutes back. I hope you feel we invested them well."

6.   **Ask a female colleague to visit class.** When she arrives ask her, "How old are you?" Then say, "You are pretty for your age." (This could also be done with a middle-aged

student, if you have one in your class.) Then ask students, "What if I had said, `You are very pretty for your race.' Would you have been offended?" Students should realize that, that would be a racist comment. Next, point out that your original compliment was an ageist comment, suggesting that people in their 40s are not as pretty as younger people. It would have been better to simply say "You are very pretty."

7.   **On the day when aging is discussed, ask students to bring a snack and a friend over 65.** While discussing aging, solicit the ideas of your guests and end with a celebratory feast. Be sure to include a name-tag for each guest, perhaps a flower, and perhaps even a banner saying, "In Celebration of Wisdom."

8.   **At the beginning of class, announce that sometime during class the name of one student will be drawn and that person will be told they have only one month to live.** That person will be asked (and perhaps given an extra credit point) to come back the next class and describe how they would spend their last month. Remind students that none of us know when death will occur. All we can do is to make the most of the moments we have.

■ BROADENING OUR CULTURAL HORIZONS

1.   **Read the following summary to students, derived from an article that appeared in the New York Times, July 23, 1990:**

A new study of right-to-die cases has found that the courts treat women very differently from men. According to the study, published in the current issue of Law, Medicine and Health Care, the courts are far less likely to give weight to a woman's wishes regarding life support than to a man's. In a study of 22 right-to-die decisions from appeals courts in 14 states, Dr. Steven Miles found that **women are consistently portrayed as less capable of rational decision-making than men.** The cases studied are the bulk of the appellate decisions involving patients who had been mentally competent, but left no written directives for their care. In such cases, judges may try to "construct" the patient's preference from evidence of his or her values.

Women are referred to by their first names, and construed as emotional, immature, unreflective and vulnerable to medical neglect while men are called by their last names, and construed as rational, mature, decisive, and assaulted by medical technology, Dr. Miles said. Only women are described as curled in a fetal position, while men are described as having contractures, the medical term.

While a 31-year-old woman's comments on life support were characterized as "offhand remarks made by a person when young," a 33-year-old man's comments are characterized as "deeply held," showing "solemn intelligent determination." The study found that in cases involving women, the courts said they could not deduce the patient's preferences regarding life support in 12 of 14 cases, while in cases involving men, the court refused to construe the patient's preferences in only 2 of 8 cases.

What are the implications of this trend for individuals of various ethnic backgrounds? How can a person be sure that her or his wishes concerning death are followed?

2.   **What are the different styles of discipline used in cultures other than the United States?** Ask students who are willing to talk about the ethnic backgrounds of their families to interview their parents or grandparents about discipline styles in their countries of origin. Other students might find willing acquaintances of a different ethnic background to interview. Discuss these differences in class.

■ SUPPLEMENTAL ACTIVITIES

TO THE INSTRUCTOR:

The purpose of these exercises is to get students thinking about the various stages of development. It is easy for people to lose sight of the fact that everyone is at *some* developmental level. It would help people to be more tolerant of others if they recognized this truth and accepted people at their own levels of development.

Exercise #1: Ages and Stages

The first exercise is based on Erikson's psychosocial stages. Students are asked to evaluate people they know, using Erikson's descriptions of the stages of development. They need to be encouraged to look at the behavior of the person first, then see what stage they fit into. The temptation may be to assume that the person is, in fact, at the stage which Erikson says is appropriate for his/her age. This may not be true. When the exercise is completed, it should be shared with class members. A good way to do this is to form groups of four. Ask the students to explain to each other what their subjects are like and why they chose to see them at the stages they did. See if the group members agree. If not, what changes would they make?

Exercise #2: Aging

The second exercise focuses attention on old age. There are many myths and stereotypes. People often see the elderly in those terms rather than as individuals who are all different, each living with and coping with a unique set of circumstances and problems. Most of all, students need to think of the elderly as persons and of old age as part of development.

The set of myths and stereotypes listed in the exercise are all false. Do a tally of the responses. See how many marked true for each item. Then ask students to explain their reasons. This should serve as a vehicle for a fruitful discussion on aging and old age.

Exercise #3: Interviewing the Elderly

A straightforward, but often valuable assignment involves having students interview an elderly person. The questions provided should ensure that the interview is informative and thought-provoking.

AGES AND STAGES: WORK SHEET

TO THE STUDENT:

This is an assignment to help you understand Erik Erikson's eight stages of psychosocial development. Review the descriptions of behaviors appropriate to each of the stages.

Select three people of different ages whom you know well. One of them should be yourself. Try to identify which of Erikson's stages best describes the person's overall behavior. Don't be influenced by the person's age. People don't always "act their age!" You need to explain your decision in each case.

Subject #1   Age_____   Stage_____

Behaviors:

Reasons:

Subject #2   Age_____   Stage_____

Behaviors:

Reasons:

Subject #3   Age_____   Stage_____

Behaviors:

Reasons:

AGING: WORK SHEET

TO THE STUDENT:

Below are ten statements about the elderly. Write TRUE or FALSE beside each one, indicating whether or not you agree.

_____ 1)   Workers should be required to retire at a set age, such as 65.

_____ 2)   Most people do not adapt well to aging.

_____ 3)   It is better for elderly persons not to wear bright colors.

_____ 4)   It is unwise for elderly persons to try to look younger by dying their hair or seeking cosmetic surgery.

_____ 5)   The elderly are not as well informed as younger persons.

_____ 6)   The lives of the elderly are generally less rewarding than the lives of younger persons.

_____ 7)   It is a greater tragedy for a young person to die than for an elderly person to die.

_____ 8)   A large percentage of the elderly are unhealthy or infirm.

_____ 9)   The elderly are less independent than younger persons.

_____ 10)   An elderly person cannot do most tasks as well as a younger person.

GROWING OLDER

Interview Questions

Select a person to interview who is at least 20 years older than you are. Take very brief notes, jotting down the key ideas. Try to focus all of your attention on the person you are interviewing. Add questions to this list if you would like.

1. When and where were you born? How many siblings did you have, if any? What was your order of birth? What do you remember about your early childhood?

2. Describe one of the happiest times of your childhood. What friends and relatives do you associate with happy times?

3. What role did animals play in your childhood? How important are animals to your adult life?

4. Describe a sad time of your childhood. Did something specific take place? How did your family suggest that pain or sadness be dealt with?

5. What was your favorite childhood toy? What was your favorite childhood book?

6. What was your best memory from high school or college?

7. What were your early career aspirations? Did you ever work in that field? What was your career?

8. What were the rules of "dating" when you were a teenager or young adult? Who was your best friend? What did you do for fun?

9. What world event had the greatest impact on your life? Why?

10. What athletic interests did you have as a teenager and young adult? Are these interests the same now?

11. Did you marry? Why or why not? Did you have children? Why or why not? Were you employed outside the home? Why or why not?

12. What did you worry about most when you were in your early 20s? In your 30s? In your 40s? Now?

13. What was the most difficult obstacle that you had to try to overcome in your life? Were you successful? Why or why not?

14. In what ways are you similar now to the way you were when you were 20? In what ways are you different?

15. If you could give advice to others younger than you, what would it be? What is the most exciting thing happening in your life at the moment?

■ JOURNAL QUESTIONS

1. In which way(s) are you the same as and different from a year ago? Five years ago? What will you be like in five years? In ten years?

2. Which of Erikson's crises have you found most difficult? Why? What resources would have helped you develop the skills to resolve the crisis in a positive direction?

3. Write your parent(s) or your child a letter describing three ways that person has helped you in your own development. Discuss the advantages and disadvantages of actually mailing the letter.

4. What kind of a relationship did you have with your parents? Why? How? What could you do (or have done) to make the relationship better? What could your parents have done? What could you now do to let go of past problems in this relationship and move on?

5. What relationship did you have with your siblings before adolescence? Why? How did your parents deal with sibling rivalry? What kind of a relationship do you have now with your siblings? If you are an only child, do you wish you had siblings? Why or why not?

6. What feelings did you have about the timing and form of your physical maturation? How did others respond? Could anything have been done to help you deal more effectively with these physical changes?

7. How do you spend your leisure time? Is this how you want to spend your leisure in your old age?

8. What do you want people to say at your funeral? What form of a memorial service do you want to have? How do you want others to grieve? If you wanted friends to be reminded of one very funny thing that happened in your life, what would it be?

9. What are the factors and events in your life that give you the greatest degree of happiness?

■ SUGGESTIONS FOR FURTHER READING

Adler, Leonore Loeb (Ed.). *Women in Cross-Cultural Perspective.* New York: Praeger Publications, 1991.

Atwood, Joan D. "10 necessary steps to stepfamily integration." *Marriage and Family Living,* 20-25, 1990.

Baker, Falcon O. *Saving Our Kids From Delinquency, Drugs, and Despair.* Harper/Collins, 1991

Barber, N. *Parenting: Roles, Styles, and Outcomes.* Nova Science Puslishers, Inc., 1998.

Bettelheim, B. *The Empty Fortress: Infantile Autism and the Birth of the Self.* Free Press, 1967.

Bolton, F., Morris, L., and McEachron, A. E. *Males at Risk: The Other side of Child Sexual Abuse.* Sage, 1989.

Caplan, Paula. *Don't Blame Mother: Mending the Mother-Daughter Relationship,* 2nd ed. Routledge, 2000.

Cooney, Teresa M. and Uhlenberg, Peter. "The role of divorce in men's relations with their adult children after midlife." *Journal of Marriage and the Family,* 52(3), 677-688, 1990.

Dobson, James and Bauer, Gary. *Children at Risk: The Fighting for the Hearts and Minds of Our Children: America's Second Civil War.* Word Books, 1994.

Elkind, D. *The Hurried Child,* 3rd ed.. Addison-Wesley, 2001.

Erikson, E. *Childhood and Society,* Trade. Norton, 1985.

Erikson, E. (ed.) *Adulthood.* Norton, 1978.

Fontana, V. J. and D. J. Besharov. *The Maltreatment Syndrome in Children—A Medical, Legal, and Social Guide.* 5th ed. Charles C. Thomas Publisher, Ltd., 1995.

Ginott, H. *Between Parent and Child.* Macmillan, 1976.

Kagan, J., Snidman, N., Arcus, D., and J. S. Reznick. *Galen's Prophecy: Temperament in Human Nature.* BasicBooks, 1997.

Kail, R. V. and J. C. Cavanaugh. *Human Development: A Life-Span View,* 2nd ed. Wadsworth Publishing, 2000.

MacDonald, Gordon. *There's No Place Like Home.* Nelson, 1990.

Matcha, D. A. *The Sociology of Aging: A Social Problems Perspective.* Boston: Allyn & Bacon, 1997.

McHale, S. M., Bartko, W. T., Crouter, A. C., and Perry-Jenkins, M. (1990). "Children's housework and psychosocial functioning: the mediating effects of parents' sex role behaviors and attitudes." *Child Development,* 61 (5), 1413-1426.

Posner, R. A. *Aging and Old Age.* University of Chicago Press, 1997.

Schaie, K. W., and S. L. Willis. *Adult Development and Aging,* 5th ed. New York: Prentice-Hall, 2002.

■ MEDIA SUGGESTIONS

Excellent films and videotapes are available from the following sources.
National Association of Anorexia Nervosa and Associated Disorders
Box 7
Highland Park, IL 60035

Parents Anonymous® Inc.
675 W. Foothill Blvd., Suite 220
Claremont, CA 91711

ADOLESCENT AND ADULT DEVELOPMENT (2002, from *Psychology: The Human Experience Series,* Coast Community College District, 30 minutes)
Explains the significance of peer relationships and Kohlberg's moral development theory. Erikson's theory on human development and Kubler-Ross's five stages of dying and death complete the overview.

ADOLESCENT DEVELOPMENT (2002, from *Psychology: The Study of Human Behavior Series,* Coast Community College District, 30 minutes)
Experts discuss what is involved in puberty and the principal features of adolescent intellectual development.

ADULT DEVELOPMENT (2002, from *Psychology: The Study of Human Behavior Series,* Coast Community College District, 30 minutes)
The various transitions of adulthood are examined.

AGING: GROWING OLD IN A YOUTH-CENTERED CULTURE (2002, Films for the Humanities and Sciences, two-part series, 30 minutes each)
This series addresses the social aspects of aging, considering the increased longevity of our aging population.

THE DEVELOPING CHILD (2001, from *Discovering Psychology Series,* Annenberg/CPB, 30 min.)
This video includes commentary on the nature/nurture debate and the study of how both heredity and environment contribute to the development of children.

EVERYBODY RIDES THE CAROUSEL (2002, Insight Media, 72 minutes)
This award-winning video features an animated view of Erik Erikson's theory of personality development.

KIDS OUT OF CONTROL (1990, Films for the Humanities and Sciences, 25 min.)
This film discussed drugs, depression, rape, and suicide. It includes a five-question quiz to help determine whether a child is experiencing healthy rebellion or is troubled and in need of help.

LETTING GO: A HOSPICE JOURNEY (2002, Films for the Humanities and Sciences, 90 minutes)
An intimate look at three patients ranging in age from 8 to 62 years of age, this program shows how hospice care helps them cope with fear and pain in the final stages of their lives, and prepares loved ones for their loss.

MATURING AND AGING (2001, from *Discovering Psychology Series,* Annenberg/CPB, 30 minutes.) This video looks at the physical and psychological changes that occur as we age, and the societal reactions to aging.

SEASONS OF LIFE (1990, PBS, Series of five 60-minute videos, with 26 integrated audiotapes, a faculty manual, and student study guides; for more information on a multi-use long term license, call 1-800-233-9910.) Tapes are chronologically organized: infancy, childhood and adolescence, early, middle, and late adulthood. The five tapes show how human life is controlled by a biological, a social, and a psychological developmental clock.

TEENS: WHAT MAKES THEM TICK? (2002, Films for the Humanities and Sciences, 43 minutes) An ABC news special with John Stossel, this video examines some of the physiological underpinnings of teenage angst.

A number of videos are available from Thomson. Videos appropriate for this chapter include the following films from the CNN TODAY Introductory Psychology Video Series:

Volume 2, Section 3: Health
      Miscarriage depression (2:03)
      Alzheimer's Boom (2:33)
      Enjoying Anorexia (2:24)

Volume 3, Section7: Human Development Across the Lifespan
      The Age Wave (9:04)

■ COMPUTER AND INTERNET RESOURCES

PSYCHNOW!

Human Development:
Adolescent Development
Adult Development, Aging, and Death

PSYK.TREK

Unit 9: Human Development
      9b: Erikson's theory of personality development
      9d: Kohlberg's theory of moral development

INFOTRAC

Subject Guide/Key Words: Psychosocial Development, Erik Erikson, Lawrence Kohlberg, Moral Development, Enuresis, Encopresis, Anorexia, Bulimia, Speech Disorders, Autism, Elkind, Menopause, Ageism, Hospice, Bereavement, Subjective Well-Being

WEB SITES

Wadsworth Online Psychology Study Center:
http://info.wadsworth.com/cooessentials9

APA Division 20: Adult Development and Aging:
http://www.iog.wayne.edu/apadiv20/apadiv20.htm

GMU's Online Resources for Developmental Psychology:
http://classweb.gmu.edu/classweb/awinsler/ordp/index.html

Marriage Survival Guide:
http://www.geocities.com/Heartland/Meadows/9082

The Commission on Domestic Violence:
http://www.abanet.org/domviol/home.html

Caregiver Survival Resources:
http://www.caregiver911.com/

CHAPTER 5

Sensation and Perception

■ LEARNING OBJECTIVES

To demonstrate mastery of this chapter the student should be able to:

1.   Explain how our senses act as a data reduction system by selecting, analyzing, and condensing incoming information.
2.   Explain how sensory receptors act as biological transducers. Define sensory coding.
3.   Explain the concept of sensory localization including the idea behind the statement "Seeing does not take place in the eyes."
4.   Define sensation and perception.
5.   Describe hue, saturation, and brightness in terms of their representation in the visual spectrum.
6.   Briefly compare the structure of the eye to a camera and explain the process of accommodation.
7.   Describe the following four conditions:
     a)   hyperopia
     b)   myopia
     c)   astigmatism
     d)   presbyopia
8.   Describe the location and explain the functions of the following parts of the eye:
     a)   lens
     b)   retina
     c)   cornea
     d)   rods (including sensitivity to light)
     e)   cones
     f)   blind spot
     g)   fovea
9.   Discuss peripheral vision. Include the structures responsible for it and how this type of vision affects night vision.
10. Discuss the following theories of color vision:
     a)   trichromatic theory
     b)   opponent-process theory (include a description of afterimage)
11. Describe color blindness and color weakness.
12. Explain the purpose of the Ishihara test.
13. Briefly describe the process of dark adaptation including the function of rhodopsin in night vision and night blindness.

14.   Explain how dark adaptation can be speeded up.

15.   Describe the process by which sound travels and what psychological dimensions correspond to the physical ones.

16.   Describe the location and explain the function(s) of the following parts of the ear:
      a)   pinna
      b)   tympanic membrane (eardrum)
      c)   auditory ossicles
      d)   cochlea
      e)   oval window
      f)   hair cells
      g)   organ of Corti
      h)   stereocilia

17.   Briefly explain how the sense of hearing works by tracing an incoming stimulus from the time it strikes the tympanic membrane until it is sent to the brain.

18.   Describe the frequency and the place theories of hearing.

19.   List and describe the three general types of deafness.

20.   Describe how cochlear implants can help overcome deafness.

21.   Describe the factors that determine whether hearing loss will occur from stimulation deafness.

22.   Describe the sense of olfaction (smell) including:
      a)   its nature
      b)   how it works
      c)   a description of the condition anosmia
      d)   a description of the lock and key theory

23.   Describe the sense of gustation (taste) including:
      a)   its nature
      b)   the four basic taste sensations
      c)   the tastes to which humans are most and least sensitive
      d)   how the vast number of flavors is explained
      e)   how it works

24.   List the three somesthetic senses and be able to describe the function of each.

25.   List and be able to recognize the five different sensations produced by the skin receptors.

26.   Explain why certain areas of the body are more sensitive to touch than other areas.

27.   List the numbers of nerve endings for each of the following: temperature, touch and pressure, and pain.

28.   Name and describe the two different pain systems in the body.

29.   List and describe three ways to reduce pain.

30.   Name and describe the functions of the structures responsible for the vestibular sense.

31.   Explain how the sensory conflict theory explains motion sickness.

32.   List and discuss the three reasons many sensory events never reach conscious awareness.

33.   Describe sensory adaptation, selective attention, and the gate control theory of pain.

34.   List and describe three characteristics of a stimulus that can make it attention-getting.

35. Explain the "boiled frog syndrome" and how it may affect the ultimate survival of humans.

36. Discuss how acupuncture may work in controlling pain.

37. Describe the visual abilities of a person who has just had his or her sight restored.

38. Describe the following constancies:
     a.   size
     b.   shape
     c.   brightness

39. Give examples of the following as they relate to the organization of perception:
     a.   figure-ground (include the concept of reversible figures)
     b.   nearness
     c.   similarity
     d.   continuation
     e.   closure (include the concept of illusory figures)
     f.   contiguity
     g.   common region

40. Explain the meaning of perceptual hypothesis.

41. Define and give an example of an ambiguous stimulus.

42. Define depth perception.

43. Describe two techniques for investigating depth perception, and describe the end results of studies with each technique.

44. Describe the following cues for depth perception and indicate in each case whether the due is monocular or binocular:
     a.   accommodation
     b.   convergence
     c.   retinal disparity

45. Describe the following two-dimensional, monocular, pictorial depth cues:
     a.   linear perspective
     b.   relative size
     c.   height in the picture plane
     d.   light and shadow
     e.   overlap (interposition)
     f.   texture gradients
     g.   aerial perspective
     h.   relative motion (motion parallax)

46. Describe the phenomenon of the moon illusion. Include in your explanation the apparent distance hypothesis.

47. Define "perceptual habit" and explain how it allows learning to affect perception.

48. Explain how the Ames room poses problems for organization and for a person's perceptual habits.

49. Describe the research that demonstrates the brain's sensitivity to perceptual features in the environment.

50. Differentiate between an illusion and a hallucination.

51.　Describe the Muller-Lyer illusion and explain how perceptual habits may account for this illusion.

52.　Explain and give experimental evidence of how motives may alter attention and perception.

53.　Explain what bottom-up and top-down processing are.

54.　Explain how perceptual expectancies may influence perception.

The following objectives are related to the material in the "Exploring Psychology" section of the text.

55.　Define the terms *extrasensory perception* and *parapsychology*.

56.　Describe the following purported psychic abilities:
　　a.　clairvoyance
　　b.　telepathy
　　c.　precognition
　　d.　psychokinesis

57.　Describe the research with Zener cards, and explain why most psychologists remain skeptical about psi abilities.

58.　Describe the concept of stage ESP.

The following objectives are related to the material in the "Psychology in Action" section of the text.

59.　Explain why most eyewitness testimony is inaccurate, including the concept of weapon focus.

60.　Explain what the term *reality testing* means.

61.　Explain Maslow's concept of perceptual awareness and discuss how attention affects perception.

62.　List seven ways to become a better "eyewitness" to life.

■ DISCUSSION QUESTIONS

1.　Why do we take our senses for granted? What can we do to better appreciate all of our sensory equipment?

2.　What features of the environment are people "wired" to detect? Why? Would it be adaptive for us to be sensitive to other features? What would they be?

3.　Is your brain sitting on a laboratory table somewhere? It is theoretically possible that your brain was donated to science some time ago. Let's say that it was preserved and recently reactivated and that a sophisticated computer is artificially generating patterns of nerve activity in the cortex by mimicking normal sensory messages in the nerves. These messages duplicate the sights, sounds, odors, and sensations of sitting in a college classroom. If this were happening--right now--could you tell? Would you be able to discover that you had no body? Defend your answer.

4.   Let's say that you would like to design a system that uses touch to convey "images" to a blind person. How would you proceed? What would be the advantages and disadvantages of using various body areas (hands, back, forehead, and so on)?

5.   In Zen Buddhism there is a familiar koan, or riddle, that says, "Last night I dreamt I was a butterfly. How do I know today that I am not a butterfly dreaming I am a man?" Can you relate this to the idea that we construct a version of reality out of the more basic world of physical energies surrounding us?

6.   How would our world be different if the majority of people could not hear? If they could not smell? If they could not taste?

7.   Some people can wiggle their ears slightly. Some scientists believe that this is a vestige of an ability that existed more prominently, earlier in human evolution. What is the ability and how was it adaptive?

8.   The eye is ingeniously constructed. Why is the eye filled with fluid rather than blood vessels? Why are there more cones than rods near the fovea? Why do cones pick up fine details better than rods? Why do some species have only rods or cones in their eyes? How might evolution have favored the development of sensitivity to movement in peripheral vision?

9.   You are planning a new airport. What form of lighting would you use to maximize safety in the landing of planes?

10.   Why is acupuncture effective in reducing pain? How do "gating" and the impact of endorphins affect the perception of pain?

11.   You are a pediatrician and must immunize small children. What could you do to reduce the pain caused by these injections?

12.   Which of the perceptual "constancies" or "organizational tendencies" would be most difficult to be without?

13.   What experiences do you feel could interfere with a child's development of depth perception? What experiences could enhance the development of this ability?

14.   Which professions would be dangerous for a person with only one eye? For a person totally lacking depth perception?

15. In your own words, explain the moon illusion and the apparent distance hypothesis. What other factors could help explain the moon illusion?

16. Why might the "earth illusion" be different from the moon illusion if you were viewing the earth from the surface of the moon? (Hint: Would the horizon on the moon appear to be as distant as it is on earth?)

17. How might the perceptual abilities of a person raised in a vertical rain forest differ from those of a person raised in a flat desert?

18. Bicyclists and motorcyclists often complain that automobile drivers act as if cyclists are invisible. What perceptual factors might cause drivers to "look right at" cyclists without seeing them?

19. A professional basketball player is at the free-throw line for the last shot in a tied championship game. What depth cues are available to him? A professional golfer is making the last putt for a $10,000 prize; what depth cues is she using? A pilot is landing at an unfamiliar airport; what cues are available to her? You are looking through a microscope with one eye; what depth cues can you use?

20. Describe a situation you have misperceived. What influenced your perceptions?

21. Why do cigarette manufacturers place the government-required health warning in the corners of their ads? How is this placement explained by theories of perception?

22. What role might habituation play in industrial accidents (especially on production lines) and in driving on arrow-straight superhighways? What changes would you make in work procedures or highway design to combat habituation?

23. Why is the nervous system structured for both adaptation and habituation? How do both of these processes contribute to our survival?

24. How dependable do you think eyewitness testimony is in a courtroom? What factors other than accuracy of original perceptions might contribute to inaccuracies in testimony?

25. If you believe that ESP occurs, what would it take to convince you that it does not? If you do not believe that ESP occurs, what would it take to convince you that it does?

26. Why do you think it is that many people have difficulty rejecting the idea of ESP?

27. Serious family, national, cultural, and international conflicts develop because of perceptual differences. Describe a conflict and how perceptual processes explain the development of this conflict.

■ LECTURE ENHANCEMENTS

Depending on the equipment available to you, there are many classroom demonstrations possible for this chapter. **You can use models to show microscopic parts of sensory systems; devices that make sound waves visible; psychophysics experiments demonstrating the sensitivity of visual, auditory, olfactory, gustatory, and kinesthetic receptors.** Students are fascinated with the chance to "see" silent, invisible processes at work. The effectiveness of these demonstrations depends on your access to up-to-date equipment and expertise for using and explaining the equipment. There is usually an exciting contrast between the interpersonal and interactional nature of the developmental chapter and the machine-orientation of this chapter. Students enjoy becoming more aware of their sensory world and you can help enhance that awareness.

1.   **The senses do not simply mirror external "reality"--they shape our experiences in a multitude of ways.** The Archimedes spiral can produce a powerful distortion of sensory experience, and thus bring home the fact that what we take for "reality" is greatly affected by the functioning of sensory systems.

   To construct an Archimedes spiral, obtain a phonograph turn-table. (The author's is a child's phonograph with the tone arm missing. It was purchased from a thrift store for less than a dollar.) Cut a large circle of white posterboard (roughly 12-15 inches in diameter). Make a hole in the middle of the posterboard disk so that it can be placed on the turntable like a phonograph record. Leave the hole small so that the disk will remain attached to the turntable when the phonograph is laid on its side for the class to see. Use a black felt-tip marker to draw a wide, bold spiral from the edge to the center of the disk. When the disk is turning, the spiral may appear to be collapsing in toward the center, or expanding outward, depending on how it is drawn. Either type of spiral will work, but the inward-moving spiral tends to produce a stronger effect. It would be interesting to make one of each to see how each works.

   Set the turntable on its side on the edge of a desk or table so that the cardboard disk can rotate freely and be seen by the class. Set the turntable at its lowest speed. Have students fixate on the center of the spiral for at least one minute. Then ask them to look immediately at some other object (a clock on the wall or your face, for example). If the collapsing spiral has been used, a figural after-effect occurs in which the object viewed after fixation appears to be expanding.

   After the "oohs" and "ahs" die down, point out that a traditional test of the reality of an event is its consensual validation. If several people have the same experience simultaneously, it is thought to be "real." If only one has the experience, it may be considered a hallucination. The question becomes, then, did the clock (or your face) actually change size, or did it not? In terms of subjective experience, an entire classroom full of people could swear in court that it did. Yet in reality it did not.

2.   **The frequently used "blind walk" helps students experience the emotional impact of a loss of vision, and of sensory loss in general.** Put students in pairs. Ask one student to close his/her eyes while being escorted around campus just outside of the classroom. After a designated period of time, switch roles. You could follow your students, listening for unusual auditory stimuli (the sound of a bird, a passerby commenting on the exercise) and quiz them on return to the classroom. Be sure to discuss how difficult it is for many people to relinquish control and totally depend on and trust their partner. Beginning the chapter with this exercise often introduces students effectively to the importance of tuning in to the many sensations that are around us.

3.   **As the text points out, "flavor," as we experience it subjectively, is actually a combination of olfaction and gustation.** This can be demonstrated relatively easily. Bring to class some apple, potato, and onion cut into tiny bits. Have a student volunteer taste bits of each while blindfolded. Discriminating between different foods should be simple in this condition. Next, test the blindfolded volunteer while he or she pinches the nostrils closed. With more olfactory cues reduced, correctly identifying the food bits should be more difficult (although not impossible). Even if they correctly identify the foods in the second test, subjects will usually report greater difficulty. Typically, they must rely more on texture than on "taste" when olfactory cues are reduced.

4.   **To demonstrate genetic differences in taste sensitivity, obtain strips of litmus paper treated with the chemical phenylthiocarbamide (PTC).** Most chemical supply houses carry this item, or the college biology department may have some in stock. It is very inexpensive. Pass out one strip to each class member. Have everyone taste the strip and ask for a description of subjective experiences. About 70 percent will have taste sensations, and about 30 percent will be genetic non-tasters. Subjectively, the chemical exists for some and is a non-stimulus for others.

5.   **In almost every classroom there are weak background stimuli that can be used to demonstrate selective attention.** The buzzing of neon lights, the hum of an air conditioner, the drone of street noise--any of these can be used to show that a stimulus may be present but not consciously perceived until attention is shifted to it. Simply stop in mid-sentence and call attention to one of these stimuli.

6.   **There is an age-old demonstration that students can do easily to illustrate that there are separate receptors for hot and cold and that temperature sensations are relative.** Prepare three containers of water: one cold, one warm, and the third lukewarm. None should be extreme, not too cold or too hot. Have students put one hand into the cold water and the other into the warm. They should observe that one hand will feel cold and the other warm and also notice that the cold or warm feeling occurs mostly at the water line, where air and water meet. This is the only place on the skin where a comparison of air and water temperature can be experienced. The relative difference is what is reported as cold or warm. After being held in the containers for a few minutes, both hands should

be put in the container of lukewarm water. Students will notice that the hand that was in cold water will feel warm, and the hand in warm water will now feel cold. Once again, a comparison of the sensations before and after is what is noted by the brain.

7.   **Similar to the above exercise, students can be asked to do an "instant coffee/brewed coffee" or a "Coke/Classic Coke/Pepsi" taste test.** Count the number of correct judgments. Be sure to take the order of presentation into account, especially if you compare diet cola to sugared cola. Individual differences (heavy coffee or soda drinkers) may also affect the results, perhaps because of sensory adaptation. The main point of this exercise is that psychophysical testing is difficult. A secondary point is that mass advertised brands may differ only marginally.

8.   **Students are often fascinated by the concept of colorblindness.** Each student could be asked to test 10 students on campus (5 males and 5 females). Students can compare the male/female frequencies they observe to the percentages stated in the text. Students can interview any color-blind or color-weak individuals they identify. Students may be disappointed to find that color-blind persons adapt well to their environment and experience only minor consequences. Nevertheless, color-blind individuals usually have at least one good anecdote about their "colorless" world to share.

9.   **Any of the following can serve as an interesting guest lecturer for this chapter: an optometrist, an ophthalmologist, a hearing specialist, a kinestheologist, an audiologist, a sports medicine physician, a dentist, a clinician from a pain clinic, anyone conducting S&P research, or a Lamaze/prepared childbirth specialist.** Students could also be given the opportunity to interview patients on sensory impairments, pain tolerance, or feelings about the upcoming birth of a child.

10.   **This demonstration requires a bit of construction.** Obtain a cardboard carton (a half-gallon ice cream carton is about right). Paint the carton flat black. Punch two small holes in the bottom of the carton, one in the center and one near the rim. Place a flashlight inside, facing the bottom, and stuff crushed newspaper around it for support. Leave a space between the lens of the flashlight and the bottom of the carton so that both holes can be lighted. Cover the center hole with opaque tape. Turn off the room lights and turn on the flashlight. Face the bottom of the carton toward the class and roll it from left to right across a tabletop. The rim light will describe a series of inverted half-circles. Next, uncover the center hole, cover the rim hole, and roll the carton again. The center light will make a straight line from left to right. You would expect, if the carton is rolled again, with both holes uncovered, the two patterns (half-circles and a straight line) would simply be superimposed on one another. Not so! Instead, the class will see a more unified and sophisticated pattern: the rim light will appear to move in complete circles around the center light. Students should be asked to account for this perceptual organization in terms of principles described in the text.

11. **For a simple illustration of convergence, have students fixate on a distant point and then bring a finger up into the line of sight.** The finger will appear "transparent" because the line of sight is nearly parallel. If students then look directly at the finger, it will once again become "solid" (convergence). A variation on this (which also illustrates retinal disparity and fusion) involves again fixating on a distant point. This time the tips of the index fingers of both hands should be brought together in the line of sight, about twelve inches from the eyes. Students should see a small "sausage" forming and disappearing between their fingertips as the two retinal images overlap.

12. **Students often underestimate the effect of the Muller-Lyer illusion because they are so familiar with it.** To demonstrate it in class, on a sheet of paper draw a horizontal line several inches long and place an "arrowhead" on one end and a "V" on the other. Be sure not to center the line within the borders of the page. Duplicate this figure and distribute it to the class. Ask the students to mark the spot that they think is the center of the horizontal line (without trying to correct for the illusion). Now fold the page so the tips of the horizontal line are matched up (to do this they will have to hold the paper up to the light), and crease the paper at the fold. Now ask them to unfold the page and compare the crease with the mark they made. The majority of the students will have erred in their bisection due to the illusion. This is a good launching point for a discussion of illusions.

13. **Demonstrate the apparent distance hypothesis by preparing two slides, drawings, or transparencies.** The circle of the moon can be on the first transparency. Overlap with a transparency that adds depth cues. If your drawing skills allow it, you may want to simply add the depth cues to an acetate as you speak.

14. **Divide students into pairs.** One student serves as subject; the other serves as experimenter. The subject will stare at a photocopy of Necker's cube. Manipulate the frequency of figure reversals by giving half of the subjects written instructions that say, "Most college students are able to see many dozens of reversals per minute." The other half are given written instructions that say, "Reversals may take place, but they are very rare." The experimenter counts the number of reversals within a 3-minute period. Collect the data. Calculate a mean for each group. Discuss why a difference between the two groups is discovered. To what extent do expectations alter perceptions?

15. **For a dramatic and time-honored demonstration of the inaccuracies of eyewitness testimony, arrange for a confederate to "make a scene" in class.** Ideally, the confederate should wear unusual or distinctive clothing (different colored socks, an outlandish hat, etc.). The confederate should charge into class, ask loudly if you are "Professor (your name)," "douse" you with a bucket full of paper clippings, and then run out. Immediately after, ask the class to write a description of your "attacker." Then compare details of the descriptions. For an interesting twist, tell students to be sure to include the color of the visitor's socks in their descriptions. In this variation, of course, the confederate wears no socks!

16.   **People of all ages enjoy watching magicians.** Invite an amateur magician to class. Your students may be willing to do the planning, and the introductions. After a short performance, you can hold a panel discussion on how easily our senses can be fooled. What perceptual principles help explain the illusions created by the magician? Involve the magician in the discussion if he or she is willing.

■ ROLE-PLAYING SCENARIOS

1.   **Imagine that you have lost one of your major senses.** Which sense would be most difficult to lose? Why? Describe this situation as if it had actually happened to you. Next imagine that you have lost only the ability to feel heat, cold, or pressure. How would you act? How would you cope?

2.   **Place yourself in each of the following scenarios:**

    a.   You are forty years old, a college professor, and have never been able to hear. You lip read and know American Sign Language. Describe your life and the reactions others have had to you.

    b.   You are forty years old, a college professor, and recently lost your hearing due to an infection that destroyed the structures of the inner ear. Describe your life and the reactions others have had to you.

3.   **You suddenly become able to hear sounds above 20 kilohertz and to see infrared and ultraviolet light.** Try to explain what you are experiencing to a person with normal sensory thresholds.

4.   **Ask a student to run through class and grab an item off a desk in the front (your purse, your wallet, your notes, etc.).** Try to express anger and surprise. While the student remains outside the class, choose a witness to question. Appoint two other students as inquisitors. These questioners should try to find out what the witness knows about the crime and which of the details provided by the witness are most reliable. Conclude by bringing the culprit back into view and discuss any inaccuracies in the witness' testimony.

5.   **Set up a debate of the proposition that "ESP is a confirmed sensory process and research in this area should receive federal financial support."** Select two students to serve as the advocates for the proposition; select two students to oppose this statement.

6.   **Ask a student to mime the role of a person who lacks depth perception and who sees the world as if it were a flat surface.**

■ VALUE-CLARIFICATION STATEMENTS

1.   Signs for public facilities should be written in Braille and positioned low enough to touch.

2.   All television shows and films should have a written text available for the deaf.

3.   All presidential and political press conferences should be required to provide a signing interpreter.

4.   Rock musicians should be prohibited from playing music at damaging decibel levels.

5.   Portable CD players with headphones should be taken off the market because of potential misuse by children and damage to the children's ears.

6.   A person with impaired depth perception should not be allowed to drive a car.

7.   It is impossible for parents to really understand how their teenage children perceive the world.

8.   Eyewitness testimony alone should never be allowed to determine the outcome of a trial.

9.   Apparent examples of ESP are really based on coincidence.

■ ONE-MINUTE MOTIVATORS

1.   **Before beginning this chapter, put a series of objects (fruit, pieces of material, something made of steel, etc.) in front of the class.** Ask students to describe these objects, in writing. The next class meeting, pass the objects around. Ask students to explore them in more depth. After they have touched and smelled each object, ask them to again describe the objects. At the next meeting, again ask students to describe the objects. This time, their descriptions should be richer and more detailed. Discuss how much sensory information there is in a single flower, leaf, or other common object.

2.   **A child's battery-operated toy musical instrument can serve as an example of a transducer:** Pressing a key converts mechanical energy into an electrical current that activates a mechanical device that makes a musical sound.

3.   **To demonstrate the idea that information is continuously flowing into our sensory system, but that it is not always attended to, play a tape of a waterfall or surf during your lecture.** Ask students whether they feel they need to pay attention to information for it to trigger some kind of sensory response.

4. **If you know a camera buff or a dynamic photography instructor, ask to have a camera taken apart for the class.** Point out the parts that function in a way similar to parts of the eye.

5. **When using plastic models for each sensory receptor, put students either in small groups or in pairs to summarize the process of sensory transduction.** Most people need quite a bit of practice learning to use the proper labels to explain the process.

6. **Ask students in pairs to observe each other's pupils.** Flip a coin to select the "subject." Darken the room for a few minutes. Suddenly turn on the lights and have students estimate how many seconds it takes their partner's pupils to return to their original degree of constriction.

7. **You can add the volley theory of hearing to your lecture by giving three students cap pistols that must be reloaded after 5 shots.** Have one student fire as quickly as possible and then reload and fire again. Then have all three students fire as quickly as they can, reloading when necessary. Stagger their starting times and you will get a continuous flow of sound.

8. **The smell of ammonia, rotten eggs, or kitty litter could (if you are somewhat sadistic) be brought to class.** Students rate the smell at the start of class and every 10 minutes after. Students will experience olfactory adaptation very quickly.

9. **Ask students to explain why individuals are often so insensitive to their own body and breath odor.** How does sensory adaptation contribute to this insensitivity? How have advertisers tried to capitalize on the situation?

10. **Show students a five-minute series of rapidly flashed abstract slides or an excerpt from an unusual, Felini-like film.** Ask them to describe what they think they saw. Discuss the diverse ways people can perceive the world.

11. **Quickly demonstrate the factors that bring order to perceptions by grouping people within the classroom.** Ask three students to stand near each other and ask a fourth to stand farther away; ask students wearing similarly colored shirts to stand together; ask students to create a large circle (note the distance between students) and then a closed circle by holding hands.

12. **Develop a 5-minute video of close-ups of common objects.** Show each close-up and have students guess what the object is. Then show the entire object. Discuss how perceptual hypotheses and figure/ground processes explain the way objects are normally perceived.

13. **Use examples from *The Man Who Mistook His Wife for a Hat* (a reference is given in Suggested Readings) to remind students that our perceptions are the result of activities in the cortex.**

14. **Ask everyone to bring to class a pair or two of sunglasses.** Bring enough foil to cover one or two lenses on each set of glasses. Conduct class as usual. At the end, discuss how students felt to only have peripheral vision, partial vision, or one eye. Discuss the effects of glaucoma, cataracts, and other visual defects.

15. **Divide students into pairs.** Ask one student to sit with eyes closed. The other student claps to the left, to the right, and above that student. The above clap should be very difficult to localize.

16. **Pictorial depth cues can be demonstrated with a series of slides or transparencies.** Ask students to name each cue and explain how it contributes to perceived depth.

17. **Ask students to use a mirror to write their name, copy a geometric design, etc.** Ask an observing student to note the nature of the errors made as their partner adapts to this new perceptual world.

18. **Send three students outside to serve as subjects.** Put three others in front of the class. Invite one subject in and ask the person to estimate the height of the middle student. Ask the middle student to remain; ask two other students to come up to the front. Invite another subject inside. The guesses should change depending on the height of the other two students as well as the height of the subject.

19. **Throughout your lecture, make a small but novel gesture every few minutes.** The gesture should be something that would draw little attention if done once. Do students become aware of the gesture as it is repeated? Or do they habituate to it? Discuss their perceptions near the end of the session.

20. **Provide students with apparent examples of "mental telepathy."** In groups have them decide how the following occurrences could be mere coincidences.

    a. "I suddenly woke up and knew that something tragic had happened to my mother. That morning I received the call that she had died at that precise hour."

    b. "My sister and I live 3,000 miles apart. We have never visited each other's homes. I didn't know what to buy her for a holiday gift but somehow knew she would like a specific set of towels. I was not surprised to learn that she had already bought one of that brand and color for her bathroom and she needed the towels I sent to complete the set."

21.   **In groups, ask students to review the 12 factors affecting the accuracy of eyewitness perception (Table 5-2) and to devise a way to run an experiment manipulating each of the factors.**

22.   **Have students visit a trial where eyewitness testimony is playing a significant role.** Ask students to report back to the class on their observations.

23.   **Find a play or film that ends tragically because two people have inaccurate perceptions of each other.** Discuss or reenact the concluding scene showing how people can try to clarify their communication. Drama or speech students may want to perform a short vignette for your class.

■ BROADENING OUR CULTURAL HORIZONS

1.   **Various cultures have different approaches to pain management.** Some groups suggest that pain should be ignored; others acknowledge pain but suggest specific ways to deal with the pain. What did the "mini-culture" of your family suggest? If you suddenly felt pain in your chest, what has your culture taught you to do? Are these behaviors adaptive or maladaptive?

2.   **Do various cultures emphasize different sensory channels to a greater or lesser degree?** For example, do some cultures place more emphasis on touch, taste, or smell than North Americans do? What does the American preoccupation with television tell us about our culture? The French reputation for cooking? The Italian tendency to touch a person when talking to her or him?

3.   **Invite a hearing-impaired and/or vision-impaired person to class.** Discuss the person's sensory world with her or him, with an emphasis on the subculture that exists among hearing-impaired and/or vision-impaired persons.

4.   **Using a world map, try to characterize the traditional cuisine of various regions as hot and/or spicy versus bland.** Do any patterns emerge? What hypotheses can be advanced to explain cultural preferences for spicy or blander tastes?

5.   **Ask students skilled in languages other than English to share with the class the alphabet of the language and a few key words.** Using Russian, Japanese, or Chinese characters is especially effective. Discuss how meaningless the characters or words may seem at first. Rewrite the letters each day on the chalkboard. By the end of the week(s), the words should become meaningful. Remind students that English appears just as meaningless at first to the non-English speaker as the characters or words appeared to the English speaker.

6.   **Ask students to watch a half-hour of Saturday morning cartoons, including the commercials.** Ask part of the class to view the shows as if they were a child raised:

        a.   On a poor ranch 100 miles from the nearest town

        b.   In a middle-class suburb of a large city

        c.   In the poorest section of a large city

        d.   In rural Guatemala

     Discuss assumptions we make about rural, suburban, and urban, and North American living and different perceptions of aggression, friendship, and materialism.

7.   **Collect photographs of arts and crafts from several cultures.** In what ways are the various styles perceptually similar? How are they different? How strongly does culture influence perceptions of beauty?

■ SUPPLEMENTAL ACTIVITIES

TO THE INSTRUCTOR:

Five classroom exercises are developed in this section to help students understand some of the concepts in this chapter. The author of the text discusses the notions of cutaneous threshold, auditory localization, and the taste sensations. These are three types of sensory experience that can be examined in the first two exercises, while the last two exercises focus on aspects of perception.

Exercise #1: Cutaneous Two-Point Threshold

This is an exercise to demonstrate the threshold for pressure on the surface of the skin. To carry out this exercise you need a subject and an experimenter and a device with two points. The two-point instrument could be a divider from a geometry set or some similar item that has two points which can be set at varying distances apart with some way to measure that distance.

This exercise can be done as a demonstration with several students selected to be subjects or by dividing up the whole class into pairs with each one alternating as subject and experimenter. The latter would require a large number of two-point instruments.

The procedure for this activity is as follows:

1. Identify the subject and experimenter. If the class is paired, each couple can determine this. If it is a class demonstration, identify several subjects and an experimenter. You should direct the demonstration and not be either the subject or the experimenter.

2. Blindfold the subject to be tested.

3. Provide the experimenter, or the whole class, with the data sheet which indicates the area of the skin surface to be tested and the type of test to make. The experimenter will touch the surface of the skin with one point or two, varying the distance between the points with each trial. The subject will respond with "one" or "two" when each contact is made.

4. Record all responses until the subject can no longer distinguish between one and two points on successive trials.

5. If this is a class demonstration, have students record the responses for each subject. If the students are working in pairs, the experimenter will record each trial. After completing the trials, the two will change places and repeat the procedure. Provide students with enough data sheets for all subjects to be tested.

6. After all testing is completed, collect the data and work out the thresholds for each part of the skin surface tested.

7. Students should note and discuss differences found among students and differences from one part of the body to the other.

8. Ask students to explain why there is a threshold and why it differs depending on the area of the body involved.

CUTANEOUS TWO-POINT THRESHOLD: DATA SHEET

TO THE EXPERIMENTER:

Some guidelines for doing this exercise--

1.   Be sure the subject is securely blindfolded.

2.   Apply even, firm, but not excessive pressure, with one point or two, as directed. You should avoid causing pain to (or breaking the skin of) the subject.

3.   Make exact measurements when setting the two points for each trial.

4.   Do not repeat any trials.

5.   Ask the subject for a response after each application of pressure.

6.   Do not give hints or clues to help the subject. Encourage the subject to make an immediate response.

7.   For each response made by the subject, put a 1 or 2 in the appropriate box.

DATA SHEET (cont.)

On the chart below, the distance (Dst) between points and the number of points (Pts) to be applied are indicated. Record the responses (Res) of the subjects in the space provided.

lower back			palm			fingertip		
Dst.	Pts.	Res.	Dst.	Pts.	Res.	Dst.	Pts.	Res.
2"	1 2 2		1 1/2"	2 1 2		3/4"	2 1 2	
1 3/4"	2 1 2		1 1/4"	1 2 2		5/8"	1 2 2	
1 1/2"	1 1 2		1"	1 2 1		1/2"	1 2 1	
1 1/4"	1 2 1		3/4"	2 2 1		3/8"	1 1 2	
1"	2 1 2		1/2"	1 2 1		1/4"	2 1 2	
3/4"	2 2 1		1/4"	1 1 2		1/8"	2 2 1	
1/2"	1 2 1		1/8"	2 1 2		1/16"	1 2 1	
1/4"	1 2 1		1/16"	2 1 2				

Exercise #2: Auditory Localization

Locating the direction of sound involves the binaural cue of time difference. Auditory stimulation reaches each ear at a different time because sound travels relatively slowly through the air. This is called the interaural time difference. This exercise will demonstrate this phenomenon. **The subject will attempt to locate a sound with only auditory cues.** Students will see that sound location will be most accurate when the interaural time difference is the greatest and least accurate when the difference is smallest. In preparation for this demonstration, students should read the section on **hearing** in this chapter with particular attention to the discussion of auditory information processing.

The only materials needed are a **blindfold, twelve noisemakers (such as a cricket clicker) that will give a clear crisp sound, and thirteen chairs.**

Procedure:

1. Set up twelve chairs in a circle to resemble the numbers on a clock. Put the thirteenth chair in the center facing six o'clock and away from the chalkboard.

2. Select as many subjects as you want to use and send them out of the room during the preparation time. You will need one, and might consider two, if time permits.

3. Select twelve persons to occupy the twelve chairs in the circle, all facing the chalkboard, and provide each with a noisemaker. Each student will be assigned a number corresponding to the numbers on a clock dial, with the student farthest from the chalkboard number six, and the student nearest the chalkboard number twelve.

4. Ask the remaining students to be recorders. Each should be provided with a data sheet.

5. Use a random procedure to determine the order of clicks. A good way would be to prepare 48 slips of paper with the numbers 1 to 12 (each number repeated four times). Draw these slips out of a hat. The order should then be put on the record sheets and on the chalkboard.

6. Admit the student subject, seat him/her in the center chair facing away from the chalkboard, and put on the blindfold. Instruct the subject to face straight ahead, listen for the sound, and indicate the location by naming a position on the clock, with 6 o'clock being directly in front and 12 o'clock behind.

7. The instructor or a student should act as experimenter and point to each location on the chalkboard, one at a time. The person seated at that location should make one clicking sound. Give time for the subject to respond and the recorders to note the location given.

8.   After all forty-eight trials are completed, students should check for the subject's accuracy at each of the twelve locations, noting the size of the error for each.

9.   If a second subject is to be used, the positions for the trials should be re-randomized.

10. On completion of the trials for all subjects, the class should determine the average size of the error at each of the twelve positions.

11. Some questions for discussion:

   a.   Is there a pattern to the error size? Where is it greatest and where is it smallest?

   b.   What is the explanation for the differences found?

   c.   Would there be any value in moving one's head when the location of a sound is ambiguous?

   d.   What would be the effect of deafness in one ear? Could the person locate a sound? Discuss reasons for a yes or no answer to this question.

(based on a demonstration by Dr. William C. Titus, Arkansas Tech University)

AUDITORY LOCALIZATION   DATA SHEET:

TRIAL	LOCATION	RESPONSE	TRIAL	LOCATION	RESPONSE
1	___	___	25	___	___
2	___	___	26	___	___
3	___	___	27	___	___
4	___	___	28	___	___
5	___	___	29	___	___
6	___	___	30	___	___
7	___	___	31	___	___
8	___	___	32	___	___
9	___	___	33	___	___
10	___	___	34	___	___
11	___	___	35	___	___
12	___	___	36	___	___
13	___	___	37	___	___
14	___	___	38	___	___
15	___	___	39	___	___
16	___	___	40	___	___
17	___	___	41	___	___
18	___	___	42	___	___
19	___	___	43	___	___
20	___	___	44	___	___
21	___	___	45	___	___
22	___	___	46	___	___
23	___	___	47	___	___
24	___	___	48	___	___

Exercise #3: Measuring Good Taste

"Measuring Good Taste" can be used as an exercise in sensory analysis. Students do need to be encouraged to think through the food they bring so that students are not tasting 10 different brands of potato chips and so that student allergies are respected.

The student assignment sheet might look like this:

Your assignment is to work as a pair to find an unusual food to bring to class. Let me know ahead of time if you have any food allergies. Research the cultural origins of the food and the traditions associated with it. Be sure that you know the ingredients. Bring enough of the food so that 10 students can have a bite. Do not bring anything that needs to be refrigerated or that could spoil. Do not bring anything that is expensive for you to prepare or purchase. I will bring napkins and utensils. Bring to class a soda so that you can refresh your taste between food samples.

You will be using this form to rate each of the foods. As you begin to taste a food, smell it carefully. Taste it slowly. Focus on the taste, the texture, the temperature of the food. Rate the food. Then the provider of that food will tell us about the cultural origins of the food and its ingredients.

Rate each food in the following way. Rate its saltiness, sweetness, and bitterness on a scale from 1-5: 1 = not very; 5 = very.

For example, if you feel it is quite salty, the rating would be a 4 or a 5. Copy the following list for each food and put your ratings in the spaces to the right of each taste quality. After the ratings are completed and the food is described, we will share our ratings. Is "good taste" fairly universal? Or learned and culturally relative? Or a little of both?

FOOD _____

SALTINESS _____

SWEETNESS _____

BITTERNESS _____

LIKING? _____

Exercise #4: Perception/Attention: The Stroop Effect

In 1935 J. R. Stroop developed an experiment, which now bears his name, on how we process conflicting sensory data. It is called the Stroop Effect. He found that conflicting sensory data slows down the process of perception and increases the chance of error. With a small amount of preparation you can do the experiment in class.

This exercise may be done as a classroom demonstration or as an all-class project. If you choose the former, select several subjects (about five would be sufficient) and ask them to leave the room. You will then bring them back, one at a time, and test them in front of the class, who will be observers and recorders. The latter method, involving the whole class, would require a bit more work to prepare but should pay off in greater student interest. You would pair up the students, having one be the subject and the other the experimenter. The roles could be reversed to test the bidirectional effect.

Procedure:

1.   **Prepare three word-color sheets.** The words should be spaced equally on both the horizontal and vertical dimensions. The list and arrangement are found at the end of this exercise. Each of the sheets will be a list of four colors: yellow, blue, green, and red. They will be presented in identical order but in different ways.

   a.   **List #1:** This list will be done in black or blue ink. All will be the same color.

   b.   **List #2:** This list will not be words but color patches. Each patch will be the color of the word on the list. These patches can be done with crayons or markers, and should be small rectangles of color with no words.

   c.   **List #3.** The words on this sheet should be the same as on List #1, except that the words should be printed in color. The color used should always be different from the color named in the word.

2.   **If this is to be a classroom demonstration, prepare your subjects, experimenters, and recorders.** Otherwise, pair up the students in the class and identify the subjects and experimenters, who will also act as recorders. Each experimenter will need a watch which will measure seconds for timing the subject. The three sheets should be placed face down in front of the subject in order of presentation. Reading each list will constitute a trial. In each case, the subject will be instructed to read the list from left to right from the top line down, as quickly as possible. When finished, the subject should say, "done." The experimenter will time the reading of each list and note it on the data sheet.

3.   **Present List #1 and ask the subject to read the words in order.** When presenting List #2, ask the subject to name the color on the patches in the same order as before. For List #3 ask the subject to name the color of the ink in which each word is printed.

4.   **Collect the data for all subjects and work out a class average for each of the three lists.** If the Stroop Effect has occurred, you should find that the subjects took about the same amount of time to read lists 1 and 2 and longer for 3.

5.   **If you have time, reverse the roles of experimenter and subject and repeat the experiment.** The only difference would be in reading List #3. The new subject would be asked to read the words on the third list instead of identifying the color of the word. This may provide a different average time when compared with the average time for the first subjects.

Some questions for discussion:

1.   Was the Stroop Effect evident? Explain how it manifested itself.

2.   How can you account for the differences in average time?

3.   Did the change in the reading of List #3 produce a different average time? How great was the difference? How could it be explained?

(Based on a demonstration by William C. Titus, Arkansas Tech University.)

THE STROOP EFFECT: COLOR-WORD LIST

YELLOW	YELLOW	BLUE	YELLOW
GREEN	RED	YELLOW	GREEN
GREEN	BLUE	RED	YELLOW
RED	GREEN	BLUE	RED
GREEN	BLUE	GREEN	BLUE
BLUE	RED	RED	YELLOW

THE STROOP EFFECT: DATA SHEET

| SUBJECT | TIME (in seconds) | | |
	LIST #1	LIST #2	LIST #3
1			
2			
3			
4			
5			
6			
7			
8			
9			
10			

Exercise #5: Mental Telepathy, or It's in the Cards

You can easily demonstrate an ESP experiment looking for evidence of telepathy by using the Zener cards. The cards can be made if no real deck is available. The Zener cards are made up of five symbols, one of which is on each card. You should have 25 cards in the deck, five of each symbol. If you make your own, use heavy cardboard so the symbol cannot be seen through the back. Select five symbols that are easily distinguishable from each other. For example, you should not use a square and rectangle as two of the symbols because of possible confusion. The cards and symbols need to be small enough to be easily shuffled and large enough to be easily seen by the whole class when shown.

Duplicate the data sheet which follows so that each student in the class can participate as a subject. The sheet has a place for students to respond to each of five trial runs through the deck. The student can also tally the responses and work out the percentage of correct answers.

Procedure:

1. **Distribute** a response sheet to each member of the class and explain how it is to be used.
2. **Shuffle the deck of cards** thoroughly in full view of the class and place the deck face down on the table.
3. **Pick up one card at a time,** look at it carefully for about two seconds, and place it face down on a new pile. Do not let students see the face of the card. While concentrating on the card, try to shut out any distracting thoughts. If you are preoccupied with running the demonstration, have a student, prepared beforehand, do the telecommunicating.
4. **Give the students time to write** down on their data sheets the symbol which they think you saw on the card. Note the correct symbol on your own record sheet. Proceed through the deck in the same way.
5. **After completing a trial** (one run through the deck), shuffle the cards thoroughly and go through the stack again. Repeat this until you have completed five trials, being sure to shuffle the cards before each one. Also, be sure you have kept an accurate record of each card for each trial run.
6. **After the fifth run through the deck,** give the students the correct listing of cards so they can score their sheets.
7. **Ask the students to total the number** of correct responses for each of the five trials. They can work out the percentage for each run by dividing the number right by 25 and multiplying by 100.
8. **Then ask them to total the number** right for all five trials. Divide this total by 125 and multiply by 100 to get a percentage for the whole experiment.

Discussion: Ask the students to discuss their findings. They should first determine what they could expect to score by chance alone, i.e. by guessing. Then they can compare their scores with the chance score to see if they did as well, poorer, or better. Do those who did better have ESP? In this case, do they have the power of telepathy? What would happen if you did it many more times? Of what value is it to do better than chance?

TELEPATHY: DATA SHEET

TRIALS	1	2	3	4	5
1					
2					
3					
4					
5					
6					
7					
8					
9					
10					
11					
12					
13					

TRIALS	1	2	3	4	5
14					
15					
16					
17					
18					
19					
20					
21					
22					
23					
24					
25					

■ JOURNAL QUESTIONS

1. Blindness is a severe sensory disability. Other than true physical blindness, in what other ways may a person be "blind." Do you think that you have any "blind spots" in your intellectual or emotional life?

2. What is the worst physical pain you have experienced? What were the circumstances? What could others have done to ease your pain? What could you have done?

3. What pleasant thoughts and memories do you associate with certain smells or tastes?

4. Have you ever experienced the equivalent of a "runner's high"? If so, under what conditions? If not, try to explain the interest (if not addiction) of some people to running. Do they run because it feels so good to run or because it feels so good when they stop?

5. Try to describe all of the sensations that you are aware of at this moment. What happens to your description as your attention shifts from sense to sense?

6. Describe a time you jumped to the wrong conclusion about a situation. Why did you or others "misperceive" the situation? What was the consequence of the misperception? What could have been done at the time to have prevented it from happening?

7. If you were to look through a department store catalogue (such as a Sears catalogue) what items would most gain your attention? What does this tell you about your interests and motives?

8. Describe a time you felt you experienced some form of ESP. What other explanations can you give for the events you have described?

9. Have you ever been a witness to a crime or accident? To what extent were you "coached" to remember the incident in a certain manner? Include informal coaching by others witnesses, those with something at stake in the accident and so on.

■ SUGGESTIONS FOR FURTHER READING

Atchison, D. A., and G. Smith. *Optics of the Human Eye.* Butterworth-Heinemann, 2000.

Bloomer, C. M. *Principles of Visual Perception.* London: Herbert Press, 1990.

Escher, M. C. *The Magic of M. C. Escher.* Abrahms, 2000.

Goldstein, E. B. *Sensation and Perception,* 6th ed. Wadsworth, 2002.

Hansel, C.E. M. *The Search for Psychic Power: ESP and Parapsychology Revisited.* Prometheus Books, 1989.

Horgan, John. "See Spot See Blue; Curb That Dogma! Canines Are Not Colorblind." *Scientific American,* 262, p. 20, January 1990.

Kare, M.R. and Maltes, R. D. "A Selective Overview of the Chemical Senses." *Nutrition Reviews,* 48, 30, February 1990.

Keller, H. *Story of My Life.* Doubleday, 1991.

MacKay, Donald. *Behind the Eye.* Bladewell Publishers, 1991.

Marks, D. and R. Kamman. *The Psychology of the Psychic.* Prometheus Books, 2000.

Nathans, Jeremy. "The Genes for Color Vision." *Scientific American,* 260, 42, February 1989.

Randi, J. *Flim Flam!* Prometheus, 1988.

Robinson, J. O. *The Psychology of Visual Illusion.* Dover Publications, 1999.

Sacks, O. *The Man Who Mistook His Wife for a Hat and Other Clinical Tales.* Touchstone Books, 1998.

Sacks, O. *Seeing Voices: A Journey into the World of the Deaf.* Vintage Books, 2000.

Sekuler, R. and R. Blake, R. *Perception.* McGraw-Hill, 1994.

Sharpe , L. T. and K. R. Gegenfurtner. *Color Vision: From Genes to Perception.* Cambridge University Press. 1999.

Smith, Jeff. *The Frugal Gourmet: On Our Immigrant Ancestors.* Avon Books, 1992.

Tart, Charles, ed. *Altered States of Consciousness.* Psychological Processes, 1990.

Wolman B. B. et al., eds. *Handbook of Parapsychology.* McFarland & Co., 1986.

■ MEDIA SUGGESTIONS

COLOR (2000, Films for the Humanities and Sciences, 23 min.)
The perception of colors, the relationship between psychological responses and physical phenomena, and how colors are used in inks and paints.

THE MIND'S EYE (2000, from the *Brain Story* series, Films for the Humanities and Sciences, 50 min.)
Drawing on the experiences of people with rare forms of brain damage, this program featuring Dr. Susan Greenfield reveals the tricks and shortcuts used by the brain to construct its version or illusion of reality.

THE SENSES: SKIN DEEP (2000, Films for the Humanities and Sciences, Inc., 26 min.)
This film looks at those sense receptors that depend on contact with the immediate world: taste buds, touch sensors, and olfactory cells. These senses lie in the skin--the largest organ of the body--which also senses heat, pain, and pressure. The complex world beneath the skin is seen from the viewpoint of the root.

SENSATION AND PERCEPTION (2000, from *Discovering Psychology Series,* Annenberg/CPB, 30 min.)
How visual information is gathered and processed, and how our culture, previous experiences, and interests influence our perceptions.

SENSATION AND PERCEPTION (2000, Insight Media, 30 min.)
This video illustrates how information about the world is gathered by sensory receptors and interpreted by the brain.

SENSATION AND PERCEPTION (2000, from *Psychology- the Study of Human Behavior Series,* Coast Community College District, 30 min.)
Demonstrates construction of reality from senses, interpretation and organization into meaningful patterns by the brain.

SENSATION AND PERCEPTION (2000, from *Psychology- the Human Experience Series,* Coast Community College District, 30 min.)
Demonstrates how our senses gather information about the world around us. Perception is also covered in depth.

SMELL AND TASTE (2000, Films for the Humanities and Sciences, 30 min.)
Life without smell and taste is almost unimaginable. Think of the important connections between smell and memory. Does a certain odor evoke fond remembrances? This program from *The Doctor Is In* travels into the nose and mouth to find out what causes these sometimes wonderful, sometimes dreadful sensations.

A number of videos are available from Thomson. Videos appropriate for this chapter include the following films from the CNN TODAY Introductory Psychology Video Series:

Volume 2, Section 1: The Brain
    Smell Memory (2:21)

Volume 3, Section 2: Sensation and Perception
    Elderly Taste (2:02)
    Sleep and Hearing (1:34)

Volume 4, Section 7: Vision
    Visual Impairment and the Artificial Eye (2:04)

■ COMPUTER AND INTERNET RESOURCES

PSYCHNOW!

Sensation & Perception:
Vision and Hearing
Chemical and Somesthetic Senses
Perception

PSYK.TREK

Unit 3: Sensation and Perception
       3a: Light and the eye
       3b: The retina
       3c: Vision and the brain
       3d: Perception of color
       3e: Gestalt psychology
       3f: Depth perception
       3g: Visual illusions
       3h: The sense of hearing

INFOTRAC

Subject Guide/Key Words: Sensation and Perception, Sensory Localization of Function, Gustation, Color Vision, Inner Ear, Hearing Loss, Olfaction, Vestibular, Visual Perception, Gestalt, Depth Perception, Visual Accommodation, Visual Illusion, Extrasensory Perception, ESP, Parapsychology, PSI

WEB SITES

Wadsworth Online Psychology Study Center:
http://info.wadsworth.com/cooessentials9

Clarion University WWW Resource Pages:
http://river.clarion.edu/sandp/sandp.html

Seeing, Hearing, and Smelling the World:
http://www.hhmi.org/senses

Sensation and Perception Links Page:
http://www.uwsp.edu/acad/psych/sh/330links.htm

Richard Hall's Guided Exploration:
http://www.umr.edu/~rhall/class/sap/sapsurfprogram/surfprogramindex.html

Virtual Tour of the Ear:
http://ctl.augie.edu/perry/ear/hearmech.htm

Perception Online:
http://www.perceptionweb.com/index.html

Extrasensory Perception:
http://www.hope.edu/academic/psychology/myerstxt/esp/esp.html

Parapsychology Sources on the Web:
http://www.ed.ac.uk/~ejua35/parapsy.htm

CHAPTER 6
States of Consciousness

■ LEARNING OBJECTIVES

To demonstrate mastery of this chapter the student should be able to:

1. Define consciousness and explain what waking consciousness is.
2. Define and describe "altered state of consciousness." Include a description of the meaning and uses of altered states of consciousness in other cultures.
3. Describe the limitations of sleep learning.
4. Define the term biological rhythm and explain its relationship to sleep.
5. Define and describe the term microsleep.
6. Describe the general effects of 2 or 3 days of sleep deprivation. Name and describe the condition that occurs when a person is deprived of sleep for a longer period of time.
7. Explain what circadian rhythms are and what bodily functions are related to them.
8. State how long the average sleep-waking cycle is. Explain how we tie our sleep rhythms to a 24-hour day.
9. Describe the normal range of sleep needs. Describe how the aging process affects sleep.
10. Explain how and why shift work and jet lag may adversely affect a person. Explain how the direction of travel (or of rotating shifts) affects rhythms and how to minimize the effects of shifting one's rhythms.
11. Describe how the brain's systems and chemistry promote sleep.
12. Briefly describe each of the four stages of sleep. Include a description of the brain waves associated with each and those associated with wakefulness.
13. Describe the cyclical nature of the sleep stages.
14. Name and differentiate the two basic states of sleep. Explain how the relative amounts of each of these two sleep states can be influenced by events of the day.
15. State how long dreams usually last.
16. List the physiological changes that occur during REM sleep, including a description of REM behavior disorder.
17. Explain the concept of REM myth.
18. Describe the probable functions of REM sleep.
19. List and briefly describe the twelve sleep disorders that are found in the DSM-IV. (See Table 6-1.)
20. Define insomnia. Describe the effects of nonprescription and prescription drugs on insomnia.
21. List and describe the characteristics and treatment of the three types of insomnia.

22. List and briefly describe six behavioral remedies that can be used to combat insomnia.
23. Characterize the following major sleep disturbances of NREM sleep.
    a. somnambulism
    b. sleeptalking
    c. night terrors (include a differentiation between night terrors and nightmares)
    d. sleep apnea (include a description of SIDS)

The following objectives are related to the material in the "Exploring Psychology" section of the text.

24. Explain Calvin Hall's view of dreams.
25. Explain how Freud viewed dreams, and present the evidence against his view.
26. Describe the activation-synthesis hypothesis concerning dreaming.

27. Give the general definition of hypnosis and then describe how it is that the general definition is not accepted by all psychologists.
28. Trace the history of hypnosis from Mesmer through its use today.
29. State the proportion of people who can be hypnotized
30. Explain how a person's hypnotic susceptibility can be determined. Include a brief description of the dimensions of the Stanford Hypnotic Susceptibility Scale. (See Table 6-2.)
31. List the four common factors in all hypnotic techniques. Explain why all hypnosis may really be self-hypnosis.
32. Explain what the basic suggestion effect is.
33. Explain how hypnosis can affect:
    a. strength
    b. memory
    c. amnesia
    d. pain relief
    e. age regression
    f. sensory changes
34. List three areas in which hypnosis appears to have its greatest value, and then state a general conclusion concerning the effectiveness of hypnosis.
35. Using the five characteristics of the stage setting outlined in the chapter, explain how a stage hypnotist gets people to perform the way they do in front of an audience.
36. Name and describe the two major forms of meditation.
37. Describe the relaxation response.
38. Describe what is known about the effects of meditation.
39. Explain what sensory deprivation is. Include a discussion of the positive and negative effects of this procedure.
40. Define the term psychoactive drug.
41. Differentiate physical dependence from psychological dependence.

42. Describe the following frequently abused drugs in terms of their effects, possible medical uses, side effects or long-term symptoms, organic damage potential, and potential for physical and/or psychological dependence.
    a. amphetamines (include the term amphetamine psychosis)
    b. cocaine (include the three signs of abuse)
    c. MDMA
    d. caffeine (include the term caffeinism)
    e. nicotine
    f. barbiturates
    g. GHB
    h. tranquilizers (including the concept of drug interaction)
    i. alcohol (include the concept of binge drinking)
    j. hallucinogens (including marijuana)
43. Compare the efficacy of quitting smoking "cold turkey" versus cutting down or smoking low-tar cigarettes.
44. List and explain the three phases in the development of a drinking problem.
45. Generally describe the treatment process for alcoholism. Name the form of therapy that has probably been the most successful.
46. Explain why drug abuse is such a common problem.

The following objectives are related to the material in the "Psychology in Action" section of the text.

47. List and describe the four processes identified by Freud which disguise the hidden meaning of dreams.
48. Contrast Hall's and Cartwright's views of dream interpretation.
49. List the eight steps for remembering dreams.
50. Explain how Perls viewed dreams and how he suggested that people interpret them.
51. Describe how one could use dreams to aid in problem solving. Include a description of lucid dreams and how they have been used in the problem solving process.

■ DISCUSSION QUESTIONS

1. How would your life change if you needed to sleep 15 hours per day? How would it change if you only needed 2 hours a day? Would you give up sleep if you could?

2. Have you ever gone without sleep for an extended period? If so, what were your reactions? Your greatest difficulties?

3. Describe a recent dream you have had. How does it relate to your daytime experiences and feelings? What additional meanings can you find in it? Do you think that recording your dreams would be worthwhile?

4. Do environmental factors affect whether one is a "day" or a "night" person? Have you switched from one to the other at any time in your life? Are you more comfortable with one pattern or the other, regardless of environmental influences?

5. Is the onset of sleep more like passively taking your foot off the accelerator? Or is it more like actively shifting into another gear (form of consciousness)? Explain.

6. Have you ever solved a problem in your dreams? How much control do you have over what you dream?

7. Respond to the statement, "The REM state is not sleep at all; during REM we are paralyzed and hallucinating." Do you agree?

8. Compare and contrast the three theories of dreaming. In what specific ways and under what conditions could all three theories be correct?

9. Why would amphetamines be helpful in treating narcolepsy?

10. If you have ever seen a stage hypnotist or participated in a hypnosis demonstration, how did your experience compare with Barber's analysis of stage hypnosis?

11. Have you ever been in a situation that produced sensory deprivation (such as a commercial "flotation center" or a radar room)? How did you react? Why do you think brief sensory deprivation is restful and longer periods are stressful?

12. Do you think that seeking altered states of consciousness is "natural"? What altered states does our culture accept? About which states is it ambivalent? What altered states does it clearly reject? How do you think such differences developed?

13. If a person is primarily interested in relaxation and quieting mental activity, what alternative forms of "meditation" might he or she find helpful?

14. What is the difference between "tolerance" and "addiction"? How would you test a drug abuser to see if either or both conditions are present?

15. Do you agree or disagree with the idea that prohibition of drug use leads to adulteration, black markets, organized crime, unwillingness of abusers to seek help, and greater injury through imprisonment than is caused by the drugs themselves? What arguments can you give to support your position?

16.   In the novel *Brave New World,* Aldous Huxley described an imaginary drug called soma that made people feel continuously happy and cooperative. If such a drug existed, what controls would you impose on its use? Why? If a drug that could enhance creativity were discovered, what use would you allow for it? What about a drug to improve memory?

17.   A friend of yours suggests that the conclusions drawn about the long-term effects of marijuana are "correlational" and that other factors cause these effects. What other factors could play a significant role?

18.   What would be the combined physical and psychological effect of cocaine, alcohol, and marijuana abuse? Why do some people engage in polydrug abuse?

19.   How would you define the difference between drug use and drug abuse?

20.   In view of their addictive qualities, should advertising be allowed for tobacco and alcohol? Should American tobacco companies be allowed to promote smoking in other countries where there is less public awareness of the health hazards of tobacco?

21.   If you had a totally free hand, how would you handle this country's drug abuse problem?

22.   Do you believe that Ecstasy (MDMA) is a dangerous drug? Why or why not?

23.   Should marijuana be made legal for medicinal uses?

■ LECTURE ENHANCEMENTS

1.   **The Charcot Pendulum makes a good demonstration of the core elements of hypnosis.** Prepare three pendulums by tying a small weight to one end of three foot-long strings. A nut, pendant, washer, fishing sinker, or ring works well. In class ask for volunteers. Have them stand in front of the class. Each should hold a string (with attached weight). Proceed by giving suggestions similar to these:

> The Charcot Pendulum has long been used as a prelude to hypnosis. Today I will not be hypnotizing you, so just relax. For the pendulum to work, you must be able to concentrate and focus your attention as I instruct you. Begin by holding the pendulum at arm's length and at eye level. Focus your attention on the pendulum. Notice its texture and the way the light reflects from its surface. Relax and take a deep breath. Watch the pendulum and focus on it intensely. Let everything else fade away until the pendulum is at the very center of your attention. Now I'd like you to begin to use your concentration to move the pendulum. Do not move your hand or body. Just apply the energy of your concentration to the pendulum. Try to push it away from you. Each

time it moves away push again, with your eyes, with your attention. Push and release, push and release. Follow it with your eyes as it begins to move. Each time it swings out, push and release. It's as if a magnet were pushing and releasing, pushing and releasing. Relax and follow it with your eyes. Let it swing wider and wider. Push, release (and so forth).

With continued suggestions such as these most subjects will respond by swinging the pendulum in a broad arc. When questioned they will deny that they consciously moved the hand. The major point here is that the pendulum seems to move of its own accord, aided only by the "concentration" of the subjects. In this respect the experience is similar to hypnosis. Suggestion brings about a temporary suspension of reality-testing and conscious intention--a change essential to hypnosis.

2.   **Invite the manager or foreperson of a local plant or military base, or a fire-fighter to class to speak about factors taken into account when scheduling employees for all-night or rotating work shifts.**

3.   **In small groups, ask students to share recent dreams and the extent to which dreaming is related to physical exhaustion and psychological stress.** Students can devise their own system for the categorization of dreams. They can then collect data from the entire class on dreaming patterns.

4.   **Divide the class into thirds.** Ask each group to discuss one of the three general approaches to dreams (Cartwright/ Freud/ Hobson & McCarley). Ask each group to select a spokesperson to describe a recent dream and interpret it from that groups point of view. Have the class discuss whether dreams are meaningful.

5.   **A very interesting class discussion can usually be generated from comparisons of individual differences in sleep patterns and unusual experiences associated with sleep.** Look for people who:
    a.   Sleep very little or much more than average

    b.   Have been deprived or sleep for long periods

    c.   Have done shift work or have maintained unusual sleep/working cycles

    d.   Have a relative or acquaintance who has had sleep disturbances such as somnambulism, night terrors, narcolepsy, sleep apnea, or insomnia

    e.   Have done problem-solving in dreams

    f.   Have had lucid dreams

    g.   Have kept a dream journal or attempted dream control

6.   **There are now hundreds of "sleep centers" around the country for the diagnosis and treatment of sleep disorders.** If one is near you, you may be able to arrange a guest speaker or a field trip. For information on the nearest sleep center contact: Dr. William Dement, ASDC, Stanford University School of Medicine, Stanford, CA 94305.

7.   **Invite the director of a sleep clinic or a drug abuse clinic to describe his/her program.** Ask a recovering alcoholic to share the nightmares he/she may have experienced after quitting drinking. Ask an AA member to explain why this program has been successful for many alcohol abusers. At some other time, you may want to discuss AA's limitations.

8.   **While many students express great interest in the topic of sleep and dreams, it is a subject about which they have many misconceptions.** J. Palladino and B. Carducci developed A Sleep and Dream Information Questionnaire designed to assess student awareness of current findings in sleep and dream research. This questionnaire can provide an interesting and informative way to introduce students to this material. Student responses can also be used to tailor lectures to meet the needs of the class. Finally, after students take the questionnaire, the instructor can discuss the items in class, thus giving students immediate feedback. Copies of the questionnaire, an appendix entitled "Explanation of Items Comprising the Sleep and Dream Information Questionnaire", and reprints are available from Joseph Palladino, Department of Psychology, University of Southern Indiana. For more information see J. J. Palladino and B. J. Carducci, "Students' Knowledge of Sleep and Dreams," *Teaching of Psychology,* Vol. II (3), October 1984.

9.   **For a simple but dramatic demonstration of the fakery involved in much stage hypnosis, try the following.** Tell the class that one of the most reliable phenomena available with hypnosis is anesthesia or pain analgesia. Tell them that earlier you used self-hypnosis to make your hand totally insensitive to pain, and that now you need only use a post-hypnotic cue to produce numbness. Stroke your hand as if you were putting on a glove, and explain that this is the cue. Pinch your hand a few times as if testing to see if it has become numb. Ask the class to watch carefully as you strike a match (a paper match, not a wooden match) and hold the flame to the palm of your outstretched hand. The trick, of course, is to keep the match moving at all times. (You may want to practice this at home first!) It is quite possible to leave very impressive "scorch" marks (actually soot) on your hand without experiencing any pain. Explain to the students what you have done and point out that many examples of stage hypnosis rely on similar deception and a lack of questioning by the audience.

10.   **The spectacular stage trick of suspending someone between two chairs (pictured in this chapter) is worth repeating in class.** Have a volunteer recline as shown. Be sure the head and feet touch the backs of the end chairs. Ask the subject to lift, and remove the middle chair. The subject should have no difficulty maintaining this position. Now place a book on the subject's upper abdomen (diaphragm area). With the volunteer's permission, lean on the book with both hands to show that the subject can support extra weight without hypnosis. Then note that the upper abdomen is the only place a hypnotist could actually stand or sit on the suspended subject. For obvious reasons the entertainer is not going to position himself/herself on the subject's knees, pelvis, or chest. The only workable position is just a few inches from the front edge of the chair--which is why subjects can so readily support the weight.

11.   **Ask students to search the Internet for articles on the use of hypnosis for the solving of crimes.** Print and make copies of the articles. Ask students to critically evaluate whether the memories were actually recalled or reconstructed. Discuss the problems of using hypnosis in court. (See Chapter 8 in the text for more information.)

12.   **Debate Statement: "If a drug is a recognized part of a religious ceremony, its use should be protected by the Bill of Rights."** Students can discuss the preceding debate statement in pairs or in small groups. Then they can be provided with the information on the Native American Church, after which the issue can be discussed further. This is also a good launching point for a discussion of cultural differences in patterns of drug use and attitudes toward drugs.

The Native American Church

The Native American Church (also called Peyotism or the Peyote Religion) is a widespread religious movement among North American Indians. The name of the religion comes from the use of the Peyote cactus tops as one of the sacraments of the religious ceremony. The tops contain mescaline, a drug that has hallucinogenic effects.

Many Indian groups have actively practiced this religion from the mid-19th century through current times. The religion first developed among the Kiowa and Comanche of Oklahoma. After 1891, the religion spread rapidly as far as Canada, and it is now practiced among more than 50 tribes. In 1965 it is estimated that one-third of the Oklahoma Indians practiced this religion. The Native American Church reports to have over 225,000 members.

The Native American Church combines Indian and Christian beliefs. Members believe in one supreme God (the Great Spirit) who guides men through "spirits." For example, the traditional water bird or thunderbird is the spirit that carries prayers to God. Christians see Jesus as God's messenger; often peyote itself is viewed as the vehicle God created for communicating with mankind. The process of eating peyote helps people commune with God and with the spirits of people who have died and to receive spiritual strength, help, and healing. The ritual usually takes place in a tepee, with tribe members gathered around a crescent-shaped, earthen altar mound and a sacred fir. At around 8 PM Saturday, the tribe "Chief" begins the ceremony of prayer, singing, the sacramental eating of peyote, a series of water rituals, and time for meditation. The ceremony continues through the night.

At midnight, special songs are sung, and testimonials are expressed until dawn. The ceremony ends with a communion breakfast on Sunday morning. Church members are encouraged to follow "the Peyote Road". The life values include the importance of the family, of giving and supporting others, and of maintaining self-support through steady work and avoidance of alcohol.

This religion has been persecuted by the non-Indian culture since its inception. It was banned by government agents in 1888 and later by 15 states. In the 1960s anthropologists and others confirmed that the use of peyote is central to the beliefs of this religion. The right of the Native American Church to express its religion has been upheld in several state supreme courts.

■ ROLE-PLAYING SCENARIOS

1.   **You own a travel agency and you are planning a 5-day business trip to New York City for one of your clients.** What factors would you take into account when scheduling the flights? What can your client do to minimize jet lag?

2.   **Why should a student try to get a REM-filled night of sleep the evening before a major exam?** Tell a fellow student about the value of sleep and variations in sleep quality.

3.   **What arguments would you present to a friend to convince her or him to stop smoking?**

4.   **What arguments would you present to a friend to convince him or her to stop using a recreational drug like Ecstasy? Marijuana?**

5.   **Once a person has succeeded in quitting smoking for a month, what would the person have to do to maintain this change in behavior?** Give your friend some suggestions.

6.   **Act out the role of a person who is increasingly abusing alcohol but continues to ignore the warning signs.**

7.   **You are running an "alcoholism rehabilitation" clinic.** What factors would you take into account in planning the therapy for a specific client? Imagine talking to a prospective client.

8.   **How would you go about trying to convince an alcoholic friend or relative to get treatment?** What could you do before the person "hits bottom"?

■ VALUE-CLARIFICATION STATEMENTS

1.   It is unrealistic to think that people will ever stop experimenting with ways to alter consciousness.

2.   Most people could reduce their sleep time to about 6 hours per night without a significant loss of alertness or productivity.

3.   It is less likely a marriage will last if one spouse is a "day" person and the other is a "night" person than if their circadian rhythms are similar.

4.   People who sleep more than eight hours are lazy or depressed, or they are probably using sleep to avoid some responsibility in their life.

5.   Dreams are simply random neurological activity and mean absolutely nothing.

6.   The use of cocaine should be decriminalized.

7.   Random drug testing should be required at all places of employment.

8.   A person should be able to do anything he/she wants to his or her own body, including using addictive drugs.

9.   It is hypocritical of adults to say that moderate alcohol consumption is acceptable for them but not for teenagers.

10.   Marijuana should be legalized and sold in the same way that nicotine and alcohol are sold.

■ ONE-MINUTE MOTIVATORS

1.   **Spend five minutes overloading the class with a videotape, a musical tape, three students reading different news stories aloud, and a thinking task or puzzle.** Contrast this with five minutes of the most dreary and monotonous lecture you have ever

given. Have students discuss their reactions to these brief samples of too much and too little stimulation. Suggest that each of us attempts to find an "optimal level of arousal" that is appropriate to the task we are trying to do.

2. **Ask students to close their eyes while you say, "Your body is becoming heavy . . ."** **etc.** Ask students if they felt at all hypnotized. If not, was their consciousness changed in other ways?

3. **Ask students to predict their hypnotic susceptibility before they read this chapter.** Then bring several students to the front of the class and make some of the suggestions from the *Stanford Hypnotic Susceptibility Scale.* Identify students who responded to most of the suggestions as good hypnotic subjects.

4. **Take students on the following meditative walk, and discuss any alterations in consciousness they experience.**

> Try to get comfortable in your seat. Close your eyes and begin deep breathing. Inhale through your nose, and then exhale through your mouth, sitting deeper and deeper in the chair with each breath. Continue deep breathing as I talk. If your mind wanders away from what I am saying, let your thoughts go for a moment, then pull them back. Imagine that you are in a beautiful green meadow. You can feel the warm but shaded sun on your arms and your legs. Your feet are bare, and you are walking down a dirt path. Your right foot is on the warm, soft dirt; your left foot is on cool grass. Watch yourself walk. Look at the rhythm of your movement as you focus on your left foot, then your right, then your left, then your right. Continue walking until you get to the end of the meadow and begin hearing and smelling the ocean. Watch yourself come out into a very warm clearing where suddenly the beach is in front of you. You walk down four warm, wooden steps, first putting your left foot, then your right, then your left, then your right. Once on the beach you pause and listen very carefully to the surf. Hear the waves build up, break, roll into shore, and pull back out. Begin walking into the surf. Watch yourself get closer and closer to the water. Now you are on crusty sand that was wet a few hours ago. Hear it crunch as you walk. Now you are on moist sand; feel the coolness. Now you have stepped into the cool, very pleasant water. Watch yourself walking farther into the water. Feel the water at your ankles, then at your mid-calf, then at your knees, and finally at your mid-thigh. Pause to listen to the surf, to hear the birds, to smell the sea. Take from a pocket in your shorts a list of ten worries that you have. Read that list very slowly: 1,2,3,4,5,6,7,8,9,10. You realize that you haven't even thought about those worries since you began your walk in the meadow. You realize that there is nothing you can do now to deal with these issues. You take your list and you tear up the biodegradable paper and toss the shreds on the sea beside you. You watch your

worries scatter, the ink fading, and you let go of all worries for the moment. Then you look up at the sun and feel the glorious warmth on your face and your arms. You turn and begin walking back to the shore, feeling the water at your thighs, then at your knees, then at your mid-calf, and then at your ankles. When you get to the shore, you see a very special person about one hundred feet from you at the end of the beach. This is the person in your life who is most able to comfort, support, and inspire you. You watch yourself approach this person; you watch yourselves embrace; you hear yourself describe one problem that you did not think you could handle yourself but you hear yourself resolve the issue. You turn and leave your friend, stronger, more assertive, more competent than before.

4. **Ask a student to role-play the feelings of the cocaine addict.** Others in class could verbalize the feelings of the addict's spouse, children, parents, and employer.

5. **Set up a debate on the topic of MDMA (Ecstasy), with one side taking the position that MDMA is a harmful drug and the other side taking the position that it is no more harmful than alcohol.**

■ BROADENING OUR CULTURAL HORIZONS

1. **What meaning or importance does American culture give to dreams?** Do you think that this applies to other cultures? Do you think that it is appropriate?

2. **The members of many cultures seek altered states of consciousness as pathways to enlightenment and personal power.** What are the predominant means of altering consciousness in our culture? Are any of them potential pathways for personal growth?

3. **Since hypnosis depends on suggestion, do you think that a person could be hypnotized if he or she grew up in a culture that did not recognize this state or have a name for it?** How much are we prepared to be hypnotized by believing that hypnosis exists?

4. **In what ways is the "passive, alert" state sought in meditation at odds with mainstream values in North American culture?**

5. **What role do drugs play in American culture?** In your life? To what extent is your use of drugs (including non-prescription drugs) an expression of cultural patterns and values?

6. **What cultural values do you think would increase the likelihood of drug use or abuse?** What similarities would you guess would exist among drug abusers in various cultures, regardless of their gender, race, or ethnic background?

■ SUPPLEMENTAL ACTIVITIES

TO THE INSTRUCTOR:

This chapter in the text has a varied collection of topics. It is good to engage the students in looking at some experiences they have had that fall into one or another of these categories. Two types of altered states have been singled out for these exercises. You could select any others that appeal to you. The main objective is for students to become aware of their own experiences and begin to examine them more objectively. Understanding the dynamics of these experiences makes them more meaningful.

Exercise #1: Dreaming

Everyone dreams but few people remember their dreams, and those who do find that the memory of the dream seems to fade away soon after awakening. To analyze the dream, the student must record it as soon as possible after waking. Suggest that students purchase a book or use the forms provided for this exercise. Students should write down the substance of a dream each day for about a week. The following items should be recorded each time that dreaming has occurred:

1. The main actions and events in the dream, including persons, known or unknown, who appear.

2. Events of the day (or days) prior to the dream that were significant to the student, even if they seem unrelated to the dream. Ask them to pay particular attention to major events and also to those thoughts or activities which preceded going to bed. After doing this for a couple of days, students should become adept at it.

    After these items have been collected for a few days, ask students in class to form groups of three to discuss the dreams. Group discussion is best because individuals often do not see connections between their own dreams and past events, but others do because they are not personally involved. Some of the more interesting findings should be shared with the whole class.

    Compare the findings in class with the discussion about dreams in the text. Do they support the author's ideas about dreams and their origins?

Exercise #2: Relaxation

Altered states such as hypnosis and meditation require the subject to relax. Relaxation is not always easy to achieve, and most people need to work at it to do it successfully. Biofeedback techniques can help people learn to relax and gain control of their bodies. Students can discover how easy it is to relax, even in the classroom, by a simple exercise. Having experienced the benefits of relaxation of the whole body, the students will want to do it again. They will find it easier to cope with stress and anxiety if they can gain control of their bodies through relaxation.

1. **This exercise requires students to:**
    a. Clear their minds of all thoughts
    b. Consciously relax their muscles
    c. Breathe deeply and regularly
    d. Concentrate on relaxing and breathing

2. **Procedure:**
    a. Ask students to sit comfortably in their chairs and close their eyes.
    b. Ask them to clear their minds of all thoughts, try not to think about anything, and listen to your voice.
    c. Tell them to breathe deeply and slowly in and out, in and out. You should set the pace very carefully so they hold each breath and exhale slowly.
    d. Tell the students to continue to do this as they begin to relax their muscles. First relax the toes, feel the toes relaxing. Then move to the feet, thighs, back, fingers, arms, chest, etc., progressing to the top of the head.
    e. Remind them periodically to keep breathing deeply in and out.
    f. As the exercise proceeds, you can interject relaxing scenes such a tree swaying in the breeze, blue water on a lake, waves lapping at a shore, etc.
    g. This exercise should take only about five minutes. To terminate it, stop talking and let the students sit quietly for a minute or two. Gradually each one will return from the activity relaxed and refreshed.

3. **Discussion:**
    a. Ask students to comment on:
        1) how they felt after the exercise,
        2) what they felt during the exercise,
        3) their confidence (or lack of it) in the exercise before it started,
        4) their feeling about the effectiveness of the exercise after it is over.
    b. Discuss the use of relaxation as a way to deal with stress in daily life.

DREAMING: DATA SHEET

TO THE STUDENT: Record on this sheet the answers to the following questions about your dreams. Write your responses as soon as you awake in the morning.

1.   What dream(s) did you have last night? What happened? What people or animals were present?

2.   What were you doing or thinking about immediately before going to bed?

3.   What significant experiences did you have yesterday or in the last few days?

4.   Are you anticipating any important events today or in the next few days? What are they?

■ JOURNAL QUESTIONS

1. Spend 24 hours keeping a consciousness journal or use a tape-recorder for dictating brief notes about the content of your "stream of consciousness." What thought patterns do you notice?

2. Describe a time when you wanted to stay awake, but sleep finally won out. What was the situation? How did you feel about losing control over your own consciousness?

3. Spend five days monitoring what you perceive to be your circadian "high" point. Have you ever slept with, lived with, or traveled with a person with the opposite kind of circadian pattern? How well did you get along?

4. Record your sleeping patterns for a week. Write down the key events of the day, the time you turn the lights off, how long you think it takes you to go to sleep, the number of times you awaken and how long you think you are awake, the quality of your sleep, and if dreams are present, the general theme. What patterns do you see by the end of the week?

5. Describe any experience you have had with consciousness altering drugs. What was the drug? What was the setting? Were other people present? What expectations did you have? What were the short-term effects? What were the long-term effects?

6. Most people engage in some moderately compulsive behavior that they feel they have little control over and where the consequences of the behavior are ignored. Describe your compulsion (or the compulsion of someone you know well). Does this give you any insight into the compulsive behavior of someone who abuses drugs?

7. Keep a dream journal. What do the patterns of your dreams seem to say to you about your behavior and emotional life?

■ SUGGESTIONS FOR FURTHER READING

Aldrich, Michael S. "Narcolepsy." *The New England Journal of Medicine,* 323, p. 389, August 9, 1990.

Dolnick, Edward. "What dreams are (really) made of: The Psychiatrist and a Neuroscientist Allan Hobson suggests replacing the traditional Freudian view." *The Atlantic,* 266, p. 41, July, 1990.

Faraday, Ann. *Dream Power.* Putnam Press, 1997.

Gackenbach, Jayne and Bosveld, Jane. *Control Your Dreams.* Harper Mass Market Paperbacks 1994.

Gibson, H. D. *Hypnosis in Therapy.* Psychology Press, 1991.

Huxley, A. *The Doors of Perception and Heaven and Hell.* Harper/Collins, 1990.

Julien, R. M. *A Primer of Drug Action*, 8th ed.. W. H. Freeman, 2000.

Kuhn, C., Swartzwelder, S., and W. Wilson. *Buzzed: The Straight Facts About the Most Used and Abused Drugs from Alcohol to Ecstasy.* W. W. Norton & Company, 1998.

Laberge, S. and H. Rheingold. *Exploring the World of Lucid Dreaming.* Ballantine Books, 1991.

Leonard, K. E. and H. T. Blane. *Psychological Theories of Drinking and Alcoholism,* 2nd ed. Guilford Press, 1999.

Loftus, E. F. "Alcohol, Marijuana, and Memory." *Psychology Today,* March 1980: 42-56, 92.

Ray, O. S. *Drugs, Society, and Human Behavior*, 9th ed. McGraw-Hill, 2001.

Van de Castle, R. L. *Our Dreaming Mind.* Ballantine Books, 1995.

Vogler, R. E. and W. R. Bartz. *The Better Way to Drink.* Harbinger, 1985.

Wallace, B. and L. E. Fisher. *Consciousness and Behavior*, 4th ed. Allyn and Bacon, 1999.

Winson, Jonathan. "The meaning of dreams." *Scientific American,* p. 86-96, November, 1990.

■ MEDIA SUGGESTIONS

ADDICTION (2002, Films for the Humanities and Sciences, 23 min.)
This program explains current research into why people become addicted, what puts them at risk, and what the best treatments may be.

BODY RHYTHMS (2002, from *Psychology-The Study of Human Behavior Telecourse,* Coast Community College District, 30 min.)
Provides vivid examples of various biological rhythms and mental states and describes research on the stages of sleep.

CONSCIOUSNESS (2002, from *Psychology-The Human Experience Telecourse,* Coast Community College District, 30 min.)
Illustrates how our consciousness and awareness vary throughout a typical day, including a look at circadian rhythms.

DREAMS: THEATRE OF THE NIGHT (2002, Films for the Humanities and Sciences, 26 min.)
This film explains why dreams occur and describes the function and meaning of dreams, from the perspective of Freud to current theorists. A sleep research lab is shown as well as PET scans of the dreaming brain. A therapy session on the meaning of dreams is described, including the physiological, chemical, and psychological reasons for dreams from many different perspectives.

DRUGS: USES AND ABUSES (2002, 8-part series, Films for the Humanities and Sciences, 17-39 min. each)
An in-depth look at various classifications of legal and illegal drugs, including the history, effects, and varieties of each drug.

THE FINAL MYSTERY: WHAT IS CONSCIOUSNESS? (2002, from the *Brain Story* series, Films for the Humanities and Sciences, 50 min.)
Dr. Susan Greenfield examines the phenomenon of consciousness, using discussion and case histories.

THE INTERPRETATION OF DREAMS (2002, Films for the Humanities and Sciences, 52 min.)
An analysis of Freud's ground-breaking work by several experts in the field of psychology.

THE MIND AWAKE AND ASLEEP (2001, from the *Discovering Psychology Series,* Annenberg/CPB, 30 min.)
The nature of sleeping, dreaming and altered states of consciousness, and how consciousness empowers us to interpret, analyze, and direct our behavior in adaptive, flexible ways.

THE MIND HIDDEN AND DIVIDED (2001, from the *Discovering Psychology Series,* Annenberg/CPB, 30 min.)
A look at how the events that take place below the level of consciousness alter our moods, bias our actions, and affect our health as demonstrated in repression, discovered and false memory syndrome, hypnosis, and split-brain cases.

SLEEP: DREAM VOYAGE (2002, from the *Living Body* series, Films for the Humanities and Sciences, 26 min.)
What happens to the body during sleep? This film explores the mystery of REM sleep, observes a computer display of the waves that sweep across the brain during sleep, and presents an interesting piece of footage of a cat "acting out" its dreams. The analogy of sleep to a ship on automatic pilot illustrates how some functions must and do continue while the conscious brain is asleep.

UNDER THE INFLUENCE: THE SCIENCE OF DRUG ABUSE (1999, Insight Media, 25 min.)
This video examines questions of effect, addiction and the human hunger for mind-altering substances.

A number of videos are available from Thomson. Videos appropriate for this chapter include the following films from the CNN TODAY Introductory Psychology Video Series:

Volume 1, Section 5: Health
    Sleep Studies (2:17)
Volume 3, Section 2: Sensation and Perception
    Sleep and Hearing (1:34)
Volume 4, Section 1: Drugs
    Parents' Teen Smoking (1:31)
    Celebrity Addiction (2:57)

Heroin Kids (1:55)
Binge Drinking (2:07)
Volume 4, Section 2: Sleep
    Sleepy Kids (1:31)
    Sleep Deprivation (2:12)
    Weightless Dream (2:44)

■ COMPUTER AND INTERNET RESOURCES

PSYCHNOW!

The Brain & Consciousness:
Sleep and Dreaming
Psychoactive Drugs

PSYK.TREK

Unit 4: Consciousness
        4a: Biological rhythms
        4b: Sleep
        4c: Abused drugs and their effects
        4d: Drugs and synaptic transmission

INFOTRAC

Subject Guide/Key Words: altered states, sleep, sleep deprivation, circadian rhythms, stages of sleep, jet lag, melatonin, REM sleep, night terrors, nightmares, somnambulism, dreams, hypnosis, meditation, sleep disorders, sleep apnea, insomnia, SIDS, drug addiction, stimulants, depressants, cocaine, caffeine, nicotine, barbiturates, alcohol, marijuana, hallucinogen, GHB, MDMA

WEB SITES

Wadsworth Online Psychology Study Center:
http://info.wadsworth.com/cooessentials9

National Sleep Foundation:
http://www.sleepfoundation.org/

Dreams and Lucid Dreaming:
http://www.nursehealer.com/Dream.htm

Meditation and Mandalas:
http://www.catanna.com/mandala.htm

National Institute on Alcohol Abuse and Alcoholism:
http://www.niaaa.nih.gov/

Addiction Resources:
http://www.well.com/user/woa/aodsites.htm

Mothers Against Drunk Driving (MADD):
http://www.madd.org

Higher Education Center for Alcohol and Other Drug Prevention:
http://www.edc.org/hec/

NCADD: National Council on Alcoholism and Drug Dependence, Inc.:
http://www.ncadd.org/index.html

History of Hypnosis:
http://ks.essortment.com/hypnosishistory_rcdg.htm

Frequently Asked Questions Regarding the Study of Hypnosis:
http://www.psywww.com/asc/hyp/faq0.html

Psychology and Hypnotism Links:
http://www.gla.ac.uk/~gbza22/hypnotism.html

Wadsworth Online Psychology Study Center:
http://psychology.wadsworth.com/study

National Sleep Foundation:
http://www.sleepfoundation.org/

Dreams and Lucid Dreaming:
http://www.nursehealer.com/Dream.htm

CHAPTER 7

Conditioning and Learning

■ LEARNING OBJECTIVES

To demonstrate mastery of this chapter the student should be able to:

1. Define learning.
2. Define reinforcement and explain its role in conditioning. (See also Table 7-1.)
3. Differentiate between antecedents and consequences and explain how they are related to classical and operant conditioning. (See also Table 7-1.)
4. Give a brief history of classical conditioning.
5. Describe the following terms as they apply to classical conditioning:
   a. neutral stimulus (NS)
   b. conditioned stimulus (CS)
   c. unconditioned stimulus (US)
   d. unconditioned response (UR)
   e. conditioned response (CR)
6. Describe and give an example of classical conditioning using the abbreviations US, UR, CS, and CR.
7. Explain how reinforcement occurs during the acquisition of a classically conditioned response. Include an explanation of higher order conditioning.
8. Explain classical conditioning in terms of the informational view.
9. Describe and give examples of the following concepts as they relate to classical conditioning:
   a. extinction
   b. spontaneous recovery
   c. stimulus generalization
   d. stimulus discrimination
10. Describe the relationship between classical conditioning and reflex responses.
11. Explain what a conditioned emotional response (CER) is and how it is acquired. Include definitions of the terms phobia and desensitization.
12. Explain the concept and the importance of vicarious classical conditioning.
13. State the basic principle of operant conditioning.
14. Contrast operant conditioning with classical conditioning. Include a brief comparison of the differences between what is meant by the terms "reward" and "reinforcement." (See also Table 7-2.)
15. Explain operant conditioning in terms of the informational view. Explain what response contingent reinforcement is.

16. Describe how the delay of reinforcement can influence the effectiveness of the reinforcement.
17. Describe response chaining and explain how it can counteract the effects of delaying reinforcement.
18. Explain why superstitious behavior develops and why it persists.
19. Explain how shaping occurs. Include a definition of the term successive approximations.
20. Explain how extinction and spontaneous recovery occur in operant conditioning.
21. Describe how negative attention seeking demonstrates reinforcement and extinction in operant conditioning. (See also Table 7-3.)
22. Compare and contrast positive reinforcement, negative reinforcement, punishment, and response cost punishment and give an example of each.
23. Differentiate primary reinforcers from secondary reinforcers and list four of each kind.
24. Discuss two ways in which a secondary reinforcer becomes reinforcing.
25. Discuss the major advantages and disadvantages of primary reinforcers and secondary reinforcers (tokens, for instance), and describe how tokens have been used to help "special" groups of people.
26. Define social reinforcers. Name two key elements that underlie learning and explain how they function together in learning situations.
27. Define feedback, indicate three factors that increase its effectiveness, and explain its importance in learning.
28. Briefly describe some ways in which conditioning techniques can be used to help people learn to conserve our energy resources.
29. Describe the following kinds of instruction and discuss their application in learning and teaching: programmed, computer-assisted, and interactive CD-ROM.
30. Compare and contrast the effects of continuous and partial reinforcement.
31. Describe, give and example of, and explain the effects of the following schedules of partial reinforcement:
    a. Fixed Ratio (FR)
    b. Variable Ratio (VR)
    c. Fixed Interval (FI)
    d. Variable Interval (VI)
32. Explain the concept of stimulus control.
33. Describe the processes of generalization and discrimination as they relate to operant conditioning.
34. Explain how punishers can be defined by their effects on behavior.
35. List and discuss three factors that influence the effectiveness of punishment.
36. Differentiate the effects of severe punishment from mild punishment.
37. List the three basic tools available to control simple learning.
38. Discuss how and why reinforcement should be used with punishment in order to change an undesirable behavior.
39. List six guidelines that should be followed when using punishment. (See *Using Psychology*.)
40. List and discuss three problems associated with punishment.

41. Explain how using punishment can be habit forming and describe the behavior of children who are frequently punished.
42. Define cognitive learning.
43. Describe the concepts of a cognitive map and latent learning.
44. Explain the difference between discovery learning and rote learning. Describe the behavior of the students who used each in the Wertheimer study.
45. Discuss the factors that determine whether observational learning (modeling) will occur.
46. Describe the experiment with children and the Bo-Bo doll that demonstrates the powerful effect of modeling on behavior.
47. Explain why what a parent does is more important than what a parent says.

The following objectives are related to the material in the "Exploring Psychology" section of the text.
48. Briefly describe the general conclusion that can be drawn from studies on the effects of TV violence on children. Explain why it would be an exaggeration to say that TV violence causes aggression.
49. Describe the procedures and results of Williams' natural experiment with TV.

The following objectives are related to the material in the "Psychology in Action" section of the text.
50. List and briefly describe the seven steps in a behavioral self-management program. Explain how the Premack principle may apply.
51. Describe how self-recording and behavioral contracting can aid a self-management program.
52. List four strategies for changing bad habits.
53. Briefly describe the eight strategies of self-regulated learning.

■ DISCUSSION QUESTIONS

1. Over the years, balloons have occasionally popped in your face when you were blowing them up. Now you squint and feel tense whenever you blow up a balloon. What kind of conditioning is this? What schedule of reinforcement has contributed to the conditioning? How could you extinguish the response?

2. You are in charge of a group of fifth-grade children that meets regularly for recreation. Other members of the group have excluded a younger girl and a very shy boy from activities. How could you use reinforcement principles to improve this situation? (Include techniques aimed at both the excluded children and the group.)

3. Sometimes "generalized fears" are adaptive; other times they are maladaptive. Give an example of each type of phobia.

4. Often siblings rejoice in the fun of trying to break the younger child of a fear of spiders or water by throwing the child in a pool or dangling a spider in the child's face. Would you expect these procedures to work? Why or why not?

5. In what ways do advertisers attempt to use both classical and operant conditioning to get us to buy their products? Describe commercials that use each type of conditioning.

6. What role has reinforcement had in your selection of a major? Friends? A job? The clothes you wore to school today?

7. You have a friend who checks the coin return slot every time he/she walks by a phone booth. Very rarely is a coin discovered. How do you explain this behavior?

8. From an operant conditioning perspective, why is it important for parent to "catch kids being good" and praise them?

9. From your point of view, what would be the ideal way to be paid at a job? Should pay be weekly, hourly, daily? Should it be tied to work output? Should rewards other than money be offered? If you owned a business what would you consider the ideal way to pay your employees?

10. What are the problems in using primary reinforcers to change behavior? What are the problems of using secondary reinforcers? If you wanted to teach your roommate, spouse, or child a new behavior, which would you use? Why?

11. You are trying to teach your dog to use a newly installed doggie door instead of scratching holes in your expensive screen door. How do you begin? What do you do if the dog never even gets near the door?

12. Whether a person tries to lose weight, stop drinking, or stop smoking, more often than not the unwanted behavior returns. Why? What should clinics or support groups try to do to make the behavioral changes more long-lasting?

13. A child in the grocery store has a temper tantrum. His/her embarrassed father scolds the child and then quiets the child by giving the child a candy bar. Is this punishment or reinforcement? What kind? What other options did Dad have to keep this behavior from happening again in the future? Who is conditioning whom in such circumstances, and what kind of reinforcement or punishment is each receiving?

14. Can you think of anything you do that is not affected in some way by learning?

15. How could you include more feedback or more immediate feedback in your study habits?

16.   If you could change procedures to enhance learning in an elementary school classroom, what would you do? What changes would you make in a high school classroom?

17.   What is the ideal timing of punishment? Why? Aren't most inappropriate behaviors discovered long after they have taken place? How should these behaviors be punished?

18.   Corporal punishment has been banned in many schools. In your opinion, what would be the pros and cons of banning corporal punishment in homes?

19.   Describe a behavior you learned by observation. What were the advantages of learning in this way? What were the disadvantages? What changes would have made the model you observed more effective?

20.   What kind of an experiment would you do to assess the effects of TV violence on infants and small children? What ethical questions would you need to answer?

21.   Over the last few years, many musical, athletic, religious, and political "heros" have admitted involvement in drugs, sex, or illegal activities. Explain "hero worship" in terms of cognitive, conditioning, and imitative processes. Who is your favorite hero? Why?

22.   Choose a bad habit you would like to break. How could you apply the principles discussed in this chapter to breaking the habit?

23.   What incompatible responses can you think of that could be performed in public to prevent the following behaviors: smoking, knuckle cracking, swearing, fingernail biting, hand wringing, eyelash plucking?

24.   In your opinion, should TV programs come with a violence rating scale or a rating system like that used for movies? What, if anything, would you suggest be done about the quality of TV programs and the amount of violence they contain?

■ LECTURE ENHANCEMENTS

Short demonstrations of conditioning help students learn the processes and vocabulary. Students experience a great sense of satisfaction actually changing the behavior of others, especially their instructor. They usually have strong feelings about issues of punishment, child rearing, willpower, and violence on television. These feelings work well in debates or value clarification activities. These often heated debates are especially effective in courses with a diverse student population.

1.   **Demonstrate classical conditioning by bringing in a balloon bouquet.** Ask students to notice the response of people in the front row to the balloons. Then pull out a long darning needle and wave it around the balloons. Hand it to a student in the front row. Ask

for it back. Ask a student to describe the reaction to the needle. Then use it to pop the balloon. Wave it around the remaining balloons again and pop another balloon. Discuss student reactions in terms of classical conditioning. Test for a reaction at the next class meeting and discuss extinction.

2. **The best demonstration of operant conditioning is to bring a Skinner box and a rat or pigeon to class.** In lieu of that, an entertaining (if somewhat artificial) illustration of shaping can be done with a human subject—you! Students provide reinforcement in this case by tapping their pens or pencils on their desks. Leave class for a few moments to allow the class to choose a response or a series of responses for you to perform. When you return, begin moving around the room. Students should tap each time you perform a response that approximates the final desired pattern. Your task, of course, is to keep the tapping as loud as possible (it's a little like playing "hot, warm, and cold"). The result can provide a hilarious interlude and a surprisingly instructive experience.

3. **Law enforcement agencies now use dogs to locate drugs and bombs.** How might such dogs be trained in these skills? Would you use shaping? How might generalization and discrimination fit into this kind of training?

4. **B. F. Skinner published *Walden Two* in 1948.** It was the story of a model community based on behavioral engineering. That is, he applied the "technology of behavior", which he developed, to a community situation to show how an ideal community could exist if operant conditioning principles were applied. Organize the class into groups of 5 or 6 students and ask them to try to visualize and plan such a community. They should specify how the behavioral principles would be used and what kind of behaviors could be expected from the participants. They should try to think in terms of the details of daily life in the community as well as the overall welfare and spirit of the group. What behavior would they want to reinforce? The groups should then come together and share their ideas as a class.

5. **The text discusses the way in which conditioned emotional responses can become phobias.** Generally those who have a phobia cannot identify its origins. However, some can do so, and often family members will relate the phobias to some experience the person had in early childhood. Ask students to generate a list of fears that they or their friends or relatives have. Try to restrict the list to only those fears that are intense and irrational (phobias) rather than other more common fears shared to some degree by most people. Ask those who contribute these items to try to recall or find out how they were acquired. Did the fear come from some legitimate unpleasant or painful experience, or did it come about vicariously? Some fears are learned from experience with the feared object. Sometimes children take on fears of their parents or some other person by imitation. Many of the fears will have no evident explanation. Be sure to discuss classical and operant conditioning principles in connection with these learned fears.

6.   **Give students an assignment to shape a specific behavior of a friend or someone with whom they live.** Students should record the baseline frequency of the behavior and choose a reinforcer (typically praise) for altering the behavior. During the shaping period students should continue to record the frequency of the behavior to document any changes. In class, students can report on their successes and failures and discuss the difficulties of using operant conditioning in the "real world."

7.   **Feedback is essential for effective human learning to take place.** To illustrate this and to introduce the concept of biofeedback, locate three class members who do not know how to wiggle their ears but think they might be able to learn. Have all three come to the front and face the class so that their ears are visible. Have them try for about a minute to master this skill. If anyone succeeds too easily, replace him/her with a new subject. When you have three subjects who clearly cannot wiggle their ears with more than minimal success, give each a hand mirror. Ask them to hold the mirror so that they can see their ears. Most will succeed with the addition of the feedback provided by the mirror.

8.   **The role of modeling in learning often seems so self-evident to students that they may not fully appreciate its importance in learning theory.** To bring home the idea that modeling has a powerful and pervasive impact on human learning, invite a student to the front of the class and ask him/her to tell you verbally how to tie your shoe. Untie one of your shoes (make sure you're wearing shoes with laces), and follow the subject's instructions explicitly. Be sure not to lead, interpret, or show any signs of previous shoe-tying skill. If you are very literal in your interpretation of the student's instructions, the point will be made: In many cases learning would be virtually impossible or incredibly inefficient were it not for observational learning.

9.   **One very good way to illustrate the existence of cognitive maps involves asking students to draw a map of the campus, or the layout in general of the community in which they live.** Selected maps can then be projected on a screen and compared to one another and/or to formal maps.

10. **The general approach of the "Psychology in Action" section in this chapter provides a good way to review learning principles.** Have students submit anonymous examples of troublesome habits (their own or those of family and friends). Select from these the most interesting and, at the next class meeting, ask students to apply chapter concepts by suggesting ways to alter the troublesome behaviors.

11. **Ask students to apply reinforcement principles to a "real world " problem such as waste recycling.** How would they engineer better paper recycling on a university campus? In a college dorm? In a selected neighborhood?

> In actual experiments of this sort several techniques have proven effective. These include "recycling contests" (in which groups compete for a small cash award

financed by selling the recycled paper), and raffles in which each bag of paper submitted for recycling earns a raffle ticket and a chance to win a small weekly prize. (E. S. Geller, J. L. Chaffee, and R. E. Ingram, "Promoting Paper Recycling on a University Campus," *Journal of Environmental Systems,* 1975, 5, 39-57.)

12.   **Depending on the size of your classes and your relationship with students, your involvement in behavioral change may be limited to study habits and academic goals or it may involve more personal changes of a clinical nature.** Whether the issue is study habits, parenting behaviors, exercise, drug consumption, or a similar topic, a contract can be written to commit the student to a change in behavior. Students can complete the contract for extra credit or a grade. Students can also be encouraged to work with a friend or relative, helping that person change a behavior. A typical contract can be written as follows:

Behavioral Contract

The behavior I am concerned about is

_____

The situation where I perform this behavior most often is

_____

The people I perform this behavior most often with are

_____

The mood I am in when I usually perform this behavior is

_____

The reason I think I perform this behavior is

_____

The feelings I usually have after performing this behavior are

_____

The reactions of other people to this behavior are

_____

The immediate disadvantages of this behavior pattern are

_____

The long-term negative consequences of continuing this pattern are

_____

Other behaviors I could engage in to satisfy the same need include

_____

I plan to reduce the frequency of the undesirable behavior by

_____

I plan to increase the frequency of the more desirable behavior by

_____

I plan to change this behavior within the following time frame

_____

I agree to try to change the above behavior in the way described. Because an attempt to change is the first step in a permanent change, I agree to be honest in sharing the results of my efforts.

Signed_____

Witness_____

■ ROLE-PLAYING SCENARIOS

1. **Have students describe typical discipline problems they have encountered with children.** Choose an example and have a student enact an "unenlightened" punitive response to the child's behavior. Then have another student role-play a more constructive use of punishment. A third student can role-play a reinforcement-based strategy.

2. **Verbalize the thoughts of an employee who is being paid an hourly wage, a weekly salary, a monthly salary, a salary plus a production bonus, and a person paid on a piece-work basis.**

3. **Role-play a person playing a slot machine programmed on a FR-5 schedule; an FR-10 schedule; a VR-1 minute schedule; a completely random schedule.** Say aloud what you are thinking on each schedule.

4. **Describe a minor behavior problem that a friend, roommate, or relative has.** Explain to that person how he or she could use conditioning principles to alter the behavior.

■ VALUE-CLARIFICATION STATEMENTS

1. A person can cease having an extreme fear if they just try.

2. Physical punishment should only be used to stop a behavior that is endangering a person's life.

3.   Practice makes perfect.

4.   Actions speak louder than words.

5.   Any behavior can be changed, as long as we are patient enough to change it slowly.

6.   Spare the rod.

7.   Rock videos that combine sex with violence should be taken off television.

8.   Children's television programming should be screened for violence and aggression.

9.   Bad models exceed good models on prime-time network television shows.

■ ONE-MINUTE MOTIVATORS

1.   **Begin the unit by asking students about their favorite foods.** Discuss briefly why they like these foods and whether they also eat these foods often. Use this as a preface to concepts of classically conditioned feelings and to the effect that reinforcers have on behavior.

2.   **Demonstrate reflex pupil dilation with a flashlight, the patellar reflex with a small rubber mallet, and the blink reflex by using a turkey baster to direct a puff of air to the eye.**

3.   **In pairs, have students answer these questions.** Why does your:
   - a.   Dog drool when you open the can of food before the food is given to him?
   - b.   Friend flinch before you tickle her or him?
   - c.   Little sister tremble at the sound of a dentist's drill?
   - d.   Fellow student begin blushing before he/she is called on to give a speech?

4.   **Ask students to describe superstitious behaviors they have observed in televised sports events.** Is it possible that these behaviors actually lead to reinforcers? What makes them superstitious?

5.   **To demonstrate negative reinforcement and operant escape, give half of the class this assignment:** "As soon as you have written the alphabet backward three times, raise your hand and then write it a fourth time." Give this assignment to the other half: "As soon as you have written the alphabet backward three times, go outside and wait for further instructions." You will find those escaping from the boredom writing much more quickly than those with no escape option.

6.   **Give students a five-minute quiz on the preceding chapter.** Collect all of the quizzes and place them in the trash. When students protest, discuss how frustrating it is to not receive knowledge of results, whether in terms of class exams, feedback at work, praise from friends, or even a thank you note when you send someone a gift.

7.   **Have students stand and face the back of the room.** Have one student come to the front of the class and mime the motions needed to fry an egg (place pan on stove, turn on burner, add oil, pick up egg, crack egg open, add salt and pepper, turn with spatula). As the student does this, she should try to tell the rest of the class what motions to make, to do what she is doing--without making any reference to cooking or to any objects. Ask students to guess what they are learning to do. When one does, discuss the model's frustration with verbal instruction and have her repeat the demonstration for those students who didn't guess what they were learning to do. Can they guess now what they were learning to do?

8.   **Show a short sequence of commercials recorded from commercial television and discuss the kinds of role models that are being presented.**

■ BROADENING OUR CULTURAL HORIZONS

1.   **Have students help you make a list of symbols that have emotional meaning for a specific group of people.** For example, religious, political, or sexual symbols (words, objects, gestures) can provoke emotional responses. Explain these associations in terms of classical conditioning.

2.   **What is the relationship between stimulus generalization and discrimination and gender, ethic, or racial stereotyping, prejudice, and discrimination?** In what ways are these processes similar and different?

3.   **Cultural norms develop because a specific behavior is reinforced.** Can you identify some behaviors that are typically reinforced in the United States that are not reinforced in other cultures? (For example, Korean businesspersons rarely smile at customers, because people who smile in public are thought to look like fools.)

4.   **Some cultures focus on and invest much time in game-playing.** Interview friends of yours about their attitudes toward game-playing. What types of games did their parents play? Was the outcome of the game primarily the result of chance or skill? What reinforced this behavior? If a person "lost" the game, what would be the consequences?

5.   **Stereotypes have developed about the "work ethic" of different cultures.** Does your ethnic group or culture focus more on immediate or delayed reinforcers?

6. **What view did your parents, your extended family, and friends of your parents take toward physical punishment?** What cultural factors explain why some parents spank and other parents talk?

7. **Have students research various cultures for methods of punishing criminal behavior.** Do some methods seem to be more effective than others?

■ SUPPLEMENTAL ACTIVITIES

TO THE INSTRUCTOR:

The first **two exercises** which follow give the students an opportunity to have some first-hand experience with the concepts being studied. In the first, students will observe or participate in classical conditioning of the eyeblink response. In the second, the students will try to identify instances from their own experience in which they were conditioned to respond in a new way. The **third exercise** is an interesting way to illustrate how a simple learned skill is acquired. The exercise should result in a typical learning curve if the task is not too easy or too hard.

Exercise #1: Classical Conditioning of the Eyeblink Response

I. **Introduction:**

Students should have read the section in the text on classical conditioning and received classroom instruction to clarify the concepts involved. They should be clear on what is to happen in this demonstration. The purpose is to condition the eyeblink response to the sound of a clicker. Some other noisemaker may be substituted such as a buzzer or bell.

II. **Apparatus:**

The apparatus for this exercise is easy to get together. A clicker or noisemaker is needed. One that makes a clear, sharp sound is best. The apparatus to deliver a puff of air to the eyes is a little more difficult. You need a piece of rigid plastic tubing attached to a stand. The stand can be made or clamp stands can be borrowed from the chemistry lab. Flexible plastic tubing (about 3 feet long) should be attached to the rigid tube at one end and to a squeeze bulb at the other. A kitchen baster will deliver a generous puff of air for this purpose.

III. **Procedure:**

A. Organize the class into teams of three. One will be the subject, one the experimenter, and the third will be the recorder. If time permits, the students can rotate these roles so each one has an opportunity to be the subject.

B.   Seat the subject and set up the apparatus so that the tip of the rigid tube will be about two inches from his/her eyes. The experimenter should be behind the subject, holding the clicker and the squeeze bulb. The recorder should sit directly in front of the subject. Throughout the experiment the recorder will note whether or not the subject blinked at each trial.

C.   Begin the experiment by presenting the subject with a puff of air and observe the eyeblink response. This should be done at least twice to be sure that the puff of air (unconditioned stimulus) is producing the eyeblink (unconditioned response). Space the trials at fifteen-second intervals. A watch with a large second hand should suffice as a timer.

D.   The conditioning trials should be done as follows. Click the noisemaker and immediately after (not at the same time) present the puff of air. Wait about fifteen seconds and repeat. Do this fifteen times. This should be sufficient to establish the eyeblink (now a conditioned response) to the sound of the noisemaker (the conditioned stimulus). The recorder will note the eyeblink for each trial on the data sheet.

E.   After the fifteen conditioning trials, continue with fifteen more, presenting only the noisemaker with no puff of air. The recorder will note the presence or absence of the eyeblink at each trial. It should be possible to see when extinction has occurred.

F.   At this point the experiment could be concluded, or some variations could be tried. Here are some possibilities:
   1.   Give the subject a rest period and then resume trials with only the clicker and see if spontaneous recovery will occur.
   2.   Present the puff of air only occasionally while continuing clicking trials, then stopping the US to see how long it takes for extinction to occur.
   3.   See if more than fifteen conditioning trials will result in slower extinction.

G.   **Discussion questions:**
   1.   What is the change in behavior in this exercise?
   2.   Why did it occur?
   3.   Why did extinction take place?
   4.   Does this kind of "learning" have a real value in our lives?

CLASSICAL CONDITIONING--HUMAN EYEBLINK: DATA SHEET

TO THE STUDENT:

Record accurately what you observe. In this exercise it will be the presence or absence of an eyeblink when the stimuli are presented to the subject. You should be sure not to communicate your expectations to the subject. Simply record what you see.

ACQUISITION PHASE		EXTINCTION PHASE	
TRIAL	BLINK (Y OR N)	TRIAL	BLINK (Y OR N)
1		1	
2		2	
3		3	
4		4	
5		5	
6		6	
7		7	
8		8	
9		9	
10		10	
11		11	
12		12	
13		13	
14		14	
15		15	

Exercise #2: Conditioning as a Personal Experience

Students should be asked to identify personal experiences in which they were conditioned. It might require some speculation on their part as to how it came about. However, it is important for them to realize the extent to which this type of learning occurs in their lives. If students use the classical conditioning model, Figure 7-3, they can see how the change in behavior occurred. For the operant conditioning experiences, they need to pay attention to the concept of reinforcement, or consequence of a response, when producing examples.

The students should be instructed to identify the source of motivation for the behavioral change and what is being associated in each example.

The data sheet that follows can be duplicated and given to students to write their examples. Many of the examples will be wrong the first time. You can help them to understand these concepts by going over the examples, showing them what is wrong, and suggesting how they could be done better. Then ask the students who were unclear to write some new examples.

CONDITIONING AS A PERSONAL EXPERIENCE: DATA SHEET

Instances of classical and operant conditioning occur in everyday life. Your assignment is to think of two personal examples of each type of conditioning that you have experienced and briefly describe each one. Do not use examples found in the text or presented by your instructor in class. In each example, identify where the association bond is and what the motivation is for the change in behavior.

CLASSICAL CONDITIONING

1.

2.

OPERANT CONDITIONING

1.

2.

Exercise #3: The Learning Curve

I.   Introduction

The purpose of this exercise is to give students an opportunity to see how learning follows a typical learning curve. This can be done by charting the progress of a student learning to follow a maze, provided the maze is not too easy or too complex.

II.   Procedure

A.   Divide the class into groups of three for this exercise. Designate one to be the subject, another the timer, and the third to be the recorder. Rotate the students so that all three will have an opportunity to be the subject.

B.   Provide each group with 45 copies of the maze, three data sheets, and three of each of the two graphs. Be sure that each group has a watch with a second hand to time the trials.

C.   Discuss with the students the way to do the timing, how to score the maze (time and errors), and how to plot points on the graphs.

D.   Sit back and enjoy a brief respite while the students go to work. Be sure they complete their trials and complete the data sheets while doing the exercise. It would be best to have them plot the graphs while in the classroom so they can help each other and seek your assistance, if needed. Once all three students have completed the exercise, each student should plot the data for all three subjects on the same graph. Different colors could be used to identify each.

III. Discussion

A.   Did a learning curve occur? What was its shape?

B.   What conclusions can you draw about maze learning in general?

C.   Would similar curves appear in the learning of other types of material?

D.   Is what you have learned from this exercise of any value to you in your learning?

Bring the class together to go over the results. Try to find out what problems were encountered and what results appeared. Then ask students to discuss the questions above. You may have some of your own to add or substitute.

THE LEARNING CURVE: DATA SHEET

Record the time for each trial and the number of errors made on each. Try to be as accurate as possible in timing the subject and recording errors. Before starting, number the maze sheets from 1 to 15 and have the subject use them in order. An error is made each time the subject raises the pencil, enters a blind alley, or crosses a line. Crossing a line and returning into the path constitutes one error (not two) since the line has to be recrossed to enter the path.

TRIALS	1		2		3	
	SECS.	ERRORS	SECS.	ERRORS	SECS.	ERRORS
1						
2						
3						
4						
5						
6						
7						
8						
9						
10						
11						
12						
13						
14						
15						

THE LEARNING CURVE: GRAPH I--LEARNING

TO THE STUDENT: Plot the times for each trial on the graph. Join the points to produce a learning curve. The horizontal axis represents the number of trials, and the vertical, the number of seconds per trial.

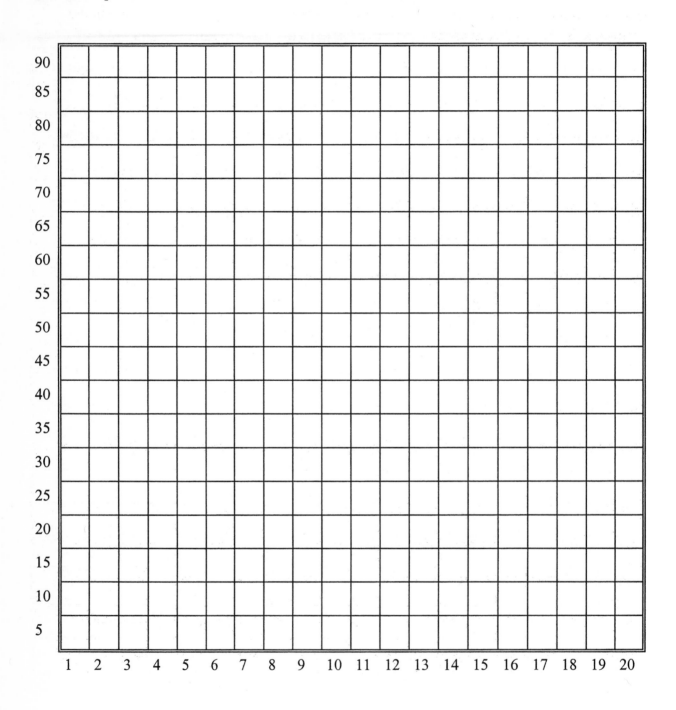

THE LEARNING CURVE: GRAPH II--ERRORS

To the Student: An error is made each time the subject raises the pencil, enters a blind alley, or crosses a line. Crossing a line and returning into the path constitutes one error (not two) since the line has to be recrossed to enter the path. Plot the number of errors made on each trial. Join the points to produce an error curve. The horizontal axis represents the number of trials, and the vertical axis, the number of errors.

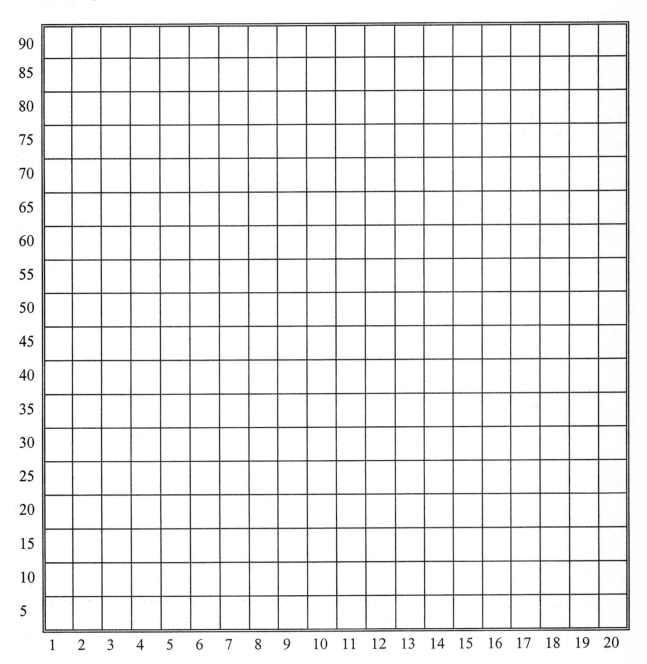

THE LEARNING CURVE: MAZE LEARNING

To the Student: Follow the maze from the center to the exit. Do not raise your pencil from the paper once you begin. If you cross a line or go into a blind alley, return to the point where the error was made without lifting your pencil from the paper. Work as quickly as you can.

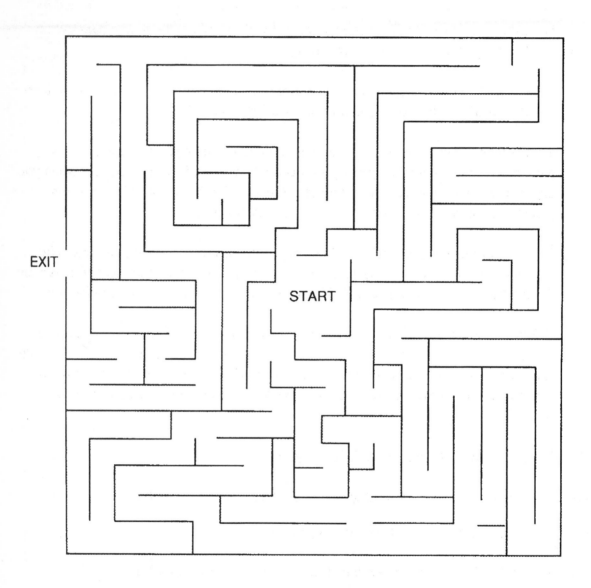

■ JOURNAL QUESTIONS

1. Describe what you consider to be a normal fear you have and describe a fear of yours that you think is a phobia. Where and how did each of these develop? How do each of these affect your life? What could you do to try to "extinguish" the fear? The phobia?

2. Describe your "favorite" TV commercial or TV show. Why do you like it so? What conditioning process explains your feelings?

3. What fears have you learned vicariously from family and friends? How do these fears affect your life? What could you do to extinguish this fear?

4. Think of a number of situations from your childhood where you felt rewards and punishments were not contingent upon specific behaviors. How did you feel when you did something desirable and you did not get recognition for that act? When you got punished in some way even when you did not do anything wrong?

5. Think of a time when you effectively managed the behavior of an animal or another person using some of the suggestions for effective punishment. Were you effective for the short term? For the long term? What could you have done to be more effective?

6. Did you ever experience what you would now consider as an adult to be "excessive physical punishment"? If so, what were the circumstances? How did you feel about the adult who punished you? Have you found yourself doing any of the same behaviors? What do you think you could do to try to break what some people call a "circle of abuse"?

■ SUGGESTIONS FOR FURTHER READING

Bower, G. H. and E. R. Hilgard. *Theories of Learning,* 5th ed. Prentice-Hall, 1981.

Chance, P. *Learning and Behavior,* 5th ed. Wadsworth, 2003.

Comstock, G. *Television in America.* Newbury Park, CA; Sage Publications, 1991.

Domjan, M. *Principles of Learning and Behavior,* 5th ed. Wadsworth, 2003.

Drowatzky, J. N. *Motor Learning: Principles and Practices,* 2nd ed. MacMillan, 1981.

Evans, Richard I. *Albert Bandura: The Man and His Ideas--A Dialogue.* New York: Praeger, 1989.

Goodall, Jane. *Through a Window.* Houghton Mifflin, 2000.

Leahey, T. H. and R. J. Harris. *Learning and Cognition,* 4th ed. Prentice-Hall, 1997.

Martin, G., and J. Pear. *Behavior Modification: What It Is and How to Do It,* 6th ed. Prentice-Hall, 1999.

Pavlov, I. *Conditioned Reflexes.* Dover Press, 1984.

Pew, T. W. Jr. "Biofeedback Seeks New Medical Uses of Yoga." *Smithsonian,* December, 1979.

Pearce, J. M. *Animal Learning and Cognition.* 2nd ed. Psychology Press, 1997.

Rubinstein, E. A. "Television and the Young Viewer." *American Scientist,* November-December, 1978.

Schwartz, B. *Psychology of Learning and Behavior*, 5th ed. W. W. Norton, 2001.

Schwartz, M. S. *Biofeedback: A Practitioner's Guide,* 3rd ed. Guilford Publications, 2002.

Skinner, B. F. *Behavior of Organisms.* Wiley, 1938.

—. *Beyond Freedom and Dignity.* Knopf, 1971.

—. *The Shaping of a Behaviorist.* Knopf, 1979.

—. *Walden Two.* Prentice Hall/MacMillan, 1976.

■ MEDIA SUGGESTIONS

ANIMALS: HOW SMART ARE THEY? (1988, Films for the Humanities and Sciences, 26 min.)
This film compares the learning abilities of chimps, the famed gorilla Koko, and dolphins at the University of Hawaii. Research is asking whether language is defined by grammar, syntax, or creativity and whether humans are fundamentally different in terms of learning processes. The value and ethics of animal research are discussed.

B.F. SKINNER'S KEYNOTE ADDRESS: LIFETIME SCIENTIFIC CONTRIBUTION REMARKS (2002, APA, 18 min.)
Behavioral psychologist B. F. Skinner presented this keynote address at the 1990 APA Annual Convention. In Dr. Skinner's last public appearance, he expresses his belief that the proper role for psychological science is the analysis of behavior. He speaks about the path psychology has followed over the years, from early introspection methods to three kinds of variation and selection, including natural selection, the evolution of operant conditioning, and the evolution of culture. VHS-format.

CLASSICAL AND OPERANT CONDITIONING (2002, part of *The Psychology of Learning* series, Films for the Humanities and Sciences, 52 min.)
This program explains the nature of Behaviorism, so central to the study of human behavior, and its important applications in clinical therapy, education, and child-rearing. The program clearly explains, discusses, and illustrates the complex Classical and Operant conditioning theories of Pavlov and Skinner, and features archival footage of laboratory work with dogs and present-day research using rats in Skinner boxes, as well as numerous examples of conditioning in everyday life.

FURTHER APPROACHES TO LEARNING (2002, part of *The Psychology of Learning* series, Films for the Humanities and Sciences, 52 min.)

This program explores alternative approaches and explanations of learning, including Latent Learning, Learning Sets, Insight Learning, Ethology, Social Learning, and Neuroscience. The program emphasizes the recent move towards a Cognitive Theory of Learning and examines the current research in this area. The program includes archival film featuring B. F. Skinner and Dr. Robert Epstein, who demonstrated apparent "insight" learning in pigeons using behaviorist techniques. Skinner, speaking just before his death, claims that reinforcement rather than higher mental processes is at work in learning. The cognitive behaviorists think differently.

IVAN PAVLOV (2002, Insight Media, 30 min.)

This simulated interview between Ivan Pavlov and thinking skills scholar Edward de Bono focuses on the revolutionary nature of Pavlov's research and the impact his work has had on our understanding of behavior.

LEARNING (2002, from *Psychology- The Study of Human Behavior Series*, Coast District Telecourses, 30 min.)

Focuses on classical conditioning, operant conditioning and real-world applications to behavioral psychology.

LEARNING (2002, from *Discovering Psychology* series, Annenberg/CPB, 30 min.)

The basic principles of classical and operant conditioning. Includes discussion of how Pavlov, Thorndike, Watson, and Skinner have influenced today's thinking.

LEARNING: CLASSICAL AND OPERANT CONDITIONING (2002, from *Psychology- The Human Experience Series*, Coast District Telecourses, 30 min.)

This video discusses Pavlov's classical conditioning experiment and how it demonstrates the process of learning by an association or relationship.

LEARNING: OBSERVATIONAL AND COGNITIVE APPROACHES (2002, from *Psychology- The Human Experience Series*, Coast District Telecourses, 30 min.)

This video covers the topics of observational learning and cognitive processes in learning.

A number of videos are available from Thomson. Videos appropriate for this chapter include the following films from the CNN TODAY Introductory Psychology Video Series:

Volume 1, Section 7: Learning
      Virtual Rat (2:44)

Volume 2, Section 6: Learning
      Head Games (2:29)

■ COMPUTER AND INTERNET RESOURCES

PSYCHNOW!

Learning & Cognition:
Classical Conditioning
Operant Conditioning
Observational Learning

PSYK.TREK

Unit 5: Learning
       5a:Overview of classical conditioning
       5b:Basic processes in classical conditioning
       5c:Overview of operant conditioning
       5d:Schedules of reinforcement
       5e:Reinforcement and punishment
       5f:Avoidance and escape learning

INFOTRAC

Subject Guide/Key Words: Behaviorism, Classical Conditioning, Operant Conditioning, Token Economy, Reinforcement Schedules, Positive Reinforcement, Negative Reinforcement, Punishment, Stimulus Control, Discovery Learning, Observational Learning

WEB SITES

Wadsworth Online Psychology Study Center:
http://info.wadsworth.com/cooessentials9

Internet Sites on the Behaviorist Approach:
http://www.acs.ryerson.ca/~glassman/behavior.html

Indiana University Learning and Cognition Web Resources:
http://education.indiana.edu/~p540/webcourse/web.html

AmoebaWeb Psychology Resources: Learning:
http://www.vanguard.edu/faculty/ddegelman/amoebaweb/index.cfm?doc_id=866

Psychology Tomorrow Internet Sites:
http://www.weber.edu/wmcvaugh/cyb_learning.html

Positive Reinforcement:
http://server.bmod.athabascau.ca/html/prtut/reinpair.htm

CHAPTER 8
Memory

■ LEARNING OBJECTIVES

To demonstrate mastery of this chapter the student should be able to:

1. Explain how memory functions like a computer. Include definitions of encoding, storage, and retrieval.
2. Describe sensory memory. Explain how icons and echoes function in this memory system.
3. Explain the function of selective attention in short-term memory. Describe this memory system in terms of capacity, permanence, how information is stored, and susceptibility to interference.
4. Describe long-term memory in terms of permanence, capacity, and how information is stored.
5. Explain what dual memory is.
6. Explain what is meant by "the magic number seven (plus or minus two)."
7. Describe chunking (recoding) and rehearsal, and explain how they help memory. Describe the difference between maintenance and elaborative rehearsal.
8. Discuss the permanence of memory, including the work of Penfield.
9. Explain how memories are constructed. Include the concepts of constructive processing and pseudo-memories.
10. Discuss the effects of hypnosis on memory.
11. Briefly describe how long-term memories are organized including the network model and redintegrative memories.
12. Differentiate procedural (skill) memory from declarative (fact) memory. Differentiate the two kinds of declarative memory--semantic memory and episodic memory.
13. Explain the tip-of-the-tongue phenomenon.
14. Describe and give an example of each of the following ways of measuring memory:
    a. recall (include the serial position effect)
    b. recognition (compare to recall and include the idea of distractors)
    c. relearning (include the concept of savings)
15. Distinguish between explicit and implicit memory. Describe how the concept of priming can demonstrate the existence of memories outside the realm of awareness.

The following objectives are related to the material in the "Exploring Psychology" section of the text.

16.   Describe the concept of internal imagery and explain how it differs from eidetic imagery.
17.   Describe eidetic imagery and its effects on long-term memory. Describe some examples of people with exceptional memories and the role of learned strategies in memory retrieval.

18.   Characterize memory loss as demonstrated by Ebbinghaus's curve of forgetting. Discuss his findings as they relate to cramming *versus* spaced review.
19.   Discuss the following explanations of forgetting:
        a. encoding failure
        b. decay of memory traces
        c. disuse (give three reasons to question this explanation)
        d. cue-dependent forgetting
        e. state-dependent learning
        f. interference (list and explain the two types of interference and how they are investigated in the laboratory)
        g. repression (and differentiate it from suppression)
20.   Describe the false memory syndrome.
21.   Describe flashbulb memories and explain how they may be formed.
22.   Define anterograde and retrograde amnesia. Describe the role of consolidation in memory, and explain how electroconvulsive shock (ECS) can affect it.
23.   Name the structure in the brain that is responsible for switching information from STM to LTM.
24.   Discuss how memories are recorded in the brain by describing how learning is related to engrams, transmitter chemicals, and brain circuits.
25.   Describe each of the following in terms of how it can improve memory:

a. memory strategies	j. overlearning
b. knowledge of results	k. spaced practice
c. recitation	l. sleep
d. rehearsal	m. hunger
e. selection	n. extending how long you remember
f. organization	
g. whole versus part learning	o. review
h. serial position effect	p. using a strategy for recall
i. cues	

26.   List and describe the four strategies of a cognitive interview.

The following objectives are related to the material in the "Psychology in Action" section of the text.

27.   Define mnemonics and explain the four basic principles of using mnemonics.
28.   List and describe three techniques for using mnemonics to remember things in order.

■ DISCUSSION QUESTIONS

1. What type of classroom testing do you prefer? Why? What would you consider an ideal way to be tested? ("Never" does not count as an answer!)

2. Would you like to have a memory like the man studied by A. R. Luria? What would be the advantages and disadvantages of such a memory? Mr. S. could not recognize faces. Can you explain why? If, as an adult, you retained eidetic memory, how would you use it?

3. If you were forced to give up either STM or LTM, which would you choose? Think carefully about your answer.

4. What do you think is the most important strategy for maximizing short-term memory? Why?

5. Describe the types of long-term memory. Give an example of something you know that fits into each category.

6. Why do people forget? Compare and contrast the various theories of forgetting. Which process makes the most sense to you? Why?

7. What is the relationship between cue-dependent forgetting and memory networks?

8. We have seen that there are several reasons for forgetting. Which does the use of mnemonics most directly combat? How would you minimize the other major causes of forgetting?

9. What role could adrenaline play in state dependent learning?

10. In 1989 a woman was raped and beaten in a notorious case of "wilding" that took place in New York City's Central Park. After she recovered, she couldn't remember events just prior to or during the attack and she could not identify her assailants. Why?

11. If scientists perfect a drug that improves memory do you think it should be widely available? Would you want to try it? If a drug were perfected that could cause selective forgetting of memories, would you support its use for victims of rape, assault, disaster, or a horrifying accident?

12. A person has a tumor in the hippocampus; what changes in that person's memory would you anticipate?

13.   What mnemonic strategies have you used in studying? Which have been most helpful? How could a person with limited mental imagery use mnemonics?

14.   What have you done to cope with remembering longer zip codes and telephone numbers?

15.   Describe a case of mistaken identity you have seen in the news. What aspect of memory contributed to the mistake?

16.   In view of the text's discussion, do you think memories that occur during hypnosis should be allowed as evidence in court? One expert has suggested videotaping sessions during which witnesses or victims are questioned under hypnosis. If such tapes were available to juries, do you think testimony based on hypnosis would be more trustworthy? Why or why not?

17.   How is redintegration related to cognitive hierarchies or networks? In what ways could redintegration explain the different types of long-term memory?

18.   You are writing a book called *Three Steps to a Terrific Memory*. What will you use as the three key processes? What specific recommendations would you make for improving memory?

■ LECTURE ENHANCEMENTS

1.   **To illustrate the limited capacity of short-term memory, read a series of random digits to the class.** Instruct the students to listen to the numbers and, after you stop, to write down as many as they can remember. Begin by reading a series five-digits long:

	5 1 9 2 3
Then try six:	9 1 9 2 5 8
seven:	9 8 2 2 9 3 1
eight:	3 8 5 4 9 6 5 7
nine:	3 8 0 4 7 1 3 6 9
ten:	5 3 2 1 9 6 1 2 1 6

Reread the digits so the students can check their accuracy. The seven (plus or minus two) bit capacity of short-term memory should become quite apparent to the students.

2.   **Chunking can greatly extend the capacity of short-term memory.** This can be shown by instructing half the class in a chunking strategy while allowing the other half to memorize more haphazardly. Hand out to half the class an instruction sheet which reads:

A long list of words will be read to you. Try to memorize the entire list using "raw" memory ability. You should listen to the list and try to remember as much as you can, but do not attempt to apply any system or special technique in memorizing the list.

The second half of the class should receive a sheet which reads:

A long list of words will be read to you. Try to memorize the entire list. Your task will be easier if you memorize the words in groups of three. Try to form a mental image that includes the first three items as read and then try to form a new image for each following set of three. For example, if the first three words were, "skate, bone, and piano," you might picture a roller-skate with a bone in it on top of a piano.

After students have read their respective instructions, read the list below from left to right. Read loudly and clearly, allowing a relatively long pause between words:

CAR	TREE	TOOTH	PENCIL	WATCH	CHAIR	VIOLIN
FLOWER	HOUSE	BICYCLE	RECORD	PIZZA	BOOK	DISH
NAIL	TOWEL	APPLE	MATCH	FISH	SKY	SHOE

Wait a moment after completing the list, and ask students to write as many items as they can remember.

Notice that there are 21 items on the list. Students who use the chunking strategy will have only seven chunks to contend with, which should be a manageable number for most. To determine if chunking improved retention, compute the mean number of items recalled by each group.

3. **To demonstrate forgetting, the limited memory storage of short term memory, and interference, read 10-15 digits from the list below.** Before you begin, tell students that when you say "begin" they are to say the alphabet aloud until you say "stop." Immediately after you say "stop," they are to write, in reverse order, as many of the digits as they can remember. Try this after interference periods of 1, 3, 5, 7, 10, and 15 seconds. By the time you reach a fifteen second delay, very few class members will be able to remember even the final digit.

        5 1 9 2 3 2 2 7 2 9 8 2 3 9 6 4 0 4 5 8 1 2 1 5 6 5 4 5 6
        9 1 9 2 5 8 4 6 2 5 7 8 1 9 6 5 3 2 8 7 7 7 5 1 2 4 6 2 1
        2 1 4 5 4 8 4 7 4 9 6 5 4 7 2 5 4 1 8 7 6 5 4 2 3 1 5 9 8
        1 2 5 4 3 2 6 5 1 4 8 7 9 5 6 2 3 1 5 4 7 8 2 5 1 3 4 5 7

4. **The lists below offer a simple illustration of the effects of meaningfulness on the organization and retention of information.** The nonsense syllables in List A are rated

as having 40 percent association value. List B is made up of meaningful, but unrelated words. In addition to being meaningful, the words in List C can be organized into a sentence. Divide the class into thirds. Give a different list to each person. Give everyone the same amount of time to learn the list. Then ask students to turn the paper over and to write down as many of the syllables as they can remember.

LIST A	LIST B	LIST C
JEK	DEN	THE
VEH	MIX	BOY
XIB	WON	AND
YAP	BUY	HIS
BIV	GET	DOG
MUP	HOW	MET
GEW	RUN	OLD
HIX	POD	MAN
WEG	CAP	WHO
CIH	FIT	HAD
QEZ	NET	ONE
FIK	TOY	HAT

5.   **One of the simplest and most obvious indications of organizational structure in memory is clustering (the tendency for related words to appear together in a free-recall situation).** To demonstrate clustering, ask students to memorize the following list:

APPLE	HAMMER	SUMMER	RED	PEACH	SAW
SPRING	YELLOW	BANANA	WINTER	BROWN	LEMON
PLIERS	AUTUMN	GREEN	PLUM	WRENCH	FALL
BLUE	SCREWDRIVER				

A satisfactory means of presentation is to read the list slowly. Afterward ask them to write as many items from the list as they can recall, in any order. Then ask them to circle adjacent items representing clusters from the categories: fruit, tools, seasons, and colors. Students with particularly good examples of the clustering effect should be encouraged to share them with the class.

6.   **To demonstrate the serial position effect, the following word list should be read aloud fairly quickly (to avoid the use of mnemonic devices by the students).** After one reading, ask the students to write down as many of the items as they can remember.

Then present the list to the students using an overhead projector and check by a show of hands how many remembered each item. More students will recall the first and last portions of the list than the middle, showing the serial position effect.

Use the following list of words:

house	*cheese*	*star*	*pen*	*dish*
book	*highway*	*melon*	*horse*	*uncle*
class	*ocean*	*doorway*	*model*	*moustache*
creature	*cloud*	*prairie*	*train*	*plastic*

7. **A discussion of mnemonic strategies and examples can provide skills of lasting value to students.** It may be useful to begin by asking for examples of terms or information students have had difficulty learning in other classes. With the help of the class you can then devise a mnemonic strategy for each. Names also make good examples. For interest, use names from the class roster, making transformations such as these: **Aaron = hair on, Carifiol = care if I oil, Chomentowski = show men to ski, Sellentin = sellin' tin,** and so forth.

The mnemonic device of loci, or places, was developed by Simonides. In this approach, each item to be remembered is pictured in association with familiar locations--around the home, along a street, on campus, or on parts of the body.

To show how powerful mnemonic strategies can be, have the class call out a list of thirty objects. As each object is added, encourage students to imagine it placed on, or associated with, a part of the body. For example, if the first item is "pencil," students might imagine a pencil stuck between their toes; if the second is "bird," a bird might be imagined in place of the foot, and so forth. Identify a body part to be used with each new item as it is added. The following loci work well: toes, foot, heel, ankle, calf, knee, thigh, hip, waist, navel, ribs, chest, fingers, palm, wrist, forearm, ear, forehead, hair. This provides 29 loci, so the last item must be remembered by rote. After the list has been practiced once through, **ask the class to recall it** by trying to picture the object associated with each body part. Nearly all the items will be remembered by most class members--a unique experience for many of them.

8. *Psychology Today* **has surveyed its readers regarding their earliest memories.** Ninety-six percent of the respondents reported having memories prior to the age of six, with 68 percent reporting recall for events occurring when they were two or three. Further, a surprising 7 percent said they had memories prior to age one, and a few even claimed to have prenatal recollections as well as memories of their own birth! While some of the early memories were of traumatic experiences (such as the birth of a sibling, being injured, or the death of relatives or pets), the majority of recollections were of more mundane things (like being given a bath, having a picture taken, or being pushed in a

swing). Interestingly, most of the memories involved images rather than events. People remembered things like curtains blowing in the breeze, a light shining on someone's face, and a mobile hanging in the air. This is probably because small children generally lack the language skills necessary to encode a complicated series of events. Many psychologists, in fact, believe that it is rare for people to remember things that occurred before they were able to talk.

Since students are usually fascinated by their own early lives, **you can generate a high amount of interest in this topic** by asking them to write the answer to the same question *Psychology Today* asked its readers: "What is your earliest memory and how old were you?" Before starting, your students need to be cautioned to try to make sure that it is a real memory and not something they've been told about or seen in photograph albums, etc. After they've finished, you should have them read some of the responses for the class. For more details see E. Stark, "Thanks for the Memories," *Psychology Today,* November, 1984.

9.   **Ask students to take home the early memories they recorded in the preceding exercise.** They should then attempt to confirm the accuracy of their memory by interviewing parents or other relatives. Does their account match that given by others? Does it match too closely? Has the relative ever told the student about the event? How confident are students that they really remember the event and that they didn't just hear about it later? Discuss the difficulties of knowing if a memory is accurate or not.

10.   **The following exercise provides another demonstration of the effect of meaningfulness on memory.** Prepare three handouts as shown below. Ask students to attempt to memorize the words listed on **Handout A**. Then give them **Handout B** and have them practice the words again, this time with some meaningful context. Finally, give them **Handout C** and have them try to consolidate their learning. By the time they get to the third presentation, they should know the lists well and they should have some insight into the organizational value of meaningfulness.

Handout A:
Read the following list of words carefully. Try to remember as many words as you can.

Gather	End
Separate	Ball
Spray	Tie corners
Push	Walk
Wait	Run
Pull	Hold
Fasten	Jerk
Pile	Unravel

Handout B:
Read the following paragraphs carefully. Try to remember the words that are underlined.

<u>Gather</u> everything and carry it to one room. <u>Separate</u>. <u>Spray</u>. Check the temperature. Add the powder. <u>Push</u> the button. <u>Wait</u> for thirty minutes. Open the lid. <u>Pull</u> everything out and place in a basket. <u>Walk</u> outside and find the rope. <u>Fasten</u> each piece, overlapping <u>corners</u> just slightly. About two hours later, unpin everything, put it back in the basket, and fold and put in piles. Carry one <u>pile</u> back to each room.

Find the <u>end</u> from the <u>ball</u>. <u>Tie</u> it to the <u>corners</u> of the wood. <u>Walk</u> to the top of a hill. As you <u>run</u> down the hill, <u>hold</u> onto the <u>ball</u> gradually letting the long <u>end</u> go. <u>Jerk</u> the <u>ball</u> up if the <u>corners</u> of the wood swoop down. Continue to <u>unravel</u> the <u>ball</u>.

Handout C:
The following paragraph describes the process of doing laundry. Read the paragraph carefully. Try to remember the words that are printed in bold type.

Gather everything and carry it to one room. **Separate**. **Spray**. Check the temperature. Add the powder. **Push** the button. **Wait** for thirty minutes. Open the lid. **Pull** everything out and place in a basket. **Walk** outside and find the rope. **Fasten** each piece, overlapping **corners** just slightly. About two hours later, unpin everything, put it back in the basket, and fold and put in piles. Carry one **pile** back to each room.

The following paragraph describes the process of flying a kite.

Find the **end** from the **ball**. **Tie** it to the **corners** of the wood. **Walk** to the top of a hill. As you **run** down the hill, **hold** onto the **ball** gradually letting the long **end** go. **Jerk** the **ball** up if the **corners** of the wood swoop down. Continue to **unravel** the **ball**.

■ ROLE-PLAYING SCENARIOS

1.   **Your classmates are going to ask you questions about yourself.** Answer as if you lacked short-term memory. How do you feel about your memory deficit?

2.   **You have just awakened from a coma and have no memory of the past month or of what caused your coma.** How do you feel? What do you want to know?

3.   **You are an attorney questioning a witness whose memory you want to challenge.** What questions can you ask the witness to demonstrate the unreliability of memory?

4.   **You are a professor advising an older student who has returned to college.** The student is having trouble preparing for exams. What advice can you give the student for improving memory?

■ VALUE-CLARIFICATION STATEMENTS

1. Testimony obtained with hypnosis should be used in court.

2. When a person can't remember information for a class, it is usually because the information was not really learned in the first place.

3. Students could remember course information better if instructors would help them visualize the ideas more often.

4. A person should never stay up all night studying for a morning exam.

5. People who say they have a "photographic memory" are really people just like us who have learned memory strategies.

6. Even if a "memory pill" could be manufactured, that pill should be illegal.

■ ONE-MINUTE MOTIVATORS

1. **During the last five minutes of class before beginning this chapter, weave into your lecture/discussion an announcement of a quiz for the next class session (or write the announcement in some obscure corner of the chalkboard).** Only one or two people should notice. Begin class by asking students to take out a piece of paper for the quiz. When students protest, begin a discussion of why we often fail to remember, including inattention and failure to record the information in the first place.

2. **Use a tachistoscope to flash images quickly to demonstrate sensory memory.** Read a series of words to the class to be remembered. Ask them to think about their initial processing of the words. Are they aware of an echo? Do they silently rehearse the words? Do they attempt to chunk them in some way? Do they try to link them to knowledge in long-term storage?

3. **Ask each student to state his or her favorite musical group and favorite food.** Have students try to remember each classmate's favorites. Discuss to what extent students used visual cues, the order of the information, and chunking to remember the information. What mnemonic strategies would make this task easier?

4. **To demonstrate redintegrative memory, ask students to try to remember the activities, demonstrations, and discussions that took place at an earlier class session.** Then show them a photograph you took in class that day (if you did take any earlier) or tell them what major national and local news events took place that day. As one memory leads to another, discuss how important memory cues are.

5.   **Give students two comparable lists of terms.** Ask students to recall one list and give them a recognition test for terms from the other list (embed the terms in a longer list and have students circle those that they learned). Compare their memory scores.

6.   **Ask a student to tell what her or his hobby is (or favorite movie, food, sport, color, etc.)** The next student repeats what the first student said and adds his or her own information. Continue in this way until 10 students have spoken. Students will find that they remember what the first few students said and the person just before their turn. Discuss the serial position effect.

7.   **Add a few posters to the classroom.** Do not draw attention to them. Take them down and ask the class about them. Discuss how difficult it is to remember if we never encoded the information in the first place. Share strategies for selective listening and note-taking.

8.   **Ask students to report a "flashbulb" memory that is especially vivid for them.** What role did emotion play in the formation of the memory? Have they rehearsed and retold the memory unusually frequently? How can flashbulb memories be explained?

■ BROADENING OUR CULTURAL HORIZONS

1.   **Members of cultures that trade beads can recall the color patterns of long strands of beads; those who herd cattle can remember and recognize dozens of individual animals.** Can you name some types of information that is easily remembered in our culture, but that might be difficult for a member of another culture to encode? (For example, the year and make of a number of automobiles.) In what ways does cultural experience prepare us to remember some things easily and others with difficulty?

2.   **Why might a person who speaks English and Spanish equally well prefer to read or study physics in English, and to learn poetry in Spanish?**

3.   **You are visiting a foreign country.** You speak the language, but you are very unfamiliar with the culture. You stop a passerby on the street and ask for directions. Why might you find it difficult to remember the directions and why might your helper have trouble giving them?

4.   **Talk to people in your class or on campus who were born in another country.** Ask them how they remember the number of days in each month, for example, or any other information you remember with a mnemonic device. What device do they use? Is it very different from the device you were taught?

5. **Why is it often difficult for new immigrants to learn a country's monetary system?** (Consider perceptual effects, such as a dime being smaller than a nickel, as well as memory.)

■ SUPPLEMENTAL ACTIVITIES

TO THE INSTRUCTOR:

The **two exercises** included in this section deal with the importance of making information meaningful to maximize storage and recall. Efficiency in learning, good retention, and significant recall depend on a number of factors, one of which is meaning. The **first** exercise is a simple demonstration to show that organization of information increases meaning and recall.

The **second** exercise shows how varying degrees of meaning result in corresponding amounts of recall. This is a take-home exercise. Students should follow the directions given, gather the data, answer the discussion questions, and then meet in class for a review of the concepts involved.

Exercise #1: Organize for Meaning

I. **Introduction**

This exercise is intended to show that when information is organized in a meaningful way it is learned, retained, and recalled more easily. You should be sure to relate this exercise, and the discussion before and after it, to the study habits of the students. They may not see the value of what they learn here unless it is pointed out. It is even better if they can be led to conclude this for themselves.

Two handouts are provided for this exercise. They should be distributed in such a way that half of the class gets *Handout #1*, and the other half gets *Handout #2*. A good way to do this would be to stack the handouts ahead of time alternating #1 and #2 in the pile.

List #1 contains a set of terms that are organized in a logical meaningful way. List #2 has no particular logic, meaning, or order to the presentation. Only the form and raw content are the same as #1.

II. **Procedure**

A. Explain to the class that they will be given a brief learning task. Ask them to do their best on it, so they can see a learning principle at work.

B. Distribute the handout sheets, alternately stacked, to the students, face down. Give each student a data sheet for responding, also face down.

C. Ask the students to turn the list over and study it for forty-five seconds.

D. At the end of the time period, instruct the students to turn the list face down and write as many words as they can remember on the data sheet. Give them about two minutes to do this.

E. Ask the students to check their work to see how many they got right.

F. Total the number right for those who had lists #1 and #2 separately, and find the mean for each group. Those who studied list #1, which was organized in a meaningful way, should receive a higher mean score than those who did list #2.

III. **Discussion**

A. What is the difference between the two lists? You should project the two lists together on an overhead projector so the students can compare them.

B. Why is there a difference in performance on the two lists?

C. Some students who had the second list, the one lacking organization, will still do as well as or better than those in the other group. Identify those persons and try to find out what they did to recall so much. This could lead to some interesting discussion of memory techniques.

D. Can what has been found in this exercise apply to the study habits of the students? Discuss ways to make it work for them.

ORGANIZE FOR MEANING: LIST #1

FOOD

Meat		Vegetables		Fruit	
beef	pork	green	yellow	small	large
ground	chops	beans	carrots	grapes	apples
steak	ribs	peas	squash	berries	oranges
roast	loin	broccoli	rutabaga	cherries	melons

ORGANIZE FOR MEANING: LIST #2

food

ribs   squash   oranges

peas	berries	chops	grapes	steak	carrots
large	apples	beef	melons	cherries	rutabaga
yellow	meat	beans	green	roast	pork
ground	vegetables	loin	small	fruit	broccoli

ORGANIZE FOR MEANING: DATA SHEET

TO THE STUDENT:

Write as many words from the list you have studied as you can, in any order. If you are not sure, you can guess.

1._____

2._____

3._____

4._____

5._____

6._____

7._____

8._____

9._____

10._____

11._____

12._____

13._____

14._____

15._____

16._____

17._____

18._____

19._____

20._____

21._____

22._____

23._____

24._____

25._____

26._____

27._____

28._____

Exercise #2: Meaning and Memory

TO THE STUDENT:

A. **Background and Purpose**

Psychologists have found that meaningful information is easier to remember than that which is not. This is because it is associated with information that is already in memory. The purpose of this project is to show that material which is higher in association value is easier to store in memory and recall.

B. **You will be testing subjects with three word lists.** One list has high association value, the second has medium value, and the third has low association value. Each subject will be given all three lists; however, they should be given one at a time, at separate times, with some time interval between the administration of each list. The subjects will be asked to write down as many words as they can remember after hearing the list once.

C. **Directions**

1. Select three subjects for this study. They should be over ten years of age.

2. You need to meet with each subject three times to administer each of the three word lists.

3. Provide the subject with a pencil and sheet of paper.

4. Give each subject the high association word list first, then the medium list, and finally the low. Each should be given separately with a time interval in between.

5. Read the word list to the subject. Read the words in order, slowly, about one word per second.

6. The subject should listen carefully. After you complete reading the list, have the subject write down as many as (s)he can remember. Do the same for each list.

7. Record the results for each subject on each word list. Find the average number of words recalled correctly for each type of list.

8. Answer the questions about your results, discussing what you found, and relating it to the material on memory in the text.

MEANING AND MEMORY (cont.)

WORD LISTS

High	Medium	Low
the	bee	yad
dog	nor	cif
ate	can	mul
two	but	bix
and	fee	pog
did	lob	zel
not	sit	riv
eat	old	mib
for	doe	daf
you	run	hib

RESULTS

SUBJECT	SCORES (number of correct words)		
	HIGH	MEDIUM	LOW
1.			
2.			
3.			
AVERAGE SCORE			

MEANING AND MEMORY (cont.)

D.   **Discussion**

1.   **Based on the data you gathered,** to what extent does association play a part in memory? Give reasons for your answer based on what you have learned about remembering and forgetting.

2.   **What are the implications** of an associationistic theory of memory for student learning?

3.   **Give some examples** of how a student might organize his/her study to take advantage of the association value inherent in the material.

■ JOURNAL QUESTIONS

1.   What is your earliest happy memory? How old were you? Where were you? What were you doing? What is your earliest unhappy memory? Does this memory predate or follow your earliest happy memory?

2.   What were you doing the day Desert Storm began, John Kennedy was killed, John Lennon was killed, President Reagan was shot, the Space Shuttle exploded, or the Federal Building in Oklahoma was bombed? Can you remember your first day of school or your first date? Describe the details. Are you able to recall days in your psychology class with the same vividness? Why not?

3.   Have you ever been in an accident and lost some memories? What happened? What did you forget? How long did it take before some memories started to return? Which memories came back first?

4.   If you have ever been to a high school reunion, were you able to remember names? If so, how?

5.   What do you do to try to remember information in short-term memory? What specific strategies do you employ? Under what conditions are these strategies most successful?

6.   What do you do to remember information in long-term memory? Under what conditions are you most successful?

7.   Describe one of the most embarrassing moments for you when your memory system malfunctioned. What was the situation? Why weren't you able to remember?

8.   What mnemonics did you learn as a child? Were they helpful? Do you use mnemonic devices now in your classes? Are there times they interfere rather than help?

■ SUGGESTIONS FOR FURTHER READING

Anderson, J. R. *Learning and Memory: An Integrated Approach.* John Wiley & Sons, 2000.

Best, J. B. *Cognitive Psychology*, 5th ed. Brooks/Cole & Wadsworth, 1999.

Bower, G. H. "Mood and Memory." *American Psychologist,* 1981, 36: 129-148.

Cermak, L. S. *Handbook of Neuropsychology, 2 ed.: Memory and Its Disorders.* Elsevier Science, 2000.

Coward, L. Andrew. *Pattern Thinking.* New York: Praeger, 1990.

Donahoe, J. W. and D. C. Palmer. *Learning and Complex Behavior.* Allyn and Bacon, 1994.

Harris, J. E. and P. E. Morris. *Everyday Memory: Actions and Absent-Mindedness.* Academic Press, 1986.

Hunt, R. R. and H. C. Ellis. *Fundamentals of Cognitive Psychology,* 7th ed. McGraw-Hill, 1999.

Klatzky, R. L. *Memory and Awareness: An Information-Processing Perspective.* W. H. Freeman, 1984.

Linton, M. "I Remember it Well." *Psychology Today,* July, 1979: 81-86.

Loftus, E. F. *Memory.* Addison-Wesley, 1980.

Loftus, E. F. and K. Ketchem. *The Myth of Repressed Memory: False Memories and Allegations of Sexual Abuse.* St. Martin's Press, 1996.

Luria, A. R. *The Mind of a Mnemonist.* Harvard University Press, 1988.

Lynch, G. "A Magical Memory Tour." *Psychology Today,* April, 1984: 29-39.

"Memory: A whiff of chocolate helps." *The New York Times,* July 10, 1990, p. 88.

McGaugh, J. L. "Preserving the Presence of the Past: Hormonal Influences on Memory Storage." *American Psychologist,* 1983, 38: 161-174.

Neath, I. *Human Memory: An Introduction to Research, Data, and Theory.* Wadsworth, 1998.

Neisser, U. and I. E. Hyman. *Memory Observed: Remembering in Natural Contexts.* Worth, 1999.

Roediger, Henry L., III. "Implicit memory: Retention without remembering." *American Psychologist,* 45 (9), 1043-1056, 1990.

Schul, Taacov and Burstein, Eugene. "Judging the typicality of an instance: Should the category be assessed first?" *Journal of Personality and Social Psychology,* 58, p. 964, 1990.

Spear, N. E. and D. Riccio. *Memory: Phenomena and Principles.* Allyn and Bacon, 1994.

Tulving, E. *Elements of Episodic Memory, Series 2.* Oxford University Press, 1986.

Tulving, Endel and Schacter, Daniel L. "Priming and Human Memory Systems." *Science,* 247, p. 301, 1990.

■ MEDIA SUGGESTIONS

FALSE MEMORIES (2002, Films for the Humanities and Sciences, 52 min.)
Elizabeth Loftus and other scientists call into question the accuracy of memory and the dangers of recovered "repressed" memories.

MEMORY (2002, from *Psychology: the Study of Human Behavior Series,* Coast Community College District Telecourses, 30 min.)
Explains research in the nature and workings of memory; defines amnesia and Alzheimer's disease.

MEMORY (2001, Insight Media, 30 min.)
This program examines how memories are formed, stored, and recalled.

REMEMBERING AND FORGETTING (2001, from the *Discovering Psychology Series,* Annenberg/CPB, 30 min.)
A look at how images, ideas, language, and psychical actions are translated into codes, represented in memory, and retrieved when needed.

THE STUDY OF MEMORY (2002, Films for the Humanities and Sciences, 74 min.)
From *The Psychology of Learning Series,* this film describes the history of research in memory and the basic terms used in studying memory. Current research, reasons for forgetting, and memory improvement exercises are included.

A number of videos are available from Thomson. Videos appropriate for this chapter include the following films from the CNN TODAY Introductory Psychology Video Series:

Volume 1, Section 2: The Brain
      Memory Drugs (1:59)

Volume 2, Section 1: The Brain
      Smell Memory (2:21)

Volume 3, Section 4: Human Memory
      Alzheimer's Babies (1:36)

■ COMPUTER AND INTERNET RESOURCES

PSYCHNOW!

Learning & Cognition:
Memory Systems
Forgetting

PSYK.TREK

Unit 6: Memory & Thought
   6a: Memory encoding
   6b: Memory storage
   6c: Physiology of memory

INFOTRAC

Subject Guide/Key Words: Human Memory, Short-Term Memory, Long-Term Memory, Sensory Memory, Hypnosis and Memory, Procedural Memory, Declarative Memory, Semantic Memory, Episodic Memory, Flashbulb Memory, Recall and Recognition, Explicit and Implicit Memory, Forgetting, Amnesia, Memory Disorders, Alzheimer's, Proactive Interference, Retroactive Interference, False Memory Syndrome, Memory Consolidation, Engram, Mnemonics, Mnemonist

WEB SITES

Wadsworth Online Psychology Study Center:
http://info.wadsworth.com/cooessentials9

AmoebaWeb Psychology Resources: Memory:
http://www.vanguard.edu/psychology/webmemory.html

Newton's Apple: Memory:
http://ericir.syr.edu/Projects/Newton/11/memory.html

False Memory Syndrome Foundation:
http://advicom.net/~fitz/fmsf/

Recovered Memories of Sexual Abuse:
http://www.jimhopper.com/memory

Therapeutic Recovery of Memory:
http://web.lemoyne.edu/~hevern/nr-mem.html

Alzheimer's Disease Internet Sites:
http://www.hc.cc.tx.us/library/alzheim.htm

CHAPTER 9
Cognition, Intelligence, and Creativity

■ LEARNING OBJECTIVES

To demonstrate mastery of this chapter the student should be able to:

1.   Define the terms cognition and cognitive psychology.
2.   List the three basic units of thought.
3.   Describe mental imagery (including the concept of mental rotation and a description of what happens in the brain during visual imaging). Explain how both stored and created images may be used to solve problems.
4.   Explain how the size of a mental image is important.
5.   Explain how kinesthetic imagery aids thinking.
6.   Define the terms concept and concept formation, explain how they aid thought processes, and describe how they are learned. Define the term conceptual rules.
7.   Define the terms conjunctive concept, relational concept, and disjunctive concept.
8.   Explain the importance of prototypes.
9.   Explain the difference between the denotative and the connotative meaning of a word or concept, and describe how the connotative meaning of a word is measured.
10.   Define the term semantic differential and briefly discuss how using inaccurate concepts may lead to thinking errors.
11.   Define semantics and explain how semantic problems may arise.
12.   Briefly describe the following three requirements of a language and their related concepts:
       1) symbols
           a) phonemes
           b) morphemes
       2) grammar
           a) syntax
           b) transformation rules
       3) productivity

The following objectives are related to the material in the "Exploring Psychology" section of the text.
13.   Describe the research involving attempts to teach primates (especially Washoe, Sarah, and Kanzi) to use language. Describe the criticisms and practical value of such attempts.

14.   Compare and contrast mechanical solutions with solutions through understanding.

15.   Define the term heuristic and contrast it with random search strategies.

16.   Describe the process of insight as a problem solving technique.

17.   List and describe the three abilities involved in insight.

18.   Explain how fixation and functional fixedness block problem solving, and give an example of each.

19.   List and explain four common barriers to creative thinking.

20.   Define the term artificial intelligence and state upon what fact it is based.

21.   Explain how computer simulations and expert systems are used.

22.   Explain the differences between experts and novices.

23.   Describe Binet's role in intelligence testing.

24.   Define intelligence.

25.   Explain what an operational definition of intelligence is.

26.   Generally describe the construction of the Stanford-Binet Intelligence Scale.

27.   Define intelligence quotient, and use an example to show how it was computed. Explain the purpose of deviation IQ scores.

28.   Distinguish the Wechsler tests from the Stanford-Binet tests.

29.   Define the term culture-fair test, and explain how IQ tests may be unfair to certain groups.

30.   Distinguish between group and individual intelligence tests.

31.   Describe the pattern of distribution of IQ scores observed in the general population.

32.   Discuss the relationship between IQ and achievement.

33.   Briefly describe Terman's study of gifted children. State how successful subjects differed from the less successful ones.

34.   List seven early signs of giftedness.

35.   Describe Gardner's broader view of intelligence and list the eight different kinds of intelligence he discusses.

36.   State the dividing line between normal intelligence and retardation (or developmental disability) and list the degrees of retardation.

37.   Differentiate between organic and familial retardation.

38.   Explain how the twin (identical and fraternal) studies can be used to support either side of the heredity/environment controversy.

39.   Describe the evidence that strongly supports the environmental view of intelligence.

40.   Describe the studies that indicate how much the environment can alter intelligence.

41.   Discuss how the heredity/environment debate is currently viewed.

42.   Describe the following four kinds of thought:
       a) inductive
       b) deductive
       c) logical
       d) illogical

43.   Describe the following characteristics of creative thinking:
       a) fluency
       b) flexibility
       c) originality

44. Explain the relationship of creativity to divergent and convergent thinking. Describe how the ability to think divergently can be measured.

45. List and describe the five stages of creative thinking, and relate them to a problem that you have solved.

46. List five conclusions about creative people.

47. Define intuition.

48. Explain the following errors made when using intuition:
    a) representativeness
    b) underlying odds (base rate)
    c) framing

The following objectives are related to the material in the "Psychology in Action" section of the text.

49. Briefly describe the relationship between intelligence and wisdom.

50. Describe eight practical steps for encouraging creativity.

51. Describe the process of brainstorming, and explain how it can be used to solve problems.

■ DISCUSSION QUESTIONS

1. If you suddenly lost your ability to mentally represent external problems, what changes would you have to make in your behavior?

2. In what ways does a large vocabulary make a person a more effective thinker?

3. In your opinion, are chimps that are trained to use hand signs really using language? Why or why not?

4. Describe a time when you have used imagery to solve a problem. What are the advantages and disadvantages of imagery in comparison to other modes of thought?

5. How do differences in connotative meaning contribute to arguments and misunderstandings? Do you think connotative meaning could or should be standardized?

6. The text implies that animals communicate, but do not use language in the human sense. Do you agree? Can you give an example of animal communication that qualifies as a language?

7. In what ways is an artificial intelligence program similar to and different from a word processor, the computerized engine control of an automobile, and a robot that builds cars?

8.   To what kinds of tasks do you think artificial intelligence should be applied? Would you be comfortable with computerized medical diagnosis, for instance? What about the launch of a nuclear attack?

9.   In what ways do you think our society encourages the development of different intellectual skills in males and females?

10.   What advantages or disadvantages would you expect to be associated with knowing your own IQ? With having a teacher know your IQ? With having your parents know your IQ?

11.   How might public education be restructured to encourage full intellectual development for all children? How might grading be changed to reflect broader definitions of intelligence?

12.   How would you define "gifted"? Why are definitions important? What are the negative consequences of defining intelligence and giftedness at all?

13.   How would you feel about the application of eugenics to human reproduction? Can you think of circumstances under which you would or would not consider it acceptable?

14.   The debate over the relative importance of heredity and environment in determining intelligence has raged for decades. Why do you think the debate has lasted so long and attracted so much interest? If the heritability of IQ could be known with certainty, what difference would it make?

15.   An organization called the Repository for Germinal Choice in Escondido, California, serves as a sperm bank for Nobel Prize winners and others possessing high IQs. Dozens of babies have now been produced by artificial insemination from the sperm bank. Do you regard this as wise or unwise, ethical or unethical, foolish or inspired?

16.   What perceptual habits could contribute to barriers in problem-solving?

17.   Think of the most creative person you know. What is that person like? How does he or she differ from your less creative acquaintances?

18.   In what ways is creativity different from intelligence?

19.   In your opinion, should measures of divergent or creative thinking be used to select students for college admission? Why or why not?

20.   You are the president of an advertising company. You want to hire a new account executive who is extremely creative. How would you go about identifying this person?

21.   Can you provide a real-life example of each of Tversky and Kahneman's concepts (representativeness, base rates, and framing)?

■ LECTURE ENHANCEMENTS

We all make assumptions about our own intelligence and the intelligence of others. Group activities can give students a chance to work together in a cooperative, non-threatening environment to solve thinking and creativity problems. Students should leave this chapter with specific strategies and skills for solving problems and they should feel more competent for having studied these concepts. They should also be encouraged to examine the assumptions they make about the intelligence of others. Students can be reminded that each culture defines intelligence and creativity uniquely and that it is very difficult to develop culture-free measures of thinking.

1.   **The research team of Sue Savage-Rumbaugh, Duane Rumbaugh, and Sarah Boysen has advanced a cogent argument against the notion that true language usage has been achieved by apes trained in ASL or computer language systems.** For a critical and thought-provoking appraisal of primate language programs, see their article, "Do Apes Use Language?" in *American Scientist,* Jan.-Feb. 1980: 49 or the more recent "Language and Apes" in *Psychology Teacher Network*, pp. 2-5, 9, 1994.

2.   **The semantic differential provides an interesting look at the subtleties and similarities of the connotative meanings of words.** To illustrate, duplicate the semantic differential scales shown in the text and give copies to the class. Then have them rate words such as: **MOTHER, FATHER, MONEY, SEX, LOVE, STUDENT, PROFESSOR, COLLEGE, POLITICS, LIBERAL,** etc. To what degree are connotations shared? Do individual differences in connotative meanings match students' perceptions of themselves, their interests, and values?

3.   **To impress upon students the arbitrary nature of operational definitions of intelligence, have them write a list of skills or capacities they believe an intelligence test should measure (e.g., memory, computation, verbal ability, etc.).** Ask a student to read his or her list, and no matter how long it is, ask, "Is that all that's meant by intelligence?" Then call on others to add to the list. When the class has exhausted all its additions, point out that the definition is still vague, limited, and arbitrary. Also ask students to imagine how all these abilities might be tested by one or several tests. It might also be interesting to note the degrees to which student definitions of intelligence have been shaped by their many years of exposure to schooling.

4.   **The quotations and notes which follow are almost sure to stir up worthwhile class discussion:**

    a.   "One thing I know. The IQ test does not truly measure intelligence. Our tests focus on such narrow things, the ability to acquire knowledge. What of human feelings? Are not these also important?" (Samuel C. Kohs, who helped develop the Stanford-Binet while a student of Lewis Terman.)

    b.   Economist Thomas Sowell of Stanford University has found that during World War I, the IQs of European and Asian immigrants were nearly identical to black IQs today. Due to acculturation, education, and upward mobility, these immigrant groups now have IQs at or above the national average. Presumably, when socioeconomic and educational differences between blacks and whites are narrowed, the black-white gap will close as well.

    c.   From a psychologist testifying for the defense in the Larry P. case (a lawsuit concerning the placement of an African-American child into a class for mentally retarded students on the basis of a culturally biased IQ test alone): "...the surest and most effective action the Negro community could take by itself to achieve equality and education and jobs would be to limit dramatically the birthrate in those families providing the least effective environment for intellectual development." On the other hand, Professors Phillip Kunz and Evan Peterson of Brigham Young University have data suggesting that, "children in lower socioeconomic classes have lower grade point averages than those in the middle or upper class, regardless of family size."

    d.   "I don't see any use for IQ tests during public school, except when a child has difficulty in learning. In that case, they are a valuable diagnostic tool. They can indicate a person lacks some ability to understand the world around them (sic)." Arthur Jensen speaking in 1980.

    e.   "Absolutely wrong," and "biological nonsense" were but a few denouncements by Nobel Prize winners when they learned of the Repository for Germinal Choice set up by a U.S. businessman as a bank for sperm contributed by Nobel laureates. Three women have reputedly been fertilized with the sperm. One of the contributors was Dr. William B. Shockley.

    f.   "The evidence about college entrance tests as predictors of academic success is no longer a subject of legitimate dispute...Most educators are quite familiar with the fact that the scores work in more cases than not, popular belief to the contrary notwithstanding." (William W. Turnbull, President of ETS in a 1974 speech.) According to figures ETS presented in 1977, the average accuracy of

ETS aptitude tests in predicting first-year grades is seldom better than random predictions.

Percentage of Predictions in which Random Predictions with a Pair of Dice Is as Accurate as an ETS Test:

SAT (college)............................88%
LSAT (law school)....................87%
GRE (graduate school)..............89%
GMAT (business school)...........92%

The compilation of ETS validity studies found that high school grades alone are about twice as good as the SAT in predicting college grades. (Quote and table from "The Reign of the ETS" by Allan Nairn and Associates, *The Ralph Nader Report on the Educational Testing Service*.)

  g.   Warner Slack and Douglas Porter of Harvard Medical School reported in the May 1980 Harvard Educational Review that coaching substantially improves scores on the SAT. ETS denies that coaching affects test results. Slack and Porter hold that the SAT tests measure "little-used vocabulary and tricky math," and that tutoring can raise scores enough to make the difference between acceptance and rejection to college.

5.   **To help students appreciate the difficulty in understanding what intelligence is, propose the following as measures of intelligence.** Ask the students to decide which would be best:

  a.   A standardized IQ test;
  b.   A person's college GPA;
  c.   Giving the person $100 to invest and seeing how much (s)he has after twelve months;
  d.   Leaving the person out in the wilderness for three days with only an axe and a box of matches;
  e.   Giving an extensive exam of general knowledge;
  f.   How much information on a particular topic the person can find on the Internet;
  g.   A person's grade in his/her course in psychology.

There will likely be a good deal of disagreement about which would be best. Most students will know someone whom they consider to be very bright but who has done poorly in college or high school. Ask them how they know the person is bright in the first place. What are their criteria? Challenge the class to propose a better way to measure intelligence.

6.   ***Mednick's Remote Associates Test* (RAT) is a good example of a creativity test that combines divergent and convergent thinking.** The RAT consists of groupings of three words. The words in each group have a single word in common associated with them.

The object is to find that word. For example, if the words were, "shake, cow, and carton," the common element is "milk" (milkshake, milk cow, and milk carton). The items below are similar to the RAT. They may be used in class to raise the question of what distinguishes creative thought from other types of problem-solving. The class may also want to discuss whether or not the RAT actually tests creativity.

1) ball   home   naval   6) ball   shake   lotion
2) stream   goose   town   7) puff   whipped   ice
3) dance   ladder   door   8) bowling   cushion   hair
4) dog   pepper   rod   9) sun   bulb   sky
5) sand   mouse   door   10) wrench   stove   line

Answers for the preceding items are: 1) base 2) down 3) step 4) hot 5) trap 6) hand 7) cream 8) pin 9) light 10) pipe.

7.   **Is "brainstorming" really superior to individual problem-solving for producing creative solutions?** A small in-class experiment may shed some light on this issue for students. Begin by dividing the class in half. Form four-person groups out of one-half of the class. If possible, separate the groups from the remaining individuals. Beforehand, prepare a brief summary of brainstorming from the discussion in the text and give it to the four-person groups to read. Tell the students their task is to imagine as many possible uses for a brick as they can. Groups are to work according to the rules for brainstorming. Individuals are to work by themselves. At the end of a five-minute period, collect the lists of uses, and arbitrarily group the solutions of individuals by fours. Then compare the number of uses generated by the brainstorming groups to the number produced by groups of four individuals working independently. In addition to determining if the cross-stimulation produced more ideas, the originality of group and individual solutions can be compared.

After discussing brainstorming, you may wish to use this exercise to illustrate the value of breaking sets. Write the following attributes on the board: weight, color, rectangularity (sharp edges, flat surfaces), porosity, strength, roughness, storage and conduction of heat, electrical insulation, hardness. Then ask students to try adding to their lists of uses by considering each of the listed attributes. Does this increase the number, flexibility, and originality of their answers? (Source: Adams, J.L. *Conceptual Blockbusting.* Perseus Books, 2001.)

8.   **There are many ways in which fixation in problem-solving can be illustrated.** A typical problem you may wish to pose to students is this: How could you put your left hand completely in your right hand pants pocket and your right hand completely in your left hand pants pocket at the same time while you are wearing the pants? The answer is to put the pants on backward, whereupon the task becomes quite easy. Students often miss this solution due to conventions about the "right" way to wear a pair of pants.

A large number of problems similar to the preceding are offered by Eugene Raudsepp in a *Psychology Today* article. They cannot be reprinted here, but the article will provide you with an excellent collection of creativity problems for class use. The article appears in the July 1980 issue of *Psychology Today*: 71-75, 88-90.

9. **It is always an interesting exercise to form students into groups and have them brainstorm a new product.** Students should describe the size, type, function, cost, potential market, and so forth.

■ ROLE-PLAYING SCENARIOS

1. **You are the Director of a "Gifted and Talented" Program.** Explain to a group of parents how you select elementary students to be a part of your program.

2. **You are a psychologist who has just tested a child and found that his IQ is 95.** Tell his parents what to expect and how they should view their child's score.

3. **You are a parent who has just found out that your child is mildly mentally retarded.** What kind of questions do you have for the professional who has just informed you of this fact? What kind of concerns do you have for your child's future? For your future?

4. **You are the parent of a 10-minute old healthy infant.** Explain to a nurse what you plan to do from this moment on to encourage the intellectual development and creativity of your child.

5. **You are the 12-year-old child of a pair of pushy, yuppie parents.** You understand that they are supposed to encourage your intellectual development; but you feel that being grounded for your first "B" is a little extreme. Tell them your feelings.

■ VALUE-CLARIFICATION STATEMENTS

1. It is cruel to take chimps from their natural environment to teach them sign language.

2. Amniocentesis shows that the fetus will never develop into an adult with an IQ over 50. This fetus should be aborted.

3. Most females do have special insight into "life" -- commonly called woman's intuition.

4. Children should be pushed to learn; otherwise, they will never be able to compete well in the adult world.

5. In the "real world" creativity is more important than intelligence.

■ ONE-MINUTE MOTIVATORS

1.   **Ask students to spend a few moments summarizing the contents of their thoughts just before class began.** What elements of thinking were present?

2.   **Ask students to process these numbers:** 15 X 2 X 7 divided by 3 - 20 (the answer is 50); to think of all the words they can make from the letters THINK; to say (without looking) how many circles there are on the back of one-dollar bill; to say what dogs, cats, parakeets, and goldfish have in common. Do students use different elements of thought to answer these questions?

3.   **Bring an unusual object to class.** Keep the object covered. Allow students to ask questions about the object until they can identify it. How much did they rely on language? Concepts? Imagery?

4.   **Ask a student to describe how to get to the bookstore,** the nearest theater, how to run a special football formation, or to describe what he/she did yesterday, and to describe feelings about a recent holiday. Ask a few students to watch the degree to which hand movements took place.

5.   **Categorize these concepts as conjunctive, disjunctive, or relative:** "yellow fruit", "American state capitals", "female vocalists", "all-star athletes", "under", "spouse", "student", "west".

6.   **Ask students to make a list of entertainers, politicians, athletes, or other prominent people.** Rate each person according to the semantic differential categories.

7.   **Flash a series of slides that show atypical chairs, vases, trees, animals.** Discuss prototypes.

8.   **Ask students to develop a list of oxymorons ("government intelligence", "jumbo shrimp").** Discuss semantic problems.

9.   **Ask students to describe the specific problem-solving strategies that they used to select this course,** and that they would use to select a job, a book, or a movie.

10.   **Walk through the eye, the ear, the neuron, or the brain by moving chairs and creating a chalk diagram on the floor.** Ask students to do this mentally; then do it physically. Discuss whether adding muscular responses to the image increases the understanding of the part of the body.

11.   **Ask students to write a short IQ test that their instructor will flunk.**

12. **Describe the smartest person you have known.** Do you think that person would score high on an IQ test? Or did they possess other kinds of intelligence?

13. **All of us have talents to share.** What is yours?

14. **Brainstorm unusual uses for a brick, ways to conserve water, uses for discarded "pop-top" tabs.** Analyze potential solutions in terms of fluency, flexibility, and originality.

■ BROADENING OUR CULTURAL HORIZONS

1. **Ask each student to think of 5 different groups of people.** The groupings can be based on physical qualities, age, gender, ethnic or racial background, etc. Create columns describing each group's socioeconomic status, happiness, creativity, intelligence, with an emphasis on family, value of independence, honesty, and industriousness. Ask students to rate the likelihood (1 = not likely; 7 = very likely) that these qualities would exist in an individual member of each group. Have students share their ratings in pairs. Then discuss the ways in which informal concepts of what various groups are like can color our attitudes toward individuals. Discuss stereotypes as a type of over-simplified concept.

2. **To what extent does cultural or ethnic background affect the kinds of prototypes we use to categorize objects and events?** Would these prototypes affect the way we think?

3. **Discuss the ways in which connotations can be culture-specific.** Ask students for examples of misunderstandings they have encountered that can be traced to differences in connotative meanings.

4. **Ask students who speak English as a second language** to discuss their feelings about learning and using a new language and about what effect this has had on their thinking.

5. **Invite a person to class who is fluent in American Sign Language.** Would a non-hearing person "perceive" the world differently than a hearing person because of using a different language structure? Teach students to sign the words to a current popular song.

6. **What cultural "rules" or values could contribute to functional fixedness?** Why are some cultures regarded as more inventive than others?

7. **Discuss with students if it is possible to develop a "culture-free" test.** If a test cannot be culture-free, can it be "culture fair"?

■ SUPPLEMENTAL ACTIVITIES

TO THE INSTRUCTOR:

The **first two exercises** which follow show the effects on behavior of mental set. **The third exercise** gives students a chance to sample one component of the type of thinking abilities measured by intelligence tests.

Solving problems may become difficult or impossible because of a predisposition, or set, to see the problem in a particular way or to try to solve it by a predetermined method. Students should readily see that they have fallen into this trap when they do the first two exercises.

The first exercise involves a story problem that is sure to baffle the listeners because of the obvious (but faulty) solution. The second exercise establishes a mental set in the first five problems. Because of the set which is now established, the students will have a harder time doing the next three.

Exercise #1: It Pays to Tip

This is a classroom exercise which demonstrates the effect of set on thinking and problem-solving. Students should be asked to read the section on mental set in the text prior to this exercise. You should have a stopwatch or some other timing mechanism to inform students of the time it takes them to solve the problem. The value of this exercise lies in the discussion of the students' attempts at problem-solving and the evident mental set which made the problem difficult or impossible to solve.

I.   **Procedure**

      A.   Ask students to have a sheet of paper and pencil or pen handy for problem-solving purposes. Advise them that you are going to read a story and ask a question. They are to solve the problem and note the time, in seconds, that it took them to find the solution.

      B.   After reading the story, watch the time and note the elapsed time in ten-second intervals on the chalkboard, as the students work on the solution.

      C.   Stop the exercise after five minutes regardless of how many are finished.

      D.   The following story should be read slowly and clearly while the students listen:

            Three friends went to a restaurant to have a leisurely drink and lunch. They finished their meal and paid their bill while lingering over coffee and conversation. The bill came to $30.00, so each paid $10.00 to the waiter, who went off to pay the bill. The bartender, who handled the cash register, noticed that the waiter had charged full price for the drinks, which were on a two-for-one special. The actual bill should have been $25.00, so he gave the waiter $5.00 and told him to return the money to the customers. On the way back to the table the waiter decided that since the diners did not know they had been overcharged, he would return one dollar to each and keep $2.00 for himself. That is exactly what he did. Now each of the diners had paid $9.00 for the food and drinks, and the waiter kept $2.00. Three times nine equals 27 plus 2 equals 29. Where is the other dollar?

(There is no "other dollar." Twenty-five dollars went to the restaurant, three to the diners, and two to the waiter.)

II   Discussion

A.   Find out how many solved the problem.

B.   Ask students to discuss how they tried to find a solution. See how many ways were tried.

C.   Discuss what factors made it difficult to solve this problem.

D.   See if students can see how mental set can be a factor in their day-to-day experiences.

Exercise #2: Measure for Measure

Beginning with an apology to Shakespeare for that title, we can also give thanks to Luchins for his classic experiment with the water jars. **The subject is given a set of three jars of varying sizes and a goal to achieve.** The person is to fill and empty the three jars until the goal of a specified number of pints of water is attained. Since the goal is never identical to the capacity of any of the three jars, some strategy needs to be developed to end up with the exact amount specified. Suppose, for example, the subject were given a 20-pint jar, a 4-pint jar, and a 3-pint jar and had to end up with exactly 10 pints of water. The solution requires the subject to fill the 20-pint jar and then pour out 3 pints twice and four once, leaving 10 pints. It could be written as $20 - 3 - 3 - 4 = 10$.

I.   Procedure

A.   Explain the exercise to the class, indicating the type of problem being presented. Students should be given the demonstration item above and shown how to record their answer on the data sheet.

B.   Distribute a data sheet to each student.

C.   Write the problems given below on the chalkboard, one at a time, asking the students to record their solution after each one.

D.   After all eight are completed, discuss items 1 - 5. Two elements are needed for a correct solution to each of these items. The correct amount of water remaining is essential. Also, the way it was arrived at is important because it will demonstrate mental set. In each case manipulation of the jars of water was needed to arrive at the exact amount.

E.   Now go on to items 6 - 8. These can be solved directly without manipulation of the amounts of water. However, after solving 1 - 6, students will probably try manipulation first and may never see the direct method. (Note that for item 6 seven plus eight equals 15.)

WATER JAR SIZE				
PROBLEM	A	B	C	GOAL
1	20	31	2	7
2	20	57	3	31
3	5	48	8	27
4	20	100	11	58
5	3	84	7	67
6	7	38	8	15
7	4	17	3	7
8	9	29	6	15

(From: Luchins, A.S. "Mechanization in Problem-Solving: The Effect of `Einstellung.'" *Psychological Monographs,* 54 (Whole Number 248), 1942.)

II.   Discussion

A.   Discuss the trial-and-error method needed to learn the best way to solve the problem when starting out.

B.   Have students identify the mental set which was established by the first five items.

C.   How many made the shift to the easy way to solve items 6 - 8? How many stuck to the "old-fashioned way," learned while doing items 1 - 5?

D.   Discuss the extent to which mental set plays a part in our everyday lives.

MEASURE FOR MEASURE: DATA SHEET

TO THE STUDENT:

In the space provided show any calculating that you need to do to arrive at a solution. You will have two minutes to do each problem. Your instructor will demonstrate how the problems are to be done and how your answer should be written.

ITEM	SOLUTION	CALCULATIONS
1		
2		
3		
4		
5		
6		
7		
8		

Exercise #3: Analogies

This exercise can serve at least two purposes. One is to arouse interest in the topic of intelligence. The second is to illustrate the use of analogies as a measure of this ability. Most tests of mental ability use some items of this kind, acknowledging that this is a measure of intelligence. The *Miller Analogies Test*, used as an entrance examination into some graduate programs, is a series of one hundred analogies. Charles Spearman's theory of intelligence describes operations of general intelligence (g) which can be measured by analogies. Simply stated, an analogy requires the subject to see a relationship in the first half of a statement and to apply it in the second half. Spearman referred to these operations as eduction of relations and eduction of correlates. This test is timed. Spearman believed that speed of response is a factor in intelligence. On this test, students get four minutes with the understanding that most will not finish. This should make the test more discriminating at the top levels.

I.   **Procedure**

      A.   **Giving the test**

            1.   Make enough copies of the test so that each student will have one.

            2.   Without discussion distribute the tests, placing them face down on the students' desks. Ask them not to look at the test until told to do so.

            3.   When everyone is ready, ask them to turn over the test and read the directions as you read them aloud.

            4.   After the directions have been read, do the examples with the students. Point out the correct answer in the first. Ask a student to give the answer to the second. Clear up any questions before continuing.

            5.   Tell the students to begin. After four minutes ask them to stop and put their pencils down. DO NOT ALLOW STUDENTS TO CONTINUE IF NOT FINISHED.

            6.   Ask the students to put their names on the test papers, and collect them. Do not leave the test with the students if you plan to use it again.

      B.   **Scoring the test**

            1.   Check the items and find the number of correct responses for each student. The scoring key follows.

2.   Work out the mean and standard deviation for the class. If you have given it to several classes, include all scores. The larger the number of scores, the more meaningful the results. You can develop a set of percentiles for the group which will tell each student how (s)he did in relation to all those who have taken the test.

3.   You can convert the mean and standard deviation into T-scores with a mean of 100, and you will have a deviation IQ score.

4.   Report the results to the students in a way that maintains the confidentiality of their scores, but do not return the tests.

II.   **Discussion**

A.   You can discuss the test items for validity.

B.   You can discuss the results obtained and what they mean.

C.   The simple statistics used can also be explained to show how data is assembled and interpreted by psychologists.

III.   **Analogies Scoring Key**

1.	kitten	11.	deaf	21.	betray
2.	herd	12.	sap	22.	rim
3.	shoe	13.	finished	23.	client
4.	light	14.	81	24.	vice
5.	door	15.	author	25.	L
6.	quart	16.	cuff	26.	Wednesday
7.	fruit	17.	seed	27.	laziness
8.	floor	18.	sparrow	28.	create
9.	trees	19.	chairperson	29.	surface
10.	dust	20.	48	30.	run

(based on the Laycock Mental Abilities Test, S.R. Laycock, University of Saskatchewan, Canada)

ANALOGIES

TO THE STUDENT:

Read each item, then find and circle the word which best completes the statement. First, do the sample items. If you do not understand what to do, ask your instructor. You will have four minutes to complete the test.

SAMPLES:

1. Day is to night as yes is to--perhaps, no, maybe, if.

2. Ship is to ocean as car is to--land, desert, forest, lake.

DO ALL OF THE FOLLOWING LIKE THE SAMPLES

1. Dog is to puppy as cat is to--mouse, dog, rat, kitten.

2. Sheep are to flock as cattle are to--herd, pack, bunch, group.

3. Head is to hat as foot is to--toe, hair, shoe, knee.

4. Dry is wet as heavy is to--light, hard, soft, firm.

5. Handle is to hammer as knob is to--lock, key, door, brass.

6. Sugar is to pound as milk is to--cream, quart, sweet, barrel.

7. Table is to furniture as apple is to--fruit, cherry, seed, leaf.

8. Wash is to face as sweep is to--broom, nail, floor, straw.

9. Book is to pages as forest is to--wood, trees, leaves, deer.

10. Chat is to flat as must is to--how, cow, shop, dust.

11. Eye is to blind as ear is to--hear, deaf, wax, hearing.

12. Man is to blood as trees are to--leaves, branches, sap, water.

ANALOGIES (cont.)

13. Die is to dead as finish is to--finishing, finishes, will finish, finished.

14. 8 is to 64 as 9 is to--54, 81, 90, 45.

15. Picture is to painter as book is to--author, artist, school, library.

16. Neck is to collar as wrist is to--hand, cuff, coat, elbow.

17. Peach is to pit as apple is to--peel, red, tree, seed.

18. Fish is to trout as bird is to--sing, nest, sparrow, tree.

19. Trial is to judge as meeting is to--rules, speakers, chairperson, hall.

20. 3 is to 12 as 12 is to--24, 36, 48, 60.

21. Promise is to break as secret is to--betray, keep, guess, trust.

22. Lake is to shore as plate is to--horizon, beach, rim, ford.

23. Doctor is to patient as lawyer is to--judge, trial, prisoner, client.

24. Honesty is to virtue as stealing is to--vice, lying, criminal, trial.

25. H is to C as Q is to--P, M, L, N.

26. Monday is to Saturday as Friday is to--Tuesday, Sunday, Wednesday, Thursday.

27. Success is to ambition as failure is to--loss, defeat, energy, laziness.

28. Discover is to invent as exist is to--find, create, know, remove.

29. Point is to line as line is to--surface, curve, dot, solid.

30. Evolution is to revolution as crawl is to--baby, stand, run, creep.

■ JOURNAL QUESTIONS

1.   Which of the elements of thought do you rely on the most? Do you make much use of images? Or do you tend to think more in language, symbols, or concepts? Do you have any awareness of muscular imagery in your thinking?

2.   What feelings and images do you associate with the words "exam", "mother", "sex", "flag", "cross", and "blood". How do your feelings compare with the denotative meanings of these words?

3.   Do you have a pet? To what extent do you think your animal (or the pet of a close friend) has the capacity to "think"?

4.   Give an example of a time you solved a problem through "trial and error." What other strategies do you use? How could you have solved this problem more effectively? What heuristics might have helped?

5.   Who is the most "insightful" person you have ever known? In what situations do you behave most "insightfully"?

6.   The "average" IQ is 100. What do you think your IQ is? Why? What experiences have you had over your life that makes you think of yourself as a very smart or a not-so-smart person?

7.   Do you know friends who were part of the "gifted" program in elementary or high school? If you were a part of this program, how did you feel? If you were not a part of it, how did you feel?

8.   Were you raised in a "stimulating" or a "boring" environment? Did your childhood environment add to or take away from your intellectual development?

9.   How creative do you think you are? Why? What experiences have made you feel you are/are not creative?

10. Describe a time when intuitive thinking served you well. Describe a time when it got you in trouble or let you down.

11. Do you believe intelligence is inherited or learned? Support your position.

■ SUGGESTIONS FOR FURTHER READING

Anderson, J. *Cognitive Psychology and its Implications,* 4th ed. W. H. Freeman, 1995.

Best, J. B. *Cognitive Psychology,* 5th ed. Wadsworth, 1999.

Bramsford, J. D. and B. S. Stein. *The Ideal Problem Solver: A Guide to Improving Thinking.* W. H. Freeman, 1993.

Chomsky, N. *Rules and Regulations.* Columbia University Press, 1980.

Cronbach, L. *Essentials of Psychological Testing,* 5th ed. Harper and Row, 1990.

deBono, Edward. *Lateral Thinking: Creativity Step-by-Step.* HarperCollins, 1990.

DeLuce, J. and H. T. Wilder (Eds.). *Language in Primates: Perspectives and Implications.* Springer-Verlag, 1983.

Ellis, A. and G. Beattie. *The Psychology of Language and Communication.* Guilford Press, 1986.

Eysenck, H. J. and L. Kamin. *The Intelligence Controversy.* Wiley, 1981.

Garcia, J. "IQ: The Conspiracy." *Psychology Today.* April 1972: 40-43.

Gardner, H. *Art, Mind, and Brain: A Cognitive Approach to Creativity.* Basic Books, 1984.

Herrnstein, R.J., and C. Murray. *The Bell Curve.* New York: Free Press, 1994.

Johnson, Lynn G. and Hatch, J. Amos. "A descriptive study of the creative and social behavior of four highly original young children." *Journal of Creative Behavior,* 24 (3), p. 205, 1990.

Koberg, D. and J. Bagnall. *The Universal Traveler*, New Horizons Ed. Crisp, 1991.

Mayer, R. *Thinking, Problem Solving, and Cognition,* 2nd ed. W. H. Freeman, 1992.

Miller, G. A. *Language and Speech.* W. H. Freeman, 1981.

Montagu, A. *Race & IQ.* Oxford University Press, 2001.

Osgood, Charles E. and Oliver C.S. Tzeng, (Eds.) *Language, Meaning, and Culture.* New York: Praeger, 1990.

Patterson, F. and E. Linden. *The Education of Koko.* Henry Holt & Co., 1988.

Premack, D. "Animal Cognition." *Annual Review of Psychology* (34) 1983: 351-362.

Rosenthal, R. and L. Jacobson. *Pygmalion in the Classroom.* Irvington Publications, 1992.

■ MEDIA SUGGESTIONS

INTELLIGENCE (2002, from *Psychology—The Study of Human Behavior Telecourse,* Coast Community College District, 30 min.)
This program graphically demonstrates differences between the intellectually gifted and the developmentally disabled.

INTELLIGENCE, CREATIVITY, AND THINKING STYLES (2000, Films for the Humanities and Sciences, 29 min.)
An interview with intelligence expert Robert Sternberg, in which he discusses the "single trait notion" of intelligence and his triarchic theory of intelligence.

INTELLIGENCE AND CREATIVITY (2002, from *Psychology—The Human Experience Telecourse,* Coast Community College District, 30 min.)
This program explores what intelligence means in different environments and cultures, discusses nature vs. nurture, and biases of intelligence testing.

INTELLIGENCE AND CREATIVITY (2001, Insight Media, 30 min.)
This video investigates the effects of nature and nurture on intelligence, and probes the history and criticisms of intelligence testing.

INTELLIGENCE: A NEW DEFINITION FOR THE INFORMATION AGE (2000, Films for the Humanities and Sciences, 77 min.)
This program critically examines intelligence and technology in today's world.

LANGUAGE AND COGNITION (2002, from *Psychology—The Human Experience Telecourse,* Coast Community College District, 30 min.)
This program explores the fact that most animals have the ability to communicate, but only humans have language, symbols for objects, actions, ideas, and feelings.

LANGUAGE DEVELOPMENT (2001, from *Discovering Psychology Series,* Annenberg/CPB, 30 min.)
The development of language and the study of how children use language in social communication.

TESTING AND INTELLIGENCE (2001, from *Discovering Psychology Series,* Annenberg/CPB, 30 min.)
A description of the field of psychological assessment.

UNLOCKING LANGUAGE (1998, Insight Media, 29 min.)
In this video, an evolutionary linguist, a neurologist, a geneticist, a neuropsychologist, a developmental cognitive neuroscientist, and a professor of communication explore the birth, development, and transmission of language.

A number of videos are available from Thomson. Videos appropriate for this chapter include the following films from the CNN TODAY Introductory Psychology Video Series:

Volume 3, Section 7: Intelligence and Psychological Testing
      Emotional Intelligence (7:01)

■ COMPUTER AND INTERNET RESOURCES

PSYCHNOW!

Learning & Cognition:
Cognition and Language
Problem Solving and Creativity

INFOTRAC

Subject Guide/Key Words: Cognition and Thought, Synesthesia, Visual Imagery, Concept Formation, Chomsky, Sign Language, Primate Language, Artificial Intelligence, Human Intelligence, IQ tests, Intelligence Testing, Gifted Children, Mental Retardation, Heredity and Intelligence, Divergent Thinking, Giftedness, Multiple Intelligences, Heuristics

WEB SITES

Wadsworth Online Psychology Study Center:
http://info.wadsworth.com/cooessentials9

AmoebaWeb Psychology Resources: Cognitive Psychology:
http://www.vanguard.edu/faculty/ddegelman/amoebaweb/index.cfm?doc_id=856

IQ Tests:
http://www.psychtests.com/cgi-bin/search/htsearch

Braintainment:
http://world.brain.com/

What's Your Emotional Intelligence Quotient?
http://www.helpself.com/iq-test.htm

The ARC: A National Organization on Mental Retardation:
http://thearc.org/

American Mensa:
http://www.usa.mensa.org/

Creativity Web:
http://www.ozemail.com.au/~caveman/Creative/

Psychology Links: Language and Cognition:
http://www.tamiu.edu/coah/psy/langcog.htm

International Dyslexia Association:
http://interdys.org/

National Aphasia Association:
http://www.aphasia.org/

A Guide to Artificial Intelligence Web sites:
http://www.gemstate.net/Susan/linksAI.htm

CHAPTER 10
Motivation and Emotion

■ LEARNING OBJECTIVES

To demonstrate mastery of this chapter the student should be able to:

1.   Define motivation.
2.   Describe a motivational sequence using the need reduction model.
3.   Explain how the incentive value of a goal can affect motivation, and describe how incentive value is related to internal need.
4.   List and describe the three types of motives and give an example of each.
5.   Define homeostasis.
6.   Discuss why hunger cannot be fully explained by the contractions of an empty stomach.
7.   Describe the relationship of each of the following to hunger:
    a.   blood sugar
    b.   liver
    c.   hypothalamus
        1.   satiety system (ventromedial hypothalamus)
        2.   blood sugar regulator (paraventricular nucleus)
        3.   neuropeptide Y (NPY)
        4.   glucagon-like peptide 1 (GLP-1)
8.   Explain how a person's set point is related to obesity in childhood and adulthood.
9.   Explain the relationship between how much a person overeats and the person's obesity.
10.   Describe the relationship between emotionality and overeating.
11.   Explain the paradox of "yo-yo" dieting.
12.   Explain what is meant by behavioral dieting, and describe the techniques which can enable you to control your weight.
13.   Describe the impact of cultural factors and taste on hunger.
14.   Explain how a taste aversion is acquired, give a practical example of the process, and briefly explain why psychologists believe these aversions exist.
15.   Describe the essential features of the eating disorders anorexia nervosa and bulimia nervosa. Explain what causes them and what treatment is available for them.
16.   Name the brain structure that appears to control thirst (as well as hunger). Differentiate extracellular and intracellular thirst.
17.   Explain how the drive to avoid pain and the sex drive differ from other primary drives.
18.   Briefly describe the impact of hormones and alcohol on the sex drive.
19.   Describe the evidence for the existence of stimulus drives for exploration, and manipulation, curiosity, and stimulation.

20. Explain the arousal theory of motivation including the inverted U function.
21. Relate arousal to the Yerkes-Dodson law and give an example of it.
22. Describe the two major components of test anxiety and describe four ways to reduce it.
23. Define need for achievement (nAch) and differentiate it from the need for power.
24. Describe people who are achievers, and relate nAch to risk taking.
25. Describe the research of Russell, Rowe, and Smouse concerning the effectiveness of subliminal perception
26. Explain the influences of drive and determination in the development of success for high achievers.
27. List (in order) the needs found in Maslow's hierarchy of motives.
28. Explain why Maslow's lower (physiological) needs are considered prepotent.
29. Define meta-need and give an example of one.
30. Distinguish between intrinsic and extrinsic motivation, and explain how each type of motivation may affect a person's interest in work, leisure activities, and creativity.
31. Explain what is meant by the phrase, "emotions aid survival."
32. List and describe the three major elements of emotions.
33. List the eight primary emotions proposed by Plutchik and explain his concept of mixing them.
34. Explain how a person may experience two opposite emotions simultaneously.
35. Describe, in general, the effects of the sympathetic and the parasympathetic branches of the ANS during and after emotion.
36. Describe the relationship between pupil dilation and emotion.
37. Define "parasympathetic rebound" and discuss its possible involvement in cases of sudden death.
38. Describe the cost of suppressing emotions.

The following objectives are related to the material in the "Exploring Psychology" section of the text.
39. Explain how the polygraph detects "lies."
40. Discuss the limitations and/or accuracy of lie detector devices.

41. Discuss Darwin's view of human emotion.
42. Briefly describe cultural and gender differences in emotion.
43. Describe the evidence that supports the conclusion that most emotional expressions are universal.
44. Define kinesics.
45. List and describe the three emotional messages conveyed by facial expressions and body language.
46. Explain how overall posture can indicate one's emotional state.
47. Briefly describe the James-Lange theory of emotion.
48. Briefly describe the Cannon-Bard theory of emotion.
49. Briefly describe Schachter's cognitive theory of emotion and give experimental evidence to support his theory.

50.   Describe and give an example of the effects of attribution on emotion.
51.   Briefly describe the facial feedback hypothesis.
52.   Discuss the role of appraisal in the contemporary model of emotion.

The following objective is related to the material in the "Psychology in Action" section of the text.

53.   Describe the concept of emotional intelligence and how it may enhance one's life.
54.   List five emotional intelligence skills.
55.   Briefly describe the benefits of positive emotion.

■ DISCUSSION QUESTIONS

1.   Which of the primary drives do you consider the strongest? Why? Which occupies the greatest amount of your time and energies? How could the strength of the primary drives be determined for animals?

2.   Discuss some of the factors that contribute to overeating at Thanksgiving or a similar feast.

3.   What would be some of the disadvantages of trying to control eating by burning out (ablating) the lateral hypothalamus?

4.   It is noon in July in the desert. You have been sweating in the sun and enjoying the warmth. You are suddenly thirsty. Why? What should you do about it?

5.   The sex drive is not essential for individual survival, and it can be easily interrupted by any of the other primary drives. Why do you think so much energy is directed toward sexuality in our culture?

6.   Why do most menopausal women report no significant reductions in sexual arousal and activity?

7.   In what ways have you observed the stimulus motives at work in human behavior? Does learning contribute to curiosity or needs for stimulation?

8.   You are the manager of a professional football team. You tell the team, "You've got to get up for this game." Explain your statement in terms of the ideas from this chapter.

9.   Does the American emphasis on competition (in your opinion) encourage achievement or discourage it? (Consider the effects, for example, when only one person can be considered the "winner" in many situations.)

10.   How could you apply the concept of incentives to improve your motivation to study?

11. In *Lady Windermere's Fan*, playwright Oscar Wilde said, "In this world there are only two tragedies. One is not getting what one wants, and the other is getting it. The last is the real tragedy." What do you think Wilde meant? Where does your motivation come from?

12. If you had a guaranteed income, would you "work?" What do you think you would spend your time doing? For how long? What, if anything, does this reveal about sources of intrinsic motivation?

13. How has our culture contributed to eating problems such as obesity, anorexia nervosa, and bulimia? In some cultures, a degree of fatness is considered desirable as a hedge against starvation. Do we label people "fat" when they are perfectly healthy?

14. Do you consider yourself more emotional or less emotional than average? What role has learning played in the development of your emotional life? (Consider the influence of family, friends, and culture.)

15. In what ways have emotions contributed to your enjoyment of life? In what ways have they caused problems for you?

16. There is an element of truth to each of the theories of emotion. What parts of each seem to apply best to your own emotions?

17. What would be the advantages and disadvantages of being emotionless? (You might use Mr. Spock from the "Star Trek" movies, Mr. Data from "Star Trek: The Next Generation," or Mr. Tuvok from "Star Trek: Voyager" as a model for answering this question.)

18. In your opinion, what limits, if any, should be placed on the use of lie detection devices by businesses? By the military? By government?

19. Did you learn "body language" from your parents? How similar are your facial and hand gestures to theirs?

20. An atmosphere of competition and evaluation pervades many schools. How might this contribute to test anxiety? Do you think that the amount of testing done in schools should be increased or decreased? What alternatives would you propose if testing were decreased?

■ LECTURE ENHANCEMENTS

1.   **To explore the idea of incentive value, give students play money.** Write various goals on the chalkboard, such as: "How much would you pay to lose 10 pounds? To have a regular sex partner? To get an 'A' in this class? To get a well-paying job? To improve a personal relationship? To live to the age of 100?" Then conduct an auction. Ask students to explain why they bid as they did.

2.   **The "Attitudes Toward Eating" survey that follows can be completed individually by students.** The purpose is not to formally score the scale, but rather, to alert students to the types of behaviors associated with eating disorders. However, students who agree with many of the items may realize that they may have an eating disorder, so be prepared to refer them to a campus clinic or eating disorders program if either is available.

     This questionnaire is based on ideas from D. M. Garner and D. E. Garfinkel (Toronto General Hospital, Toronto, Canada). It has been used successfully to predict the likelihood a client will develop anorexia nervosa and/or bulimia nervosa. For more information, see *Handbook of Psychotherapy for Anorexia and Bulimia* (Garner and Garfinkel, 1984, Guilford Press).

Attitudes Toward Eating

DIRECTIONS: Select the number that describes how frequently you behave this way or have these feelings about your behavior. Write that number to the left of each statement.

1 = never 2 = rarely 3 = sometimes 4 = usually 5 = always

_____   1. I feel terrified about being overweight.
_____   2. I don't eat even when I am feeling physically hungry.
_____   3. I am preoccupied with thoughts about food.
_____   4. I experience eating binges and find it difficult to stop eating.
_____   5. I cut my food into a specific number of small pieces.
_____   6. I am aware of the calorie content of the foods I eat.
_____   7. I eat foods rich in grain carbohydrates but low in fat. (For example, bread, rice, potatoes).
_____   8. I feel that others would prefer if I ate a greater quantity of food.
_____   9. I vomit after I have eaten.
_____   10. I feel extremely guilty after eating.
_____   11. I often think about wanting to be thinner.
_____   12. I am aware of the number of calories I burn up when I exercise.
_____   13. Other people think I am too thin.
_____   14. I am upset when I discover fat on my body.
_____   15. I eat very slowly in comparison to others.

_____ 16. I avoid foods that contain sugar.

_____ 17. I eat foods manufactured for dieters.

_____ 18. Food seems to control most of my life.

_____ 19. I demonstrate great self-control when around food.

_____ 20. Others seem to pressure me to eat.

_____ 21. I think too often about food.

_____ 22. I feel uncomfortable after eating sweets.

_____ 23. I am always trying to cut down on the amount of food I eat.

_____ 24. I enjoy the feelings of having an empty stomach.

_____ 25. I enjoy tasting new foods, even if the food is high in calories or fat.

3.   **Ask students to bring to class their favorite diet.** Make a few copies of the best and worst examples. Give the diets to small groups of students for discussion. Ask them to predict the short-term and long-term effectiveness of each diet.

4.   **An exercise can be developed around the results of a projective approach to assessing nAch.** Find a somewhat ambiguous photo in a magazine and ask students to write a short story telling what led up to the situation portrayed, what is happening now (including the feelings of the characters), and what will happen next. Stories can be scored (rather loosely) for the number of references to achievement themes and imagery (references to striving, trying, goals, excellence, success, planning, achievement, and so forth). Interview students with unusually high nAch as a basis for discussion and illustration. Other themes that can be interesting to look for are power, affiliation, and fear of success.

5.   **Have the class rate the importance of each of the following clusters of needs on a 10-point scale (1 = of little importance to me; 10 = extremely important to me).** Which cluster gets the highest rating? Where does this place the individual on Maslow's hierarchy of motives? Does this placement correspond to his or her self-perception? In what way does one's culture affect the area of emphasis on the hierarchy? Do students agree with Maslow's ordering of needs?

    a. A safe and secure house, dependable income, good health, predictable future, general sense of security.

    b. Respect from colleagues or co-workers, valued by others in the community, self-respect, and self-esteem.

    c. Perfection, justice, beauty, truth, autonomy, meaningfulness, simplicity.

    d. Close circle of family or friends, loved and cared for by others, loved by a special person, accepted in the community.

e. Good food, drink, sex, physical comfort, rest and vigorous activity, good night's sleep, life's physical pleasures.

It is fairly obvious that the items represent (in this order): **1)** safety and security; **2)** esteem and self-esteem; **3)** self-actualization (meta-needs); **4)** love and belonging; and **5)** physiological needs. The items are likely to be transparent even for a naive subject. Therefore, to get the most out of this exercise, it should probably be given before students have studied the material in Chapter 10 but discussed when the chapter has been read.

6. **Try to show how Maslow's theory helps us understand everyday problems.** How could an owner of a business use the hierarchy of needs to understand her employees, and how could she change conditions to improve morale and increase productivity? How could the theory apply to your own classroom, to problems between parent and child, boyfriend and girlfriend, etc?

7. **Discuss the notion of willpower with students.** This is a problem for many people. Most of us have "too little" of it, whatever it is. Have the students examine this concept in the light of the theories they have been studying. Behaviorists would say there is no such thing; our actions are simply the result of association and reinforcement. The notion of motivation as a force to generate behavior would be unacceptable to a behaviorist. Willpower, from a cognitive point of view, is an internal force that moves a person in some direction. Behavior is powered by strong needs, or guilt, or anxiety. How would humanistic psychologists view this concept? Using this kind of discussion, you should be able to get students to see how these theories explain behavior more clearly. Instead of willpower, you could use conscience as the concept to be discussed.

8. **A good way to clarify the cognitive view of emotion is to seek examples from the class in which they were "fooled" by an emotional situation,** so that an initial reaction of fear or apprehension gave way to relief or laughter. Point out that the foundation of physiological arousal remained--only the perception or interpretation changed.

9. **If you can obtain a galvanic skin response instrument, you can show the sympathetic nervous system in action:** Attach the sensors to the fingers of a volunteer and have the class ask some provocative questions. (You may need to screen them ahead of time to avoid being provoked or embarrassed yourself.) Even without a verbal response from the subject, the GSR will show an increase in the level of moisture on the skin (perspiration) due to sympathetic nervous system arousal.

10. **You have discussed the polygraph and how it works.** Students are aware of its usefulness and its limitations. Raise some questions with the class about its use and abuse. Ask them to respond to the following questions:

a. How would you react if your employer were to demand regular polygraph tests of all employees?

b. Should the polygraph be used to check up on government officials?

c. What do you think about "lie detecting" in the future? How will it be different?

■ ROLE-PLAYING SCENARIOS

1. **You are a person who finds it impossible to gain weight.** You are very tired of people asking you if you are anorexic and treating you as if you are emotionally unstable.

2. **You just lost fifty pounds.** You are receiving positive feedback about your appearance, but you don't seem to be any happier than you were before.

3. **You are the director of an eating disorders clinic.** How would you decide who needed out-patient care? What kind of a program would you suggest? What kind of follow up would you provide? How would you measure "success"?

4. **You are a politician running for a student government office.** Describe to the class why you think you should be elected.

5. **You are the first person from your family to graduate from high school and now you are starting college.** You know you can succeed, but there is a part of you that is afraid of the responsibilities that success in college can bring. Tell you best friend about these feelings.

6. **You have just taken a polygraph exam at your place of employment.** The polygraph operator says that you failed and that you are suspected of stealing. You know that you are innocent. Defend yourself.

■ VALUE-CLARIFICATION STATEMENTS

1. Success is 1 percent inspiration and 99 percent perspiration.

2. Children should not be paid for getting good grades.

3. The results of polygraphs should be admissible in court.

4. Any new employee should not be required to take a lie detector test before starting a new job.

5. If a person consistently exercises, he or she can lose weight.

6.   Bulimia nervosa is a symptom of a larger problem--an inability to delay gratification.

7.   It would be better if humans never felt emotion.

8.   Subliminal stimuli in advertising should be banned.

■ ONE-MINUTE MOTIVATORS

1.   **Depending on the season and your classroom, you can demonstrate homeostasis by turning the thermostat in your room up or down** and waiting until a student complains and asks you to alter the temperature.

2.   **Provide students with many baskets of chips and salty peanuts.** Be sure that no one has any liquid in class to drink. Wait until one student asks to run outside for a drink of water. Discuss intracellular thirst.

3.   **Give students the first five minutes of class to complete a large wooden or a jigsaw puzzle.** Stop students before the puzzle is complete and return to lecture/discussion. Be sure the puzzles are within touching distance of many students. Ask a student before class to count the number of times students reach out to complete the puzzles. Discuss human curiosity and manipulation needs. You may also want to discuss the motivational properties of frustration that results from interrupted goal-seeking.

4.   **Arrange students in pairs.** Ask half of the pairs to engage in five minutes of aerobic exercise. Ask the other half to meditate. Then give each pair some pick-up sticks. Each pair decides who is the observer and who is the subject. Count the number of sticks that can be carefully picked up. Discuss optimal arousal.

5.   **Play a quick series of games with points.** Ask trivia questions, guess numbers, or the like. Keep track of each student's points. Ask students to share feelings about winning and losing with a person sitting near them. What does this say about each person's need to achieve?

6.   **Ask students working in pairs to conduct an entire conversation using only facial expressions and gestures.** How much was understood? Why?

7.   **Ask students to spend one day intentionally smiling.** Ask them to jot down their feelings and the reactions of others to them. Share feelings the next day of class.

8.   **Call on people for impromptu speeches.** Break a balloon or turn on a buzzer just prior to pulling out a name. Discuss the role of anxiety and arousal as they relate to the fight/flight reaction. Remind students that these are normal reactions and that the challenge is to channel such responses into adaptive behaviors.

9. **There are some brief and fairly well designed quizzes on the Internet to measure emotional intelligence.** One of these sites is at http://quiz.ivillage.com/health/tests/eqtest2.htm. Assign this quiz to students, and reassure them that their results are confidential. Ask them to examine the results and determine if they agree with the assessment.

■ BROADENING OUR CULTURAL HORIZONS

1. **Some cultures encourage people to eat a sweet, fat, high-variety diet.** Other cultures encourage more savory, low fat, and less varied foods. Ask students to study the eating habits of different cultures. Is the Far Eastern diet becoming westernized? Or is the western diet becoming easternized?

2. **Ask students to bring to class the most unusual ethnic foods they can find.** Ask students to taste the foods; then have the provider describe the food and its cultural background.

3. **What cultures would you expect to have the least frequency of anorexia?** Why are most people with eating disorders female? As women play a more prominent role in business, will this gender difference change? How? Why or why not?

4. **Imagine a society without ads for food.** People can only eat what they raise. Money can be used to buy tangible objects or services but it cannot be used to buy food. What kinds of eating disorders would occur?

5. **What cultural biases may exist in the Zuckerman Sensation-Seeking Scale?** What assumptions does this scale make about human behavior?

6. **Make a list of all of the ways a culture could reinforce social behaviors.** What social behaviors do you perform? How are these reinforced? Do different ethnic groups and sub-cultures encourage different social behaviors?

7. **Look at your own family culture.** What forms of success are you encouraged to work toward? Do you think that other cultures share the same goals or define "success" in the same way?

8. **Are Maslow's motives universal?** Imagine a culture where social needs were more important than self-actualization needs. How would you test the universality of self-actualization? Are there many different ways self-actualization can be expressed?

9. **Most colleges have an increasingly diverse student population.** Imagine that you are one of five student government leaders wanting to put together a recycling campaign. One student is a 40-year-old Indian man; another is a 25-year-old single woman; another

is a 32-year-old white, single father; another an 18-year-old man; and finally a
22-year-old married Japanese woman. How would you go about motivating this diverse
group of people?

■ SUPPLEMENTAL ACTIVITIES

TO THE INSTRUCTOR:

The exercises that follow are designed to give students an opportunity to evaluate motivation in
an objective manner. They should be able to see how a psychologist tries to assess motivation.
At the same time, they should become aware of the difficulty of doing it scientifically and
getting hard data to work with. **Exercise #1** deals with the need for achievement. This is near
and dear to the hearts of students since they spend a great deal of time and energy in pursuit of
goals that will satisfy this need. Students should be able to arrive at a need level for themselves
and also see what characteristics are found in people who have high and low need levels.
Exercise #2 is intended to help students see the way in which Maslow's hierarchy of needs
functions in their lives. Students should begin to see that they are "on the road" and not yet "at
the destination" as far as personality development is concerned. **Exercises #3 and #4** provide
ways for students to explore linkages between emotion and behavior. Emotions are interesting to
study and discuss in class because they touch everyone. Each person has a unique experience
with emotions and, in the right circumstances, is willing to discuss them with others. The
classroom climate needs to be accepting before students will share feelings with each other.
They will often trust the teacher and reveal their thoughts and feelings. **Exercise #3** should be
non-threatening and will open up discussion of some personal experiences. In this exercise
students are asked to identify some fears that they have, and they are then asked to think about
ways to reduce them. **Exercise #4** illustrates the way that some words take on emotional
overtones. People show this by their behavior when they are confronted with these words or
ideas.

Exercise #1: nAch(oo!)

Pardon the pun! But just as the sneeze is a precursor of a cold, so some behaviors indicate the
existence of a need and the intensity of the drive to satisfy it.

I.   **Introduction**

       The items in this exercise describe some behaviors which are related to achievement
       motivation. People do not experience them all to the same degree, but put together they
       can be an indicator of the strength of the need for achievement. Have the students
       respond to the scale, total the points on all items, and report their scores. The highest
       possible score is 50 points; the lowest would be 10. On the scale achievement motivation
       could be evaluated as follows:

High: 40 - 50   Medium: 20 - 40   Low: 10 - 20

This could leave some people on the borderline with scores of 20 or 40. Other factors may need to be taken into account to determine in which group the student belongs. Students should be put at ease about this exercise. Be sure they understand that the results will not affect their standing in the class nor will it be a basis for personal judgments.

II.   **Procedure**

   A.   Distribute the scale to the students. Ask them to read the directions and follow them. They should be given as much time as needed--about 10 minutes.

   B.   Ask students to total their ratings to arrive at a score for the scale. They should note their own scores for future reference.

   C.   Collect the scales for further analysis.

   D.   Prior to the next class develop the following data:

      1.   Find a mean score for the class.
      2.   Identify the high and low achievers.
      3.   Pick out the items which distinguish most clearly between high and low achievers. You do this by identifying those items that all or most low achievers scored lowest on and high achievers scored highest on.

III.   **Discussion**

   A.   Make copies for the students of the items identified as common to high and low achievers. Discuss achievement motivation using these items as a starting point. Begin by asking students why they responded as they did.

   B.   Ask students if they felt this scale adequately sampled their achievement motivation. Could it be improved? How? (For this discussion you could put a copy of the scale on an overhead projector.)

MOTIVATION--NEED FOR ACHIEVEMENT (nAch)

TO THE STUDENT:

This is a five-point rating scale. Your responses should be based on how you feel about each item at the present time. This is not an evaluation of your work in this course, and your responses will be anonymous. Try to respond as accurately as you can. Rate each item as follows:

not characteristic of me	1
seldom characteristic of me	2
sometimes characteristic of me	3
usually characteristic of me	4
very characteristic of me	5

1.   I tend to be competitive and strive to excel in most activities I undertake. _____

2.   I often go out of my way to take on outside responsibilities in the college _____ and community.

3.   When thinking about the future, I emphasize long-term goals more than _____ short-term goals.

4.   I get bored easily by routine.   _____

5.   I tend to get upset if I cannot immediately learn whether I have done well_____ or poorly in any situation.

6.   I am generally not a gambler; I prefer calculated risks.   _____

7.   In choosing a career, I would be more interested in the challenge of the _____ job than in the pay.

8.   When I cannot reach a goal I have set for myself, I strive even harder to _____ reach it.

9.   If given the choice, I would prefer a highly successful stranger as a _____ co-worker to a friend as a co-worker.

10. I believe people should take personal responsibility for their actions.   _____

TOTAL FOR THIS SCALE   _____

Exercise #2: Needs: A Hierarchy

I.   **Introduction**--This is an exercise that should help students understand Maslow's hierarchy of needs. The goal is to have students examine their own experiences and find ways in which they satisfy needs at each of the five levels. They should use everyday examples such as the following:

A.   **Physiological needs**

1.   the need to get a sweater when the classroom is cold
2.   the need to get a cup of coffee after a "long, hard class"

B.   **Safety needs**

1.   stocking up on canned tuna so it will be there when needed
2.   putting a double lock on the front door

C.   **Love and belonging needs**

1.   joining the French Club at college
2.   checking on your best friend when she or he is sick

D.   **Esteem needs**

1.   working hard to get good grades
2.   helping mother with dishes after supper

E.   **Need for self-actualization**

1.   taking dancing lessons to be better at it
2.   volunteering to work with handicapped children at the park district pool

II. **Procedure**

A.   Pass out the worksheets to students to use for this exercise.

B.   Group the students in threes so they can discuss their experiences and select those that fit each level more easily.

C.   Ask students to produce their own list after sharing and discussing their ideas. Each student should produce his/her own list.

D.   Allow about ten minutes for this part of the exercise, then ask them to return to their own places.

E.   Now ask the students to evaluate these levels and try to see where they are at the present time. Each student should try to determine the level at which (s)he has the most difficulty and why. They should be asked to explain this in the space provided at the end of the worksheet.

F.   Have students turn in the worksheet for your review. You should not grade the sheet, but read it and make supportive comments on what is said. You will learn a good deal about your students from this exercise.

HIERARCHY OF NEEDS: A WORKSHEET   NAME_____

TO THE STUDENT:

In the space provided, try to identify and record some things that you do which are intended to satisfy needs at each level. Provide several examples of each. You can discuss this with your group members, but put down your own behavior, not theirs.

1.   Physiological needs

2.   Safety needs

3.   Love and belonging needs

4.   Esteem needs

5.   Need for self-actualization

Indicate the level of needs that you feel takes up most of your time and energy at the present time. At what level do you find yourself functioning most of the time? Explain what you do at that level and why it is keeping you occupied at present.

Exercise #3: Personal Fears

I.   **Introduction**

This exercise is intended to get students to think about their own fears. Fears can be a serious problem if they affect the quality of life of an individual. Often people don't face up to their fears but instead develop a lifestyle that avoids confronting situations that might cause feelings of fear to occur.

In doing this exercise students can, in a non-threatening way, assess their fears and try to evaluate the effect they have on their lives. If they are willing to share some of these with the class, they will have an opportunity to think them over and perhaps do something to change.

II.   **Procedure**

A.   Hand out to students a copy of the fear intensity scale which follows this exercise.

B.   Ask students to record on the scale those fearsome things, events, or situations that they can think of. They should place these items on the scale where they think they should fall. Each item should be clearly stated.

C.   Students should then be asked to think about ways to reduce the fears. Begin with the top item and work on down.

III. **Discussion**

A.   It would be good to start off some discussion in class by asking students to volunteer to give their top-rated fear. If a cooperative environment exists, students will try to help each other with suggestions.

B.   Be sure to bring in some psychological principles. You could have them explore the possibility of using techniques for extinction of unwanted behavior and reinforcement and shaping of new behaviors.

C.   Either individually or in groups, students should think of ways to change this behavior. Ask them to write down ideas for changing their fear behaviors.

PERSONAL FEARS: INTENSITY SCALE

INTENSE	100-
	95-
	90-
	85-
	80-
	75-
	70-
STRONG	65-
	60-
	55-
	50-
	45-
	40-
MILD	35-
	30-
	25-
	20-
	15-
	10-
WEAK	5-

TO THE STUDENT: Indicate on the scale the intensity of some of your fears. Below, write some of the reasons for the more intense fears and some ideas you have for changing them.

Exercise #4: Words and Emotion

I.   **Introduction**

Words and numbers, as symbols, have no special significance in themselves besides their designated meaning. However, they take on added meaning and/or value as they are used in a culture. A number sequence such as 38-22-36 may have no special significance in itself, but when the number sequence is attributed to anatomical measurements, it takes on additional meaning. Word association techniques are used for diagnostic purposes because words are both motivational and emotional. Freud used word association in his psychoanalytic approach to behavior problems. Free association is initiated by words that have emotional content for the patient.

Some psychologists have found significance in not only the word or words used but also to the length of time taken to respond and the behavior of the subject while responding. This exercise is designed to determine whether words which are emotional in content produce a different behavior from neutral words. For this study, the variable under observation will be the length of time between the stimulus word and the response.

II.   **Procedure**

A.   Make copies of the word list and data sheet for the students in the class.

B.   Divide the class into groups of three. Ask each group to identify a subject who is immediately sent out of the room. The other two in each group should divide up the work to be done; one will be the experimenter and the other the timer.

C.   Distribute a copy of the word list to each experimenter. Ask the experimenters to read over the directions while you read them aloud. Be sure both experimenters and timers know what they are to do. Review the role of each as follows:

1.   experimenter - present one word at a time, waiting after each for a response from the subject

2.   timer - use a watch with a large second hand or a stopwatch. Note the period of time between the stimulus word and the reaction time. Do not stop timing until the subject has given a complete word. Utterances such as, "uh," laughter, remarks such as, "That's a tough one," are not responses.

D.   Instruct the students to work out the average response time for the neutral words and the emotionally-laden words.

III.   **Discussion**

Some questions that can be raised with students should include the following:

A.   Was there any difference in response time between the neutral and emotional words? If a difference occurred, how do you account for it?

B.   Were there any differences between response times for the neutral words? Were reaction times any different to neutral words given after an emotional word than to those after a neutral word? If so, can you explain why?

C.   Does the level of association value make a difference in response time?

D.   If no significant differences occurred between the two means, does that mean that emotional connotations do not affect reaction time?

WORDS AND EMOTION: WORD LIST

TO THE EXPERIMENTER:

Read the following list of words to the subject, one at a time. Pause after each word to give the person time to respond. Give the recorder time to write the response and time. Emotion-laden words are designated by an asterisk (*).

Say to the subject:
I am going to give you a list of words, one at a time. After each word say the first word that comes into your mind. My partner will write down what you say. Here is the first word.

1.   cloud

2.   rape*

3.   leaves

4.   chair

5.   brother

6.   failure*

7.   flower

8.   communism*

9.   dog

10.   abortion*

11.   holiday

12.   paper

13.   table

14.   chocolate*

15.   groceries

WORDS AND EMOTION: WORD LIST

TO THE RECORDER:

Be sure to note the *exact time* (number of seconds) between the stimulus word given by the experimenter and the response of the subject. Also, make a note of the response in the appropriate place. Emotion-laden words are designated by an asterisk (*).

STIMULUS WORD	RESPONSE	RESPONSE TIME
1. cloud		
2. rape*		
3. leaves		
4. chair		
5. brother		
6. failure*		
7. flower		
8. communism*		
9. dog		
10. abortion*		
11. holiday		
12. paper		
13. table		
14. chocolate*		
15. groceries		

MEAN response time for: NEUTRAL WORDS _____

EMOTIONAL WORDS   _____

■ JOURNAL QUESTIONS

1. Describe a time when were you pushed to the limits of your endurance.

2. Make a list of your five key "needs." What drives the responses you take to reach a specific goal?

3. Can a person get too much of a "good thing"? Or could receiving a large quantity of "something" alter a person's perception and definition of a "good thing"?

4. Keep a "hunger pang journal." For three days try to avoid eating at habitual times and in response to external cues. Instead, delay eating until your body says that you are hungry.

5. What emotional states predict when you will overeat or undereat?

6. How long can you recline without doing anything? If you haven't tried this recently, give yourself a few hours to recline (no sleeping allowed). How does it feel? What kinds of thoughts did you have?

7. Do you perceive yourself to be an under-achiever, over-achiever, or at-ability achiever? For which specific abilities? Why?

8. Which level of needs in Maslow's hierarchy do you spend the greatest time satisfying? Keep a "motives" log as you move through the day from one level to another.

9. Make a list of those things you do daily that you would stop doing if it weren't for extrinsic reward. What activities are most intrinsically rewarding for you?

10. How moody are you? What cues do you give others to let them know "now" is not a good time to ask for a favor? Do you feel that you handle emotion well?

■ SUGGESTIONS FOR FURTHER READING

Bennett, W., and J. Gurin. *The Dieter's Dilemma.* HarperCollins, 1992.

Berlyne, D. E. *Conflict, Arousal, and Curiosity.* McGraw-Hill, 1960.

Brody, N. "Social Motivation." *Annual Review of Psychology,* (31) 1980: 143-168.

Darwin, C. *The Expression of Emotions in Man and Animals.* University of Chicago Press, 1965 (first published in 1872).

Dickinson, G. E., Leming, M. R., and A. C. Mermann. *Dying, Death, and Bereavement,* 5th ed. Dushkin/McGraw-Hill, 2000.

Franken, R. E. *Human Motivation,* 5th ed. Wadsworth, 2002.

Geen, R., R. Arkin, and W. Beatty. *Human Motivation.* Brooks/Cole, 1995.

Grossman, S. P. "The Biology of Motivation." *Annual Review of Psychology,* (30) 1979: 209-242.

Kubler-Ross, E. *On Death and Dying.* Scribner, 1997.

LaFreniere, P. *Emotional Development: A Biosocial Perspective.* Wadsworth, 2000.

Lepper. M. R. and D. Greene. *The Hidden Costs of Reward.* Erlbaum, 1978.

Lykken, D. T. *A Tremor in the Blood: Uses and Abuses of the Lie Detector.* Plenum Press, 1998.

McClelland, D. *Human Motivation.* Cambridge University Press, 1998.

McGee, M. G. and M. Snyder. "Attribution and Behavior: Two Field Studies." *Journal of Personality and Social Psychology,* (32) 1975: 185-190.

Orbach, S. *Fat Is a Feminist Issue.* Berkeley Publishing Group, 1994.

Plutchik, R. *The Psychology and Biology of Emotion.* Addison-Wesley, 1994.

Seligman, M. "Fall into Helplessness." *Psychology Today,* June 1973: 43-48.

■ MEDIA SUGGESTIONS

EATING DISORDERS (2002, Films for the Humanities and Sciences, 26 min,)
This film describes the personality profile of an individual more likely than others to develop anorexia, the symptoms of the disease, and the treatments available.

EMOTION (2002, Coast Community College District Telecourses, 30 min.)
Part of the *Psychology - The Study of Human Behavior Series*, this video illustrates the universality of certain human emotions.

EMOTION (2001, Insight Media, 30 min.)
This study of emotion looks at what constitutes an emotion and looks at key studies on the universality of emotions.

EMOTIONAL INTELLIGENCE (Insight Media, 28 min.)
This video addresses the relationship between coping and health, using the concept of emotional intelligence.

GENDER AND THE INTERPRETATION OF EMOTION (2002, Films for the Humanities & Sciences, 25 min.)
A report on an extensive investigation on the differences between men and women in the thoughts and feelings they ascribe to others.

MOTIVATION (2000, Coast Community College District Telecourses, 30 min.)
Part of the *Psychology - The Study of Human Behavior Series*, this video describes what motivates people to think, behave, and make choices.

MOTIVATION (2002, Insight Media, 30 min.)
This program offers an in-depth exploration of the biological and social theories of motivation, including Bandura's work on self-efficacy.

MOTIVATION AND EMOTION (2001, from the *Discovering Psychology Series,* Annenberg/CPB, 30 min.)
A review of what researchers are discovering about why we act and feel as we do, from the exhilaration of love to the agony of failure.

OBESITY: PAIN AND PREJUDICE (2002, Films for the Humanities & Sciences, 40 min.)
The problem of obesity is discussed against the backdrop of the recent trial of a San Francisco mother convicted of child abuse after her seriously overweight daughter died as a result of obesity.

THE SILENT HUNGER: ANOREXIA AND BULIMIA (2002, Films for the Humanities & Sciences, 46 min.)
This program specifically examines anorexia nervosa, bulimia nervosa, and binge eathing syndrome. Interviews with seven females who have all suffered from eating disorders, the father of a woman who died as a result of her disorder, and health professionals are included.

WHAT IS MOTIVATION? (Insight Media, 30 min.)
This video, with a business theme, looks at the classic theories of Taylor, Maslow, and MacGregor.

A number of videos are available from Thomson. Videos appropriate for this chapter include the following films from the CNN TODAY Introductory Psychology Video Series:

Volume 2, Section 3: Health
> Enjoying Anorexia (2:24)

Volume 3, Section 6: Intelligence and Psychological Testing
> Emotional Intelligence (7:01)

■ COMPUTER AND INTERNET RESOURCES

PSYCHNOW!

Motivation & Emotion:
Motivation
Emotion
Coping with Emotion
Stress and Health
Human Sexuality

PSYK.TREK

Unit 8: Motivation & Emotion
       8a: Hunger
       8b: Achievement motivation
       8c: Elements of emotion
       8d: Theories of emotion

INFOTRAC

Subject Guide/Key Words: Human Motivation, Emotion, Homeostasis, Hypothalamus, Eating Disorders, "Yo-yo" Dieting, Anorexia, Bulimia, Human Sexuality, Arousal Theory, Need for Achievement, Maslow, Intrinsic and Extrinsic Motivation, Biology of Emotion, Polygraph, Body Language, Emotional Intelligence, Kinesics, Human Sex Drive, Subliminal Perception

WEB SITES

Wadsworth Online Psychology Study Center:
http://info.wadsworth.com/cooessentials9

AmoebaWeb Psychology Resources: Emotion and Motivation:
http://www.vanguard.edu/faculty/ddegelman/amoebaweb/index.cfm?doc_id=860

The Center for Eating Disorders:
http://www.eating-disorders.com/

Overeaters Anonymous:
http://www.overeatersanonymous.org/

APA Public Communications: Controlling Anger:
http://www.apa.org/pubinfo/anger.html

Emotions and Emotional Intelligence Bibliography:
http://trochim.human.cornell.edu/gallery/young/emotion.htm

CHAPTER 11

Personality

■ LEARNING OBJECTIVES

To demonstrate mastery of this chapter the student should be able to:

1. Define the term personality and explain how personality differs from character and temperament.
2. Discuss the stability of personality.
3. Define the term trait.
4. Describe the trait approach and the type approach to personality, and explain the shortcoming of the type approach.
5. Explain the concepts self-concept and self-esteem and how they affect behavior and personal adjustment.
6. Briefly describe cultural differences in self-esteem.
7. Define the term personality theory.
8. List and describe the five broad perspectives of personality included in this chapter.
9. Characterize the general approach to the study of personality taken by a trait theorist.
10. Distinguish common traits from individual traits.
11. Define and give examples of Allport's cardinal traits, central traits, and secondary traits.
12. Distinguish between surface traits and source traits, and state how Cattell measures source traits.
13. Explain how Cattell's approach to personality traits differed from Allport's approach.
14. Discuss the five-factor model of personality.
15. Explain what a trait-situation interaction is.

The following objectives are related to the material in the "Exploring Psychology" section of the text.
16. Explain how twin studies are used to assess the relative contributions of heredity and environment to personality.
17. Discuss how the similarities in the personalities of twins can be explained.
18. Assess the relative contributions of heredity and environment to the makeup of personality.

19. List and describe the three parts of the personality according to Freud.
20. Describe the dynamic conflict between the three parts of the personality, and relate neurotic and moral anxiety to the conflict.

21. Describe the relationships among the three parts of the personality and the three levels of awareness.

22. List and describe Freud's four psychosexual stages. In your answer include an explanation of fixation and the corresponding age range for each stage.

23. Discuss the positive and the negative aspects of Freud's developmental theory.

24. Explain how behaviorists view personality and traits. Include a definition of the term situational determinants.

25. Explain how learning theorists view the structure of personality. Include in your discussion the terms habit, drive, cue, response, and reward.

26. Explain how learning theory and social learning theory differ. Include in your discussion a description of the terms psychological situation, expectancy, reinforcement value, and self-reinforcement.

27. Explain how self-reinforcement is related to self-esteem and depression.

28. Using the behavioristic view of development, explain why feeding, toilet training, sex training, and learning to express anger or aggression may be particularly important to personality formation.

29. Describe the role of identification, imitation, and social reinforcement in the development of sex-appropriate behavior.

30. Briefly explain how the humanists set themselves apart from the Freudian and behaviorist viewpoint of personality.

31. Describe the development of Maslow's interest in self-actualization.

32. Using at least five of the characteristics of self-actualizers listed in your text, describe a self-actualizing person. From the original list of eleven, evaluate yourself and explain what may be helping or hindering your self-actualization.

33. List and briefly explain or describe (where applicable) eight steps to promote self-actualization.

34. Describe Rogers's view of the normal or fully functioning individual.

35. Describe Rogers's view of an incongruent person.

36. Explain how "possible selves" help translate our hopes, dreams, and fears and ultimately direct our future behavior.

37. Explain how "conditions of worth," "positive self regard," and "organismic valuing" may affect personality formation.

38. Discuss the following assessment techniques in terms of purpose, method, advantages, and limitations:
    a. unstructured and structured interviews (include halo effect)
    b. direct observation (include rating scales, behavioral assessment and situational testing)
    c. personality questionnaires (include validity, reliability, and a description of the MMPI-2)
    d. honesty tests
    e. projective tests (include descriptions of Rorschach, TAT)

39.   Describe the personality characteristics of sudden murderers, and explain how their characteristics are related to the nature of their homicidal actions.

The following objectives are related to the material in the "Psychology in Action" section of the text.

40.   List and describe the three elements of shyness.
41.   State what situations usually cause shyness.
42.   Compare the personality of the shy and the non-shy. Include the concepts labeling and self-esteem.
43.   List and discuss the three major areas that can help reduce shyness.

■ DISCUSSION QUESTIONS

1.   If you could select only three personality traits, which would you consider most basic? Why?

2.   If you were selecting candidates for an extended space flight, how would you make your choices? What could you do to improve the accuracy of your judgments of candidates' personalities?

3.   Do you think that there is such a thing as "national character"? That is, do all Germans, all French, all Americans, all Canadians, and so forth, have some traits that are common to their national group? How likely is it that these perceived traits, if any, are actually stereotypes?

4.   Do you know anyone who seems to have a cardinal trait? What do you think are the central traits of your personality? Secondary traits?

5.   Can a person become "type cast" with respect to personality? Why? How? What can a person do to change how she or he is categorized by others?

6.   Compare and contrast Allport and Cattell's theories of personality. How are their ideas similar and different?

7.   Do you think that animals have personalities? Defend your answer.

8.   How could the personality of a child affect and shape the child's environment? How might expectations about twins affect the way the twins develop?

9.   Why do you think that media coverage of reunited twins (those separated soon after birth and reunited as adults) has exaggerated the role of genetics in human behavior and personality?

10.   Can you describe an action you performed recently that seems to represent operation of the id, ego, or superego? How would a behaviorist or a humanist interpret the same event?

11.   Can you cite a behavior or an experience that seems to support the existence of the unconscious or of unconscious motivation?

12.   Can you cite observations that support Freud's scheme of psychosexual stages? Can you cite observations that contradict it?

13.   Is "Mr. Clean" an anal-retentive?

14.   As a child with whom did you identify? What effect did this have on your personality? How does imitation differ from identification?

15.   Freud thought that adolescent males who clash with adult male authority figures (teachers, ministers, policemen, and so forth) are experiencing a carryover of the Oedipus conflict. What do you think?

16.   Recent studies show that teachers continue to treat boys and girls differently. Why is it so difficult to change these behaviors?

17.   What experiences have you had that have contributed to personal growth? What experiences set you back or were otherwise negative in their effects? Which personality theory best explains the differences between these experiences?

18.   Presently, what are the most prominent "possible selves" you visualize? How have these self-images influenced your behavior?

19.   Which theory of personality seems to best explain your personality?

20.   How would Freud explain the value of projective tests?

21.   Have you ever been interviewed or given a personality test? How accurate did you consider the resulting assessment of personality?

22.   Under what circumstances would you consider a personality test an invasion of privacy? Do you think it is acceptable for personality tests to be used to select job applicants?

23.   Which methods of assessing personality would be most appropriate for each major view of personality?

24.   How would Freud explain the shy personality? How would Skinner, Rogers, and Maslow explain shyness?

■ LECTURE ENHANCEMENTS

1.   **For an ambitious exercise, administer a complete personality inventory to class members.** Appropriate tests are the *Guilford-Zimmerman Temperament Survey* and the *Sixteen Personality Factor Questionnaire*. These tests can be attained from NCS Pearson, Inc., 1-800-627-7271, extension 5151.

An excellent alternate source of psychological tests is a classic trade book by Rita Aero and Elliot Weiner, titled *The Mind Test* (New York: William Morrow, 1981). This book includes a variety of scales and questionnaires appropriate for class administration. Some of the areas covered are personality, stress, fear, anxiety, depression, marriage, vocation, and interpersonal relationships. Most of the scales presented were drawn from journal articles and are of good quality. The following listings are particularly suitable for classroom use: *Locus of Control Scale, Self-Consciousness Scale, Death Concern Scale, Marital Adjustment Test, Beck Depression Inventory, Interest Check List, Social Interest Scale,* and the *Assertion Questionnaire.*

Many personality tests are available on the Internet, if one is careful about the selection. The Keirsey Temperament Sorter can be found at http://www.keirsey.com, and the Big Five Personality Test can be found at http://www.outofservice.com/bigfive/.

As an alternative to in-class testing, plot the personality profiles of one or two individuals (real or hypothetical) on the rating forms for one of the tests mentioned above. Duplicate the profiles for class distribution or present them with an overhead projector. Discuss the meaning of the various scales and the picture that emerges of the individual's personality.

2.   **Students can simulate a Rorschach test by making their own inkblots.** The instructor should bring a large bottle of a dark-colored liquid and an eyedropper. Ask students to fold a sheet of paper in half, then open it up. Put a few drops of the liquid into the fold and close it, pressing it flat. More than one application of drops may be needed to create a blot that is symmetrical and large. Students can then compare blots and discuss what they see.

An additional exercise might be to ask students to show their blots to several persons not in their class and record their responses. They should ask their subjects to respond to both the overall image and to particular parts of it.

Student discussion of the results should center on similarities and variations in responses with some speculation on reasons for this.

3. **It might be wise in connection with this chapter to remind students of the problems associated with easy acceptance of overly generalized and self-contradictory personality descriptions.** These are frequently found in magazine articles, popular psychology books, and online on the Internet. A recent example is an online test (available at http://www.colorquiz.com/) purporting to analyze personality on the basis of one's color preferences, loosely based on some early work by psychologists studying the impact of color. As with many such "tests," the descriptions given are fairly general and could apply to anyone. Here's a sample of a similar test result to share with your class:

> If your choice is red, you are an aggressive, extroverted person with strong desires and a craving for action. You are energetic, impulsive, and have a tremendous drive for success. You are quick to take sides and make judgments. However, you are not unreasonably stubborn, and in fact, may sometimes be too easily swayed in your feelings and attitudes. You dislike monotony in any form, and your search for activity may sometimes make you appear fickle. You tend to lack perseverance but may reach success through sheer energy and force of personality.

4. **Interest in environmental influences on personality traits can be heightened through the effects of birth order.** An exercise that dramatizes the differences in ordinal position consists of arranging students in small groups by birth order. Have students get into groups of only children, first-borns, middle children, and last-borns. Have each group select a recorder and give them about fifteen minutes to list what the group members consider to have been the advantages and disadvantages of their birth positions. After they are finished, have the recorder read the list aloud to the rest of the class. This exercise usually generates a great deal of interest and a lively discussion.

5. **To convey the flavor of the Freudian view of unconscious thought patterns, meanings, and associations, try having students follow a chain of associations to see where it leads.** Begin by asking the class to write the first word or thought that occurs to them when they hear one of these words: mother, father, death, birth, money, love, failure, breast, gun, rival. (Choose words you consider most interesting or likely to produce interesting responses.) After the first association has been written, ask students to write their first association to that word or idea. Continue through a series of eight or ten associations, then select a few papers for discussion. The linkages and endpoints can be fascinating.

6. **For a further investigation into Freudian dynamics, have students complete the statements that follow.** Can the resulting statements be categorized as id, ego, or superego responses?

I want to...	One should never...
If I could do anything, I would...	I won't ever...

Why do I...?	Realistically, I...
My plan is to...	I can't seem to...
I think a responsible person...	Ideally I...

7.   **To illustrate the importance of situational determinants of behavior, you might find it interesting to share this bit of information with students:** L. R. Kahle of the University of Michigan has reported that nearly half of the male students he tested cheated when they were deliberately given a chance to change test answers. Kahle used hidden pieces of pressure-sensitive paper to find out which students did or did not change answers on the test. You may want to discuss this finding in conjunction with the concepts of the psychological situation, expectancy, and reinforcement value.

8.   **Another good way to illustrate situational determinants and the behavioral view is as follows:** Instruct students to keep a careful record for a day of each person they talked with. Students should include a brief description of the circumstances, setting, nature of the interaction, and apparent reinforcement (information, approval, needed goods, etc.) provided by interacting with others. When the records are brought to class, ask students to discuss the external variables influencing how "sociable" their personalities appeared on the day in question.

9.   **You can give the students a chance to experience a projective test by preparing a TAT-like card.** Find a picture that is ambiguous and which can be copied. It should fit on an 8 1/2 x 11" sheet of paper. Make copies so that each student can have one. Ask the students to write a story about the card. What is going on in the scene? What led up to the action? What will happen next? When they are finished, ask the students to look over their responses. Look for themes and motives, such as aggression, achievement, love, anger. Students should be asked to share some of their stories with others. Ask other students to look for themes and motives in the reader's story.

■ ROLE-PLAYING SCENARIOS

1.   **What would the id, ego, and superego say in each of these situations?** What would you do in these situations?

   a.   You can't decide whether or not to eat a huge, very fattening hot fudge sundae after an already filling dinner.
   b.   You have been invited to a party the night before your psychology final exam.
   c.   You just found a wallet with $20 in it on campus. There is no identification in the wallet.
   d.   Your family is having a party on the same day when your friends are getting together.

2.   **Myrtle is trying to stop smoking.** But all it takes is the sight of matches and the craving returns. Speaking as a behaviorist, give her some hints about things she could do to make quitting easier.

3.   **You are interviewing for a job.** What nonverbal cues usually accompany the following thoughts? Pose for these thoughts: "I really care about this job." "I have the skills to do this very well." "I don't think this job pays enough." "I have been fired from other jobs; I hope they don't find out." "I don't want this job at all—just the experience of interviewing."

4.   **In pairs, have one person role-play a convicted murderer awaiting sentence and the other person role-play the attorney.** Switch roles. How did you feel in each role? Is it possible to empathize with another person while rejecting their behavior?

5.   **You are a psychologist seeing a client who gets extremely anxious whenever he is near a woman who has red hair, like his mother's.** Explain his feelings to him as a Freudian psychologist might. Next, explain his feelings from a social learning perspective.

6.   **Your usually quiet and reserved 12-year-old daughter is suddenly getting into fist fights at school.** Her sudden explosions of rage worry you. What should you say to her?

7.   **Act out an exaggerated form of direct and flippant "opening lines."** What should a person say to start a conversation? Practice using " open-ended questions."

8.   **You are majoring in medicine because your parents have always pressured you into becoming a doctor.** You aren't really happy in this field, and have begun to have some health problems and a lot of anxiety. How would you explain your feelings using Carl Roger's humanistic theory?

■ VALUE-CLARIFICATION STATEMENTS

1.   A person's personality does not change greatly from one situation to another.

2.   It is a bad idea to dress identical twins identically.

3.   Our real personality is primarily unconscious and something we may never really know.

4.   Freud's concepts of the anal-retentive and anal-expulsive personalities make absolutely no sense at all.

5.   Most people put themselves down too often.

6.   Children should be pushed to be toilet trained by the age of two.

7.   Parents should give their children "genderless" toys.

8.   Children's dolls should be anatomically correct.

9.   Humans are basically good.

10.   When all is said and done, people choose their own personality traits.

■ ONE-MINUTE MOTIVATORS

1.   **Ask students to check items on the Adjective Checklist in the text that they believe describe their personality.** Before the next class session, students should ask their best friend to check items on a duplicate list. Ask students to discuss the ways in which their choices differed from those made by their friend. This can be related to personality traits, testing, or self-concept.

2.   **How does our society reinforce the traits students used to describe themselves?**

3.   **Interview a set of identical twins.** Talk to each twin separately (with one waiting outside class). In what ways do they feel they are similar and different? Then bring them together for a joint discussion.

4.   **Have a conversation with a student who is directed to act unsocialized.** Discuss how difficult it is to put aside our socialization.

5.   **To demonstrate the preconscious, ask students to dredge up their earliest memory of a family holiday celebration.**

6.   **Give each student a 3 X 5" card.** Ask students to write three statements of self-praise for some behavior done frequently during the week. Pass these around the class so everyone can read each other's statements. Read a few of the statements. Then ask students to take their own card home and to place it in a visible location for a week. A week later discuss whether students noticed the card and whether they think it had any impact on their view of themselves.

7.   **Ask students to write a joke on a 3 X 5" card.** Ask for a group of volunteers to read through the cards and quantify the number of jokes that they perceive to be "hostile" versus "not hostile." Is it difficult to think of unhostile humor? Are jokes perpetuated because they express unconscious hostility? Because of the rewarding effects of

tension-release? Because of the social reinforcement of making others laugh? Because they express or enhance one's self-image?

8. **Develop a file of 8 1/2 X 11" pictures from magazines (or a series of slides).** Show students one picture or slide and ask each person to write a story. Ask students to share their story with the class or with the person next to them. Were there any sexual or aggressive interpretations? Did people fabricate bizarre interpretations? How do psychologists know whether a person taking a personality test is telling the truth or lying?

9. **Ask each student to engage another student in a five-minute conversation.** Repeat the same procedure with three other people. Ask students how they felt about the dialogue? Did they feel shy? Did they act shy? What did they do effectively in the conversation? What could they have done more effectively?

10. **Sophie Tucker once said, "From birth to 18, a girl needs good parents, from 18-35 good looks, from 35-55, a good personality, and from 55 on CASH."** Type this four ways: using "girl," "boy," "woman, "man." Distribute the forms randomly to the class and discuss whether the statement is true. Interestingly, many men in the class will find the term "boy" offensive but "girl" appropriate. Discuss gender-based differences in personality and expectations.

■ BROADENING OUR CULTURAL HORIZONS

1. **Who are your heroes?** Who do you identify with? How has this affected your self-concept? How has your culture helped define your heroes and models? Would other cultures make heroes of the same people we do?

2. **Imagine a society where people are rewarded when they give to the poor, live humbly, and stay physically fit.** What common traits would you expect to find in such a society? What do you think are the common traits of American society?

3. **How universal are Freud's concepts?** Would the strength and the role of each of Freud's structures of personality differ in various cultures? For instance, aren't some cultures more pleasure-oriented than others? Don't some acknowledge more libidinal energy than others? Could a boy develop a conscience if he never felt any rivalry with his father?

4. **Cultures vary widely in their views of toilet-training and breast-feeding.** What patterns are considered normal and desirable in mainstream American culture? What variations are you aware of in cultural or ethnic groups with which you are familiar?

5.   **Researchers traveling in China claim that they have never encountered a shy Chinese child.** What kinds of cultural differences do you think would account for this observation? How would you change our culture to reduce the incidence of shyness?

■ SUPPLEMENTAL ACTIVITIES

The **first two exercises** that follow are related to personality and should be of interest to the students. The first requires the student to involve others in exploring his/her personality traits and needs to be done outside class. The second can be done in class or at home by the student. Self-examination is always intriguing to the students. The **third and fourth exercises** in this section should engender student interest in knowing more about personality because they both deal with ways to look at one's own personality. Interest in the topic and classroom discussion should be easy to develop after one or both of these exercises. The third exercise requires students to rate themselves on a number of personality traits. They are instructed to rate themselves as they see themselves at the moment and then as they would like to be. The purpose is to get a measure of the discrepancy between their self-image and their self-ideal. They are asked to think and write about what they have found. The fourth exercise also focuses on self-concept. This time students should arrive at an idea of the type of self-image they have. This will give a global, or overall impression of how they see themselves (at least, that is the hope!)

Exercise #1: Personality Traits

The purpose of this exercise is twofold. The first is to force the students to think about traits and to try to determine which are important. The second is to give each student a chance to see that his/her view of the self may not be the same as what others see or think is important.

This exercise is complete with instructions, a rating sheet, and a summary sheet to collect all the ratings. The student is given directions and some questions to stimulate thought. You may wish to add to these.

You will need to duplicate sufficient copies of the rating sheet so that each student will be able to rate him/herself and have three or four raters. Each student will need one copy of the directions and the summary sheet.

Exercise #2: Personality Types

This is an Introversion-Extroversion scale developed by the author of this text. It can be administered to students in class or as a take-home project. It should generate interest in personality types and illustrate a typical self-report instrument.

Once the scores are obtained, you should give students an opportunity to discuss the results. They will have some immediate reactions to the validity of the scale based on their scores and their perceptions of themselves.

Another interesting classroom activity would be to plot all the scores on a single scale to see what kind of distribution would be found in the whole class. A graph could be constructed that would give the students an idea of the variability that exists.

PERSONALITY TRAITS: INSTRUCTIONS

TO THE STUDENT:

Attached is a list of terms that describe personality traits that are commonly found in the population. You can probably think of many others, but stick with these for this exercise.

The purpose of this exercise is to compare your own ratings of yourself with the ratings of others. Do others see you in the same way that you see yourself? Follow the directions to discover this.

1.   Make several copies of the list of terms. Ask three people to each separately rate you on the list of traits. You should also rate yourself. Select a variety of people to do the rating, such as a family member, friend, co-worker, neighbor, teacher, spouse, etc.

2.   You and each of your raters should select and check off 20 traits that describe you best. It may be hard to stick to 20, but force yourself (and your raters) to do so.

3.   On the summary-rating sheet, check off your choices and the choices of each of the raters.

4.   Now you can compare how you see yourself with the way others see you. You can also compare the responses of the different raters. They may not all agree with you or with each other!

PERSONALITY TRAITS: RATING SHEET

Rater's I.D._____ (Rater may wish to be
anonymous.)
Identification of personality traits of _____

Instructions: Check the twenty (20) traits from this list that best describe the person named above. Your
evaluation should be based on behavior that you have observed.

__boastful	__generous	__optimistic	__shy
__candid	__good-natured	__orderly	__sincere
__clumsy	__gracious	__outgoing	__skeptical
__compulsive	__grouchy	__patient	__sloppy
__considerate	__headstrong	__perceptive	__sly
__cooperative	__honest	__persistent	__smart
__cordial	__idealistic	__persuasive	__sociable
__courageous	__imaginative	__pessimistic	__studious
__courteous	__kind	__prejudiced	__suspicious
__crafty	__logical	__prideful	__tactful
__daring	__loyal	__punctual	__tense
__dependable	__mature	__reasonable	__truthful
__diligent	__methodical	__rebellious	__understanding
__efficient	__modest	__reliable	__unselfish
__energetic	__naive	__respectful	__vain
__ethical	__neat	__sarcastic	__versatile
__forgetful	__nervous	__sexy	__warm
__friendly	__open-minded	__short-tempered	__wholesome

PERSONALITY TRAITS: SUMMARY SHEET

In order to compare your own rating of yourself with the ratings of others, put your own twenty (20) checks on this chart first. Then put each rater's checks in the boxes provided.

	RATERS			
	ME	1	2	3
boastful				
candid				
clumsy				
compulsive				
considerate				
cooperative				
cordial				
courageous				
courteous				
crafty				
daring				
dependable				
diligent				
efficient				
energetic				
ethical				
forgetful				
friendly				
generous				

	RATERS			
	ME	1	2	3
good-natured				
gracious				
grouchy				
headstrong				
honest				
idealistic				
imaginative				
kind				
logical				
loyal				
mature				
methodical				
modest				
naive				
neat				
nervous				
open-minded				
optimistic				
orderly				

PERSONALITY TRAITS: SUMMARY SHEET (cont.)

	RATERS						RATERS			
	ME	1	2	3			ME	1	2	3
outgoing						sincere				
patient						skeptical				
perceptive						sloppy				
persistent						sly				
persuasive						smart				
pessimistic						sociable				
prejudiced						studious				
prideful						suspicious				
punctual						tactful				
reasonable						tense				
rebellious						truthful				
reliable						understanding				
respectful						unselfish				
sarcastic						vain				
sexy						versatile				
short-tempered						warm				
shy						wholesome				

PERSONALITY TRAITS: EVALUATION

Now you need to evaluate the results. The following questions should help you.

1.   Overall, does your selection of traits present a favorable or unfavorable picture of your personality?

2.   Do the traits identified by your raters present a favorable or unfavorable picture?

3.   How different are the traits selected by your raters from yours? In what ways do they differ?

4.   How do you explain the difference?

5.   Which of your traits appear to be most positive based on all ratings?

6.   Which of your traits appear to be most negative based on all ratings?

7.   What do you think about this type of evaluation of personality? Explain what you mean.

INTROVERTED? EXTROVERTED? WHICH ARE YOU?

TO THE STUDENT: To find out, mark true (T) or false (F) next to each of the statements below, and then follow the scoring instructions.

____ 1)   I tend to keep in the background at social events.

____ 2)   I prefer to work with others rather than alone.

____ 3)   I get embarrassed easily.

____ 4)   I generally tell others how I feel regardless of how they may take it.

____ 5)   I really try to avoid situations in which I must speak to a group.

____ 6)   I am strongly motivated by the approval or interest of others.

____ 7)   I often daydream.

____ 8)   I find it easy to start conversations with strangers.

____ 9)   I find it difficult to make friends of the opposite sex.

____ 10)   I particularly enjoy meeting people who know their way around the social scene.

____ 11)   I would rather read a good book or watch television than go out to a movie.

____ 12)   I would rather work as a salesperson than as a librarian.

____ 13)   I spend a lot of time philosophizing and thinking about my ideas.

____ 14)   I prefer action to thought and reflection.

____ 15)   I am often uncomfortable in conversations with strangers.

____ 16)   I am mainly interested in activities and ideas that are practical.

____ 17)   I would prefer visiting an art gallery over attending a sporting event.

____ 18)   I enjoy open competition in sports, games, and school.

____ 19)   I make my decisions by reason more than by impulse or emotion.

INTROVERTED? EXTROVERTED? WHICH ARE YOU? (cont.)

____ 20)   I have to admit that I enjoy talking about myself to others.

____ 21)   I like to lose myself in my work.

____ 22)   I sometimes get into arguments with people I do not know well.

____ 23)   I am very selective about who my friends are.

____ 24)   I make decisions quickly and stick to them.

SCORING:

1.   Go through the odd-numbered items and add the number of true and false responses. Put the numbers in the appropriate boxes.

2.   Go through the even-numbered items, adding the true and false responses. Enter the numbers in the proper boxes.

3.   Add only the ODD-false items to the EVEN-true items.

4.   The total thus obtained should be marked on the introversion-extroversion scale.

ODD ITEMS	True	False			
		True	False	EVEN ITEMS	
	TOTAL				

INTROVERT			EXTROVERT	
0	6	12	18	24

Exercise #3: "To Dream the Impossible Dream"

TO THE INSTRUCTOR:

This exercise should help students to see the difference between the way they are (or think they are) and the way they would like to see themselves. Often people don't realize there is a real difference even though they know that they fall short of what they think they ought to be. This should make the concepts clearer and more understandable.

Procedure:

1.   Discuss self-concept and self-ideal so students know what they are and how to determine the level of each.

2.   Explain the purpose of the rating sheet and provide one for each student.

3.   Read the directions to the students as they read them. Clear up any questions about what to do.

4.   Once students have completed both ratings, ask them to subtract the lowest rating from the highest and note the difference in the space at the right of each scale. The difference will be either zero, if both evaluations are the same, or they will be one or more units apart. Do not be concerned about which is higher or lower. (There should be no negative difference.)

5.   Ask students to respond, in writing, to the discussion sheet. It is important for each one to think out the meaning of the scores for him/herself. If the discussion is oral, only some will respond, and many will tend not to examine their scores or the concepts critically.

6.   Once the scales are done, and the responses turned in, some general discussion is useful to give students a chance to express their feelings and questions.

DREAM THE IMPOSSIBLE DREAM: RATING SCALE

TO THE STUDENT:

I.   **Rating Scale**

On a separate sheet you will be given a personal profile to complete. On it, there are fifteen rating scales, each measuring a personality trait. Each trait is on a nine-point scale with opposing aspects of the trait indicated at each end. You should do three things in the following order:

A.   Circle the number on each scale which best describes where you believe you are at present regarding the trait indicated. Do all fifteen in this way.

B.   Then do all fifteen again. This time mark an X over the number that best describes where you would like to be or hope to be some day in regard to each trait.

C.   Finally, indicate the size of the difference between the two marks for each trait in the space on the right.

D.   Work out the average of the differences. To do this, add up all fifteen differences as indicated in the spaces on the right. Divide that number by fifteen. That will give you the average.

II.   **Discussion**

After completing the rating scales and the calculations as directed above, write a brief response to each of the following:

A.   As you look over all fifteen scales, do the differences between your present status and your ideal vary greatly?

B.   Which traits had the largest differences and which had the smallest?
        largest: smallest:

DREAM THE IMPOSSIBLE DREAM: RATING SCALE (cont.)

3.   How do you feel about those traits where larger gaps exist between how you see yourself (your self-image) and where you would like to be (your self-ideal)?

4.   Do any of the larger differences exist because someone else has imposed the ideal on you? Or, have you accepted someone else's idea of what you should be, rather than deciding for yourself?

5.   Indicate those traits which you would like to change and feel could be changed to narrow the difference. What would you do differently?

6.   What do you think of the overall picture of yourself that you have identified? Do you see problems because of the size of the difference?

(based on an exercise by Wayne Weiten, College of DuPage, Glen Ellyn, IL)

SELF-CONCEPT vs. SELF-IDEAL: RATING SCALES

1.   Decisive   Indecisive   ____
      9   8   7   6   5   4   3   2   1

2.   Tense   Relaxed   ____
      9   8   7   6   5   4   3   2   1

3.   Easily Influenced   Independent Thinker ____
      9   8   7   6   5   4   3   2   1

4.   Very Intelligent   Not Very Intelligent ____
      9   8   7   6   5   4   3   2   1

5.   In Good Physical Shape   In Poor Phys. Shape ____
      9   8   7   6   5   4   3   2   1

6.   Undependable   Dependable   ____
      9   8   7   6   5   4   3   2   1

7.   Deceitful   Honest   ____
      9   8   7   6   5   4   3   2   1

8.   A Leader   A Follower   ____
      9   8   7   6   5   4   3   2   1

9.   Unambitious   Ambitious   ____
      9   8   7   6   5   4   3   2   1

10.   Self-confident   Insecure   ____
      9   8   7   6   5   4   3   2   1

11.   Timid   Adventurous   ____
      9   8   7   6   5   4   3   2   1

12.   Extroverted   Introverted   ____
      9   8   7   6   5   4   3   2   1

13.   Physically Attractive   Phys. Unattractive ____
      9   8   7   6   5   4   3   2   1

14.   Lazy   Hardworking   ____
      9   8   7   6   5   4   3   2   1

15.   Good Sense of Humor   Poor Sense of Humor ____
      9   8   7   6   5   4   3   2   1

Exercise #4: Who Am I?

I. Introduction

This exercise on self-concept is built around Louis Zurcher's *Twenty-Statement Test (TST)*. The students are asked to complete the statement, "I am..." twenty times. Then they are asked to categorize the statements into the four categories as outlined on the Interpretation Sheet. Zurcher found that the TST statements of an individual often fall into one category more than the others. He labeled the four categories as follows:

Category 1: the physical self
Category 2: the social self
Category 3: the reflective self
Category 4: the oceanic self (selfhood independent of the preceding three categories)

II. Procedure

A. Pass out the **Response Sheets** to the students. Ask them to follow the directions and complete the forms.

B. When they have finished, pass out the **Interpretation Sheet** and ask them to follow the directions. Circulate and help those who are uncertain about how to categorize a statement.

C. Ask them to indicate in which category their answers predominate.

III. Discussion

A. How do most students see themselves? Is there a majority in any one category?

B. Speculate on why the results came out as they did.

C. Zurcher says that a balance among all four components would be best for a person. Ask students if they agree and why.

IV. Reference

For more information consult, L. A. Zurcher's *The Mutable Self,* Sage, 1977.

WHO AM I?: RESPONSE SHEET

TO THE STUDENT:

Complete each of the twenty "I am" statements below. Complete each sentence saying something about yourself. Do not be too concerned about exactness. Say whatever you think of as it occurs to you.

1.   I am_____

2.   I am_____

3.   I am_____

4.   I am_____

5.   I am_____

6.   I am_____

7.   I am_____

8.   I am_____

9.   I am_____

10.   I am_____

11.   I am_____

12.   I am_____

13.   I am_____

14.   I am_____

15.   I am_____

16.   I am_____

17.   I am_____

18.   I am_____

19.   I am_____

20.   I am_____

WHO AM I?: INTERPRETATION SHEET

TO THE STUDENT:

You now have a difficult job to do. You need to classify each of your statements into one or another of four categories below. Read over all four categories. Be sure you understand what they are. Ask your instructor if you need clarification. Put each of the item numbers under the heading that seems most appropriate based on the descriptions below:

Category 1: Physical or traditional identification--includes one's sex, age, address, religion, etc. For example, "I am a woman," "I am a Green Thing from Mars."

Category 2: Social relationships--family, occupation, membership, etc. For example, "I am a student," "I am a middle child."

Category 3: Situation-free behavior--likes, dislikes, attitudes, etc. For example, "I am a lover of music," "I am for nuclear disarmament."

Category 4: Identity--this is how you describe yourself. You say who you are. For example, "I am a citizen of the world," "I am a living individual," "I am a person."

Place the number for each of the twenty statements in the columns below as you make your decision about which category is best.

Category 1	Category 2	Category 3	Category 4
_____	_____	_____	_____
_____	_____	_____	_____
_____	_____	_____	_____
_____	_____	_____	_____
_____	_____	_____	_____
_____	_____	_____	_____
_____	_____	_____	_____
_____	_____	_____	_____
_____	_____	_____	_____

■ JOURNAL QUESTIONS

1. If you could divide the people of the world into three categories, what would your categories be?

2. In what ways would our society deem you to be a "good" person? What unique qualities do you have that are not recognized by our society?

3. Where do you study? What could this say about your personality?

4. What traits do you have? How are these behaviors affected by your current life situation?

5. What childhood experiences were key in the development of your personality?

6. Which part of your personality is most dominant--the id, the ego, or the superego? When? What kind of anxiety do you experience according to Freud? How would Freud categorize your personality?

7. How did your parents handle your toilet training? If you don't remember, ask one of your parents or a sibling.

8. What did your parents do to shape your personality?

9. Think of a habit you have that you are proud of. How did it develop? How would Dollard and Miller explain this behavior?

10. Think of a habit you are not proud of. What cues could you try to pay attention to as a way to change this behavior?

11. Think of someone from your childhood who provided you with inconsistent affection or responsiveness. How did that affect the person's "reinforcement value" and your behavior?

12. What "conditions of worth" were applied to you as a child?

13. What are you willing to change in your life? What are you not willing to change, at least not now?

14. How self-actualized do you feel you are? Using a 1-7 point scale, rate the degree to which the ten characteristics of self-actualizers seem to apply to you.

15. To what extent do you consider yourself shy? How has this part of your personality developed? Under what circumstances do you feel more or less shy? Are you more publicly or privately self-conscious?

■ SUGGESTIONS FOR FURTHER READING

Adler, A. *The Science of Living.* Doubleday, 1929.

Aero, R. and E. Weiner. *The Mind Test.* Morrow, 1981.

Allport, G. *Pattern and Growth in Personality.* ITP, 1961.

Bandura, Albert. *Social Foundations of Thought and Action: A social cognitive theory.* Englewood Cliffs, New Jersey: Prentice-Hall, 1986.

Canfield, John W. *The Looking-Glass Self: An Examination of Self-Awareness.* New York: Praeger, 1990.

Cattell, H. B. *The 16PF Personality in Depth.* Institute for Personality & Ability Testing, 1989.

Cattell, R. B. *The Scientific Analysis of Personality.* Penguin, 1965.

Cronbach, L. J. *Essentials of Psychological Testing,* 5th ed. Harper and Row, 1990.

Fadiman, J. and R. Frager. *Personality and Personal Growth,* 5th ed. Prentice-Hall, 2001.

Freud, S. *An Outline of Psychoanalysis.* Norton, 1984.

Lindzey, G. and C. S. Hall. *Theories of Personality,* 4th ed. Wiley, 1997.

Jones, E. *The Life and Work of Sigmund Freud* (3 vols.). Basic Books, 1981.

Kagan, J. *Galen's Prophecy: Temperament in Human Nature.* Basic Books, 1997.

Kagan, J. "Temperamental contributions to social behavior." *American Psychologist,* 44 (4), 1989: 668-674.

Lanyon, R. I. "Personality Assessment." *Annual Review of Psychology,* (35) 1984: 667-701.

Loevinger, J. and E. Knoll. "Personality: Stages, Traits, and the Self." *Annual Review of Psychology,* (34) 1983: 195-240.

Maddi, S. R. *Personality Theories: A Comparative Analysis,* 6th ed. Brooks/Cole, 1996.

Mahoney, J. J. "Reflections on the Cognitive Learning Trend in Psychotherapy." *American Psychologist,* (32) 1977: 5-13.

Mischel, W. *Personality and Assessment.* Analytic Press, 1996.

—. *Introduction to Personality,* 6th ed. Wadsworth, 1998.

Olds, L. E. *Fully Human.* Prentice-Hall, 1981.

Pervin, L. A. *Personality,* 7th ed. Wiley, 1997.

Pleck, J. H. *The Myth of Masculinity.* MIT Press, 1983.

Rogers, C. R. *On Becoming a Person.* Peter Smith Pub. , 1996.

Zimbardo, P. G. *Shyness: What It Is, What to Do About It.* Perseus Press, 1990.

■ MEDIA SUGGESTIONS

BIRTH ORDER AND ITS EFFECTS (1997, Films for the Humanities and Sciences, 18 min.)
Heredity, environment, intelligence, and family birth order all help shape the personality throughout the formative years and into adulthood. Each position in a family can influence how a child interacts with other family members and friends. This program examines the only child, the firstborn, the middle child, and the youngest child, giving insight into behaviors and attitudes that seem to be shaped by birth order

BODY DOUBLES: THE TWIN EXPERIENCE (1997, Films for the Humanities and Sciences, 51 min.)
The study of twins is vital to research in biology and psychology. Twins separated at birth and later reunited are often quite similar. This similarity begs the notion that personality is formed by experience, and suggests that personality is genetically predetermined. This brilliant HBO documentary—with powerful interviews with numerous twins, including those conjoined, and a history of twin research from Josef Mengele to the University of Minnesota Twin Research Center—offers vehement arguments for and against this idea.

THE INTERPRETATION OF DREAMS (1996, Films for the Humanities and Sciences, 52 min.)
Few figures have had so decisive an influence on modern cultural history as Sigmund Freud, psychology's grand theorist—yet few figures have also inspired such sustained controversy and intense debate. In this program, Freud historian Peter Swales; Freudian psychoanalyst Barbara Jones; Peter Kramer, author of *Listening to Prozac;* and others analyze *The Interpretation of Dreams,* the concepts it contains, and the growing movement to reject them. Biographical details, dramatizations of Freud at work, and archival footage and photos add a personal dimension A Discovery Channel Production.

PERSONALITY (2002, from *Psychology- The Study of Human Behavior,* Coast Community College District, 30. min.)
This video introduces major theories of personality.

PERSONALITY THEORIES (2002, from *Psychology—The Human Experience Series,* Coast Community College District, 30. min.)
This video explores the three major theories of personality—Freudian, humanistic, and social-cognitive perspective—by examining the life of the former president of South Africa, Nelson Mandela.

PERSONALITY TRAITS AND ASSESSMENT (2002, from *Psychology—The Human Experience Series,* Coast Community College District, 30. min.)
This video looks at the ways we can evaluate and assess the many parts of our individual personalities.

SIGMUND FREUD (1995, Insight Media, 50 min.)
This video explores the career of Freud, from his early beginnings, elements of his theory, and his falling out with Jung.

THEORIES OF PERSONALITY (1994, Insight Media, 20 min.)
Interviewing clinical and research psychologists, this video examines five theories of personality: psychoanalytic (Freud, Jung, Erikson, and Adler), humanistic (Maslow, May, and Rogers), social-learning (Pavlov, Thorndike, Bandura, and Skinner), cognitive (Kelly), and trait (Allport, Cattell, and Eysenck). It also considers whether or not personality is stable over time.

A number of videos are available from Thomson. Videos appropriate for this chapter include the following films from the CNN TODAY Introductory Psychology Video Series:

Volume 4, Section 6:
        Freud (1:27)

■ COMPUTER AND INTERNET RESOURCES

PSYCHNOW!

Personality and Abnormal Psychology
Theories of Personality
Assessment

PSYK.TREK

Unit 10: Personality
        10a: Freudian theory
        10b: Behavioral theory
        10c: Humanistic theory
        10d: Biological theory

INFOTRAC

Subject Guide/Key Terms: Personality Theory, Personality Type, Introversion, Extraversion, Personality Trait Theory, Personality Trait, Five-Factor Model, Behavioral Genetics, Psychoanalytic Theory, Freud, Rotter and Expectancies, Locus of Control, Self Esteem, Maslow, Self-Actualization, Carl Rogers, Personality Tests, Personality Questionnaires, Honesty Tests, Shyness

WEB SITES

Wadsworth Online Psychology Study Center:
http://info.wadsworth.com/cooessentials9

Sigmund Freud and the Freud Archives:
http://plaza.interport.net/nypsan/freudarc.html

AmoebaWeb Psychology Resources: Personality:
http://www.vanguard.edu/faculty/ddegelman/amoebaweb/index.cfm?doc_id=869

Great Ideas in Personality:
http://www.personalityresearch.org/

The Personality Project:
http://fas.psych.nwu.edu/personality.html

Personality Tests on the WWW:
http://www.2h.com/Tests/personality.phtml

CHAPTER 12
Health, Stress, and Coping

■ LEARNING OBJECTIVES

To demonstrate mastery of this chapter the student should be able to:

1. Describe health psychology including its focus.
2. Define the terms behavioral medicine and lifestyle diseases.
3. List eleven behavioral risk factors that can adversely affect one's health.
4. Define the term disease-prone personality.
5. Briefly describe the research demonstrating the relationship of health-promoting behaviors and longevity.
6. Describe the impact of refusal-skills training, life skills training, and community health campaigns on illness prevention.
7. Define the term wellness by listing the characteristics of wellness.
8. Explain the similarity between your body's stress reaction and emotion.
9. List four aspects of stress that make it more intense and damaging.
10. Describe burnout. List and describe the three aspects of the problem.
11. Describe three things that can be done to help reduce burnout.
12. Give an example of how primary and secondary appraisal is used in coping with a threatening situation.
13. Explain how the perception of control of a stressor influences the amount of threat felt.
14. Differentiate problem-focused coping from emotion-focused coping and explain how they may help or hinder each other.

The following objectives are related to the material in the "Exploring Psychology" section of the text.

15. Describe the impact of traumatic stress, and list five ways to cope with reactions to traumatic stress.
16. Briefly describe what happens when traumatic stresses are severe or repeated.

17. List and describe the two different kinds of frustration.
18. List four factors that increase frustration.
19. List and describe five common reactions to frustration (see Figure 12-3).
20. Explain how scapegoating is a special form of displaced aggression.
21. Describe and give an example of each of the following four types of conflict:
    a. approach-approach

  b. avoidance-avoidance

  c. approach-avoidance (include the terms ambivalence and partial approach in your response)

  d. double approach-avoidance (include the term vacillate in your response)

22. Define the term defense mechanism. Discuss the positive value of defense mechanisms.

23. Describe the following defense mechanisms and give an example of each:

  a. denial   d. regression   g. compensation

  b. repression   e. projection   h. sublimation

  c. reaction formation f. rationalization

24. Describe the development of learned helplessness and relate this concept to attribution and depression.

25. Explain how learned helplessness may be prevented from spreading.

26. List three similarities between learned helplessness and depression.

27. Discuss the concept of hope and its relationship to mastery training.

28. Describe the six problems that typically contribute to depression among college students.

29. List the five conditions of depression and describe how it can be combated.

30. Discuss the relationship between life changes and long-term health. Describe the SRRS. Explain how hassles are related to immediate health.

31. Distinguish between psychosomatic disorders and hypochondria.

32. Name several of the most common types of psychosomatic problems.

33. List the causes of psychosomatic disorders.

34. Discuss biofeedback in terms of the process involved and its possible applications.

35. Differentiate between Type A and Type B personalities. Students should note the twelve strategies for reducing hostility and be able to apply them.

36. Describe what a hardy personality is and list the three ways such people view the world.

37. Explain the concept of the General Adaptation Syndrome. List and describe its three stages.

38. Explain how stress affects the immune system.

The following objectives are related to the material in the "Psychology in Action" section of the text.

39. Define the term stress management. Briefly discuss the College Life Stress Inventory.

40. List the three responses that are triggered by stress and discuss the stress management techniques that can be used to diminish or break the cycle of each response.

41. Define stereotyped response and give an example of it.

42. Discuss three effective ways to avoid frustration.

43. List four things to remember when dealing with conflict or a difficult decision.

■ DISCUSSION QUESTIONS

1. How could you reduce conflict or avoid an unfortunate decision in the following situations: choosing a school to attend, choosing a major, deciding about marriage, choosing a job, buying a car?

2. Calculate your life change score using the Social Readjustment Rating Scale in the text. If your score is elevated, what could you do to reduce the chances of illness? If it is low, what could you do to put more excitement in your life?! Can you see any relationship between periods of illness you have had and the number of life changes or hassles that preceded them?

3. What do you consider the most prominent sources of stress in our society? What do you think should or could be done to combat these stresses?

4. Over a decade ago, journalist Alvin Toffler predicted that large numbers of people would become victims of "future shock." According to Toffler, future shock is a condition of shattering stress and disorientation brought on by overly rapid social change. In your view, is there any truth to the idea that we are "future-shocked" or that we may be in the near future?

5. How would you integrate the concept of problem and emotion-focused coping into the process of making a decision? What should you do first, second, and third to cope with stress?

6. How should you go about deciding which stressors you can and cannot control?

7. Explain why you agree or disagree with the following statement (attributed to the famous Professor P. T. Barnumandbailey Circuits): "Television is the opiate of the people. If all the TV tubes in the United States suddenly went blank, the mental health of the nation would crumble because people could no longer escape their problems by watching television."

8. How could you best deal with the following sources of frustration: delays, losses, lack of resources, failure, rejection?

9. Many people report becoming extremely frustrated as they learn to use a computer. Why? In what way can this frustration be explained by the concepts of stress?

10. Gay bashing and acts of racial and religious prejudice have increased in frequency over the last few years. Why?

11. The defense mechanisms listed in this chapter were described in psychodynamic terms, that is, in terms of the balance of forces within the personality. Can you advance a learning theory explanation for any of the defenses? (Hint: Think in terms of avoidance learning and the rewards connected with defensive responses.)

12. What are the advantages and disadvantages of using defense mechanisms? Do you think it would be possible for a person to be completely free of defense mechanisms?

13. In what ways do schools, parents, and the government encourage feelings of helplessness? In what ways do they (or could they) add to feelings of confidence, competence, or "hope"?

14. Some state lottery winners have reported that their life is more stressful than prior to winning the money. Why? How?

15. What is the SRRS? What does it measure? In what ways has this instrument been criticized? In what way is the instrument biased? How would you go about developing a more "accurate" predictor of illness?

16. Describe the principles of biofeedback. How effective is biofeedback? Why? For what kind of problems would biofeedback be most effective?

17. What are the advantages and disadvantages of being a Type A person? What is a Type B person like? How are these two personalities similar to and different from the "hardy" personality?

18. In view of the relationship between smoking and health, should the government continue to give a large yearly subsidy to tobacco growers? Why or why not?

19. Why do you think the relationship between behavioral risk factors and health is so widely ignored? How important is health to you? How do your acquaintances rationalize their unhealthy behaviors? How do you?

20. Why do support groups help people deal with the elements of burnout? How do support groups help people reduce stress?

21. How might stress be related to the recent increase in murders committed by students and employees in schools and offices?

■ LECTURE ENHANCEMENTS

1.   **Although everyone has plenty of experience with frustration and can provide numerous examples, creating a little frustration in class can dramatize the subject and encourage discussion.** The music department on your campus may own a device called an *Echoplex* (or a similar device). Internally it has a continuous tape loop which allows auditory input to be delayed for short time intervals for replay. You will also need a microphone, a small amplifier, and a speaker. Connect and adjust the equipment so that a word spoken into the microphone is heard from the speaker with a delay of about one-half second. The resultant delayed auditory feedback makes it virtually impossible to speak into the microphone without tremendous interference and frustration. (This effect is similar to the interference caused by the echo of a poor public address system in a large auditorium.) Invite a student to the front of the class and ask him/her to tell the class some things about him/herself (college major, interests, what he or she has been doing for the last few days, etc.). The speaker should speak into the microphone, and the speaker volume should be as loud or slightly louder than his/her voice. Under these conditions, the speaker will stutter, stammer, and become thoroughly frustrated. Allow the tension to build, and then interview the student about the frustration experience.

2. **Obtain a large, narrow-mouthed jar.** You will also need two metal rods about three-sixteenths inch in diameter and eighteen inches long. (These may be obtained at most hardware stores; welding rods also will work well.) Place a marble or ball-bearing in the bottom of the jar. In class, ask if someone would like to play a game. Tell the volunteer that he/she has one minute to use the metal rods to lift the ball out of the jar. The jar may not be picked up or touched; the lifting must be done directly with the rods. To make things more interesting you might offer to add five points to the student's last test score for succeeding within the time limit. Be sure to test the task first before using it in class. If the dimensions are right, it hovers right on the edge of possibility—and is devilishly frustrating. Discussion can clarify conditions under which frustration is likely to occur.

3. **To introduce the topic of conflict, it might again be valuable to create a little conflict in class.** Ask if someone would like to play a "game of chance" with you. Tell the volunteer that you are going to flip a coin. If it comes up heads, three extra points will be added to the student's last test score. If it is tails, five points will be subtracted from the last test score. Give the student a few moments to decide if he/she still wants to play. Then discuss the approach-avoidance conflict that has been created.

    If the student declines or wins, ask if anyone else wants to play. Tell this volunteer that he/she must guess if heads or tails will appear when you flip the coin. If he/she guesses wrong, five points will be deducted from his or her last test score; if he/she guesses right, three points will be deducted. When the student says he/she does not want to play, tell him/her that choosing not to play will result in ten points being subtracted from his or her last test score. This should produce a good spontaneous display of emotion. Force the choice and discuss the conflict created (avoidance-avoidance). After demonstrations such as these, it is probably best to announce that three points will be added to each volunteer's grade for class participation and that the supposed effects of their decisions will be ignored.

4. **Type A personality characteristics can be illustrated in this way:** Give each student three pages completely covered with random digits. (These can be duplicated from a table of random numbers.) Tell students that their task is to cross out as many single, odd digits as they can after you say, "begin." Start students and let them work for thirty seconds. Have students count the number of digits crossed out. Announce that students will get a second try at the task, and have each student write down his or her goal for the second trial. Give the class thirty seconds to work. Students should again record their scores and set a goal for the third test. This completes the demonstration, since it is not necessary to conduct the third test; the point of this exercise is the goal-setting.

    On the board make a distribution of the number of digits students set as a goal for the third test. Research has shown that on similar tasks Type A's and Type B's do not differ on average performance. However, Type A's consistently set higher goals than Type B's. This pattern of goal-setting seems to reflect the Type A's preference for a rapid pace of activity. Students whose announced goals were at the top of the distribution are presumably Type A's; those at the bottom, Type B's. (Based on B. R. Snow. "Level of Aspiration in Coronary Prone and Non-Coronary Prone Adults." *Personality and Social Psychology Bulletin* (4) 1978: 416-419.)

5. **The "Hassles and Uplifts Scale" shown here can be completed by students individually.** Either a class discussion can take place or students can be encouraged to share the details of their hassles and uplifts in small groups. [NOTE: The questionnaire is similar to the ideas of Delongis, Folman, and Lazarus, published in the *Journal of Personality and Social Psychology,* 1988, Vol. 34(3), 486-495.]

Hassles and Uplifts Scale

HASSLES are things that annoy or bother a person. **UPLIFTS** are events that are pleasurable or satisfying. Sometimes an event is only a hassle OR only an uplift; sometimes the event can be both a hassle AND an uplift. Complete this questionnaire at the end of the day just before bed. Think of the extent to which each event of the day was a hassle AND/OR an uplift. Write the number to the left to describe the degree to which it was a hassle; write the number to the right to describe to what extent the event was an uplift.

For both scales 0 = not at all   1 = somewhat 2 = quite a bit 3 = to a great extent

A HASSLE		UPLIFT
_____	1. Your child/children	_____
_____	2. Other relatives	_____
_____	3. Your spouse or significant other	_____
_____	4. Sexual expression	_____
_____	5. Your friends	_____
_____	6. Your fellow workers or your work	_____
_____	7. Enough money for necessities	_____
_____	8. Enough money for recreation	_____
_____	9. Your smoking or drinking habits	_____
_____	10. Your health or physical appearance	_____
_____	11. The air quality or noise of your environment	_____
_____	12. Political or social issues	_____
_____	13. Housework and/or yardwork	_____
_____	14. Debts or investments	_____
_____	15. Taxes and legal matters	_____
_____	TOTAL	_____

Add up the points in the "hassle" column. Add up the points in the "uplift" column. Subtract the "hassle" total from the "uplift" total. Compare your answer to the answer of others in your class. What does this score tell you about the quantity of stress in your life? What does it tell you about the specific source of most of your stress? What can you do to reduce the hassles in your life? What if you don't have many hassles--but you don't have many uplifts either? What, if anything, should you do?

6.   **Ask students to bring to class an oral thermometer, preferably a digital thermometer.** Divide students into pairs. Ask one person to serve as subject and to hold the thermometer in his/her palm. The other student instructs his/her partner to lower the temperature of the palm. When the temperature goes down, this person should say, "getting cooler." Record the temperature every minute for five minutes. Switch roles. The second time, ask the subject to increase the temperature of the palm. Record the temperature in the same way. Calculate a mean for each instruction and discuss the averages with the class.

■ ROLE-PLAYING SCENARIOS

1.   **Act out a scene of emotion-focused coping.** Contrast it with an "instant replay" done using problem-focused coping. Issues to be enacted could include: spousal disagreement over money or children, dealing with spending too much money, caught in a traffic jam, preparing to give a speech.

2.   **Ask each student to describe a conflict he/she is dealing with at the moment.** Ask two others to play the two forces that are literally pushing and pulling the person in two different directions. As a trio ask students to discuss the feelings that result from conflicts.

3.   **Have students try the following:**

   a. Role play being a person who is homeless, who rents an apartment, who owns a condo, who owns a home, and a person who is an affluent public figure. In what ways do each of these people feel caught by their economic circumstances?

   b. In what ways do the following people feel caught by their social circumstances: a person in a marriage of ten years, single (no children), a single parent, a divorcee (no kids), and a divorcee with two children and a joint custody agreement?

   c. In what ways do the following people feel caught by their physical circumstances: a very tall person, a very small person, a person with a physical impairment, a person lacking intellectual skills, and a person lacking emotional stability?

4. **Role play being hassled by a teacher, a student, a parent, a child, and a boss.** What strategies should a person use for dealing with hassles?

5. **Role play a Type A talking to a Type A, a Type A to a B, a Type A to a hardy personality, and a Type B to a hardy personality.** Which conversation was the most frustrating? Why?

6. **Ask students to write a list of difficult situations to deal with (cheating, stealing, tax evasion, participating in gossip, and so forth).** Ask students to role-play "refusal" behaviors.

7. **You are a student government leader who wants to develop a campus-wide health campaign.** What specific behaviors do you want to change? How would you go about doing it?

■ VALUE-CLARIFICATION STATEMENTS

1. Our society is no more stressful than society was a hundred years ago.

2. When a person is frustrated, he/she should act on the anger in a constructive way.

3. People who repress their anger eventually explode.

4. Public elementary schools tend to encourage feelings of helplessness in many students.

5. It is difficult to succeed in today's society unless one becomes a Type A personality.

6. Cigarettes should be illegal.

7. Hard alcohol should be made illegal.

8. The drinking age should be raised to 25.

■ ONE-MINUTE MOTIVATORS

1. **Suddenly give students a pop quiz or lecture very rapidly.** They will quickly tell you that the quiz isn't fair or to speak more slowly. Begin talking about stress.

2. **Ask students how many would be excited to receive a "C" in this class, to weigh 140 pounds, to receive $5000 as a full-time salary, and so forth.** Some would be excited and pleased; others will be disappointed; discuss primary appraisal.

3. **Ask students to interview each other, making a list of activities found to be "boring," "relaxing," "fun," and "stressful."** Most likely many activities will be listed in different categories by different people. Discuss perceptual differences in primary appraisal.

4. **Put students in groups of six.** One person stands in the middle. The other five put their arms around the waists of the people on either side. The person in the center has one minute to break out of the circle. Count backwards for the final 10 seconds. Usually you will see students increase the vigor of their attempts during the last few seconds. Caution students against expressing their frustration aggressively.

5. **Use a pillow to be the recipient of displaced aggression.** Ask students to think of someone they're angry at while briefly pounding the pillow. Do they feel better? Why or why not?

6. **Have students help you make a list of humorous rationalizations for not having studied psychology.** Discuss the value and costs of rationalization and other defenses.

7. **Ask students to make a list of life changes that have taken place over the last month.** Share the list with other students.

8. **Ask students to make an honest estimate of the amount that they spend on alcohol and tobacco for one week.** Collect the amounts and total them; then multiply by 52.

■ BROADENING OUR CULTURAL HORIZONS

1. **Poverty is the norm in many cultures and it is a continuing problem for many in the U.S.** Discuss the helplessness that occurs with poverty. How do the poor feel? What can be done to help each of us feel less helpless in dealing with poverty?

2. **Depression is much more common among women then men.** Why? What social and environmental factors contribute to depression? Could men be just as depressed as women--but select different behaviors for dealing with this emotion?

3. **Rewrite the "Life Change Units" scale in terms of the principal stressors of the poor.** Would the stressors be the same? Would the rankings be the same? Why or why not?

4. **What cultural values would encourage Type A behavior?** Type B behavior? More hardy personalities? Why?

5. **Some cultures, especially those marked by poverty and privation, place a high value on stoicism and quiet tolerance of suffering.** How does this compare with the hardy personality? How might it be adaptive? How is it maladaptive?

6. **How might the actions of the terrorists in the Middle East be related to stress?** In blaming the U.S. for their social ills, what defense mechanism(s) might be in effect?

■ SUPPLEMENTAL ACTIVITIES

The exercise that follows should provide students with a good deal of thought-provoking material. It is based on the idea that stress in a person's life can lead to a crisis, to illness, and/or accidents. Changes in one's life, whether positive or negative, can be stressors. Because we live through these events one by one, we may not put them together or see how much stress we are under at any particular time. This questionnaire forces the student to look back over the past year to see what stressful events occurred. *The Social Readjustment Rating Scale* is reproduced in Chapter 12 of the text. It is Table 12-6. Students are asked to take from that list any events which they have experienced over the last twelve months. The total score can then be interpreted by the values given on the interpretation sheet.

Exercise #1: Stress in Your Life

TO THE INSTRUCTOR:

I. **Procedure**

   A. Provide all students with a **Data** sheet, an **Interpretation and Reaction** sheet, a **Health Problems** sheet, and a **Discussion** sheet.

   B. Ask them to go over the list of life events in Table 12-6 of Chapter 12 in the text. It is the *Social Readjustment Rating Scale* (SRRS). They should pick out those events which apply to them and record them on the data sheet.

   C. Instruct students to get a total of the LCU's and proceed with the **Interpretation and Reaction** sheet.

   D. Finally, ask the students to check off the health problems from the list provided and arrive at a total.

   E. Ask students to complete the **Discussion** sheet and submit it with the figures for the their total LCU's and their total health problems. This can be done anonymously.

F.   Select the 25% of the LCU scores that were the highest and the 25% that were the lowest. Find the average of LCU's from the high group and the low group. Find the average number of health problems for the high and low groups. See what differences there are, and let the class discuss these.

STRESS IN YOUR LIFE: DATA SHEET

TO THE STUDENT:

This data sheet consists of two parts. The first is an inventory of significant life events that you have experienced in the last twelve months. **Table 12-6** in your text lists forty-three life events which could add stress to your life. No doubt you could think of others. For this exercise, restrict yourself to those listed in the Table. You will see that each event has a value, stated in Life Change Units (LCU's). Go through the list in Table 12-6 and pick out those events which you have experienced over the past year (12 months). List them below with their corresponding units. Then total the LCU scores and compare yours with the standards given on the interpretation sheet.

SIGNIFICANT LIFE EVENT	LCU
---------------------	-----
---------------------	-----
---------------------	-----
---------------------	-----
---------------------	-----
---------------------	-----
---------------------	-----
---------------------	-----
---------------------	-----
---------------------	-----
---------------------	-----
---------------------	-----

Total: -----

STRESS IN YOUR LIFE: INTERPRETATION

Interpretation of the LCU score is based on samples of subjects who have been given the *Social Readjustment Rating Scale*. See if you fit the description of those who had scores similar to yours.

SCORE	DESCRIPTION
0 - 150	Persons scoring in this range should be suffering very little stress. Their chances of suffering illness or crisis are small.
150 - 199	Scores in this range indicate that you are experiencing MILD stress with a possibility of crisis or illness being fairly low--about 33%.
200 - 299	Scores in this range indicate a MODERATE stress situation. This could result in a greater possibility of accident, illness, or some other crisis - about 50%.
300 or more	Those scoring in this range are experiencing high levels of stress and therefore run a much higher risk of crisis or illness. This is considered a major risk area, about 80% chance of experiencing some problems.

My LCU score _____

REACTION: Indicate how you feel about the significance of your score. Are you surprised? Did you expect it to be higher? Or lower? Has this been a typical year for you?

STRESS IN YOUR LIFE: HEALTH PROBLEMS

Below is a list of health problems that are common in the population. You will recognize many as old friends. Try to think back over the past twelve months and see if you can recall having had some of these. Check off all of those that you can remember.

___ allergies	___ diarrhea	___ minor accident
___ appendicitis	___ earache	___ muscle strains
___ asthma	___ eye problems	___ nausea
___ athlete's foot	___ flu	___ nerves (anxiety)
___ backache	___ hay fever	___ sexual problems
___ blisters	___ headaches	___ shortness of breath
___ bloody nose	___ hearing loss	___ sinus problems
___ boils	___ hernia	___ skin disease
___ bruises	___ high blood pressure	___ skin rash
___ chest pains	___ hives	___ sleep problems
___ colds	___ indigestion	___ sore throat
___ constipation	___ injury to joints	___ stomach problems
___ cough	___ insomnia	___ tonsillitis
___ cuts	___ kidney problems	___ ulcers
___ dental problems	___ major accident	___ urinary problems
___ depression	___ menstrual problems	___ vomiting
___ other		

TOTAL HEALTH PROBLEMS _____

STRESS IN YOUR LIFE: DISCUSSION

TO THE STUDENT:

Enter your LCU score and your total number of health problems in the space provided. Then write brief comments on the discussion questions.

LCU score   _____

Health Problems   _____

1.   In which of the four LCU categories did you find yourself? Does this seem to fit in with your idea about your stress level and possibility of crisis or illness?

2.   How does your level of health problems compare with your LCU score? Do you see any relationship between the two?

3.   Are you taking any significant steps to reduce the stress level in your life? Do you see any need to do so?

■ JOURNAL QUESTIONS

1. Describe your most stressful life experience. Why was it stressful? How did you deal with the situation? What could you or others have done to make it less stressful?

2. Which is more frustrating to you--external or personal frustrations? Why?

3. Describe a time in your life when you dealt with frustration through aggression and withdrawal. Did these reactions help or did they make the frustration worse?

4. Give an example of each of the defense mechanisms from your own life.

5. In what ways do you feel caught and helpless? What strategies have you learned to cope with these feelings? Are these strategies effective or ineffective?

6. Describe times in your life when you felt depressed. Describe the feelings, the situation surrounding the depressions, and the ways you tried to cope with the depression.

7. Make a list of 20 or more things that went well this week for you or things that you did well. You must list at least 20 items.

8. With respect to stress, which "type" of personality do you most identify with? What genetic and environmental factors have "made" you this "type"?

■ SUGGESTIONS FOR FURTHER READING

Andre, Rae. *Positive Solitud: A Practical Program for Mastering Loneliness and Achieving Self-fulfillment.* Universe.com, 2001.

Biracree, Tom and Nance (1991). *Over Fifty: The Resource Book for the Better Half of your Life.* Harper/Collins.

Cherey, L. "The Man Who First Names Stress." *Psychology Today,* March 1978: 64.

Davis, M., M. McKay, and E. R. Eshelman. *The Relaxation and Stress Reduction Workbook,* 5th ed. New Harbiner, 2000.

Dienstfrey, Harris. *Downshifting: Reinventing Success on a Slower Track.* Harper/Collins, 1991.

Dollard, J. *Frustration and Aggression.* Greenwood Publishing Group, 1980.

Dreher, Diane. *The Tao of Inner Peace.* Plume, 2000.

Dyer, W. W. *No More Holiday Blues.* Harper/Collins, 1993.

Dyer, W. W. *Ten Secrets for Success and Inner Peace.* Hay House, 2002.

Feinstein, David and Mayo, Peg Elliott. *Rituals for Living and Dying.* HarperCollins, 1990.

Freedman, Arthur and DeWolf, Rose. *Woulda, Coulda, Shoulda: Overcoming Regrets, Mistakes, and Missed Opportunities.* HarperCollins, 1992.

Hojat, Mohammadreza and Crandall, Rick (Eds.). *Loneliness: Theory, Research, and Applications.* Sage Press, 1990.

Kasl, Charlotte Davis. *Women, Sex, and Addiction.* Harper/Collins, 1990.

Lazarus, R. S. "Little Hassles Can Be Hazardous to Health." *Psychology Today,* July 1981.

Levi, L. *Society, Stress, and Disease: Working Life.* Oxford University Press, 1982.

Levi, L. *Society, Stress, and Disease: Old Age.* Oxford University Press, 1988.

Mandler, G. *Mind and Body: Psychology of Emotion and Stress.* Norton, 1984.

Meichenbaum, D. "Stress-Inoculation Training." In *Cognitive Behavior Modification.* Plenum, 1977.

Saltzman, Amy. *Where the Mind Meets the Body.* HarperCollins, 1992.

Schafer, W. *Stress Management for Wellness.* Thomson, 1999.

Selye, H. *The Stress of Life*, 2nd ed. McGraw-Hill, 1978.

Smith, Jonathan C. *Stress Scripting: A Guide to Stress Management.* New York: Praeger, 1991.

Spodnik, Jean and David P. Cogan. *The 35-Plus Good Health Guide for Women.* HarperCollins, 1991.

Woolfolk, R. and F. Richardson. *Stress, Sanity, and Survival.* New American Library, 1986.

■ MEDIA SUGGESTIONS

HEALTH, MIND, AND BEHAVIOR (2001, from the *Discovering Psychology Series*, Annenberg/CPB, 30 min.)
How research is forcing a profound rethinking of the relationship between mind and body—a new bio-psychosocial model is replacing the traditional biomedical model.

HEALTH, STRESS, AND COPING (2002, from *Psychology- The Study of Human Behavior,* Coast Community College District Telecourses, 30 min.)
This video presents a discussion of Hans Selye's General Adaptation Syndrome (GAS), stress and physical illness, and psychological stress.

MANAGING STRESS (2002, Films for the Humanities and Sciences, 19 min.)
This program looks at positive and negative stress, the effect of these stresses on the immune system, and outlines ways to manage stress.

THE SCIENCE OF STRESS (2002, Films for the Humanities and Sciences, 50 min.)
This program explores the link between stress and illness by staging a day in the life of a lawyer. Various professionals in the health field comment on his stress factors and the way he handles them. Type A and Type B personalities are discussed.

STRESS, HEALTH, AND COPING (2002, from *Psychology- The Human Experience,* Coast Community College District Telecourses, 30 min.)
This video chronicles a breast cancer survivor who employs successful coping strategies to aid in maintaining good health in stressful situations.

A number of videos are available from Thomson. Videos appropriate for this chapter include the following films from the CNN TODAY Introductory Psychology Video Series:

Volume 2, Section 4: Mental Health and Stress
    Honduras Mental Stress (1:54)

Volume 3, Section 8: Stress, Coping, and Health
    Elderly Depression (1:37)

■ COMPUTER AND INTERNET RESOURCES

PSYCHNOW!

Motivation and Emotion:
Coping With Emotion
Stress and Health

PSYK.TREK

Unit 11: Abnormal Behavior & Therapy
    11f: Types of Stress
    11g: Responding to Stress

INFOTRAC:

Subject Guide/Key Words: Health Psychology, Stress and Health, Lifestyle Diseases, Psychological Stress, Stress Reaction, Hans Selye, Burnout, Coping with Stress, Scapegoating, Psychological Defense Mechanisms, Learned Helplessness, Psychosomatic Disorders, Psychoneuroimmunology, Stress Management

WEB SITES

Wadsworth Online Psychology Study Center:
http://info.wadsworth.com/cooessentials9

AmoebaWeb Psychology Resources: Health Psychology:
http://www.vanguard.edu/faculty/ddegelman/amoebaweb/index.cfm?doc_id=862

The American Institute of Stress:
http://www.stress.org/

Stress Management Resources on the Internet:
http://www.selfgrowth.com/stress.html

Association for Applied Psychophysiology and Biofeedback:
http://www.aapb.org/

The Medical Basis of Stress, Depression, Anxiety, Sleep Problems, and Drug Use:
http://www.teachhealth.com/

CHAPTER 13

Psychological Disorders

LEARNING OBJECTIVES

To demonstrate mastery of this chapter, the student should be able to:

1. Present information to indicate the magnitude of mental health problems in this country.
2. Define psychopathology.
3. Describe the following ways of viewing normality including the shortcoming(s) of each:
   a. subjective discomfort
   b. statistical abnormality
   c. social nonconformity (include the concept of situational context)
   d. cultural relativity
4. Discuss gender bias in judging abnormality.
5. State conditions under which a person is usually judged to need help.
6. Explain the dangers of social stigma when using psychiatric labels.
7. Generally describe each of the following categories of mental disorders found in the DSM-IV:
   a. psychotic disorders
   b. organic mental disorders
   c. substance related disorders
   d. mood disorders
   e. anxiety disorders
   f. somatoform disorders
   g. dissociative disorders
   h. personality disorders
   i. sexual and gender-identity disorders
8. List the four general risk factors that may contribute to mental disorders.
9. Distinguish the term insanity from true mental disorder.
10. List and briefly describe the ten different types of personality disorders. (See Table 13-3)
11. Describe the distinctive characteristics, causes, and treatment of the antisocial personality.
12. Define anxiety.
13. Outline the four features of anxiety-related problems.
14. State what is usually meant when the term "nervous breakdown" is used.
15. Differentiate an adjustment disorder from an anxiety disorder.
16. Define the key element of most anxiety disorders.
17. Differentiate generalized anxiety disorders from the two types of panic disorders.

18.   Describe the following conditions:
    a.   agoraphobia
    b.   specific phobia
    c.   social phobia
    d.   obsessive-compulsive disorder
    e.   stress disorder
        i.   acute stress disorder
        ii.   post-traumatic stress disorder
    f.   dissociative disorders
        i.   dissociative amnesia
        ii.   dissociative fugue
        iii.   dissociative identity disorder
    g.   somatoform disorders
        i.   hypochondriasis
        ii.   somatization disorder
        iii.   pain disorder
        iv.   conversion disorder

19.   Discuss how each of the four major perspectives in psychology views anxiety disorders.
    a.   psychodynamic
    b.   humanistic-existential (include the concepts of self-image and existential anxiety)
    c.   behavioral (include the terms self-defeating, paradox, avoidance learning, and anxiety reduction hypothesis)
    d.   cognitive

20.   Define what is meant by the term psychosis.

21.   Define delusion.

22.   Define hallucination and name the most common type.

23.   Describe the emotion, communication, and personality changes that may occur in someone with a psychosis. Include an explanation of the frequency of occurrence for these changes.

24.   Differentiate an organic from a functional psychosis.

25.   Describe dementia.

26.   Briefly describe Alzheimer's disease, including its incidence, symptoms, and neurological concomitants.

27.   Describe the characteristics of delusional disorders, including each of the five delusional types.

28.   Describe a paranoid psychosis. Explain why treatment of this condition is difficult.

29.   Generally describe schizophrenia.

30.   List and describe the four major types of schizophrenia.

31.   Explain how paranoid delusional disorder and paranoid schizophrenia differ.

The following objective is related to the material in the "Exploring Psychology" section of the text.

32.   Describe the general relationship between violence and mental illness.

33.   Describe the roles of the following three areas as causes of schizophrenia:
        a. Environment
                i.   prenatal problems and birth complications
                ii. psychological trauma
                iii. disturbed family environment
                iv. deviant communication patterns
        b. Heredity
        c. Brain Chemistry
                i.   dopamine
                ii. CT, MRI, and PET scans

34.   Discuss the stress-vulnerability model of psychosis.

35.   Describe the characteristics of depressive disorders. Include a description of dysthymia and cyclothymia.

36.   List and describe the three major mood disorders.

37.   Explain the difference between major mood disorders and dysthymia and cyclothymia.

38.   Generally describe the likely causes of mood disorders.

39.   Define and briefly discuss the symptoms of maternity blues and postpartum depression.

40.   Define seasonal affective disorder (SAD), list five major symptoms, and briefly describe the treatment of SAD.

41.   List and describe the two basic kinds of treatment for psychosis.

The following objectives are related to the material in the "Psychology in Action" section of the text.

42.   Discuss how each of the following factors affects suicide rates: season, sex, age, income, marital status.

43.   List the eight major risk factors that typically precede suicide. Discuss why people try to kill themselves.

44.   Name/identify the twelve warning signs of suicide.

45.   List four common characteristics of suicidal thoughts and feelings.

46.   Explain how you can help prevent suicide.

■ DISCUSSION QUESTIONS

1.   Can you think of a behavior that would be considered "abnormal" under any possible set of circumstances?

2.   What are the advantages and disadvantages of having discrete categories for defining psychological problems?

3.   How might your perception of a person change if you knew he or she were an "ex-mental patient"?

4.   To what extent does "maladjusted" or "sick" mean "different from me"?

5.   In the 1950s, a book called the *Age of Anxiety* was published. Using the categories of abnormal behavior, how would you label our current decade? What would need to take place for it to be a decade of "mental health"?

6.   Are standards of "normality" in our society broad enough to accommodate varying life-styles?

7.   In what ways might our ultra-competitive society contribute to the development of a sociopathic personality?

8.   Briefly summarize the features of psychosis. Are "normal" behaviors completely without these qualities? Compare these to the qualities of normal functioning. Are psychotic behaviors different from normal behavior in terms of kind or degree?

9.   Some psychologists suggest that the majority of American families are dysfunctional. Can we expect that the incidence of schizophrenia will increase? Why or why not?

10.   The majority of families with a member who exhibits schizophrenic behaviors do not have other members with a history of schizophrenia episodes. Why?

11.   Under what circumstances would you consider it reasonable for a stranger to be involuntarily committed? A friend? A close relative? Yourself?

12.   In your opinion how could a person experiencing a severe "problem in living" be most effectively helped?

13.   Should a mental patient have the right to refuse medication? To demand legal counsel and alternative medical opinions? To refuse to work in a mental hospital or to choose the work that will be done? To communicate by phone, letter, or in person with anyone at any time? To keep personal property (including drugs, matches, pocketknives, and other potentially harmful materials? To request an alternative to legal commitment to a mental hospital? To be represented by an independent "advocate" who is not on the hospital staff?

14.   In view of what you know about the causes of psychosis, how valid do you consider the medical model of mental illness? What are the advantages and disadvantages of such a model? What are the advantages and disadvantages of a psychological model?

15.   If the genetic component is large in major problems such as schizophrenia and mood disorders, should we try genetically to identify individuals at risk when no sure treatments are available? Should people who are close relatives of affected persons receive special counseling?

16.   The parents of John Hinkley (who attempted to assassinate President Reagan) have complained "The comedian Robin Williams has great fun making sick jokes about 'crazies' like our son John, but does he joke about muscular dystrophy or cancer? Of course not." Do you agree or disagree with the point they are making?

■ LECTURE ENHANCEMENTS

Films are often most effective when they are short, dramatic, and introduced as a way to activate the student rather than to induce drowsiness. This chapter needs illustrations, and films or videotapes can be especially valuable. Excellent clips from the many series of films for the introductory course can be used. To prevent students from distancing themselves from the concerns, issues, and plight of the mentally ill, the films can be stopped and students can be asked for their opinions or feelings. For example, after watching a film students can be asked to view the depicted behavior from the perspective of family members.

If you do not have a clinical background, consider inviting a clinical or counseling psychologist to class. Because the chapter includes vocabulary that many students are not familiar with, it is important to help students rehearse and review terms as well as address issues and controversies.

1.   **Although the emphasis in Chapter 13 is psychopathology and perspectives on abnormality, it should be useful to devote some class time to the concept of mental health.** Earlier discussion of Maslow's research on self-actualization advances one view of mental health. What do the class perceive as the basic attributes of a psychologically healthy individual? Can psychopathology be defined in the absence of some notion of health? As a starting point for discussion, you may want to present Jahoda's list of attributes:
     a.   accurate self-concept, self-awareness, self-acceptance;
     b.   self-actualization, full use of potential;
     c.   autonomy;
     d.   integration, a coherent outlook on life;
     e.   accurate perceptions of reality, social sensitivity;
     f.   competence and mastery of the environment.

(The preceding list is from M. Jahoda, *Current Concepts of Positive Mental Health,* Ayer Company Publishers, 1980.)

2. **A good way to illustrate the relativity of most definitions of abnormality is to ask the class to describe examples of odd or unusual behavior they have observed in public.** After getting several examples, return to each and ask if there is any set of circumstances under which the behavior observed might be considered normal. (For example, the person observed had lost a bet, was undergoing an initiation, was practicing a part for a play, was part of a psychology experiment, etc.) The point is that the behavior may have been truly eccentric, and perhaps pathological, but that few behaviors are universally normal or abnormal.

3. **Here are some statistics you may want to discuss with your classes:** According to recent figures, an average of thirteen teen-age youths commit suicide each day in the United States, producing a yearly total of about five thousand. Since 1960 the number of suicides in the 15-24 age range has more than doubled. In the 10-14 age range there has been an increase of thirty-two percent since 1976. There has been an increase of roughly three hundred percent in youth suicides in the last fifteen years. At one time the incidence of suicide increased directly with age, reaching a peak in the 50-70 age range. Now there is a second peak--at about age twenty. There are now more suicides in the 15-24 age group than in the 50-70 group. Suicide is the number two cause of death among the young, with accidents number one.

4. **The Audio-Visual Center at Indiana University has produced a fascinating videotape that consists of interviews with four individuals suffering from a Bipolar Affective Disorder.** In the first sequence a young woman is interviewed by a therapist while she is in the depressive phase of this disorder. This same young woman is then shown being interviewed during a manic episode. The change is so dramatic that students have great difficulty believing it is the same person. The tape then shows interviews with three different young men, each of whom is experiencing a hypomanic episode. Students find these interviews extremely interesting, and they produce a great deal of class discussion. The half-hour videotape can be obtained by writing to Indiana University Audio-Visual Center, Bloomington, IN 47401 and requesting *Bipolar Affective Disorders,* tape No. EVH 2198.

5. **If there is a chapter of the National Association for Mental Health in your area, volunteer speakers can often be arranged through this organization.** Also, interested students may themselves participate as volunteers in out-patient programs or other mental health services.

6. **For some reason, a simple description of the dangers of psychiatric labeling fails to impress many students with the profound impact such labeling can have.** The dramatization described here must be handled with great care and sensitivity, but if it is done well, it may be one of the more memorable sessions of the course. Here is what you can say and do:

"Today we have a very special opportunity. After our last meeting a student from this class approached me and said that he had been hospitalized for schizophrenia several years ago. This student has volunteered to share with us his experiences while hospitalized. I told him I thought it was an excellent idea and added a twist of my own. One of the secondary problems often associated with mental hospitalization is the stigma that follows a person afterward. Many people believe that if a person becomes psychotic, that person will be "crazy" for life. To illustrate how complete recovery from schizophrenia is, I'm going to call three people up to the front of the class. One is the student we will be talking to, and the other two don't know I'm going to call on them."

Select three students from the class and call them to the front. (It is best to select three students you know to be stable and adaptable. To avoid gender complications, select all male or all female students. In this example, male students are used.)

"In a few moments we're going to do an interesting thing. I want to prove that it is impossible to correctly identify a "former mental patient." To give you something to go on, I'm going to ask each of these people to tell us a little about themselves, their major in school, or their interests."

Have each student give his or her name and speak for one or two minutes. Then ask the class to decide which person they think was hospitalized at one point in his life. Tell them to write their choice. Just as they begin, tell them to stop and cross out anything they have written. Reveal to the class what you have done and emphasize that you selected the students because of their maturity and that you know nothing about their backgrounds. Begin discussion by interviewing the subjects. Given that each knew that he was not the former patient, his perceptions of the other two subjects are usually radically affected. Also note that what subjects choose to say about themselves under these circumstances is usually very safe and very normal. Next interview the rest of the class and discuss how labeling affected their immediate perceptions and their interpretation of the past behavior of each subject. Be sure to point out that, while many were hesitant to choose one of the subjects, most did choose because of the labeling. Finally, be sure to thank the students who participated and ask the class to show their appreciation to them.

7. **There is a case on record of four identical quadruplets all of whom developed schizophrenia.** The odds against this happening are truly staggering. Identical quadruplets occur only once in every sixteen million births, and less than half of them survive to adulthood; only one in a hundred of these is schizophrenic, and the odds against all of them being schizophrenic seem overwhelming. This case, then, could seem to provide evidence for the heritability of schizophrenia. However, you should point out to your students that the quadruplets shared many other things besides their genes. For example, they all shared their mother's uterus where they could have contracted a viral

infection or been exposed to some chemical substance. They all had the possibly brain-damaging liability of being born with very low weights. All of them were placed in incubators and spent the first six weeks of their lives in a hospital. They all grew up with constant publicity surrounding their daily activities. Finally, they all shared a father who was known for eccentric and erratic behavior and who remained extremely close to them even into adulthood. For more information, see a report on the twenty-year follow-up on this unusual and interesting case by M. S. Buchsbaum, "The Genain Quadruplets," *Psychology Today,* August 1984.

8. **If there is a mental hospital in your area, arrange to take your students on a tour of the facility.** There will be an office for volunteers in the hospital. They will set it up or direct you to someone who will. Some of the students may wish to become volunteers once they know of the opportunity. Prepare the students beforehand. You should give a thorough briefing, preparing the students for the observation. Discussion, films, or a visit by a volunteer would also help prepare the students so they get the most out of the trip. Otherwise, the students will not know what to look for, and the experience will become a matter of simply feeding their curiosity.

9. **A visit by a staff person from a local suicide prevention center, help-line, or crisis intervention team is always worthwhile.**

■ ROLE-PLAYING SCENARIOS

1. **You are a defense attorney interviewing a psychologist who has testified that your client was sane when he committed a crime.** What questions will you ask the psychologist about she reached her conclusion?

2. **You're a psychiatrist.** A woman comes to you complaining that her mother seems frightened and refuses to leave the house. Explain what the mother's problem is and help the daughter understand it.

3. **Your friend, Larry, is showing paranoid symptoms.** Suggest to Larry that he see a psychologist. What difficulty do you face in making this suggestion?

4. **You are a physician.** Your patient has suddenly lost his ability to smell. There is no damage to his nose. You want to know whether your patient has a brain tumor. Explain to your patient why you want to use a CT scan, rather than a PET scan.

5. **Tanya feels her life is meaningless and hopeless.** She has trouble functioning at work and at school. She continues to withdraw into herself more each day. How would you label her behavior? Why? What would you suggest that she do to break this pattern?

6. **Because of a terrible mix-up you have been involuntarily committed to a mental hospital.** Convince the ward psychologist that you are not psychotic and that a mistake has been made.

■ VALUE-CLARIFICATION STATEMENTS

1. Psychotic people are not responsible for their behavior and should not be prosecuted for injuring others.

2. A person could easily fake symptoms and fool others into thinking they are psychotic.

3. It is better to occasionally err by providing government assistance to people who don't need it than to withhold help from those who do.

4. A person showing a pattern of schizophrenic behaviors should not be allowed to hold a full-time job that is even somewhat stressful.

5. A person with schizophrenia should not have children.

6. All a person needs to do to stop being depressed is to think of happy events.

7. A person who admits to having attempted suicide or who has been treated for depression should be prohibited from running for President or Vice-President of the United States.

8. A person convicted of manslaughter due to uncontrolled aggression should be required to receive psychosurgery.

9. Nothing can be done to stop a person who wants to commit suicide.

■ ONE-MINUTE MOTIVATORS

1. **Prepare a list of unusual behaviors and ask students are normal or abnormal for:** A man? A woman? A person? A culture emphasizing passivity? A culture emphasizing aggression?

2. **During the late 1980s, support groups developed to assist people who were victims of abuse, neglect, alcoholism, rape, family violence, etc.** What are the advantages and the disadvantages of a "victim mind-set"?

3. **Pass a transparency around the class.** Ask students to list "worries." Share the transparency with the class. As a prelude to discussing anxiety.

4. **Lecture while standing on a table, in the corner, or while walking from desk-top to desk-top.** Or, make a repeated "fly-catching" movement with your hand as you speak. Discuss the role of social norms in defining abnormal behavior. Also discuss how minor and undramatic a behavior may be and still raise questions about a person's normality.

5. **Read definitions of major DSM-IV categories and see if students can name the defined disorder.**

6. **Have students estimate the number of parties they attended during the preceding month.** Make a frequency distribution on the chalkboard. Challenge the class to help you draw a line that defines "compulsive partying." As an alternative, collect data on the number of hours of television watched per week and define "TV addiction" by establishing a cut-off point.

7. **Ask students to help you name some humorous new phobias,** such as Muzakophobia (fear of being trapped in an elevator with insipid piped-in music playing in the background), cellulitophobia (fear that one's thighs are turning to cottage cheese), or Geraldophobia (this one's self-defining).

■ BROADENING OUR CULTURAL HORIZONS

1. **What effect might living in different parts** of town, membership in a different ethnic group, or growing up in a different culture have on perceptions of "normality?"

2. **Depression is much more frequent among females than among males.** Why?

3. **Read about a culture very different from your own.** What category of mental illness would you guess would be most frequent?

4. **Challenge students to compare the frequency of suicide in our culture to the frequency in another culture.** How would they explain the difference?

5. **Collect a few clips from *National Geographic* episodes** and ask class whether the behaviors shown would be perceived as "episodes of mental illness" within another culture.

6. **In many European countries, men's rest rooms are tended by women.** Discuss the implications this has for any attempt to create a culture-free definition of abnormal behavior.

7. **Recently, a number of Middle Eastern young persons, protesting U. S. support of Israel, have committed suicide by blowing themselves up, usually taking many innocent lives with them.** Is this a form of mental illness? If so, into what category would this behavior fall?

■ SUPPLEMENTAL ACTIVITIES

Abnormality has many different meanings. Certainly students come to this course with misconceptions and fixed ideas. To get students thinking along the same lines, you can use one or both of these exercises. By the time they are finished with the exercises and your class discussion of what they produced, they should be open to a more realistic appraisal of what is "normal" and what is not. The **first exercise** focuses on the students' ideas about what is normal. It should help them to see that there are many ways to be abnormal, depending on your definition and what you are looking for. The **second exercise** is an attempt to observe what people generally do when confronted with behavior that is outside the expected. The **third exercise** shows the dangers of labeling.

Exercise #1: What Is Normal?

In this exercise students will be asked to distinguish between what is normal behavior and what is abnormal. There are a number of ways to do this:

1. Statistically—this approach says that the mean is the norm, and any deviation from the mean is abnormal. The further one's behavior is from the mean, the less normal the person is; or, conversely, the more abnormal. Those furthest from the mean are the most abnormal. Notice that from this viewpoint, both positive and negative deviations are equally abnormal.

2. Clinically—people are judged as abnormal only if they display behaviors which deviate negatively from the norm. The greater the deviation, the greater the abnormality.

3. Humanistically—well-adjusted people are somewhat rare, and they occupy the top of the distribution: they are self-actualizers. All others are maladjusted to some degree. Those who are further down the scale are more maladjusted than those higher up.

Procedure

A. Discuss the three approaches to normality/abnormality outlined above.

B. Distribute the student worksheets for their responses.

C.   Organize the class into small groups of three or four students so they can discuss the questions and record their conclusions on their worksheets.

D.   After the students have completed the discussion, you should ask them to report their conclusions. As each group reports, the whole class can comment. This should generate a good deal of interest in the topic of behavior disorders.

E.   Collect the students' work. Be sure that each student has written something. This is the best way to get students to think about the concepts being discussed.

WHAT IS NORMAL? WORKSHEET

TO THE STUDENT:

In the space provided, report your group's decisions about each of the questions below. If you disagree with the rest of your group, indicate your disagreement and reasons. You will be asked to turn in this sheet after the discussion.

A.   List five behaviors that would be considered abnormal according to all three approaches to the question of maladjustment explained by your instructor: statistical, clinical, or humanistic:

1.

2.

3.

4.

5.

B.   List five behaviors that would be considered statistically abnormal, but not from the other two points of view:

1.

2.

3.

4.

5.

C.   List three behaviors that would be considered mentally healthy from the humanistic point of view:

1.

2.

3.

Name_____

Exercise #2: The Deviant Among Us

This exercise, if carefully planned and executed, can be very beneficial to students. The main objective is to provide an opportunity for them to observe people's reactions to deviant behavior. They will, moreover, get to try out some observation techniques and will need to look more closely at behavior than they are accustomed to doing.

The students will observe people's responses to deviant behavior. It will be their own deviant behavior! Organize the students into groups of three for this exercise. One will be the deviant behaver, and the other two will be the observers. If time and opportunity permit, they could rotate and each take a turn at being deviant.

Students should form groups and plan a deviant behavior to perform and one or more locations in which to perform it. You should monitor this closely, so that the behavior is inoffensive, and the locations are appropriate. Any mistakes here could be embarrassing and/or costly!

Suggest that the "deviant" student might join a table of two or three who are eating lunch in the cafeteria. (S)he could then be unresponsive to any gestures of friendship and/or mumble to him/herself while eating. The observers should be at a nearby table appearing to eat lunch but unobtrusively noting the behavior of those at the table. Other possibilities might be talking loudly (to no one) while walking down a crowded hall or sobbing uncontrollably in a busy lounge. Other ideas will come up. Be sure the students clear their plans with you before proceeding.

When the students return to class after completing the assignment, you should have a great discussion, including:

1.   reactions of the unsuspecting subjects to the "deviant;"

2.   the negative sanctions applied by the subjects;

3.   the feelings of your students before, during, and after the assignment was carried out;

4.   their thoughts about what it means to be normal or abnormal.

Have their ideas on that changed with this exercise?

It would be good to ask the students to write up this project as an assignment for credit. They should describe the deviant behavior, the location, the reactions of the subjects, and his/her own reactions. This is a good way to give the students a chance to deal with their feelings about this assignment.

THE DEVIANT AMONG US: WORKSHEET

1.   "Deviant" student_____

2.   Observer students_____

3.   Location_____

4.   Description of deviant behavior:

5.   Description of subjects (number, sex, approx. age, etc.):

6.   Reactions of subjects:

7. What did you learn from doing this experiment?

Name_____

Exercise #3: Psychiatric Labeling

This is an exercise that should help students to appreciate the problems created by using labels to identify the problem behaviors that people have. The persons become identified with the label, and our stereotypes take over. It is difficult for someone who has been labeled with a psychological problem to shake the image no matter how (s)he behaves.

PROCEDURE

1.   Invite a person unknown to your students to come to class to impersonate a former mental hospital patient. The person needs to be a convincing actor who will feel comfortable in front of the class. It is best to choose someone who has familiarity with a mental hospital--possibly someone who has worked or volunteered in one.

2.   Prepare your class for the visit. Tell them that this person was diagnosed as paranoid schizophrenic and has spent a couple of brief periods of therapy in a mental hospital. Students should be asked to review the appropriate material in the text and to prepare questions about hospital life. Ask them to be sensitive to the feelings of the "patient."

3.   After the speaker has departed, ask the students to discuss his/her behavior. They should look at it from a variety of points of view. Ask them to respond to questions such as those following. You may have others.

      a.   What was their impression of this person's behavior?
      b.   Did the person show any symptoms of the disorder for which (s)he was hospitalized?
      c.   Does (s)he appear to be "cured" of this disorder?
      d.   Did his/her thinking appear to be normal?
      e.   Were his/her emotions flat or inappropriate?
      f.   Did the students notice any side-effects of medication?
      g.   Were there any peculiar or unusual behaviors?

DISCUSSION

After the discussion questions above are completed, tell the students what you did. Now discuss their reactions to this revelation. Also discuss their responses to the above questions. Did labeling influence their reactions and observations?

■ JOURNAL QUESTIONS

1. Has anyone ever called you or someone you love "crazy" or "insane"? How did you feel?

2. Think of a behavior that you would label "abnormal." Which definition are you using for this labeling process?

3. Imagine that you "heard" from others in class that "someone" in your class was "psychotic." How would you feel? How would this information probably affect your behavior?

4. Have you ever known someone who abused or became dependent on drugs? How did the drugs affect their ability to function at home or at work? Were they able to eventually stop using the drugs? If so, how?

5. Do you ever feel depressed? What situations seem to make the depression worse? What do you do to try to stop feeling depressed?

6. Describe one of your irrational fears. When and how did the fear develop? How does it affect your behavior? What could be done to reduce the fear?

■ SUGGESTIONS FOR FURTHER READING

Achenback, T. and C. Edelbrock. "Psychopathology of Childhood." *Annual Review of Psychology,* (34) 1984: 227-256.

Alvarez, A. *The Savage God: A Study of Suicide.* W. W. Norton & Co., 1990.

American Journal of Psychiatry. 134 (9) 1977. A special issue devoted to the pros and cons of ECT.

Arieti, S. *Understanding and Helping the Schizophrenic.* Bruner/Mazel, 1994.

Braginsky, B. M., D. Braginsky, and K. Ring. *Methods of Madness: The Mental Hospital as a Last Resort.* University Press of America, 1982.

Carson, R. C., J. N. Butcher, & J. C. Coleman. *Abnormal Psychology,* 11th ed. Allyn and Bacon, 2000.

Cook, Ellen Piel. "Gender and psychological distress" (Special Volume on Gender Issues). *Journal of Counseling and Development,* 68 (March/April), 1990: 371.

Gottesman, I., J. Shields, and D. Hanson. *Schizophrenia Genesis.* W. H. Freeman, 1991.

Green, H. *I Never Promised You a Rose Garden.* New American Library, 1984.

Horgan, John. "Through a glass darkly: Are wearers of tinted glasses more likely to be depressed?" *Scientific American,* 262 (May), 1990: 34.

Janus, S. S. and C. L. Janus. *The Janus Report on Sexual Behavior.* John Wiley & Sons, Inc., 1994.

Kesey, K. *One Flew Over the Cuckoo's Nest.* Viking Press, 2002.

Laing, R. D. *The Politics of Experience.* Random House, 1983.

Meyer, R. *Case Studies in Abnormal Behavior,* 5th ed. Allyn and Bacon, 2000.

Nasar, S. *A Beautiful Mind: The Life of Mathematical Genius and Nobel Laureate John Nash.* Touchstone Books, 2001.

Needles, Douglas J. and Lyn Y. Abramson. "Positive life events, attributional style, and hopefulness: Testing a model of recovery from depression." *Journal of Abnormal Psychology,* 99 (May), 1990: 156.

Podvoll, Edward. *The Seduction of Madness: Revolutionary Insights into the World of Psychosis and a Compassionate Approach to Recovery at Home.* Harperperennial, 1991.

Rosenhan, D. L. "On Being Sane in Insane Places." *Science,* 179, 1973.

Ross, C. A. *Bluebird: Deliberate Creation of Multiple Personality by Psychiatrists.* Manitou Communications, 2000.

Ruiz, Dorothy (Ed.) *Handbook of Mental Health and Mental Disorder Among Black Americans.* Greenwood Press, 1990.

Schreiber, F. R. *Sybil.* Warner Books, 1995.

Seligman, M. E., Walker, E. F. and D. L. Rosenhan. *Abnormal Psychology,* 4th ed. W. W. Norton & Co., 2000.

Styron, William. *Darkness Visible: A Memoir of Madness.* Vintage Books, 1992.

Szasz, T. *The Myth of Mental Illness.* HarperCollins, 1984.

—. *The Manufacture of Madness.* Syracuse University Press, 1997.

■ MEDIA SUGGESTIONS

ANXIETY-RELATED DISORDERS: THE WORRIED WELL (2002, Films for the Humanities and Sciences, 15 min. each)
Each of the six programs in this series addresses a different condition. During powerful and moving interviews, two patients with each condition share their distressing stories of how the disorders have wreaked havoc on their lives, and how they've learned to cope. Several people have achieved a semblance of normality in their lives in spite of their dysfunctions. Leading experts in each field provide brief explanations of the condition.

DEPRESSION AND MANIC DEPRESSION (2002, Films for the Humanities and Sciences, 28 min.)
This program from *The Doctor Is In* explains the disease through the experiences of several people, including *60 Minutes* host Mike Wallace; Kay Redfield Jamison, psychiatrist and author of a book on her life with manic-depressive illness; artist Lama Dejani; and State Dept. official Robert Boorstin. The program also provides an overview of medications and therapy being used.

MASKS OF MADNESS (1998, Insight Media, 49 min.)
Featuring the personal stories of recovered mental illness patients, this video explains how help comes first in the form of a label — like schizophrenia, manic depression, or personality disorder — and then as medication. It reveals the problematic side effects of many medications and highlights the increasing success of strategies that involve vitamin therapy and nutrition.

MOOD DISORDERS (2002, Films for the Humanities and Sciences, 39 min.)
Mood disorders, or affective disorders, are discussed in this program together with their symptoms and differential diagnoses. The two main classifications of mood disorders—manic and depressive—are clearly defined and differentiated according to symptoms. The persistent mood disorders cyclothymia and dysthymia are discussed, along with medical causes of mood disorders.

MULTIPLE PERSONALITY DISORDER (1999, Insight Media, 50 min.)
Multiple personality disorder remains one of the most misunderstood mental disorders today. Although it is usually triggered by abuse or trauma, there are many cases with no apparent cause behind the onset of the affliction. This program enters the minds of several people who have battled multiple personality disorder, offering an intimate look at what life is like for those who live with strangers in their own minds. It takes an in-depth look at the Sybil case.

MULTIPLE PERSONALITY DISORDER: IN THE SHADOWS (2002, Films for the Humanities and Sciences, 24 min.)
Multiple Personality Disorder (MPD) is a completely preventable medical condition. Studies show that the average MPD patient spends seven years and receives three incorrect diagnoses before receiving an accurate diagnosis and appropriate treatment. It is now recognized that MPD is the result of severe childhood trauma, usually sexual and physical abuse—and it develops as a coping mechanism in young children who develop other personalities to deal with pain, fear, and danger. As the child grows older, this dissociation ceases to be a coping mechanism and becomes a block to normal functioning. This program shows how therapy can integrate the multiple personalities and make a patient "whole" again. Following two MPD patients and health care professionals, the program traces the struggles and triumphs in treating this disorder.

NEUROTIC, STRESS-RELATED, AND SOMATOFORM DISORDERS (2002, Films for the Humanities and Sciences, 45 min.)
This program discusses the following disorders and their differential diagnoses: phobic anxiety, anxiety, obsessive-compulsive disorder, stress reactions and adjustment, and dissociative disorders. Several sub-disorders, such as Korsakov's syndrome and post-traumatic stress disorder, are also discussed.

PANIC (2002, Films for the Humanities and Sciences, 26 min.)
This film explains anxiety disorders, including panic attacks and phobias. People with phobias are interviewed and the treatment procedures are explained. The biological factors contributing to anxiety disorders are described.

PERSONALITY DISORDERS (2002, Films for the Humanities and Sciences, 26 min.)
This program looks at the most common personality disorders—paranoid, schizoid, antisocial, and emotionally unstable.

PSYCHOPATHOLOGY (2001, from the *Discovering Psychology Series,* Annenberg/CPB, 30 min.)
This video explores the major types of mental illness, including schizophrenia, phobias, and affective disorders, and the major factors that influence them—both biological and psychological.

PSYCHOTIC DISORDERS (2002, Coast Community College District Telecourses, 30 min.)
Part of the *Psychology - The Study of Human Behavior Series,* this video discusses schizophrenia, its treatment and possible causes.

SCHIZOPHRENIA AND DELUSIONAL DISORDERS (2002, Films for the Humanities and Sciences, 46 min.)
Schizophrenia, acute and transient psychoses, persistent delusional disorders, and schizoaffective disorders are examined in this program. Specific symptoms of each disorder are discussed.

SUICIDE: THE PARENTS' PERSPECTIVE (2002, Films for the Humanities and Sciences, 26 min.)
This film helps parents listen more sensitively for signs of potential suicide.

SUICIDE: THE TEENAGER'S PERSPECTIVE (2002, Films for the Humanities and Sciences, 26 min.)
This film suggests that peer groups can be successfully trained to notice signs and to give friends support. Jim Wells, a nationally recognized expert on suicide, suggests that teens don't want to die and they do want help.

UNDERSTANDING BORDERLINE PERSONALITY DISORDER (1995, Insight Media, 35 min.)
This video presents clinically relevant features of borderline personality disorder (BPD) based on DSM-IV criteria. Marsha Linehan describes the underlying causes of the disorder, emphasizing biosocial factors, and traces the development of her treatment approach, Dialectical Behavior Therapy. Viewers see segments of actual case sessions.

UNDERSTANDING PSYCHOLOGICAL DISORDERS, Parts I & II (2002, Coast Community College District Telecourses, 30 min. each)
Part of the *Psychology – The Human Experience Series,* these videos present research on both obsessive-compulsive disorders and schizophrenia, including a look at the daily lives of such patients and the prognosis for the future.

WHAT IS NORMAL (2002, Coast Community College District Telecourses, 30 min.)
Part of the *Psychology - The Study of Human Behavior Series,* this video explains the distinction between normal and abnormal behavior.

THE WORLD OF ABNORMAL PSYCHOLOGY (1992, Annenberg/CPB, 60 min. each)
This series examines the etiology and characteristics of stress, anxiety, psychosomatic illnesses, and substance abuse, as well as of sexual, mood, organic mental, schizophrenic, personality, and behavior disorders. It also explores the psychodynamic, cognitive-behavioral, Gestalt, couples, group therapy, and biomedical approaches to treatment

A number of videos are available from Thomson. Videos appropriate for this chapter include the following films from the CNN TODAY Introductory Psychology Video Series:

Volume 1, Section 1: Mental Health and Stress
    Mental health History (1:36)
    Mental Health & Traumatic Events (2:24)

Volume 1, Section 4: Genetic Mapping
    Schizophrenia Gene (4:09)

Volume 2, Section 4: Mental Health and Stress
    Honduras Mental Stress (1:54)
    Suicidal Tendencies (1:32)

Volume 3, Section 9: Psychological Disorders
    Schizophrenic Reality (4:33)

Volume 4, Section 5: Abnormal Behavior
    Serial Killer (1:52)

Volume 4, Section 6: Disorders in Childhood
    Anxiety Disorders in Kids (1:43)

■ COMPUTER AND INTERNET RESOURCES

PSYCHNOW!

Personality and Abnormal Psychology
Abnormality and Psychopathology
Non-psychotic, Psychotic, and Affective Disorders

PSYK.TREK

Unit 11: Abnormal Behavior & Therapy
    11a: Anxiety disorders
    11b: Mood disorders
    11c: Schizophrenic disorders

INFOTRAC

Subject Guide/Key Terms: Psychological Disorders, Psychotic Disorders, Psychosis, Organic Mental Disorders, Dementia, Substance-related Disorders, Mood Disorders, Affective Disorders, Dysthymia, Maternity Blues, Postpartum Depression, Anxiety Disorders, Somatoform Disorders, Dissociative Disorders, Personality Disorders, Schizophrenia, Antisocial Personality, Panic Disorder, Agoraphobia, Phobia, Obsessive-compulsive Disorder, Stress Disorder, Delusions, Alzheimer's Disease, Bipolar Disorder, Seasonal Affective Disorder, Suicide

WEB SITES

Wadsworth Online Psychology Study Center:
http://info.wadsworth.com/cooessentials9

Internet Mental Health:
http://www.mentalhealth.com

Anxiety-Panic Resource Page:
http://www.algy.com/anxiety/anxiety.html

Obsessive-Compulsive Foundation:
http://www.ocfoundation.org/

Depression Web Resources:
http://www.depressionalliance.org/links/pages/

Bipolar Disorders Portal:
http://www.pendulum.org/index.htm

The Experience of Schizophrenia:
http://www.mgl.ca/~chovil/

The Schizophrenia Homepage:
http://www.schizophrenia.com/

Mental Health Net:
http://mentalhelp.net//

CHAPTER 14

Therapies

■ LEARNING OBJECTIVES

To demonstrate mastery of this chapter, the student should be able to:

1. Define psychotherapy.
2. Describe each of the following approaches to therapy:
   a. individual therapy
   b. group therapy
   c. insight therapy
   d. action therapy
   e. directive therapy
   f. non-directive therapy
   g. time-limited therapy
   h. supportive therapy
3. Evaluate what a person can expect as possible outcomes from psychotherapy.
4. Briefly describe the history of the treatment of psychological problems, including in your description trepanning, demonology, exorcism, ergotism, and Pinel.
5. Explain why the first psychotherapy was developed.
6. List the four basic techniques used in psychoanalysis and explain their purpose.
7. Name and describe the therapy that is frequently used today instead of psychoanalysis. Describe the criticism that helped prompt the switch, including the concept of spontaneous remission.
8. Contrast client-centered (humanistic) therapy and psychoanalysis.
9. Describe client-centered therapy, including the four conditions that should be maintained for successful therapy.
10. Explain the approach of existential therapy and compare and contrast it with client-centered therapy. Name and describe one example of existential therapy.
11. Name a key aspect of existential therapy.
12. Briefly describe Gestalt therapy, including its main emphasis.

The following objective is related to the material in the "Exploring Psychology" section of the text.

13.   Discuss the limitations of media and phone psychologists and describe what the APA recommends should be the extent of their activities. Briefly describe the advantages and disadvantages of cybertherapy, and describe how videoconferencing can avoid many of the limitations of nontraditional therapy.

14.   Contrast the goal of behavior therapy with the goal of insight therapies.

15.   Define behavior modification and state its basic assumption.

16.   Explain the relationship of aversion therapy to classical conditioning.

17.   Describe aversion therapy, and explain how it can be used to stop smoking and drinking.

18.   Explain how relaxation, reciprocal inhibition, and use of a hierarchy are combined to produce desensitization.

19.   State what desensitization is used for and give an example of desensitization therapy or vicarious desensitization therapy.

20.   Explain how virtual reality exposure may be used to treat phobias.

21.   Very briefly describe eye-movement desensitization and reprocessing.

22.   List and briefly describe the seven operant principles most frequently used by behavior therapists.

23.   Explain how nonreinforcement and time out can be used to bring about extinction of a maladaptive behavior.

24.   Describe a token economy, including its advantages and possible disadvantages. Include the terms token and target behavior in your description.

25.   Describe what sets a cognitive therapist apart from other behavior therapists.

26.   List and describe three thinking errors that underlie depression and explain what can be done to correct such thinking.

27.   Describe rational-emotive behavior therapy.

28.   List the three core ideas that serve as the basis of most irrational beliefs.

29.   Describe the advantages of group therapy.

30.   Briefly describe each of the following group therapies:
      a.   psychodrama (include the terms role-playing, role reversal, and mirror technique)
      b.   family therapy
      c.   group awareness training (include sensitivity groups, encounter groups, and large group awareness training)

31.   Evaluate the effectiveness of encounter groups and sensitivity groups. Include the concept of the therapy placebo effect.

32.   Discuss the effectiveness of psychotherapy.

33.   Describe the rate at which typical doses of therapy help people improve.

34.   List the eight goals of psychotherapy, and state the four means used to accomplish the goals.

35.   List and briefly describe the nine points or tips that can help a person when counseling a friend.

36.   List and explain the seven characteristics of culturally skilled counselors.

37.   Define pharmacotherapy.

38.   List and describe the three classes of drugs used to treat psychopathology.

39.   Discuss the advantages and disadvantages of the use of pharmacotherapy in the treatment of psychosis.

40.   Describe the risk-benefit controversy for drugs such as Clozaril and Risperdal.

41.   Describe what is known about the uses and effectiveness of the following techniques in the treatment of psychosis:

      a. electroconvulsive therapy   b. psychosurgery (include the term deep lesioning)

42.   Describe the role of hospitalization and partial hospitalization in the treatment of psychological disorders.

43.   Explain what deinstitutionalization is and how halfway houses have attempted to help in the treatment of mental health.

44.   Discuss the role of community mental health centers in mental health.

The following objectives are related to the material in the "Psychology in Action" section of the text.

45.   Describe how covert sensitization, thought stopping, and covert reinforcement can be used to reduce unwanted behavior.

46.   Give an example of how you can overcome a common fear or break a bad habit using the steps given for desensitization.

47.   List and describe four indicators that may signal the need for professional psychological help.

48.   List six methods a person can use for finding a therapist.

49.   Describe how one can choose a psychotherapist.

50.   Distinguish among paraprofessionals, peer counselors, and self-help groups.

51.   Summarize what is known about the importance of the personal qualities of the therapist and the client for successful therapy.

52.   List six psychotherapy danger signals.

■ DISCUSSION QUESTIONS

1.   What preconceptions did you have about psychotherapy? Has your understanding of therapy changed? Has your attitude changed?

2.   Chapter 14 defines psychotherapy as "any psychological technique used to facilitate positive changes in a person's personality, behavior, or adjustment." Give three examples of dialogues about problems that are not a form of psychotherapy.

3.   What role does the passage of time play in a person's improvement during and after psychotherapy?

4. Do you agree with existential therapist Rollo May that there has been a loss of individual freedom, faith, and meaning in today's society? Why or why not?

5. Which form of psychotherapy do you find the most attractive? Why?

6. What similarities would Carl Rogers see in the job of being a "good therapist" and the job of being a "good parent"?

7. What psychological services are available in your area? Would you know how to find or make use of them? What factors would affect your decision to seek help?

8. Describe a time when you helped someone resolve a personal problem. Describe a time when you were unsuccessful in helping. What factors seemed to make the difference?

9. Do you think it would be right for a therapist to allow a person to make suicide an "existential choice" or an expression of "free will"?

10. Which style of therapy would you expect a computer program to most closely duplicate? If a computer were programmed to provide help for a limited problem such as test anxiety, would you find computer therapy more acceptable?

11. In your opinion, are radio psychologists engaged in education or therapy? Is talk-show psychology ethical? What value is there for listeners and callers in talking with a radio psychologist? With an online-therapist over the Internet?

12. Psychotherapy is based on trust and confidentiality. Do you think that therapists should be legally required to report dangerous thoughts or fantasies revealed by clients? If a therapist misjudges the seriousness of a client's intent to do harm, should the therapist be held legally responsible? Why or why not?

13. Under what conditions would you condone the use of behavior modification? When would you oppose it?

14. Based on the techniques described in Chapter 14, would you cooperate with a therapist who wanted to use behavior therapy? Are there some techniques you find acceptable and others not?

15. Select a bad habit you would like to break or a positive behavior you would like to encourage, and explain how you might use a behavioral or cognitive behavioral technique to alter your behavior.

16. Some critics have charged that the use of tokens in the classroom encourages students to expect artificial rewards. Behavior theorists reply that explicit rewards are better than inconsistent rewards such as praise and attention. What are the advantages and drawbacks represented by each position?

17. How do you feel about the use of behavior modification in prisons and psychiatric hospitals? Is behavior therapy any different from the involuntary administration of tranquilizers or other drugs? Why or why not?

18. Some states have tried at times to ban the use of aversive therapy techniques for severely disturbed people. Do you think that such treatment decisions should or should not be limited by law?

19. Many people develop stronger (not weaker) fears of water when pushed into the pool. Why? Under what conditions could this form of "therapy" (often called "implosive therapy") work?

20. For what kind of person and for what problems would Ellis's REBT be most effective?

21. If you were going to become a therapist, would you become a psychologist or a psychiatrist? Why?

22. What positive and negative roles do mental institutions play?

■ LECTURE ENHANCEMENTS

This unit offers many opportunities to use role-playing to demonstrate therapeutic principles. Students can be invited to come to the front of a large lecture hall to demonstrate the procedures. Students can be asked to share some of the worries, anxieties, and fears they are dealing with at this time in the semester. Students can be provided with literature on peer counseling, and the definitive differences between peer support and formal counseling can be discussed. Be prepared for an increase in requests from students for referrals.

1. **Students will undoubtedly find a visit by a clinician interesting in conjunction with the readings in this chapter.** If possible, invite a clinical colleague or clinician in private practice to class. Even if you yourself are a clinician, the inclusion of a person with different viewpoints and experiences will enrich discussion.

2. **It is not too difficult in the classroom to simulate some basic approaches to psychotherapy.** Ask for a volunteer and begin by asking the student to recount a recent dream. Select an interesting element from the dream and ask the student to free-associate

to it. Follow a few of the interesting thoughts through further free association, and make note of any apparent resistances. Point out that you are using psychoanalytic techniques, and then ask the student what he or she would like to talk about next. Shift into a non-directive style and simulate a Rogerian approach. As soon as this approach as been illustrated, begin watching for an irrational assumption in what the student is saying. When you find one, shift to the more confrontative and didactic tone of REBT. Again point out what you have done. Finally, return to some topic which has already surfaced and demonstrate the theatrical "here and now" approach of Gestalt therapy. For example, ask the student to say something to an empty chair representing a parent, roommate, lover, etc. Next ask the student to sit in the chair and answer as that person, and then to stand up and reply to the imagined person, and so forth. Conclude by reviewing and discussing all the techniques that have been illustrated.

3. **A brief illustration of one or two sensitivity techniques can be interesting. A trust walk is a good choice.** Randomly pair students and instruct them to walk to some point on campus. On the way to the chosen point, one student should be blindfolded while being guided by the second. On the way back, they should reverse roles. For a more dramatic demonstration, have a student stand with several students arranged behind him or her. The student must close his/her eyes and fall backward--to be caught by the group. This takes real trust!

4. **As various therapies are tried, modified, and developed, the possibility of controlling maladaptive behavior increases.** It is possible to foresee a time when such techniques will be perfected to the point where behavioral change, and therefore, behavioral control, will be much easier to accomplish and more certain. Ask the students to consider some questions about this because it would be possible, then, to control not only maladaptive behavior, but any behavior. Is it a good idea to go that far? Can we keep the knowledge for good purposes and keep it out of the hands of manipulators who want to exploit others? Who should decide when and how a therapeutic technique should be used? Who will protect the interests of the mentally ill who could be exploited?

5. **Invite an experienced psychiatrist who has successfully used electroconvulsive shock therapy to class to discuss its use, value, and consequences.** Students should be prepared ahead of time with good questions; otherwise, they tend, on first hearing the specifics of the procedure, to be bothered by what they imagine to be an unpleasant and painful experience since any reference to electric shock has negative connotations. Good preparation can make for a productive class discussion.

6. **To give students experience with the basic elements of systematic desensitization, it can be interesting to guide them through the steps of deep muscle relaxation.** When they are thoroughly relaxed, announce that one of the reasons you wanted them to be relaxed is that in a moment you are going to give a surprise test on behavior modification.

At that point, ask students if they were able to notice an increase in tension or anxiety when you announced the test. If they could, tell them they did not pass the item, "surprise quiz announced in class," on a hierarchy of test anxiety, and that they will have to repeat the relaxation exercises! This will allow them to see what actually occurs in systematic desensitization.

7. **For an interesting discussion starter, have two teams of students prepare a debate reflecting the opposing viewpoints of insight therapists and behavior therapists.** Another good topic for debate is the question of whether or not, or under what circumstances, behavior modification techniques should be used in schools, the military, prisons, programs for the mentally retarded, mental hospitals, and other institutional settings.

8. **If it is possible to find someone who has undergone aversion conditioning at one of the many commercial stop-smoking services, invite him/her to be a guest speaker.** Interview him/her with respect to the effectiveness of the technique, the degree of discomfort experienced, how long the effects lasted, how he or she now feels about the issue of behavior control, etc. A point worth exploring is the cost of the treatment. It could be argued that expensive and aversive procedures simply produce strong commitment to a nonsmoking regimen by creating a powerful cognitive dissonance effect, rather than actually conditioning aversions.

9. **Students' understanding of systematic desensitization is enhanced when they have an opportunity to experience it.** Another way to provide this experience is to combine Jacobson's traditional relaxation exercise with the construction of a class anxiety hierarchy. Most students seem to have an aversion to tarantulas which can provide a suitable topic for the generation of an imaginary hierarchy. Have class members combine relaxation techniques with visualization of scenes from the hierarchy. If all goes well, some students can be brought to the point of imagining, without obvious discomfort, dozens of tarantulas crawling all over them. (Jacobson's relaxation technique is described in M. Goldfried and G. Davidson, *Clinical Behavior Therapy,* Holt, Rinehart, and Winston, 1976.)

10. **A number of issues relating to diagnosis, pharmacotherapy, hospitalization, and patient rights can be addressed by asking the class to consider this hypothetical situation:**

John has spent much of the last month curled up in a fetal position under the dining room table in his apartment. A worried neighbor called the local county mental health unit. John has been hospitalized on a 72-hour hold for observation.

There are several questions for discussion:

Who should decide if he should be further hospitalized?

Should he be given drugs, with or without his consent?

When should he be released?

Who should decide: his parents, a psychiatrist, a judge, John alone?

11.   **Prepare copies of the following three hypothetical situations.** Give everyone in class one of the three cards. Students are given one week to decide whether the person needs psychotherapy, and if so, the specific person in their community who could help. Encourage students to research how much the therapy would cost, how many weeks of contact would be expected. A letter can be sent to resource people in the community "advising" them they could be receiving a barrage of calls. Not only will students learn about resources, but the instructor will have the chance to do some professional networking. If your class is large, appoint only a few researchers to do this investigation, following which they can report their findings to the class.

Xavier has trouble sleeping. He is worrying about problems at his job and feels tired at work. He is on edge most of the time and is having trouble tolerating the behavior of an abrasive co-worker. His personal relationships are not affected by the problems at work.

Jan experiences intense highs and lows. For weeks her "blues" deepen to thoughts of suicide; then she will feel her body come out of the depression and for a few weeks she will feel on top of the world. During her energetic periods, she sometimes makes poor decisions. Last week she was so certain she was going to get a job advertised in the newspaper that she spent $2,000 of her savings on new work clothes. She didn't even get an interview.

Nestor has trouble concentrating in class. Often he will find himself thinking about aviation disasters and he will hysterically laugh. He feels "evil" as if surrounded by a poisonous cloud that will contaminate anyone nearby. He'll answer questions in class but he gets distracted and ends up talking about unrelated ideas. His classmates give him looks of confusion and seem to avoid him on campus. Yesterday he was certain he smelled smoke in the classroom. When he began shouting, "Fire!" his professor removed him from class and reprimanded him saying, "Your joke wasn't funny."

■ ROLE-PLAYING SCENARIOS

1.   **Ask students to work in pairs to act out a psychoanalytic therapy session.** One partner begins by free associating--saying anything that comes to mind for about ten minutes. The other jots down the topics mentioned. At the end of the ten minutes, the "patient" is asked to elaborate about either a personal topic not mentioned or the topic

mentioned least often. Switch roles. Discuss as a pair or as a class defenses, resistance, and transference.

2. **Ask students to work in pairs.** Give one partner (the "client") a file card on which is printed a behavior that would usually trigger shock or disapproval. The other partner (the "therapist") is to respond to this issue showing unconditional positive regard, authenticity, and empathy. (Students enjoy developing the shocking examples.)

3. **In pairs, share decisions you have made this semester.** How did you make these choices? What were the consequences of these choices for you? What could be done to help you make wiser decisions and accept the responsibility for the decisions that you make?

4. **Form small "self-help groups."** Spend thirty minutes talking as:
   a. parents concerned about their teen's driving habits;
   b. parents concerned about their teen's drinking behavior;
   c. teens concerned about their parent's drinking behavior;
   d. students upset about favoritism and racism in one of their classes;
   e. employees angry about low wages;
   f. husbands confused about their domestic role in an era of woman's liberation.

5. **Role-play a family meeting.** Assign parent and sibling roles. One of the children is chairing this meeting. Ask each person to bring an issue to the family "agenda"; have the family work together to decide which issue to discuss and what to do on that particular issue.

6. **You have a friend who smokes.** You have decided that you can no longer tolerate this behavior in your presence. What would you say or do to change this behavior without destroying your friendship?

7. **A very physically fit truck driver and his highly religious wife have come to you for sex therapy.** They have been married ten years and have stopped making love. What would you ask them? What would you tell them? Which therapeutic approach would you use? Why?

8. **You have been asked to direct an experimental electronic prison.** Electronic devices monitor the behavior of inmates, open and close doors, and prevent inmates from having contact with guards and with each other. Describe to your staff the challenges you expect as the new director.

9. **You are a psychiatrist treating a patient who is exhibiting schizophrenic episodes.** Explain to the patient's relatives why you would (or would not) use pharmacotherapy?

10.   **You are the director of a halfway house for psychiatric residents.** A woman is arriving this afternoon who was able to learn to take the medicine for her mild schizophrenic episodes and to reduce stress through a token economy system in the hospital. What can you do to help her improvement in therapy generalize to the situation within your halfway house?

■ VALUE-CLARIFICATION STATEMENTS

1.   Dreams are simply random thoughts and have no meaning whatsoever.

2.   Freud's approach to therapy is the only way to get at the real causes of human unhappiness and maladjustment.

3.   Most people are not willing to accept responsibility for their own behavior.

4.   Media psychology (talk-radio, television, and online therapy) is harmful and should be banned from radio stations, television, and the Internet.

5.   Sensitivity and encounter groups are social, not therapeutic events.

6.   Aversion conditioning is an inhumane way to treat people.

7.   Psychotherapy should be made available freely to all taxpayers.

8.   The problem of therapists having sex with their clients has been blown out of proportion by the media.

9.   Anything shared in a psychotherapy session is confidential and cannot be revealed to anyone under any circumstances.

10. Electroconvulsive Shock Therapy (ECT) is too dangerous to use and should be banned.

11. If a therapist truly falls in love with his/her client, it is acceptable for a romantic relationship to develop, even while the therapist is still providing the client with therapy.

12. Tranquilizers and energizers should only be prescribed as a last resort.

13. Antipsychotic drugs should be prescribed as the first form of intervention so that psychotherapy can be most effective.

■ ONE-MINUTE MOTIVATORS

1.   **Ask students to help clarify what is the difference between a witch doctor or shaman, and a psychotherapist.**

2.   **Briefly describe the historical, economic, political, and sociological times of Freud.** If Freud were beginning his career now, how would his theory and therapy be different?

3.   **Ask students to keep a "daydream journal" by jotting in the margin of their notes the topic of any daydreams that they have.** At the end of a week, ask students to evaluate their daydreams. What are the themes? How frequently do the daydreams occur? What do the dreams say about the student's feelings toward this course or other events in their life? Do they reveal unconscious desires, as postulated by Freud?

4.   **Ask students to reflect your lecture presentation.** At the end of a few sentences, call on a volunteer to restate what you said. Invite a student who heard your ideas differently to provide his/her view. After three or four attempts to rephrase satisfactorily, it should be clear how important "reflecting" is for really understanding what we are saying to each other.

5.   **To focus on the "here-and-now," suddenly ask a student what he/she is feeling at the moment.** Continue with lecture. Ask another student. If students have trouble expressing their feelings, use Gestalt techniques to clarify their immediate experience.

6.   **Ask students to turn to the person next to them and to share "things left unsaid" to someone they care about.** If they could talk to anyone in the world to add closure to the relationship, who would they call? What would they say?

7.   **Ask students to think of something that they are currently doing that they wish they would not do.** Then pass out a rubber band to each student. Encourage them to zing themselves with the rubber band every time they think about doing that disgusting behavior. Discuss the pros and cons of aversive techniques.

8.   **Encourage students to think of five good things that happened today.** If they have been feeling depressed, is this difficult to do? Is it helpful?

9.   **Ask the class to repeat in unison, "I am a valued, competent person."** What are the limits of the "positive thinking" inherent in much cognitive therapy?

10.   **Ask students to practice active listening, clarifying, and focusing on feelings.** Students can share the activities of the previous weekend or their feelings about friends,

relatives, work, or this class. Students should find that active listening is time consuming, exhausting, and tremendously important. Most of us have not really been trained to listen to each other.

■ BROADENING OUR CULTURAL HORIZONS

1. **All societies find some mechanism for facilitating change in others.** Compare and contrast the therapeutic role of witch-doctors, folk-medicine practitioners, and religious leaders. What might all of these have in common that would help at least some people feel better?

2. **Research psychotherapy in other cultures.** What is the goal of the therapy? What techniques are used? How effective are they? For example, various drugs, herbs, chemicals, and vitamins are used in the Far East to treat "impotence," which is regarded as a psychological problem in about half the cases in America. [See Shikai, Xu (1990). Treatment of impotence in traditional Chinese medicine. *Journal of Sex Education and Therapy,* 16(3), 198-200.]

3. **Sometimes the purpose of therapy is to change a person's behavior; other times the purpose is to encourage the person to accept aspects of their own behavior more fully.** Think about differences between your culture and the culture of your parents (or your children). What behavior patterns do your parents want you to change? What behavior would you want them to accept more readily? What happens when two cultures or two generations clash in terms of whose behavior is supposed to change? How do the politics of power affect the kinds of changes that therapy encourages and the specific groups who are doing most of the changing?

4. **How important is it for a therapist to understand the ethnic group or culture of the client he or she is treating?** What kind of cultural or gender differences might make certain kinds of therapy ineffective?

■ SUPPLEMENTAL ACTIVITIES

Exercise #1: Locating Professional Help

TO THE INSTRUCTOR:
This is an enlarged version of an exercise suggested earlier. Its purpose is to give students first-hand experience in locating mental health services in his/her own area. This could pay big dividends later. Everyone needs at some time to think about getting or helping someone get professional psychological help. In a crisis or emergency, a person may not have the time or opportunity to do a thorough review of what is available in the area. Being prepared is a great advantage. Students will be surprised, when this project is completed, at the vast number of

services available in most communities. There are always many more than people expect there to be.

PROCEDURE

A. Set up one or more scenarios for the students. The following is an example. Each scenario could focus on a different type of problem. This one covers quite a few:

> You have a friend who has a serious adjustment problem. It has reached the point where (s)he can no longer do his/her work, is having serious problems with his/her family, is generally miserable and very anxious. Thoughts of suicide recur, and (s)he has started drinking heavily. (S)he knows you are studying psychology and asks you for some assistance in finding good professional help. The friend indicates that (s)he has some money, but is on a limited budget.

B. Divide the class into groups of three, asking each group to research the resources that would be available in the city and county to help the friend. They should identify specific sources of help and know something about the kind of assistance that would be provided. This means they should visit the facility, talk to personnel there, read brochures, etc. to become well informed. Provide each student with a worksheet. You may want to modify or add to the sample given.

C. Once the students have completed the research, all groups should report on the same class day. As they give their findings, compile a master list of resources in the area. This could be refined and distributed to the students.

D. Provide some incentives to the class. Give a reward, such as extra class credit, to the groups who bring in comprehensive lists. Be sure that everyone who tried hard is a winner, not just one or two. Another incentive could be having the students, when the comprehensive list is completed, distribute it to places where it could be used--the college counseling office, local churches and clergy, helping agencies in the local government, etc.

A FRIEND IN NEED: WORKSHEET

TO THE STUDENT:
You have a friend who has a serious adjustment problem. It has reached the point where (s)he can no longer do his/her work, is having serious problems with his/her family, is generally miserable and very anxious. Thoughts of suicide recur, and (s)he has started to drink heavily. (S)he knows you are studying psychology and asks you for some assistance in finding professional help. The friend indicates that (s)he has some money, but is on a limited budget.

You and your group are to research the area (extend your search to include the whole county) to find all the possible resources that might help your friend.

Complete the following:

1.   Indicate the resources which you have found. Note where you found out about each and how you checked it out.

2.   State briefly what services your friend could expect from each of the resources, who is eligible for the services, and what the fees might be. This will require a personal visit, a phone call, or, at least, reading some literature provided by the office or agency.

3.   What do you think of the possibilities of your friend getting the kind of help (s)he needs, based on what is available in your area? Explain your answer.

Exercise #2: Behavior Self-Modification

TO THE INSTRUCTOR:

This is an exercise that will get students to think about behavior modification techniques. It is a project that can be done in one class period, as it is described here, or could be more elaborate and done over a whole term. Some modification would be needed, but the basic idea is the same whichever way it is done.

Ask the students to form small groups, three per group would be ideal, and work on a plan to change a behavior. Each of the three should have a behavior to change. The group can work on each one. There is an advantage to a group rather than an individual working on the problem because it is more likely to get done if the group works on it. It also gives support to each individual in the planning and executing of the change.

In preparation for this project, you may need to review the basic concepts of operant conditioning to make sure everyone understands them. In particular, go over reinforcement so that they are clear on how it is to be applied.

PROCEDURE

1. Divide the class into groups of three to design and execute the project.

2. Distribute the instructions and worksheets for the exercise, and go over them with the students.

3. Ask students to submit their worksheets and a plan of action for your review.

4. If you feel this is worthwhile, ask the students to carry out the plan of action, once it has been reviewed and critiqued by you, and to report back to their group and to you on their progress after a specified number of weeks.

BEHAVIOR SELF-MODIFICATION: WORKSHEET

TO THE STUDENT:
In this exercise, each student will identify a behavior (s)he wants to change, and the group will help to develop a plan of action to bring this about. You should do the following:

1.   Each person in the group should identify a behavior (s)he would like to change. Keep it simple. Try something like nail-biting, smoking, a poor study habit, or overeating. You can certainly think of others.

2.   Use the outline that follows as a guide for developing your program for change. First you should describe the present situation; then you can work on changes. Keep in mind that you should try to do only what is possible. There is no point in planning what you won't carry out.

I.   **The Present Situation**

    A.   *The problem behavior:* Here you should briefly but clearly state what behavior you wish to change. It should be described exactly as it occurs.

    B.   *The stimulus cues:* These are the stimuli in your environment that have become associated with the behavior you wish to change. An example: smoking while drinking a cup of coffee. If you want to stop smoking, you will have to change that whole behavior pattern because coffee drinking and smoking have become associated. What are all the cues or stimuli that are associated with the undesirable behavior? You should try to identify as many of these as possible. It may be a good idea to do some self-observation, taking notes of the circumstances that surround the behavior you want to change.

    C.   *The reinforcements:* There will be immediate and delayed reinforcements for the behavior you want to change. Be honest about this, and try to identify what they are. For example, smoking relaxes you and makes you feel good; it looks cool; it gives you something to do with your hands; you can blow neat smoke rings, etc.

BEHAVIOR MODIFICATION: WORKSHEET (page 2)

II.   **Changes That You Plan to Make**

     A.   The new behavior that you want to develop to replace the old: Remember, you can't just stop doing something. You need to do something different in its place. An overeater doesn't stop eating, but eats differently! A smoker doesn't stop breathing, but inhales differently! Describe the new behavior. It needs to be attainable.

     B.   New stimulus cues: those objects or events you plan to associate with the new behavior to help it become established.

     C.   The reinforcements for the new behavior: These need to be immediate and long range. Plan specific reinforcements and set specific times when they will be received.

III.   **Keep accurate and detailed records to chart your progress.** Speak with the instructor about your plan and the progress you are making once you are working on the change.

■ JOURNAL QUESTIONS

1. If you have never been in therapy, what feelings do you have about people who go to therapy? What expectations would you have if you went to therapy?

2. If you (or a friend of yours) have been in therapy, what encouraged you to seek help? What problem did you bring to the therapy sessions? How did you select the therapist? What therapeutic techniques were used? How did the therapeutic process change you?

3. Keep a dream journal. Explain each dream in terms of the latent and the manifest content.

4. Who in your life seems most genuine, authentic, and empathic in responding to your concerns?

5. Think of a problem that your family (or a family you know well) is trying to work through. Would family therapy be helpful? Why or why not?

6. Think of a behavior you would like to change. Would aversion therapy be helpful? Why or why not?

7. Think of a behavior that you would like to change in someone you live with. How could you reinforce the appropriate behavior? How could you discourage the inappropriate behavior? Would tokens be helpful? Why or why not?

8. Which of Ellis's irrational beliefs do you unfortunately believe most strongly? Why?

9. If you had a major problem, who would you go to for help? What kind of help would be most effective? Why?

10. You have been deeply depressed for some time, and your therapist has suggested ECT as a treatment. How do you feel about this treatment? What hopes do you have for the outcome of treatment? What fears do you have?

■ SUGGESTIONS FOR FURTHER READING

Burton, A. (Ed.). *Twelve Therapists.* Jossey-Bass, 1972.

Corey, Gerald. *Theory and Practice of Group Counseling,* 4th ed. Brooks/Cole, 1995.

___. *Theory and Practice of Counseling and Psychotherapy,* 6th ed. Wadsworth, 1999.

Ellis, A. and M. Powers. *A New Guide to Rational Living,* 3rd ed. Wilshire, 1998.

Frankl, V. *Man's Search for Meaning.* Beacon Press, 2000.

Freud, S. *Essentials of Psychoanalysis.* Penguin, 1988.

___. *On Dreams.* Dover, 2001.

Martin, G., and J. Pear. *Behavior Modification: What It Is and How to Do It.* Prentice-Hall, 1998.

Meyers, R. *Case Studies in Abnormal Behavior.* Allyn and Bacon, 2002.

Perls, F. *Gestalt Therapy Verbatim.* Gestalt Journal, 1992.

Prochaska, J. O., and J. C. Norcross. *Systems of Psychotherapy: A Transtheroretical Analysis,* 5th ed. Brooks/Cole 2003.

Rathus, S. A. and J. S. Nevid. *Behavior Therapy.* New American Library, 1986.

Rogers, C. *Client-Centered Therapy.* Constable and Co., Ltd., 1995.

Ruitenbeck, H. M. *The New Group Therapies.* Avon, 1972.

Watson, D. and R. Tharp. *Self-Directed Behavior: Self-Modification for Personal Adjustment,* 8th ed. Wadsworth, 2002.

Wolpe, J. *The Practice of Behavior Therapy,* 4th ed. Allen & Bacon, 1992.

Yalom, Irvin D. *Love's Executioner and Other Tales of Psychotherapy.* HarperCollins, 2000.

■ MEDIA SUGGESTIONS

APPROACHES TO THERAPY (2002, from *Psychology - The Study of Human Behavior Series,* Coast Community College District, 30 min.)
This video allows viewers to observe sessions with three therapists, each of whom employs a different approach.

BELLEVUE: INSIDE OUT (2002, Films for the Humanities and Social Sciences, 76 min.)
New York City's Bellevue Hospital has a renowned psychiatric emergency center that treats 7,000 men and women annually. This gritty program takes a daunting look at the daily operation of the center by focusing on a handful of people as they struggle with their illnesses. The entire experience is presented, from arrests of the criminally insane and admissions of new patients to long-term treatment and therapy groups. In addition to working with mental disorders, doctors and nurses also confront drug and alcohol addiction in an environment where 50 percent of their patients have substance abuse problems.

DEPRESSION: OLD PROBLEM, NEW THERAPY (2002, Films for the Humanities and Social Sciences, 23 min.)
In this program, Dr. Dennis Charney, of Yale University; Lydia Lewis, of the National Depressive and Manic Depressive Association; and other mental health professionals discuss the types, symptoms, and triggers of depression as they relate both to adolescents and to adults. Promising antidepressants such as selective norepinephrine re-uptake inhibitors, Substance P antagonists, and corticotropin-releasing factor receptor antagonists are considered, as are advances in brain scan technology. The value of psychiatric counseling and peer support groups is also stressed.

DON'T PANIC: THE PROMISE OF INTENSIVE EXPOSURE THERAPY (2002, Films for the Humanities and Social Sciences, 17 min.)
Can confronting one's own worst nightmare really destroy the paralyzing power it commands? In this program, ABC News anchors Diane Sawyer and Sam Donaldson and correspondent Jay Schadler document a young woman's struggle to overcome the feelings of fear that have reduced her world to the narrow confines of her own home. Through intensive exposure therapy, an alternative to medication and psychotherapy for treating panic attacks complicated by agoraphobia, many patients return to normal living within mere days. Although the long-term benefits of the therapy are still being researched, the results are nothing short of miraculous. (17 minutes, color)

PSYCHOTHERAPY (2001, from the *Discovering Psychology Series,* Annenberg/CPB, 30 min.)
This video explores the relationships among theory, research, and practice, and how treatment of psychological disorders has been influenced by historical, cultural, and social forces.

THERAPY CHOICES (2002, from *Psychology - The Study of Human Behavior Series,* Coast Community College District, 30 min.)
This video focuses on significant alternatives to traditional individual psychotherapy, group therapy, family therapy, and self-help groups.

THERAPIES (2002, from *Psychology - The Human Experience Series,* Coast Community College District, 30 min.)
This video examines four different styles of therapy treatment for mental disorders and discusses the role of each style of therapy.

TREATING PHOBIAS (2002, Films for the Humanities and Sciences, 19 min.)
This film describes the frequency and the unpredictability of panic attacks for many people. Intervention strategies are described, including "confrontational or supportive exposure," beta blockers, and tranquilizers. The difference between a fear, a phobia, and a panic attack is clarified. Listeners are reminded that it is crucial that people talk about their fears.

A number of videos are available from Thomson. Videos appropriate for this chapter include the following films from the CNN TODAY Introductory Psychology Video Series:

Volume 1, Section 3: The Mind and Therapy
        Aversive Therapy (2:12)
        Thought Control (3:46)

Volume 2, Section 2: The Mind and Therapy
        Road Rage (2:02)

Volume 3, Section 10: Treatment of Psychological Disorders
 Depression Treatment (1:55)

■ COMPUTER AND INTERNET RESOURCES

PSYCHNOW!

Personality and Abnormal Psychology
Major Psychological Therapies

PSYK.TREK

Unit 11: Abnormal Behavior & Therapy
 11d: Insight therapies
 11e Behavioral and biomedical therapies

INFOTRAC

Subject Guide/Key Terms: Psychotherapy, Group Therapy, Psychoanalysis, Existential Therapy, Gestalt Therapy, Cybertherapy, Effectiveness of Psychotherapy, Eye Movement Desensitization, Time-out and Misbehavior, Token Economy, Cognitive Therapy, Family Therapy, Psychosurgery, Psychopharmacology

WEB SITES

Wadsworth Online Psychology Study Center:
http://info.wadsworth.com/coonessentials9

Behavior On-Line:
http://www.behavior.net

The Psychoanalytic Connection:
http://psychoanalysis.net/

Introduction to Psychotherapy:
http://www.geocities.com/psychotherapyuk/

Psychology Self-Help Resources on the Internet:
http://www.psychwww.com/resource/selfhelp.htm

Internet Mental Health Resources:
http://www.mentalhealth.com/

AmoebaWeb Psychology Resources: Therapy:
http://www.vanguard.edu/faculty/ddegelman/amoebaweb/index.cfm?doc_id=877

CHAPTER 15
Gender and Sexuality

■ **LEARNING OBJECTIVES**

To demonstrate mastery of this chapter, the student should be able to:

1.   Distinguish between the terms sex and gender. Differentiate primary from secondary sex characteristics and state (in general) what causes them.
2.   Define or describe the following terms or concepts:
    a. menarche
    b. ovulation
    c. menopause
    d. gonads
    e. estrogens
    f. androgens
    g. testosterone
3.   List and describe the five dimensions of sex.
4.   Explain how a person's sex develops. Include in your discussion a description of these conditions:
    a. androgen insensitivity
    b. hermaphroditism
    c. androgenital syndrome
    d. biological biasing effect
5.   Describe the relationship between sex and intelligence.
6.   Differentiate gender identity from gender role and explain how gender identity is formed.
7.   Discuss whether there are universal psychological differences between males and females.
8.   Define "gender role stereotypes." Discuss how these stereotypes ignore the "diversity of humanity."
9.   Describe the effects of socialization on gender roles and include a discussion of instrumental and expressive behaviors.

The following objective is related to the material in the "Exploring Psychology" section of the text.
10.   Discuss the concept of androgyny and its relationship to masculinity, femininity, and adaptability.

11. Describe the development of sexual behavior in humans and show how cultural norms influence that development. Define the term erogenous zones.
12. Explain the concept of a sexual script.
13. Discuss the differences between males and females and their degree of arousal to erotic stimuli.
14. Explain what causes increases in sex drives in males and females.
15. Describe the effects of castration, sterilization, and aging on the sex drive.
16. Discuss the frequency, importance, normality, and acceptability of masturbation.
17. Describe the factors that determine one's sexual orientation.
18. Describe the effect of heredity and hormones on one's sexual orientation.
19. Discuss homosexuality in terms of incidence, acceptability, psychological normality, and when homosexuals develop their sexual orientation.
20. Define the terms homophobia and heterosexism, and describe their significance to homosexuals.
21. List in order and briefly describe the four phases of sexual response in women and men.
22. Discuss the debate concerning possible differences between vaginal and clitoral orgasms and how the issue has been resolved.
23. Describe what is known concerning gender differences in sexual response styles in these two areas: rate of passage through the sexual phases and sexual responsiveness.
24. Explain the difference between public and private standards of sexual behavior.
25. Explain what sets true sexual deviations apart from other sexual activity.
26. Define paraphilia, and list and define eight paraphilias.
27. Describe exhibitionism, including who the offenders are, why they do it, and how one's reactions may encourage them.
28. Describe child molestation, including who does it, what the offenders are like, and the factors that affect the seriousness of the molestation.
29. List seven signs that indicate possible child molestation.
30. Briefly describe ways that children can be taught to protect themselves against molestation.
31. List six tactics of child molesters.
32. Briefly discuss the damaging effects of child molestation on the victim.
33. List the two characteristics that emerge in the picture of sexual deviance.
34. List or describe four changes that have taken place in sexual attitudes or behavior that lead some people to label the differences a sexual revolution.
35. Summarize the current status of the sexual revolution. Explain how your answer reflects on the position of the double standard in our society.
36. Describe how the changing sexual attitudes and values of the society interact with one's personal freedom. Include the term acquaintance rape.
37. Describe the research demonstrating the relationship between gender role stereotyping and rape.
38. List and discuss five rape myths.
39. Explain why rape is not viewed by experts as primarily a sexual act.

40. Briefly describe what is currently known about the factors affecting the spread of AIDS. Include in your answer a discussion of "at-risk" groups, risky behaviors, and the impact that AIDS has on sexual practices.

The following objectives are related to the material in the "Psychology in Action" section of the text.

41. Describe the following sexual problems, including the nature, cause, and treatment of each:
    a. desire disorders
        i.   hypoactive sexual desire
        ii. sexual aversion
    b. arousal disorders
        i.   male erectile disorder (include the term psychogenic)
        ii. female sexual arousal disorder
    c. orgasm disorders
        i.   female orgasmic disorder
        ii.   male orgasmic disorder
        iii. premature ejaculation
    d. sexual pain disorders
        i.   dyspareunia
        ii. vaginismus

42. Explain what is meant by referring to sex as a form of communication within a relationship.

43. List the four elements of a healthy sexual relationship.

44. List seven techniques that can be used to facilitate healthy communication in a relationship.

■ DISCUSSION QUESTIONS

1. Suppose a woman has a malfunctioning adrenal gland that is producing excess androgens. How would this affect the appearance of her body?

2. Consider that an unusual event occurred during conception: An egg containing an X chromosome is fertilized by a sperm that had only 22 chromosomes and no sex chromosome (normally there are 23). What affect would this probably have on the child's internal and external sexual organs?

3. A mother took a drug that increased her fetus' prenatal exposure to androgens. What effect would you guess this could have on her baby girl?

4. Imagine that you were born as a member of the opposite sex. In what ways would your life so far have been different? (Consider relationships, self-image, clothing, recreation, interests, career plans, and so forth.)

5. In your opinion, what are the advantages and disadvantages of distinctly different male/female sex roles?

6. Can you name any public personalities (entertainers, politicians, athletes, artists, musicians) who seem to be androgynous? Are any of your friends or acquaintances androgynous? Do you agree or disagree with Bem's assertion that these people are more adaptable?

7. How would you go about collecting data to confirm or disconfirm the existence of androgyny?

8. Mentally change your male friends to females and your female friends to males. Can you separate the "human being" or "core person" from your friends' normal gender identities and sex roles? What effect does this have on your perception of others?

9. What social learning factors explain why many women report negative reactions to sexually explicit pictures?

10. Some adults in their '30s and '40s report infrequent sexual activity. What factors could explain this pattern?

11. How would you go about planning an experiment to study the causes of homosexuality?

12. Kaplan and Singer have suggested that a "desire" stage precedes the excitement stage described by Masters and Johnson. Do you agree or disagree? Why?

13. In what ways does sexual contact differ from non-sexual touching? Do you feel that people should touch more? Why or why not?

14. Would you be jealous if your spouse or lover were touched (in a non-sexual way) by a person of the same sex? Opposite sex?

15. In recent years there has been a dramatic increase in child molestation trials involving day-care workers. Some teachers and child-care workers complain that they are now afraid to touch or hug children. Is this new reticence to touch an over-due correction or a saddening loss?

16.   Female sexual behavior appears to be changing more rapidly than male behavior. To what do you attribute the different rate of change?

17.   Recall your own education about sexuality. In what ways and at what age would you recommend that children learn about sex?

18.   The American teen pregnancy rate is alarmingly high. What do you think is the cause? What should be done to change this trend?

19.   How should a couple go about deciding whether they are ready for a sexual relationship? What can be done to reduce the frequency of STD's?

20.   Sex therapists often suggest that couples experiencing "dysfunction" often "get something" out of the problem. What do you think would be the "rewards" of sexual problems?

21.   What effect would arousal of the sympathetic nervous system have on sexual arousal? If a man found it difficult to become erect, would relaxation exercises help? Or would this make his sexual dysfunction more severe?

22.   There is no doubt that sexual abuse of children is widespread. How do you think our society should approach the problem of protecting children?

23.   Why would alcohol increase sexual dysfunction when it seems to function as an aphrodisiac?

24.   How could vaginismus be the result of classical conditioning? How is the treatment similar to systematic desensitization?

25.   You work in the critical care unit of a hospital and are assigned to an AIDS patient. Should you be worried about contracting the disease? Why or why not?

■ LECTURE ENHANCEMENTS

Our perceptions of sex and the norms guiding sexual behaviors are changing. Perhaps no other chapter in the text is more important in terms of clarifying values. The value statements should provoke dialogue, if not dramatic disagreement. If value clarification is used earlier in the semester, students will know that this classroom is a safe place for honest discussion. There are many excellent films available to begin discussions on transsexuality, homosexuality, and gender differences. Many people used to speak of the other gender as the "opposite" sex--opposite in interests, biology, and abilities. Now we speak of the "other" sex--still different in some ways but eventually to be valued equally. Perhaps the direction of gender socialization will be in the direction of cultural assimilation, where similarities are celebrated and differences are appreciated.

1. **A high-interest class exercise involves having students in small groups discuss their attitudes toward various sexual topics.** Before class, write ten to fifteen of the terms in Chapter 15 on 3 x 5 cards (e.g. masturbation, oral sex, double standard, premarital sex, etc.). Make a separate set of cards for each group. In class, assemble the students in groups of four or five and place a set of cards in front of one member of each group. That person is instructed to randomly draw a card, announce the topic, and then express his or her own attitudes and feelings about the subject. After each person in the group has expressed his/her opinions on the topic, the person next to the one who started the discussion draws a second card that again goes around the group with each person expressing his/her opinions. The exercise continues with each person taking a turn at initiating the discussion. After all the groups have finished, it is useful to conduct a general class discussion on reactions to the exercise. Most students have had few opportunities to share their feelings on these topics with others and usually find the exercise enlightening and valuable.

2. **Another way to help students explore their attitudes toward various sex-related matters is to give them a sex-topics survey.** You might like to construct your own questionnaire or else adapt the one that appeared in the July 1969 issue of *Psychology Today*. The results of this survey were summarized in the July 1970 issue of the magazine and are usually of great interest to students.

3. **A good way to introduce the topic of androgyny is to select a number of terms from the adjective checklist that appears in Chapter 15.** Write them on the board and ask students to indicate by a show of hands whether men (then women) tend to rank high or low in the quality named by the adjective. Plot two profiles to compare ratings of males and females. This should define some clear-cut "masculine" traits, "feminine" traits, and "neutral" traits--at least as they exist in the minds of many.

4. **Give students five descriptions of applicants for the manager of a small corporation:** a male with stereotypical male qualities; a male with androgynous qualities; a female with stereotypical female qualities; a female with male qualities; a female with androgynous qualities. Ask them to rank the five candidates. Who should be selected for this job? Why?

5. **A topic that usually generates lively discussion is the question of where and how students gained their knowledge of and developed their attitudes toward sexuality.** Studies have indicated that parents are often uncomfortable discussing sex with their children and leave them to gain their information from other sources.

6.   **Inviting a representative of a gay rights organization to speak to the class can give students a new perspective on the issue of homosexuality in our society.** If possible, invite a professional to discuss some aspect of his or her area of expertise. After students have accepted the person as an expert, ask, "Has being Gay (or Lesbian) affected your acceptance as a (name of profession)?" Discuss with students the effects of homophobia and the prejudices homosexual persons have faced.

7.   **Give students two forms of the following situation.** One form describes "Lynda;" the other describes "Ted."

_____ is a very attractive 25-year-old who enjoys wearing the current style of clothes, who is warm, friendly, uses touch and direct eye contact in meeting others. One night _____ is at a bar and orders for the first time a Margarita. Unaccustomed to drinking, _____ becomes mildly intoxicated and begins dancing very affectionately with a stranger. Getting a bit dizzy, _____ holds the stranger very closely for support and accepts a ride home. The stranger walks _____ to the apartment and asks to use the phone. Once inside the apartment, the stranger begins to make sexual advances, clothes are ripped off, and because of the drinking, _____ is not able to fight off the advances.

■ ROLE-PLAYING SCENARIOS

1.   **Explain to your lover or spouse why you think that he or she should be primarily responsible for cooking.** How convinced are you by your own arguments?

2.   **Summarize your mental script for a first date.**

3.   **You are the principal of an elementary school, and you have hired a superb third grade teacher who has admitted he is homosexual.** You feel you made an excellent choice but you have been asked to justify the choice to the school board. What evidence and data should you present to the board?

4.   **You are a sex therapist giving ideas to a couple having trouble coordinating their love-making.** What do you suspect is the problem? What would you suggest they do to develop a more satisfying sexual relationship?

5.   **Eloise was raised her early years by an affectionate but weak mother and a cold but hard-working father.** Her father suddenly vanished when Eloise was 12 and has not been heard from since. Now Eloise has trouble relating sexually to her husband. Why? What can be done to help Eloise and her husband?

6.   **Elmer feels he and his wife make love too often; Erica feels they don't make love enough.** Give them advice about how to resolve this conflict.

7. **Norma likes to make love quickly and go to sleep; Norman prefers to make love slowly and cuddle and chat afterward.** How should they resolve this difficulty?

8. **Veronica has dated many men and has experienced many sexual relationships.** Vincent has never been with anyone but Veronica. Veronica is tired of the missionary position; Vincent has never tried anything else. Help them talk about this issue.

■ VALUE-CLARIFICATION STATEMENTS

1. Fewer women have received the Nobel Prize than men. This confirms that on the average men are smarter than women.

2. Women are born talkers.

3. Women should be required to register for the armed services.

4. Women should be required to be trained for and used in direct combat in the armed services and police departments.

5. Even a single experience of sexual molestation will affect the typical person for the rest of his or her life.

6. Convicted pedophiles should be required to undergo drug therapy before release from prison.

7. A person convicted of rape should be sentenced to life imprisonment.

8. Convicted male sexual molesters should be required to be castrated.

9. I could never vote for a homosexual, even if he/she is obviously the best candidate.

10. If a person has a one-night sexual contact that they know will never be repeated, they still should disclose this to their spouse.

11. A hemophiliac child with AIDS should not be allowed to attend public school.

■ ONE-MINUTE MOTIVATORS

1. **Ask students to do the following:**
    List 5 traits of your personality, 5 interests, and 5 behaviors you usually engage in. Then close your eyes and imagine yourself as the other gender. Picture your "self" doing and

feeling these same things. If you had been born the other gender, in what ways would your identity be similar or different?

2. **Ask students to complete the following:**
   I feel nurtured when . . .
   I feel angry when . . .
   I feel most attractive when . . .
   I feel most vulnerable when . . .

3. **As an introduction to sexual adjustment, share with students the following story:** A couple on a vacation, tired after a long day of driving, pull into a motel, where they can only get a room with twin beds. Exhausted, they turn off the light and climb into their separate beds. Then the man whispers, "Honey--let's make love." She agrees, but as she is walking in the dark, she trips over the lamp cord and the lamp on the table by the bed crashes to the floor. "Oh, darling, are you alright? Is there anything I can do to help?" he asks. "No, I'm fine," she replies. She puts the lamp back on the table, gets into his bed, and they make love. A few minutes later, as she is walking back to her bed in the dark, she again trips on the cord and the lamp again crashes to the floor. This time he yells, "Stop that racket! Can't you see I'm asleep!"

4. **Carry a purse, wear an earring, man's neck-tie, man's hat, or some other cross-gender cue to class.** Ask students how their perceptions are affected. How do such object come to have such powerful gender-linked meanings?

■ BROADENING OUR CULTURAL HORIZONS

1. **Imagine a society where one gender is domineering, shrewd, and responsible for the home.** The other gender is team-oriented, cooperative, and the breadwinner. What would the rest of the society be like? What would the role of the family? Of competition?

2. **Many cultures have special rites of passage into puberty.** A few have circumcision rites--for both males and females. What are the rites of passage into puberty for your culture?

3. **If you could only give or receive pleasure during intercourse, which action would you prefer?** Why? How is this preference related to cultural socialization?

4. **Students can be asked to evaluate a written essay, a work of art, or an accomplishment.** With half of the class, the author can be a female name; with the other half, a male name can be used. Quickly collect the data and see if the ratings differ

because of the supposed gender of the author. Would such differences in judgments occur if the work were attributed to a person from a culture very different from our?

5. **Try to imagine a culture where one of the sexual "deviations" listed in the text is accepted as a normal behavior.** How would our society be different if this deviation were accepted as normal?

6. **All cultures differ in not only what they actually do in private but what they talk in public about doing in private.** Which sexual deviation do you feel is most loudly denounced in public? Which one is most often performed in private?

7. **Rape is more common in American culture than in many other cultures.** Why? What social factors have affected its occurrence? Do you anticipate that the frequency of rape will increase or decrease over the next ten years? Why? (The rate has remained unchanged for the last 10 years, although the number of attempts has declined.)

■ SUPPLEMENTAL ACTIVITIES

This exercise is intended to open up discussion on the topic of sexuality. Since students may feel inhibited about sharing their views and knowledge, the *Sexual Information Survey* can get them into the proper mind-set. It also becomes easier to talk about something that has become somewhat impersonal by first responding on paper.

The *Sexual Information Survey* contains a sampling of facts that are often misunderstood. Students sometimes feel very sophisticated, but have a good deal of misinformation about sex. You may want to add to the list given here. If so, simply type a second page and add it to the questionnaire.

Have the students score their own papers. If the surveys are not signed, you could collect them at the end of the period and report on the next class day, giving students an idea of how informed and misinformed they are as a group. If you use this survey in several classes, you could also get overall statistics for each item to report to the class. However, keep in mind that the survey is intended to be a discussion-starter and a means of letting the students know that they have more to learn about the topic. Its purpose is not simply to show them how uninformed they are.

The correct answers to the items:

1. T	5. F	9. F	13. T	17. T
2. F	6. T	10. F	14. T	18. T
3. T	7. F	11. F	15. F	19. F
4. T	8. T	12. F	16. F	20. T

SEXUAL INFORMATION SURVEY

This survey is intended to evaluate how much information you have about some topics that will be discussed in the section on human sexuality. You should not sign the survey so your responses will remain anonymous.

Mark each item either true (T) or false (F).

_____	1.	Sex education in school is favored by most parents.
_____	2.	There is clear evidence that the incidence of sex crimes is directly related to the availability of pornographic materials.
_____	3.	Highly educated males are more likely to masturbate than males who have very little education.
_____	4.	American culture is more restrictive regarding sexual activity than most other cultures.
_____	5.	Sexual intercourse is considered proper only in marriage in nearly all cultures.
_____	6.	Impotence in men and frigidity in women usually have no physical cause but are learned behaviors.
_____	7.	Homosexuality is caused by unsatisfactory sexual experiences in the childhood or teen years, according to most recent studies.
_____	8.	Most transsexuals and transvestites are male.
_____	9.	The sex of a child is determined at conception by the genes in the ovum of the female.
_____	10.	It is predicted by most social scientists that marriage will eventually disappear in this country.
_____	11.	A person can expect serious physical and emotional harm from excessive masturbation.
_____	12.	Venereal diseases are usually spread by prostitutes.
_____	13.	Incest taboos are found in some form in all societies.
_____	14.	Sexual arousal can occur without direct stimulation of the erogenous zones.
_____	15.	A person with a small penis is unable to stimulate the most sensitive areas of the vagina.
_____	16.	A vasectomy causes a reduction in sexual desire because male hormones are no longer produced or available.
_____	17.	Sexual desire and response are not affected by a hysterectomy.
_____	18.	A survey of women indicates that about two-thirds of those entering marriage for the first time have had an orgasm.
_____	19.	Frequency of sexual intercourse between married couples increases up to about age thirty-five and then gradually decreases to near zero by about age sixty.
_____	20.	Homosexual women have far fewer sexual partners than do homosexual men.

■ JOURNAL QUESTIONS

1. When did you first notice the development of secondary sexual characteristics? How did you feel about these changes? Did you tell anyone about the changes? If so, what did they say to you?

2. Have you ever taken the SAT? How did you perform on the verbal and the math portions? Is this the result of your genetics or your social environment? Explain.

3. What is the earliest age you remember? What were you doing? Can you even imagine yourself as anything but your own gender? Explain.

4. Were you ever considered a "tomboy" or a "sissy"? If so, how did you feel? If not, did you know any "tomboys" or "sissies"? In what ways was their social environment different from yours?

5. How aggressive are you? Are males and females different in their "inherent" aggressiveness--or are they simply socialized to express aggression in different ways?

6. If you have brothers or sisters, how did your parents treat you in comparison with your siblings? What kinds of "jobs" were you assigned as a child? Were decisions based on your unique skills, on age, or on gender?

7. What are your feelings about homosexuality?

8. Some writers suggest that women are the "more sexual gender." Why?

9. Have you ever known a person who engaged in an extra-marital affair? If so, how do you explain that person's behavior? What effect did the affair have on the person's marriage?

10. Would you (or did you) engage in premarital sex? Why or why not?

11. Have most of the cohabiting couples you know eventually married? If so, do you think that they have a better or worse chance than noncohabitators to stay married? Explain.

12. What messages did your parents send you about sexuality? If you have a religious background, what messages were you given about sexuality from your religion? How have these themes affected your behavior?

13. Have you ever wanted to peak into someone's window or to parade your skimpy bathingsuit clad body at the beach? Who do we draw the line between "normal" and "abnormal" peeking and exhibiting?

■ SUGGESTIONS FOR FURTHER READING

Bach, G. and P. Wyden. *How to Fight Fear in Love and Marriage.* Avon, 1983.

Bem. S. L. "The Measurement of Psychological Androgyny." *Journal of Consulting and Clinical Psychology,* (42) 1974: 155-162.

—. "Androgyny vs. The Tight Little Lives of Fluffy Women and Chesty Men." *Psychology Today,* September 1975: 58-62.

—. "Sex-Role Adaptability: One Consequence of Psychological Androgyny." *Journal of Personality and Social Psychology,* (31) 1975: 634-643.

Caplan, Pat (Ed.). *The Cultural Construction of Sexuality.* Routledge, 1987. Publications.

Crooks, R. L., and K. Baur. *Our Sexuality,* 8th ed. Thomson, 2002.

Ellis, A. *The Sensuous Person.* Signet, 1974.

Hall, C. M. *Women and Identity: Value Choices in a Changing World.* Hemisphere Publishing Corporation. 1989.

Hendrick, Clyde. *Close Relationships.* Sage Publications, 2000.

Hite, S. *The Hite Report.* Dell Publishing, 1989.

Hyde, J. S., and J. D. Delatamer. *Understanding Human Sexuality,* 8th ed. McGraw-Hill, 2002.

Janus, S. S. and C. L. Janus. *The Janus Report on Sexual Behavior.* John Wiley & Sons, Inc., 1994.

Kleinplatz, P. J. *New Direction in Sex Therapy: Innovations and Alternatives.* Brunner/Mazel, 2001.

"Living with AIDS." (Entire volume). *Daedalus,* 118 (2), 1989. (Especially see pp. 92-112, "The Power of Professionalism: Policies for AIDS in Britain, Sweden, and the United States.")

Masters, W., Johnson, V., and R. C. Kolodny. *Human Sexuality.* Addison-Wesley, 1995.

Nielsen, Joyce McCarl. *Sex and Gender in Society,* 2nd ed. Waveland Press, 1990.

Tavris, C. *The Mismeasurement of Woman.* Peter Smith Pub., 1999.

Tavris, C. and C. Offir. *The Longest War: Sex Differences in Perspective,* 2nd ed. Thomson, 1984.

Walker, A. E. *The Menstrual Cycle.* Routledge, 1997.

■ MEDIA SUGGESTIONS

AIDS, THE FAMILY, AND THE COMMUNITY (2002, Films for the Humanities and Sciences, 26 min.)
This film describes how AIDS is transmitted and ways AIDS is already affecting all of us in some way.

CHILD SEX ABUSERS (2002, Films for the Humanities and Sciences, 28 min.)
The typical sex abuse cycle—abused as a child, abuser as adult—is being replaced by an even more frightening scenario: more of today's abusers appear to be children. This specially adapted Phil Donahue program features mothers and their daughters who have been sexually abused by brothers, half-brothers, and neighborhood kids—one of the molesters was 13, and his victim was three. The program also features an expert who deals with abusive children, who counsels what signs to look for and what to do when it comes to abusive kids, and counsels kids who are being abused.

GENDER AND RELATIONSHIPS (2002, Coast Community College District Telecourses, 30 min.)
Part of the *Psychology - The Study of Human Behavior Series*, this video explores the complexities of emotional interactions and attachments.

GENDER AND SEXUALITY (2002, Coast Community College District Telecourses, 30 min.)
Part of the *Psychology - The Human Experience Series*, this video explores the distinction between the terms *sex* and *gender* and describes the similarities and differences between men and women.

GENDER AND REPRODUCTION: A NATURAL HISTORY (2002, Films for the Humanities and Sciences, 19-28 min. each)
Throughout the realms of living beings—in bananas and humans, in jungles and zoos, in test tubes and ocean depths—survival depends on adaptation, and adaptation on variation. And variation is the product of sexual reproduction. Through twelve half-hours of fascinating photography, the viewer observes in how many ways beings of all kinds reproduce: how male and female find one another, attract one another, couple, and produce one or more of a new generation that is alike but not identical; and how anatomical, behavioral, and social characteristics of a species are linked to the genetic goal of reproduction. 12-part series.

LOVE & SEX (2002, Films for the Humanities and Sciences, 52 min.)
This film describes the discrepancies between male and female behavior, biological sexual needs and social constraints, and between the ideal of a long-term relationship and divorce statistics. The problem of teen pregnancy is raised and the distinction between a love and a sexual relationship is discussed.

MEN, WOMEN, AND THE SEX DIFFERENCE: BOYS AND GIRLS ARE DIFFERENT (2002, Films for the Humanities and Sciences, 43 min.)
In this ABC News special, ABC News correspondent John Stossel raises questions about the nature/nurture debate, and seeks to discover if many parents' gut instincts—and the findings of many researchers and psychologists—about differences between little girls and boys have been right all along. The program speaks with parents who have tried to foster gender-neutral behavior in their children, and specialists who illustrate differences in male-female brain functions and hormones. The program also features feminists Gloria Steinem, the late Bella Abzug, and Gloria Allred, who question whether the issue of gender differences should even be raised.

RAPE: AN ACT OF HATE (2002, Films for the Humanities and Sciences, 30 min.)
Hosted by Veronica Hamel of 'Hill Street Blues,' the film describes why people rape and what potential victims (who are all of us) can do to protect ourselves. Winner of an Emmy and an American Women in Radio and Television Award.

SEX AND GENDER (2001, from the *Discovering Psychology Series,* Annenberg/CPG, 30 min.)
This video explores the ways in which males and females are similar and different, and how sex roles reflect social values and psychological knowledge.

SEX ROLES: CHARTING THE COMPLEXITY OF DEVELOPMENT (1991, Insight Media, 60 min.)
Looking at the cultural ramifications of sex roles and the myths associated with them, this video examines three theories of socialization: Freudian, cognitive-developmental, and social-learning. It analyzes how each theory views the nature-versus-nurture controversy. It also explores the impact of sex-role stereotypes on the developing child, looking at the differences these stereotypes create in scholastic achievement, interaction with peers, and expectations for the future.

A number of videos are available from Thomson. Videos appropriate for this chapter include the following films from the CNN TODAY Introductory Psychology Video Series:

Volume 1, Section 6: Gender and Sexuality
     Brain Differences (2:12)

Volume 2, Section 5: Gender and Sexuality
     Gay by Nature (5:02)

■ COMPUTER AND INTERNET RESOURCES

PSYCHNOW!

Motivation and Emotion
Human Sexuality

Social Psychology
Gender and Stereotyping

PSYK.TREK

None are appropriate.

INFOTRAC

Subject Guide/Key Terms: Gender and Sexuality, Human Sexuality, Sex Roles, Gender Roles, Sex Role Stereotype, Gender Role Stereotype, Androgyny, Sexual Scripts, Masturbation, Sexual Orientation, Homosexuality, Psychology of Rape, Paraphilia, Sexually Transmitted Disease, AIDS, Sexual Disorders

WEB SITES

Wadsworth Online Psychology Study Center:
http://info.wadsworth.com/coonessentials9

Psychology of Gender: A Brief Guide to Information Resources:
http://libweb.uoregon.edu/subjguid/women/psycgen.html

Sexual Dysfunction:
http://sexuality.about.com/cs/sexualdisorders/

AmoebaWeb Psychology Resources: Gender and Sexuality:
http://www.vanguard.edu/faculty/ddegelman/amoebaweb/index.cfm?doc_id=861

Center for Gender Studies:
http://humanities.uchicago.edu/orgs/cgs/resources.html

Gender and the Internet: Sex, Sexism, and Sexuality:
http://www.csa.com/hottopics/gender/websites.html

CHAPTER 16
Social Behavior

■ LEARNING OBJECTIVES

To demonstrate mastery of this chapter, the student should be able to:

1.   Define social psychology.
2.   Describe the research that indicates that humans have a need to affiliate.
3.   Describe the social comparison theory.
4.   List and describe four factors that affect interpersonal attraction.
5.   Describe the similarities and differences in what men and women look for in a mate.
6.   Explain how self-disclosure is important in the process of getting to know someone. Explain how overdisclosure can affect the same process.
7.   Describe Rubin's studies of romantic love.
8.   Discuss the differences between loving and liking. Include the term mutual absorption in your discussion.
9.   Define evolutionary psychology.
10.   Discuss the possible evolution of male and female mate selection.
11.   Define the following terms:
        a. social role
        b. ascribed role
        c. achieved role
        d. role conflict
        e. status
        f. norm
12.   Explain what attribution theory is and the difference between internal and external causes of behavior.
13.   Explain the fundamental attributional error.
14.   Briefly discuss the research on the double standard in attribution of male and female success.
15.   Define the term social influence.
16.   Describe Asch's experiment on conformity and list any personal factors that can influence it.
17.   Define groupthink and explain how it may contribute to poor decision-making. Describe six ways to prevent groupthink.
18.   Explain how group sanctions and unanimity affect conformity.

19. Describe Milgram's study of obedience and identify the factors that affect the degree of obedience.
20. Describe the following methods of compliance:
    a. foot-in-the-door
    b. door-in-the-face
    c. low-ball technique .
21. Define and discuss passive compliance.
22. Describe the process of assertiveness training, including the term self-assertion.
23. Describe how a person can learn to be more assertive using rehearsal, role-playing, overlearning, and the broken record technique.
24. Define attitude.
25. Describe the belief, emotional, and action components of an attitude.
26. List, describe, and give examples of six ways in which attitudes are acquired.
27. Explain why people may exhibit discrepancies between attitudes and behavior.
28. Differentiate between reference groups and membership groups.
29. Define persuasion, and list nine conditions of persuasion that can be applied to bring about attitude change.
30. Present an overview of cognitive dissonance theory, indicate its influence on attitude formation, and describe the effect of justification on dissonance.

The following objectives are related to the material in the "Exploring Psychology" section of the text.

31. List two types of forced attitude change.
32. Describe the three techniques used in brainwashing.
33. Explain how beliefs may unfreeze, change, and refreeze, and indicate how permanent the attitude changes brought about by brainwashing are.
34. Describe how cults are able to recruit, convert, and retain their members.

35. Define and differentiate prejudice and discrimination.
36. Explain how the following relate to the learning of prejudice:
    a. scapegoating
    b. direct experiences with members of the rejected group
    c. personal prejudice
    d. group prejudice
    e. personality characteristics—the authoritarian personality
37. Describe the characteristic beliefs (including ethnocentrism and dogmatism) and childhood experiences of the authoritarian personality.
38. Present the major characteristics of social stereotypes and indicate how they may lead to intergroup conflicts.
39. Describe symbolic prejudice.
40. Briefly describe the role of dehumanization in promoting violent conflicts.

41. Explain how status inequalities may lead to the development of stereotypes and how equal-status contact may reduce intergroup tension. Give an example of each situation.
42. Explain how superordinate goals can reduce conflict and hostility.
43. Explain how a "jigsaw" classroom utilizes superordinate goals and helps reduce prejudice.
44. Describe the relationship between aggression and each of the following:
    a. instincts
    b. biology
    c. frustration (include frustration-aggression hypothesis and aversive stimuli)
    d. aggression cues (include the weapons effect)
    e. social learning
45. With respect to the effects of violence on television:
    a. summarize the relationship between television violence and real life
    b. explain how television violence may teach antisocial actions, disinhibit dangerous impulses, and desensitize a person to violence
46. List six steps that parents can implement to buffer the impact of television on their children.
47. Define prosocial behavior.
48. Give an example of bystander apathy, and indicate the major factor that determines whether or not help will be given.
49. Trace the progress of an individual through the four decision points that must be passed before helping behavior is given.
50. Indicate how the presence of other people can influence apathy.
51. Define the term empathic arousal.
52. Briefly note how a person can "de-victimize" oneself.

The following objectives are related to the material in the "Psychology in Action" section of the text.
53. Define multiculturalism.
54. List seven ways to "break the prejudice habit."

■ DISCUSSION QUESTIONS

1. How do you explain the behavior of the guards in Zimbardo's prison study? What could be done to prevent this from happening in real prisons?

2. Many students hesitate to ask questions in class. How would a student explain this behavior? How would an instructor explain the behavior? How do these explanations relate to attribution theory?

3.   From all that you have learned in this class, would you say that the human need to affiliate is genetic or learned? What kind of an experiment could you run to test your hypothesis?

4.   How has physical proximity influenced your choice of friends?

5.   Think of your closest high school friends. Which theory best explains your relationships: social comparison, social exchange, or the factors underlying interpersonal attraction?

6.   Why do people often underdisclose to a friend or spouse and overdisclose to strangers? Explain these behaviors in terms of principles from this chapter.

7.   How serious, in your estimation, are problems of conformity, obedience, and passive compliance?

8.   Can you think of a personal experience in which you were subjected to group pressures similar to those in the Asch experiment? How did you feel? Did you yield?

9.   In view of the Milgram obedience experiment, do you think the civil disobedience of the civil rights and anti-war movements was justified? Why or why not?

10.   Is "blind obedience" ever necessary? Explain.

11.   If you were placed in charge of an important decision-making group, what would you do to minimize groupthink? Do you think that some types of committees or groups are especially prone to groupthink? How serious a problem do you think groupthink is in the government? In the military? In business? In schools? In community groups?

12.   Describe the various persuasive techniques for gaining compliance. Under what conditions and in what situations would each technique be most effective? Why do each of the techniques works?

13.   Which of the techniques to gain compliance do you find least ethical? Why?

14.   How has the anti-smoking campaign of the American Cancer Society made use of cognitive dissonance to discourage smoking?

15.   In what ways do magazine and television advertisements apply the principles of persuasion? (Consider the communicator, the message, and the audience.)

16.   Choose an issue you feel strongly about. State your attitudes concerning the issue. How did you come to hold your present attitudes? What types of experiences or variables influenced you?

17.   What are the principles underlying assertiveness training? What procedures are used to teach a person to become more assertive? Under what conditions do you hypothesize (guess) that these procedures are most effective?

18.   Reread the experiments performed on passive compliance. What would have been an assertive response to the situations described? An aggressive response?

19.   Kenneth Clark has said, "Prejudice is a way that human beings have of betraying the fragility of their egos." What do you think Clark meant? Do you agree?

20.   Is prejudice a personality trait or a group of behaviors? Explain your answer.

21.   What can be done to reduce symbolic prejudice?

22.   If you were asked to establish a program to end conflict between students attending two rival high schools, what steps would you take?

23.   What do you think are the superordinate goals facing the nation and the world? (To be truly superordinate a goal would have to be seen as valid by nearly everyone.) Do such goals exist? How could such a goal be converted into greater intergroup cooperation?

24.   The view that humans are instinctively aggressive "naked apes" has been quite popular. To what do you attribute this popularity? Do you consider humans naturally aggressive? What evidence can you give for or against this view?

25.   What biological and learning factors explain human aggression? Under what circumstances does frustration contribute to aggression?

26.   Studies of capital punishment show that it has either no effect on deterring homicides, or that there is a slight decline after it is abolished. How would a social learning theorist explain this decline? If capital punishment does not deter homicides, do you think it can be justified for other reasons? If so, what, in your opinion, are they?

27.   What are the advantages and disadvantages of a free press that allows violence to occur on television?

28.   Describe a situation in which you did or did not offer help to someone who was, or might have been, in need. What influenced your decision? In view of what you know about

helping behavior, can you explain why rape or assault victims are advised to shout "Fire!"?

29.   What can be done on your campus to encourage more helping behavior?

■ LECTURE ENHANCEMENTS

1.   **Provide students with a list of twenty adjectives, such as honest, courteous, punctual, assertive, generous, shy, frugal, talkative, hard-working, neat, friendly, grumpy, happy, irritable, suspicious, trusting, serious, relaxed, imaginative, self-assured.** Create a column that says "self" and another column that says "best friend." Next to each adjective in each column write either "usually," "rarely," or "it depends." Ask students to hand their sheet to the person next to them and to count the number of times they said "it depends" in each column. The fundamental attribution error predicts that they will describe themselves more often in "it depends" terms than their best friend.

2.   **A good way to introduce the topic of interpersonal attraction is to ask students to make a list of the five characteristics they look for in their friends.** In other words, what five factors are most important in determining to whom they are attracted. Student lists will typically include attributes such as honesty, sense of humor, openness, and so forth. Compare the lists produced by students to the factors identified by social psychological research: social comparison, propinquity, physical attractiveness, competence, and similarity.

3.   **Another way to begin discussion of interpersonal attraction is to divide the class into small groups by sex and ask each group to generate a list of characteristics of the ideal person to date.** After everyone has finished, ask one person from each group to read their list to the rest of the class while you write it on the board. This generally elicits a great deal of discussion and debate about the attributes that were chosen. There are usually notable differences in the types of characteristics selected by female groups as opposed to male groups. A class discussion could center on possible explanations for this sex difference in preferred characteristics.

4.   **Demonstrate critical thinking (rather than groupthink) by asking students to work in groups to develop a plan for improving the quality of instruction at your college or specific actions the community could take to improve the environment.** Ask one person in the group to serve as the "designated devil's advocate" (the DDA). Ask students to draw up a plan one day and to reevaluate the plan the next day. Did the presence of a devil's advocate add to the quality of the group's solutions?

5.   **Verbal definitions and discussion of assertive, aggressive, or excessively passive behavior do not necessarily prepare students to make appropriate responses in**

actual situations. Modeling each type of behavior can be far more effective. A worthwhile demonstration, therefore, is to have students role-play assertive, aggressive, and passive responses to various situations. Excellent sample situations, complete with dialogue, can be found in Chapter 13 of *Your Perfect Right* (8th ed.) by Alberti and Emmons, San Luis Obispo, CA, Impact Publishers, 2001.

6.   **Put students in small groups of ten.** Five people will work as a group; the other five will sit behind them observing their behavior. Give the five in the center the following instructions, "You are a committee gathered to develop a list of guidelines on the kinds of social relationships that should take place in a business office. Should single employees be able to date each other? Should supervisors be able to have relatives working under them? If a dating relationship develops between two employees, should one be transferred to a different department?" Give the group fifteen minutes to talk. Then ask the observers which group members were most persuasive, and why they succeeded in advancing their views.

7.   **According to dissonance theory, after one has made an important decision, there is a tendency to seek information that bolsters the choice made and to avoid information that contradicts it (due to the dissonance created).** Accordingly, it can be very interesting to interview a student who has recently made a major purchase (of an item such as an automobile, stereo, television, etc.). Inquire into the student's information-gathering behavior before the purchase and his or her information exposure after. Typically, people read advertisements for several brands before a purchase but, afterward, only ads for the brand they selected.

8.   **Ask each student to write on a 3 X 5 card a situation in which they would like to become more assertive.** On the back of the card the student should write what they wish they could say in that situation. Either ask the student to read their own card aloud or mix the cards up before distributing them to the class to be read. Then ask each person to repeat the general idea of the card but use his or her own words. Finally, ask students to role-play the entire situation. This can be done in pairs or in small groups.

9.   **To demonstrate that attitudes can be shaped by both information and misinformation, ask ten students to help you transmit "information."** Begin a "rumor" by selecting from a magazine a photograph of a dramatic event involving several people. Ask the first "assistant" to step outside. Show this student the picture and ask him/her to try to remember as many details as possible. Ask the second "assistant" outside to be told by the first all of the details. The story can be repeated; questions cannot be asked. Once all ten students have heard what becomes "misinformation," ask the last person to describe what he/she heard. Then present the class with the photograph. What attitudes do students think could be developed in their own lives through misinformation? What can be done to prevent rumors and falsehood from taking place?

10.   **Chapter 16 addresses the topic of the elusive emotion of love.** As a way of allowing students to explore their own ideas about this subject, they can be put into small groups and asked to write a definition of love on a 3 X 5" card or slip of paper. Then all of the groups should shuffle their cards and place them face down in the center. Each person in turn should select a card, read it aloud, and comment on the definition. After they have all been discussed, the groups should be instructed to arrive at one definition acceptable to all of the members. The group definitions should be presented to the class as a whole for discussion and debate.

11.   **To dramatize the topic of aggression, try beginning this way:** Have students stand in pairs, facing one another. Students are then to play a children's game with which they are probably familiar. One player extends his or her hands, palms down, in front of him/herself; the second player places his or her hands, palms up, touching the palms of the first player. The object of the game is for the person with his or her hands on the bottom to quickly move one or both hands over the top of the first player's hands in an attempt to slap them with a downward motion. The first player tries to avoid being slapped by moving his/her hands out of the way at the first sign of motion. If the second player is able to slap the first player's hand(s), he or she continues with hands on the bottom. If he/she misses, the players change roles so that the first player tries to slap the hands of the second. (*Note:* This game has been played by generations of children and poses little risk in class. However, if any student objects, he or she should be excused. Also, it is wise to ask students to remove any large rings they may be wearing.) This game is usually sufficiently frustrating, competitive, and mildly angering to stir up some aggressive feelings in participants. After the game has progressed for a few moments, it becomes interesting to discuss students' reactions and feelings and to ask which views of aggression seemed to relate to their experience.

12.   **One of the major problems that occurs in the study of aggression is how to define it.** Although most people seem to know what they mean by the term, when they attempt to define aggression precisely, it becomes less clear. As an example physical attacks by one individual against another are generally viewed as aggression unless the attacker is in a role in which such behavior is sanctioned (soldier, police officer). Professional football players are seen as aggressive as are used car salesmen. To highlight this problem for your students, you could give them examples of different behaviors and ask them to consider whether or not they constitute aggressive actions. For example, you could include things like someone being an avid gun collector, a married couple having an argument, and a state executioner pulling the switch on an electric chair. Attempting to decide whether each of these reflects aggression usually results in a fairly heated classroom debate and gives students some idea of the problems involved in defining the concept.

13.   **If the class is fairly small, put all the males in one group and all the females in another group.** Ask students to discuss things that bother them about the opposite sex. Ask them to select a spokesperson. Bring the groups together. Ask the men to give one example of their major complaints; ask the women to give another example. What you may discover is that both groups are annoyed by similar behaviors. To what extent do men and women misperceive one another? Do many of us have stereotypes and prejudices with respect to the other gender? What are the superordinate goals in male-female relationships?

14.   **A staged "accident" may be used to dramatize research on the inhibition of prosocial behavior.** During a lecture have an accomplice drop an arm-load of books outside the classroom door. This should be accompanied by a crashing sound and then a pained moan. All this should be out of sight of the class but clearly audible to them. Even if students have already read the discussion of prosocial behavior in the text, the majority will not respond to the "emergency." Follow this dramatization with a discussion of student experiences with real emergencies and the inhibiting effects of other bystanders.

■ ROLE-PLAYING SCENARIOS

1.   **Give students a list of achieved roles.** Ask one person to role-play one of them; the class should try to guess the role. Discuss stereotypes with the class using the following examples: student, prostitute, businessperson, plumber, mother, father, parent, teacher.

2.   **You are a police officer who pulls over your son for speeding.** What do you say? You are at a night spot and you run into your psychology instructor. What do you say?

3.   **You just became engaged to a person from a different race or culture.** Announce the exciting news to your parents, your closest friends, or your children.

4.   **Ask students to stand in a row as if waiting in line.** Ask the student at the end of the line to walk to the front and try to push in front of everyone else. Everyone in line needs to practice assertively saying "No."

5.   **You go to a store to purchase a particular sale item, but the salesperson tries to talk you into buying a more expensive version.** How do you resist? What do you say?

6.   **Practice responding assertively to verbal aggression.** What should you say if a person says to you:
        a. "You are so lazy; you never get your part of the work done."
        b. "For you, this is a great paper."

    c. "Going to school at night and working all day, it is no wonder your house is such a mess."

7. **How would you deal with each of these situations?**
   a. Your boss inaccurately evaluates you. What would you say to your boss?
   b. You only have money to pay some of your bills. What would you say to a persistent collection agent?
   c. You just received a promotion; but it would entail moving to another city. This would interfere with your spouse's job. How would you tell your boss that you don't want to move?
   d. A large company near you is polluting a nearby river. How would you tell the president that the lake must be cleaned?
   e. Your ex-spouse is behind in the child support payments. What would you say to convince him/her to pay you immediately?

8. **Role-play being a couple in "romantic love."** Then role-play a couple who have been married 15 years and have a companionate love relationship. Is it possible to combine these two styles of love?

9. **Put students in pairs.** They are to discuss what they did last weekend. Decide who is person A. That person will act as the higher-status student. Person B will act as the lower-status student. What behavioral differences take place in the way they converse with each other?

10. **Role-play an interaction between a teenage "bully" and another student.** Practice different responses to verbal aggression, such as ignoring abusive comments and assertively saying, "I'm uncomfortable when you say those things."

11. **Ask a student to huddle in a corner of the room and try to look sick or unconscious.** A second student should role-play first a passerby who decides to ignore the "wino" in the corner and then a person who decides to help someone who may be ill or injured. In both cases, the passerby should verbalize aloud the thoughts that lead to a decision to help or to ignore the person in need.

■ VALUE-CLARIFICATION STATEMENTS

1. Very few people are "real." Most people are phonies who simply play roles.

2. While we criticize politicians, politicians still have high status within our society.

3. Interracial marriages are less likely to last than same-race marriages.

4.   Police officers don't have enough power to do their job effectively.

5.   It is the instructor's responsibility to prevent cheating.

6.   It is impossible for a person to be brainwashed into doing something they don't really want to do.

7.   Parents have the right to kidnap their adult children who may become involved in a cult.

8.   Most people conform too easily to the pressures of others.

9.   It is impossible to hide the fact that a couple is romantically in love.

10.   After years of prejudice, it is now time that extra opportunities are given to minority members.

11.   It is impossible for equal-status contact to take place between groups.

12.   It is important for people to act out their aggression rather than hold it inside.

13.   Parents should prohibit their children from watching more than two hours of television per week.

14.   If a person tries to help, she or he may be sued. Thus, it is dangerous to help in an emergency.

■ ONE-MINUTE MOTIVATORS

1.   **Select a person from class who is "King/Queen for the moment."** Ask students to demonstrate subtle ways they could defer to this person and confirm this person's high status. Ask students to treat "this high status person very well" over the next two days. At the next class meeting, discuss how it felt to defer to that person. Ask the "King/Queen" how it felt to be treated royally.

2.   **Ask students to violate a social norm.** For example, they could offer to pay more than the asking price for a quart of milk or offer to help pay for a part of someone else's food while waiting in the cafeteria line. How do others react?

3.   **Ask students to turn to the two people sitting adjacent to them and to compliment each person for some behavior they observed during the semester.** The recipient of the compliment is only allowed to say "Thank you." Discuss social reinforcement and social exchange.

4.   **Ask students to describe whether they are below average, average, or above average in the following ways: physical attractiveness, friendliness, creativity, athletic ability, sense of humor, height, and weight.** Then discuss the concept of social comparison.

5.   **Ask students to write the names of people from the class that they didn't know when the class began but they know now.** Ask them to swap papers. Does proximity explain who they have gotten to know this semester? (Include proximity outside of class if the students share other classes or live in the same dorm.)

6.   **Put students in pairs.** Ask Person A to establish a specific level of disclosure and for Person B to reciprocate. What are the advantages and disadvantages of reciprocity? How should a person go about changing the level of disclosure in a dialogue?

7.   **Have a "clone" day.** Ask everyone to wear the same color clothes. Discuss how they felt conforming to this suggestion. Can a person conform without giving up their own individuality? Did students feel a need to distinguish themselves by their choice of clothing within the color constraint?

8.   **Ask students to perform a series of behaviors:** "Would you please: Put your hands on your hips. Do three pushups. Move to the back row. Hug the person sitting behind you. Sing a song. And so forth. See how long it takes until one student says, "Do I have to?" Answer, "please participate in this experiment." A few minutes later, ask them why they obeyed. Is their behavior any different from the subjects in Milgram's experiment? Under what conditions should we conform? When should we refuse to obey?

9.   **Give students a sudden pop quiz (especially if that was not a part of the original rules of the class).** When someone protests, compliment them on not being a "willing victim." Discuss under what conditions they should passively comply or actively protest.

10.   **Using a pad of yellow "stickums", write "ignore," "praise," "confront" on alternate pieces of paper.** Put one yellow sticky piece of paper on each person's forehead. Ask students to form groups and to discuss what they did last weekend. They need to treat each other according to the roles on each person's forehead. Were they able to guess their role by the way others treated them? How did it feel to be ignored?

11.   **Hold class in a large open space--a large auditorium, field bleachers, in the parking lot. Make certain that everyone is as spread out as possible.** After about fifteen minutes, ask students to move in closer. Briefly discuss feelings experienced when distant versus when crowded.

12.   **Ask students to rate their most recent love relationship according to its intimacy, passion, and commitment.**

■ BROADENING OUR CULTURAL HORIZONS

Students can be reminded that each of us brings a unique "microculture" to our social interactions. These traditions can empower or inhibit us. While some family norms need to be discarded, other traditions can be shared and celebrated. Emotional discussions can focus on "majority" power, "minority" discontent, the political impact of the new "majority minority", the pain and conflicts of new immigrants, and the complex needs of the "placeless" (often called the "homeless").

1.   **Describe the "traditions" of your home,** including favorite holidays, dinner and bedtime rituals, preferred formal language and slang, value and use of money, views toward sex, attitudes toward grandparents, religious values, etc.

2.   **What kinds of role conflicts do you guess that new immigrants experience?**

3.   **Do males and females attribute causation of events in the same way or in different ways?** How? Are attributions changing?

4.   **Make a list of twenty different cultural groups.** Who would you: Exclude from your country? Leave alone but not want face-to-face contact? Tolerate face-to-face contact? Enjoy having as an acquaintance? Enjoy becoming close friends with? Admit to marriage within your family? Marry yourself?

5.   **Put students in pairs.** Give each student one of the following:
     a. You come from a culture where cooperation is preferred to individual assertiveness. You solve problems by working as a team.
     b. You come from a culture where people are expected to use power to solve problems. If you don't have power, you are supposed to publicly submit.

     c. Then ask students to decide which current movie to go to or which local restaurant to go to. Take notes on the processes used to develop or confirm power.

6.   **What are your feelings about affirmative action hiring?** In what ways does a more culturally diverse set of employees add to the quality of the decisions made by a company?

7.   **In some cultures, marriages are arranged by relatives, rather than being based on romantic attraction.** Such marriages are just as likely to last as marriages formed by choice. Why would this be?

8. **All cultures have different approaches to love.** Why do you think that our culture emphasizes romantic love as the basis for marriage? What other cultural values does this emphasis echo?

9. **Prejudice and discrimination can take place based on gender and age.** Imagine that a person has a brain tumor and goes to a physician for treatment. What kind of treatment would you recommend? What if the person is 40 years old? Would the treatment be different if the person is 65 years old?

10. **Many people have suggested that "economic" warfare should be used during international disputes, instead of traditional weapons.** Why? What principle of group interaction does this reflect?

11. **Make a list of all of the aggression cues used by different groups of people.** Spend some time researching gangs that may be active in your area. What cues do they use to indicate power and to trigger aggression?

12. **Some cultures encourage more prosocial behavior than other cultures.** Did your family stress helping others? Does your general culture suggest that people should go out of their way to help others? Research a culture where strangers are expected to help each other.

■ SUPPLEMENTAL ACTIVITIES

The **four exercises** outlined in this section should help to get students involved in the discussion of social psychology. They should give students an opportunity to see how the concepts they are studying relate to real-life experiences. The **first exercise** deals with conformity. Social psychologists tell us that people conform to the norms or rules of a social group only to the extent that they accept the goals of the group and want to attain the objectives the group espouses. This exercise gives students an opportunity to observe and record adherence to a group norm, namely, stopping at a stop sign at a busy intersection. The **second exercise** relates to group pressure. Students will themselves be the subjects. Some will be asked a question to which they will respond using their own feelings and judgments while others will be presented with some judgments already made about the same question and then asked to express their estimates. Will the group who see previously made estimates be influenced in their judgments? Try this exercise to find out. In the **third exercise**, students will develop a heightened awareness of violence as a form of aggression and will begin to think about its causes. The **fourth exercise** focuses on the concepts of cooperation and competition. Variations of this activity have been done many times, and results generally show that even though cooperation would produce the best results for everyone, competition is most likely to occur when people have a choice, even though the result is less rewarding. It is the *Prisoner's Dilemma* game and is a rousing and intriguing exercise to do in a class.

Exercise #1: Conformity

TO THE INSTRUCTOR:

This is a project that can be done individually by each student. Ask each student to spend an
hour at an intersection that has stop signs rather than signal lights. Their task is to observe and
record the behavior of the motorists as they reach the stop sign. If it is a four-way stop, the
students should be able to collect lots of data.

Students should be given a data sheet to use so they can keep accurate records. It is a good idea
to break down the stopping behavior of motorists into all of the likely variations and record each
one. The data sheet includes the following:

1. coming to a full at the stop sign, then slowly moving up to the intersection if visibility
    is impaired, as is the law;

2. coming to a full stop, not at the sign, but at the intersection;

3. rolling to a near stop and moving on;

4. slowing down, but not stopping, while passing through the intersection;

5. driving through without slowing down or stopping.

When students return to class with their information, you can ask them to work out the
percentages for each of the alternative stopping behaviors. It would also be possible to get a set
of percentages for the whole class. See if there are differences in different types of
neighborhoods and different times of day.

CONFORMITY: DATA SHEET

TO THE STUDENT:
Find an intersection that has stop signs in all four directions.

Your task is to observe and record the way motorists behave at the stop signs. You will notice that not all drivers do the same thing. Spend an hour at the location and record all vehicles. Check the appropriate number on the chart using the following criteria. If the intersection is busy, you may need more than one data sheet.

1. Coming to a full stop at the stop sign and then slowly moving up to the intersection if visibility is impaired;
2. Coming to a full stop, not at the sign, but at the intersection;
3. Rolling to a near stop and moving on;
4. Slowing down, but not stopping, while passing through the intersection;
5. Driving through without slowing down or stopping.

TIME OF DAY_____

LOCATION_____

VEHICLE	STOPPING BEHAVIOR					VEHICLE	STOPPING BEHAVIOR				
	1	2	3	4	5		1	2	3	4	5
1						1					
2						2					
3						3					
4						4					
5						5					
6						6					
7						7					
8						8					
9						9					
10						10					

Exercise #2: Group Pressure

TO THE INSTRUCTOR:
This exercise involves a mock student survey. Tell the class that you are cooperating with a campus committee that is surveying a sample of students. Your classes have been chosen to be part of this study. Tell them that you are distributing several survey sheets to speed things up, a couple of which were used in a previous class. Start by passing out four sheets, ask them to read the directions, add their opinions, and pass the sheet on to the next person.

Prepare the sheets to be distributed before the class period. All four sheets should be copies of the **STUDENT SURVEY** form that follows. Two of them should be blank except for the instructions. The other two should already have five signatures on them, each in different handwriting. Next to the signatures should be the following estimates: $75, $80, $60, $75, $65.

After the sheets have circulated throughout the class, collect them. Find the mean for the first four responses on the two blank sheets and the mean for the first four real responses on the two sheets with fake signatures. See if there is a difference between the influenced and uninfluenced groups.

The purpose of the survey should be revealed to the students. Your discussion should center on group pressure and peer influence. However, students may also want to discuss the ethics of fooling them about the real purpose of the survey.

STUDENT SURVEY

As part of an evaluation of teaching practices, the Administrative Committee on Instructional Policy is conducting a survey of students. Your response to the following question is requested.

What do you think is a fair amount for an instructor to require students to spend on books and other materials for a typical college class?

Please write your estimate in dollars, where shown. To authenticate this survey, please write your name in the space provided. Thank you for participating.

NAME	AMOUNT
_____	_____
_____	_____
_____	_____
_____	_____
_____	_____
_____	_____
_____	_____
_____	_____
_____	_____
_____	_____
_____	_____
_____	_____

Exercise #3: Aggression on Television

Television violence has been a subject of much discussion, and lots of statistics are quoted for its frequency. Through this exercise, students have an opportunity to concentrate on this aspect of TV programming.

PROCEDURE

A.   Divide the class into small groups of three or four persons.

B.   Ask each group to consider the question of violence on television. Each group should develop a definition of violence. They should then determine what kinds of behavior they would characterize as violent. Both of these should be noted on the student data sheet which is provided at the end of this exercise.

C.   Ask each group to assign members to different shows on television. Each should observe for an hour at a time. By dividing up the day and week, they will be able to sample a variety of times without becoming slaves to the set. They should simply tally the number of violent acts they see for the hour they are viewing.

D.   At the end of a week the students in each group should put their data together, drawing up some statistics for time of day, type of show, etc.

E.   The class discussion should be lively on the day the groups report their findings.

AGGRESSION ON TELEVISION: DATA SHEET

Definition of
violence:_____
_____
_____
_____

Some examples of behavior that is evidence of violence on TV:

_____
_____
_____
_____
_____

Make a note of the programs you watched during the week and the number of violent acts you observed.

PROGRAM	DAY	TIME	NUMBER OF VIOLENT ACTS

Exercise #4: The Prisoner's Dilemma

TO THE INSTRUCTOR:

A number of interesting variables may be observed when students play the Prisoner's Dilemma game. Within the groups you will see cooperation, and between the groups there will be competition. The students' meanness to opponents will create cognitive dissonance, which will become evident in their descriptions of those against whom they compete.

The students will attempt to deal with the dissonance by referring to their opponents by derogatory or even subhuman terms. In the column where they are asked to describe the other group, students will often use terms such as "fools," "nerds," "idiots," etc.

PROCEDURE

A.   Divide the class into an even number of small groups. Usually three persons to a group would be sufficient.

B.   The game consists of four rounds of play. Two groups will be paired for each round. Change the pairing for each round.

C.   Supply each group with an instruction and payoff sheet and also a record sheet to keep track of each round.

D.   After the game is over, see how each group did to determine who won and by what strategy--cooperation or competition.

E.   An interesting aspect of the game may be the type of descriptive terms used about the opponents. You may want to collect the forms and make a list for the students to reflect on during the next class session.

F.   Students should be given an opportunity to discuss how they felt and why they played the way they did.

THE PRISONER'S DILEMMA

Two prisoners, accused of a major jewel theft, are isolated from each other and are being pressured to give evidence against each other. Since there is not enough evidence to hold either one, if they both keep silent (cooperate), they will both go free and can split the booty. However, the prosecutor is offering immunity from prosecution as an inducement for one of them to squeal (compete). The squealer the goes free and keeps the jewels all to himself. If both squeal and testify against each other, then both will go to prison.

INSTRUCTIONS

1. You will play four rounds of this game. On each round, your group will play against one other group.

2. The goal is to win as many points as possible. During each round, your group must decide whether it will cooperate (be silent) or compete (squeal) with the other group.

3. The following table indicates your payoff. Remember that the score you get will depend not only on what your group does, but also on what the other group decides to do.

4. After each round, fill in the requested information on the record sheet.

PAYOFF-TABLE

	YOUR PAYOFF IF THE OTHER GROUP:	
WHEN YOUR GROUP:	**COOPERATES**	**COMPETES**
COOPERATES	+10 POINTS	-15 POINTS
COMPETES	+15 POINTS	-5 POINTS

THE PRISONERS'S DILEMMA: RECORD SHEET

DIRECTIONS

A.   Select someone in your group to:
1.   keep a record of your groups' decisions for each round on a piece of paper,
2.   fill in the information asked for on the chart below. The information should be entered at the end of each round. The description portion should be a group decision to be sure it expresses the feelings of everyone involved.

B.   Once the round has begun, the recorder should write the group decision on a piece of paper as soon as it is made. When the instructor gives the signal, both groups should reveal their decision at the same time.

C.   At the end of each round, the recorder should enter on the chart:
1.   the decision of the group--to cooperate or compete;
2.   the number of points won or lost in that round;
3.   two or three words that describe the members of the opposing group.

D.   After the fourth round, the recorder should enter the total number of points earned. Remember to subtract the negative points from the positive ones. It is possible to end up with a negative score.

ROUND	COOPERATE OR COMPETE	POINTS + OR -	DESCRIPTION OF OTHER GROUP
1			
2			
3			
4			

TOTAL POINTS _____

■ JOURNAL QUESTIONS

1. What behaviors do others expect of you? What "ascribed" roles do you have? What "achieved" roles? When have you experienced "role conflict"? What would happen to your "status" if you violated one of these expectations?

2. How do you feel when someone compliments you? What do you say? What do you do?

3. What do you feel is most important in selecting a mate? Why?

4. What general topics about yourself would you not be willing to disclose in class? Even in private to a few friends? Even in private to your best friend? Briefly describe the issue, not the specific information.

5. How have your attitudes changed since high school? What factors explain these changes or a lack of change?

6. Under what conditions, in which situations, or for what behaviors do you most often conform?

7. In what situations would you like to become more assertive?

8. When did you first fall in love? If it was romantic love, how long did it take until you fell out of love?

9. Who do you know that you regard as a prejudiced person? What is the nature of their prejudice? How do you think their prejudice developed? What are the disadvantages of a rigid personality structure?

10. When have you felt discriminated against? What was the situation? How did you react?

11. Describe a time in your life when you were extremely frustrated. Did you consider behaving aggressively? Why or why not?

12. What are your favorite television shows? Should scenes that merge violence and sexuality be made illegal?

13. Have you ever been in need of help? What happened? What was the situation? Did anyone help you? Why or why not? How did you feel when the problem was resolved?

■ SUGGESTIONS FOR FURTHER READING

Allport, G. *The Nature of Prejudice* (25th Anniversary Edition). Perseus, 1988.

Aronson, E. *The Social Animal*, 8th ed.. W. H. Freeman, 1999.

Baron, R. A. and D. Byrne. *Social Psychology: Understanding Human Interaction*, 9th ed. Allyn and Bacon, 1999.

Festinger, L. *A Theory of Cognitive Dissonance*. Stanford University Press, 1957.

Freedman, J. L., Taylor, S. E., Peplau, L. A., and D. O. Sears. *Social Psychology,* 10th ed.. Prentice-Hall, 1999.

Hall, E. T. *The Hidden Dimension*. Doubleday: Anchor, 1990.

Harvey, J. H. and G. Weary. "Current Issues in Attribution Theory and Research." *Annual Review of Psychology,* (35) 1984: 427-460.

Himmelfarb, S. and A. H. Eagly. *Readings in Attitude Change*. Wiley, 1974.

Hyde, J. S., and J. D. Delamater. "Love" in *Understanding Human Sexuality*, 8th ed. McGraw-Hill, 2002.

Matsumoto, D. *Culture and Psychology: People Around the World,* 3rd ed. Thomson, 2000.

Phelps, S. and A. Austin. *The Assertive Woman,* 3rd ed. Impact, 1997.

Seifert, K. *Training for Assertiveness*. Ash Gate Publishing Company, 1995.

Siegel, M. "Crime and Violence in America." *American Psychologist* (38) 1983: 1267-1273.

Worchel, S., Cooper, J., Goethals, G., and J. Olson. *Social Psychology*. Thomson, 2000.

Zimbardo, P. G. and E. B. Ebbesen. *The Psychology of Attitude Change and Social Influence*. McGraw Hill/Temple, 1991.

■ MEDIA SUGGESTIONS

ATTITUDES (2002, from *Psychology – the Human Experience,* Coast Community College District, 30 min.)
This video analyzes the formation of attitudes and how they can be turned into prejudice, as well as ways to prevent prejudice and appreciate diversity.

CONFORMITY, OBEDIENCE, AND DISSENT (2002, from *Psychology – the Study of Human Behavior,* Coast Community College District, 30 min.)
This video defines conformity, discusses how people view dissent, and explains how groups use rewards and punishments to enforce conformity.

GROUP INFLUENCE (2002, from *Psychology – the Human Experience,* Coast Community College District, 30 min.)
This video explains individuality, group behavior, and deindividuation.

HELPING AND PROSOCIAL BEHAVIOR (1989, Insight Media, 30 min.)
Defining reciprocity and social responsibility, this program explores why people help each other and considers the variables that moderate altruistic behavior. It discusses modeling effects and diffusion of responsibility, and investigates how mood influences helping.

A HISTORY OF SOCIAL CLASSES (2000, Films for the Humanities and Sciences, 52 min.)
Marx divided the industrial world into two antagonistic classes: the bourgeois and the proletariat. In today's society, this simple dichotomy fails to capture the many segments of a global marketplace. From the communal hunter/gatherers and agrarian cultures; to ancient empires and medieval fiefdoms; to the technocrats, executives, laborers, and others of the stratified modern world, this program examines how each era has organized its members into social classes. Although the opportunistic meritocracy of the global marketplace has displaced earlier societal models, do older patterns of privilege still linger?

HUMAN SEXUALITY (IT'S PERSONAL) (2000, Insight Media, 28 min.)
Sexuality is an integral part of human identity and a primary factor in human behavior. This video explores the development of sexual behavior and considers the range of sexual experience and preference that exists within contemporary human society. It also examines whether fear of the AIDS virus and other sexually transmitted diseases has altered patterns of sexual behavior.

THE POWER OF THE SITUATION (2001, from *Discovering Psychology Series,* Annenberg/CPB, 30 min.)
This video examines how situational forces affect beliefs and behavior. It presents footage of Lewin's study on leadership styles, Asch's work on situational conformity, Milgram's experiment on obedience, and Zimbardo's prison study. It also includes Constructing Social Reality, which looks at how mental processes shape one's interpretation of reality.

RACE AND RACISM (2001, Insight Media, 60 min.)
Exploring how the scientific understanding of "race" affects ethical considerations and census questions, this video attempts to define racism. It ponders explanations of racism as an act of will, a disease, a bad habit, or the product of historical economic forces; questions racism as an affront to justice; addresses the social and political status of people of mixed race; and stresses the difficulty of identifying subtly racist assumptions.

SOCIAL COGNITION (2002, from *Psychology – the Human Experience,* Coast Community College District, 30 min.)
This video focuses on how people form impressions of others and on how people's behavior is affected by attitudes.

SOCIAL INTERACTION MODEL (2001, Insight Media, 60 min.)
A social interaction model clarifies the dynamics and implications of human social behavior. This video presents a social interaction model designed to elucidate the way people interact in culturally diverse settings. It focuses on the five major components of the model and shows how they overlap.

SOCIAL PSYCHOLOGY (2002, from *Psychology – the Study of Human Behavior,* Coast Community College District, 30 min.)
This video shows how people's behavior is influenced by the social roles they play and by the norms or rules governing different roles.

UNDERSTANDING PREJUDICE (1996, Films for the Humanities and Sciences, 50 min.)
This thought-provoking program discusses the nature of prejudice and the effect it has on individuals and society as a whole. Begins with a historical overview and defines key terms such as prejudice, discrimination, and bigotry. Interviews provide insight into different kinds of prejudices and stereotypes. Some topics discussed include multiculturalism, homosexuality, politically correct language, the role of the media, and religion. Hear first-hand various opinions about prejudice, personal experiences of discrimination, as well as successful approaches to promoting tolerance.

A number of Videos are available from Thomson. Videos appropriate for this chapter include the following films from the CNN TODAY Introductory Psychology Video Series:

Volume 3, Section 11: Social Behavior
        Teen Culture (2:20)

Volume 4, Section 4: Prejudice
        Dragging Death (1:42)
        Campus Segregation (2:09)

■ COMPUTER AND INTERNET RESOURCES

PSYCHNOW!

Social Psychology
Helping Others
Attribution
Social Influence: Obedience and Conformity
Attitudes and Prejudice
Aggression

PSYK.TREK

Unit 12: Social Psychology
        12a: Attribution processes
        12b: Theories of love
        12c: Attitude change
        12d: Prejudice

INFOTRAC

Subject Guide/Key Terms: Social Psychology, Psychology and Culture, Role Conflict, Interpersonal Attraction, Self-disclosure, Attribution Theory, Fundamental Attribution Error, Social Influence, Groupthink, Milgram and Obedience, Door-in-the-face, Persuasion, Cognitive Dissonance, Astrology, Prejudice, Scapegoating, Aggressive Behavior, Prosocial Behavior, Evolutionary Psychology, Multiculturalism and Psychology

WEB SITES

Wadsworth Online Psychology Study Center:
http://info.wadsworth.com/coonessentials9

Center for the Study of Group Processes:
http://www.uiowa.edu/~grpproc/

Cultic Studies:
http://www.csj.org/

Racism and Prejudice: Psychological Perspectives:
http://aps.psychsociety.com.au/member/racism/contents.html

Social Psychology Archives:
http://clan.ch/ks/CPSP1.htm

Social Psychology Network:
http://www.socialpsychology.org/

AmoebaWeb Psychology Resources: Social Psychology:
http://www.vanguard.edu/faculty/ddegelman/amoebaweb/index.cfm?doc_id=873

Cultural Psychology Links:
http://www.socialpsychology.org/cultural.htm

Evolutionary Psychology: A Primer:
http://www.psych.ucsb.edu/research/cep/primer.html

CHAPTER 17

Applied Psychology

■ LEARNING OBJECTIVES

To demonstrate mastery of this chapter, the student should be able to:

1. Define the term applied psychology.
2. Describe the typical activities of an industrial/organizational psychologist.
3. Describe the activities of personnel psychologists by defining or describing the following areas:
   a. job analysis (include the term critical incidents)
   b. biodata
   c. personal interview (include the term halo effect)
   d. vocational interest text
   e. aptitude test
   f. multi-media computerized tests
   g. assessment center
      i. situational judgment tests
      ii. in-basket test
      iii. leaderless group discussion
4. Differentiate scientific management styles (Theory X) from human relations approaches (Theory Y) to management.
5. Contrast work efficiency *versus* psychological efficiency.
6. Define the terms participative management, management by objectives, self-managed teams, and quality circles.
7. List eight factors that seem to contribute the most to job satisfaction.
8. Explain the concept of flextime.
9. Discuss the four basic coping styles in making career decisions.
10. Explain how jobs may be enriched and what should be increased as a result.
11. Define organizational culture and organizational citizenship.
12. List and describe six ways to improve communication skills.
13. List and describe six ways to be a good listener.
14. Explain the main focus of environmental psychology, including three types of environments or settings of particular interest.
15. Define personal space.
16. Define proxemics, and describe the four basic spatial norms and the nature of the interactions that occur in each.
17. Define the term territoriality.

18. Discuss the results of animal experiments on the effects of overcrowding, and state the possible implications for humans.
19. Differentiate between crowding and density.
20. Define the term attentional overload, and describe the possible effects of noise pollution.
21. Explain how environmental assessment, architectural psychology, or even simple feedback can be used to solve environmental problems.
22. List eight strategies to promote recycling.

The following objective is related to the material in the "Exploring Psychology" section of the text.
23. Explain the concepts social trap and the tragedy of the commons. Explain how they can be avoided or escaped.

24. Discuss the psychology of law and identify topics of special interest.
25. Discuss the use of mock juries to examine the ways in which jurors reach decisions. Include four major problems in jury behavior discovered by jury research.
26. Define the term scientific jury selection, and describe four techniques commonly used to assess the potential usefulness of prospective jurors.
27. Describe what is meant by the term death-qualified jury.
28. Explain the ways in which a sports psychologist might contribute to peak performance by an athlete.
29. Define the term task analysis.
30. Define the terms motor skill and motor program.
31. List and explain six rules that can aid skill learning. Include the concept of mental practice.
32. Discuss the concept of peak performance.
33. List six ways for athletes to mentally improve performance.

The following objectives are related to the material in the "Psychology in Action" section of your text.
34. Describe the main focus of a space psychologist.
35. Describe some of the human factors that space station design must take into account. Include a discussion of the difficulties involved in having astronauts from different cultures living and working together.

■ DISCUSSION QUESTIONS

1. In your opinion, what are the advantages and disadvantages of flextime?

2. If you were selecting a person for a job, how would you try to ensure that the person's skills and interests matched those required by the position?

3. How is an aptitude test different from an interest inventory?

4.   How do people maintain a sense of distance from strangers when they are in crowded situations that force them into close physical proximity?

5.   How would you attempt to show that a specific personnel selection technique is both valid and reliable?

6.   Under what economic and interpersonal conditions would Theory X management be most successful in encouraging productivity? Under what conditions would Theory Y be most successful?

7.   What are the advantages and disadvantages of participatory management? Of management by objectives? Of quality circles?

8.   What can employers do to help their employees deal with stress and make appropriate career decisions?

9.   Why do you think people tend to "mark their territories? Under what conditions is such marking most important?

10.   What can a person do in a densely packed environment to reduce feelings of crowding?

11.   Should extra money be spent constructing buildings that accommodate the needs of people--or should people learn how to satisfy their own needs within cheaper, more energy-efficient buildings?

12.   What social traps can you identify in day-to-day experience? What could be done to change them?

13.   Garrett Hardin believes that it is a mistake to send food to countries wracked by famine. According to Hardin, this only allows the population of such countries to expand so that a later, larger disaster becomes inevitable. In your opinion, is it more or less humane to supply food under such circumstances?

14.   What kinds of incentives and reinforcers would motivate people to work harder to preserve their environment?

■ LECTURE ENHANCEMENTS

1.   **Hall's list of interpersonal space zones relates easily to everyday experience and thus needs little illustration.** Just the same, a few quick dramatizations can be worthwhile. To demonstrate the boundary of intimate distance, select a subject, preferably someone slightly shy. Have this person stand with his or her back to the wall. Then arrange four volunteers in a semi-circle, five or six feet from the subject and facing him or her. Move

the semi-circle of people in toward the subject in increments of about six inches. Ask the subject to indicate at what point a noticeable difference in comfort occurs or when (s)he feels that his or her personal space is being invaded.

2. **Relatively few psychological problems have manifested themselves among space crew members thus far; however, an analysis of the situation suggests that in the future, more, rather than fewer, psychological problems will arise.** This is because, in future missions, the reward/cost ratios will reverse themselves. That is, in the early missions, the psychological and physical costs to the astronauts were quite high, but so were the rewards. However, as space flight becomes increasingly routine and the number of individuals to visit space increases, the external rewards to astronauts will undoubtedly diminish more rapidly than their costs. Therefore, as the extrinsic rewards for space flight wane, it should become increasingly important to select candidates on the basis of positive psychological characteristics. As an interesting illustration of personnel selection issues, you could ask your students to generate a list of attributes that they think the successful astronaut of the future will need to possess. For more information on this subject, see R. L. Helmreich, "Applying Psychology in Outer Space," *American Psychologist,* April 1983: 445-450.

3. **Even when classroom seats are not assigned, there is a strong tendency for students to select a particular spot at the beginning of the semester and to occupy that place for the rest of the term.** While most of them are not conscious of their territorial behavior, they can be made aware of it by being forced to sit somewhere else. At the beginning of class, simply tell the students that you want everyone to sit in a different seat for that day. Instruct the people who typically sit in the back to come up to the front and vice versa. Ask those who usually sit on the left hand side of the room to move to the right and so forth. Then proceed with the class as usual. It won't be long before you begin to notice marked changes in the students' behavior. Normally talkative students will seem subdued; those that often ask questions will be quiet; the mood of the entire class will seem altered. Stop at this point and ask the students how they feel--they generally report feeling quite anxious and uncomfortable. This effect is particularly pronounced if it is toward the end of the semester and they have had plenty of time to get used to their seats. (You may even find it necessary to allow them to return to their usual places.) You might like to conclude the demonstration with a discussion of whether human territoriality is innate or learned.

4. **Students could be asked to play the role of an environmental or architectural psychologist and redesign the classroom.** It might be useful to begin with their initial perceptions of the environment--is it seen as a friendly place or cold and forbidding? Is it spacious or crowded? Cluttered or neat? What features contribute to these impressions? Then ask them to come up with modifications in the design of the room that would make it a more comfortable and/or effective learning environment. Have them consider ambient conditions that might readily be altered like lighting, noise level, and temperature as well

as the more permanent architectural features like walls, floor, ceiling height, and windows.

5. **Geographers have studied cognitive representation of the physical environment for centuries, but it is only recently that psychologists have become interested in cognitive maps and how they influence behavior.** Maps are by nature distortions of physical space, and it is thought that these errors reveal important information about the values and interests of the map-maker. Accordingly, it might be interesting to ask your students to draw a map of their college campus. After they are finished, students can compare maps with one another or you might provide actual copies of a map of the campus. Are there certain landmarks that were included on most students' maps? Were certain parts of the campus over-represented or more detailed than others (e.g. campus center, gym, library)? Were there any major aspects of the campus environment that were completely omitted from some students' maps? Do the students agree that a map such as this provides a measure of what is important to them? For an interesting look at how maps reveal what different societies consider important, see B. Nimri Aziz "Maps and the Mind," *Human Nature,* August 1978.

■ ROLE-PLAYING SCENARIOS

1. **You are an employer interviewing a new candidate for the manager of a videotape rental store.** A "job analysis" has been done and you are looking for a candidate who can schedule and supervise employees, maintain inventory, anticipate customer rental trends, and interact in a friendly manner with customers. What "critical incidents" would this employee have to cope with? What biodata would you need?

2. **You are an employer who believes in Theory X.** You are making your annual report to your employees. What would you say?

3. **A friend of yours has adopted the "complacent" style in selecting college courses.** He/she waits until the last day of registration and enrolls in whatever courses are left. The result is that he/she has taken many courses that may not meet the requirements for a specific major. Figure out a way to motivate your friend to become "more vigilant" in selecting courses and graduating.

4. **You are the chairperson of a new water conservation program.** Give a persuasive speech to the class encouraging them to participate in your program.

■ VALUE-CLARIFICATION STATEMENTS

1.   It costs the employer too much in extra utilities and other overhead to allow flextime.

2.   Employers need to pay employees more, even if that means providing fewer psychological benefits.

3.   Students and staff should eat in the same area, not in separate areas on campus.

4.   More tax money should be spent building additional prisons as a way to reduce overcrowding among prisoners.

5.   One day a week all citizens should be required to car pool or use mass transit systems.

6.   Fines should be increased for littering.

7.   Attempts to protect the environment should not be allowed to endanger businesses, jobs, or the economy.

■ ONE-MINUTE MOTIVATORS

1.   **Give students a series of interest inventories.** Ask them to look at their scores and decide which inventory "best" describes their perception of their interests.

2.   **Ask students to answer this question:** If you wanted to take a series of interest and aptitude inventories, what specific building on campus would you go to? Who would you talk to?

3.   **If possible, arrange chairs in class very close to each other.** Ask students to move their chair to make themselves comfortable. Demonstrate different preferences in personal space.

4.   **Give students a very short ungraded pop quiz on Chapter 17.** The next class session, ask them to take a similar quiz in pairs. Which quiz did they prefer? Would it have made any difference if the quiz were actually to count for their grade?

5.   **Give students the chance to decide on the kind of a quiz, exam, or written assignment they would like for this chapter.** Either students could quickly submit their preferences and you could make the decision based on majority vote or some class time could be spent having students discuss the issue and use consensus for making the decision. Briefly discuss the differences between teaching by objectives prepared by the instructor and teaching by having students participate in developing the goals and the ways to achieve the goals.

6.   **Ask students to write down on a slip of paper something that an instructor (or that you as the instructor) could do to "enrich" this class.**

7.   **Begin class by using a front desk where a student predictably always sits. Observe the reactions of that student.**

8.   **Bring poster board to class.** On the top write, "Graffiti Board" and tack the board to the wall. Write something on it. Observe and discuss the graffiti that develops over a week or two.

9.   **Hold class in a very small area.** Try to lecture as usual. Act a bit surprised when students act restless, uncomfortable, or frustrated. Discuss how it would feel to live in a very densely packed home.

10.   **Spend five minutes attempting to overload the class with sensory stimulation.** You can ask another instructor to class and introduce your double or triple lecture by saying, "Studies show the brain can process twice as much as information as it normally processes. Accordingly, Dr. ___ and I will lecture simultaneously. Take notes as well as you can." You also could ask students to bring to class "something that makes noise." The result could be a few tape recorders, radios, flashing lights, buzzers, etc. Ask everyone to "play them" simultaneously. Do people feel overwhelmed? Why or why not? Ask half of the class to take a graded quiz while the other half makes noise. Now do they feel overwhelmed? Why or why not?

11.   **Consider coming to class explaining that suddenly you have been asked to move our class to meet outside in some uncomfortable area for the rest of the semester.** Explain that you want the class to spend a few minutes helping you list reasons why the class should not be moved. Ask them to quickly get into groups and prepare a list of reasons. Then move on to lecture. The next meeting, mention how unified the class seemed. Admit that you had lied to them. Discuss both superordinate goals and the ethics of social research.

12.   **Assign each person in class a subtopic of this chapter or all of the chapters in the book.** Ask each person to develop five objective questions to be used for review for the quiz on this chapter or for the final. Remind students that the entire class is depending on each person. Make a few copies of their questions and put them on reserve to be used for studying for the quiz or final. Discuss mutual interdependence and cooperation.

■ BROADENING OUR CULTURAL HORIZONS

1.   **Within what kind of a society would Taylor's Theory X be most common?** A capitalist, a socialist, or a communist society? Why?

2.   **Research Japanese managerial techniques.** What are the advantages and disadvantages of the Japanese management style?

3.   **Many plants employ a very diverse mixture of people originally from many different parts of the world and cultural backgrounds.** What should a plant manager do to try to help this group of people work as an effective team?

4.   **How might a person's view of the world be affected by living in a dense and crowded urban environment?**

5.   **Some cultures expect personal touching to take place during conversations; others are literally repelled by touch.** What does your culture prefer? What would you guess happens when a person from a "touchless" culture contacts a person from a "touchy" culture?

■ SUPPLEMENTAL ACTIVITIES

This **exercise** is designed to help students better understand psychology as a profession and to assess its relevance to them as a career choice.

Exercise #1: What Do Psychologists Do?

Students have many misconceptions about what psychologists do once they receive their basic education. They also have some erroneous ideas about what it takes to become a practicing psychologist. A beginning course may whet their appetites and make psychology seem like a glamorous career to pursue. Every instructor has experienced students who, after the introductory course, decide to follow a career in psychology. **A realistic appraisal of what it takes to become a qualified practitioner and a look at the work done by psychologists may help students to make a better decision regarding the next step in their education.**

There are five suggestions here, any one of which could help students along the road. Which you do will depend on time and resources. However, some activity along this line would pay dividends.

1.   If you are a university or college with a graduate program in psychology, invite faculty and/or graduate students to participate in a panel discussion. Try to get as wide a variety of backgrounds and interests as possible to reflect the diversity in the field. Have the

students prepare questions ahead of time so that the time will be spent in a productive, non-repetitive discussion.

2.   A second type of panel which, though harder to put together, may be most rewarding is to invite a group of practicing psychologists from the community. You should look for persons in school systems, mental health clinics, industry, advertising, social services, research institutes, etc. Speakers should be asked to identify their area of interest and specialization, the kind of work they do, the education required to do the work, the salary range, the career advancement opportunities, etc. Allow students to ask questions. Some questions should have been preplanned to be sure pertinent information is elicited.

4.   Provide students with an up-to-date list of careers in psychology such as that put out by the American Psychological Association. Ask them to select an area they might be interested in pursuing or that they want to know more about. Send the students to the library, career placement center, or counseling office to gather information on that particular career. They should look for educational requirements, type of work done, salary range, and career advancement opportunities. Students should submit a written report and also report on interesting aspects of their findings to the class.

4.   Since most students will not be psychologists, a different approach might be interesting to pursue. Ask students to identify their career goals. Since many will be vague about this, you may have to do some work to get every student to settle on some specific area that is, at least, of interest to them.

Now your task is to convince the students that psychologists work in their area of interest either directly or indirectly. For example, if someone says (s)he wants a career in business, you can help them discover that there are psychologists in industry, advertising, personnel selection and training, etc.

Once the students have settled on a career choice and identified a psychological service that is provided to people in that field, have them research what the psychologist does. The idea is that they should discover what psychological services they can expect from a psychologist once they enter their career.

It may be possible for students with common career goals to work together on this project. Written papers should be submitted and an oral report given to the class.

5.   Send some or all of the students to interview some persons who work in psychological careers. The class as a whole should develop questions, and the interviewees should be carefully selected.

■ JOURNAL QUESTIONS

1. What hours would you like to work? What hours do you wish your parents or some of your friends worked?

2. Sketch your spatial bubble. How much distance do you usually place between yourself and others? What situations change the size of your spatial bubble?

3. Describe the behaviors of your "favorite" and your "most disliked" past employers. Who made you work most efficiently? Who made the job most enjoyable?

4. What kind of a job would be most satisfying to you? Why? What could your current or a past employer do to enrich your job?

5. Which coping style have you used thus far in make educational and career decisions?

6. If you don't live alone, what area in your apartment or home is "yours"? How is this area "marked"? What would you do if your roommate, spouse, child, or sibling invaded your territory?

7. What social traps are you enmeshed in? How could you try to get out?

■ SUGGESTIONS FOR FURTHER READING

Altman, I. *The Environment and Social Behavior: Privacy, Personal Space, Territoriality and Crowding.* Brooks/Cole, 1975.

American Psychologist. " Special Issue: Organizational Psychology." February, Volume 45 (2), 1990.

Bechtel, R. B. (Ed.) *Handbook of Environmental Psychology.* John Wiley & Sons, 2002.

Bolles, R. N. *What Color is Your Parachute?,* 32nd ed. Ten Speed Press, 2000.

Cox, R. *Sports Psychology,* 5th ed. McGraw-Hill, 2002.

Evans, G. W. *Environmental Stress.* Cambridge University Press, 1983.

Gifford, R. *Environmental Psychology: Principles and Practice,* 3rd ed. Optimal Books, 2002.

Hirschhorn, Larry. *Managing in the New Team Environment.* Addison-Wesley, 1991.

Lamberton, L. *Human Relations,* 2nd ed. McGraw-Hill, 2002.

Leunes, A., and J. R. Nation. *Sports Psychology,* 3rd ed. Thomson, 2002.

Levine, C. "Making City Spaces Lovable Places." *Psychology Today*, June 1984.

McCormick, E. J., and M. S. Sanders. *Human Factors in Engineering and Design,* 7th ed. McGraw-Hill, 1993.

Memon, A. *Psychology and Law.* McGraw-Hill, 1998.

Milgram, S. "The Experience of Living in Cities." *Science,* (167) 1970: 1461-1468.

Muchinsky, P. M. *Psychology Applied to Work: An Introduction to Organizational and Industrial Psychology,* 7th ed. Thomson, 2003.

Poindexter, J. "Shaping the Consumer." *Psychology Today,* May 1983.

Rice, B. "Why Am I in This Job." *Psychology Today,* January 1985.

■ MEDIA SUGGESTIONS

APPLYING PSYCHOLOGY IN LIFE (2001, from the *Discovering Psychology Series,* Annenberg/CPB, 30 min.)
This video discusses some of the innovative ways psychology is being applied to practical situations and professions in areas concerning human factors, law, and conflict negotiation.

BEHAVIORAL SCIENCES (1991, Films for the Humanities and Sciences, 23 min.)
Although we are unaware of it, we behave in accordance with some very precise programs that are deeply rooted in our genetic makeup. This program explores three aspects of behavioral sciences: innate as opposed to acquired behavior, social behavior, and behavior in the workplace. In all three cases, scientists have established close links between humans and animals as testimony to the distant origin of some of our behaviors.

CAREER EVALUATION (1997, Films for the Humanities and Sciences, 15 min.)
This program shows viewers how to relate their interests, skills, education, training, values, and lifestyle to specific occupations in the world of work. Based on the common-sense notion that you do best at what you really like to do, this video shows you how to find an occupation with job requirements that closely match your interests. Having a close match between your interests and abilities and the requirements of your job results in high job satisfaction. Before making career choices, it is important to know what your career will really be like. Shows you how to research the numerous sources of career information available today. A Cambridge Educational Production.

INSIDE THE CRIMINAL MIND (2001, Films for the Humanities and Sciences, 45 min. each)
This gripping three-part series enters the world of forensic psychology to illustrate how law enforcement officers and mental health professionals get inside the criminal mind. Captivating case studies from the U.K. and the U.S. provide a real-world context for the techniques and processes described. 3-part series, 45 minutes each.

KIDS AND RACE: WORKING IT OUT (1987, Films for the Humanities and Sciences, 52 min.)
This film shows how a weekend encounter group can help nine children from diverse backgrounds discuss their feelings about stereotypes and prejudice.

LEADERSHIP AND PEOPLE SKILLS (1996, Insight Media, 22 min.)
What is the difference between a leader and a manager? What qualities characterize an effective leader? This program analyzes the particular difficulties that leaders of professionals encounter and examines different approaches and models of leadership. It offers a range of practical ideas for leading professional colleagues.

MAKING PSYCHOLOGY PART OF YOUR LIFE (2002, from *Psychology – the Human Experience,* Coast Community College District, 30 min.)
This video examines how psychology can be applied to all areas of our lives.

ORGANIZATIONAL CULTURE (1999, Insight Media, 12 min.)
The culture of an organization — its values, attitudes, beliefs, and behavioral standards — develops in the same organic way as the cultures of the individuals who comprise it, and is just as resistant to change. Designed for leaders involved in implementing change, this video teaches how to identify leverage points in the culture of an organization and utilize them to achieve greater efficiency and productivity.

SCIENCE IN THE ARENA (1993, Films for the Humanities and Sciences, 23 min.)
Since the first Olympic Games, 2600 years ago, the goal of athletes has been to win; however, methods of winning have changed. This program shows three contributions of modern science to the feats of athletes: sports psychology, which uses various psychological techniques, such as, autosuggestion, rituals, mental imagery, and relaxation, that enable athletes to extend their physical limits; better health through more careful training, with adequate periods of rest and recuperation; and genetics, which can lead to the pre-selection of athletes who are genetically likely to be winners.

UNDERSTANDING PEOPLE (1990, Insight Media, 17 min.)
This program explains principles of human behavior revealed through Maslow's Hierarchy of Needs Theory, McGregor's X & Y Theory, and the Hawthorne Studies. It explores how these principles can be applied in leadership situations to enhance effectiveness.

■ COMPUTER AND INTERNET RESOURCES

PSYCHNOW!

Social Psychology
Environmental Psychology

PSYK.TREK

None are appropriate.

INFOTRAC

Subject Guide/Key Words: Applied Psychology, Industrial/Organizational Psychology, Proxemics, Personal Space, Flextime, Aptitude Test, Job Satisfaction, Environmental Psychology, Noise Pollution, Tragedy Of The Commons, Forensic Psychology, Jury Behavior, Psychology of Jury Selection, Sports Psychology, Psychology of Careers

WEB SITES

Wadsworth Online Psychology Study Center:
http://info.wadsworth.com/coonessentials9

Human-Computer Interaction Resources on the Net:
http://www.ida.liu.se/~miker/hci/

Industrial/Organizational Psychology:
http://psychology.about.com/cs/io/

Journal of Environmental Psychology:
http://www.academicpress.com/jep

Forensic Psychology Links:
http://www.oklahoma.net/~jnichols/forensic.html

Sports Psychology Web Resources:
http://www.fitinfotech.com/books/splinks.html

AmoebaWeb Psychology Resources: Applied and Forensic Psychology:
http://www.vanguard.edu/faculty/ddegelman/amoebaweb/index.cfm?doc_id=854

SOSIG: Organizational Psychology:
http://www.sosig.ac.uk/roads/subject-listing/World-cat/indpsych.html

Internet Survival Guide of Industrial/Organizational Psychology:
http://allserv.rug.ac.be/~flievens/guide.htm

APPENDIX A
Helpful References for Teaching Psychology

■ TACTICS, RESOURCES, DEMONSTRATIONS

Publications from the American Psychological Association

> *Activities Handbook for the Teaching of Psychology.* Washington, D.C.: APA, Vol 4, 1999.
>
> McGovern, T. V., ed. *Handbook for Enhancing Undergraduate Education in Psychology.* Washington, D. C.: APA, 1993.
>
> Meltzoff, J. *Critical Thinking About Research: Psychology and Related Fields.* APA, 1998.
>
> Puente, A. E., Matthews, J., & Brewer, C., eds. *Teaching Psychology in America: A History.* Washington, D. C.: APA, 1992.
>
> *Teaching of Psychology Newsletter.* A Publication of Division 2 of the APA.

Eble, K. E. *The Craft of Teaching: A Guide to Mastering the Professor's Art,* 2nd ed. San Francisco: Jossey-Bass, 1994.

Eison, James. "Confidence in the Classroom: Ten Maxims for New Teachers." *College Teaching,* 38(1), 21-25, 1990.

Erickson, S. C. *The Essence of Good Teaching.* San Francisco: Jossey-Bass, 1984.

Gardner, R. M. *Exercises for General Psychology.* Minneapolis: Burgess, 1980.

Gleitman, H. "Introducing Psychology." *American Psychologist* (39), pp. 421-427, 1984.

Griggs, R. A. (Ed.). *Handbook for Teaching Introductory Psychology,* Vol. 3. Erlbaum, 2002.

Hilsen, L. "How to Jump Start Discussions." *The Teaching Professor*, August/September, p. 7, 1991.

Hoover, K. *College Teaching Today.* Boston: Allyn-Bacon, 1981.

Lowman, J. *Mastering the Techniques of Teaching,* 2nd ed. Jossey-Bass, 2000.

Lucas, Ann F. "Motivating faculty to improve the quality of teaching." *New Directions for Teaching and Learning,* 37, 5-15, 1989.

Matthews, J. R., A. M. Rogers, and C. J. Scheirer. "Selected Resources for College Teachers of Psychology." *Teaching of Psychology* (13), pp. 3-7, 1986.

McKeachie, W. J., and G. Gibbs. *Teaching Tips*, 10th ed. Houghton-Mifflin, 1998.

Pintrich, Paul R. "Student learning and College teaching." *New Directions for Teaching and Learning,* 33, 71-861988.

Radford, J. and D. Rose (eds.). *A Liberal Science: Psychology Education Past, Present, and Future.* Open University Press, 1990.

Seldin, P. "Evaluating college teaching." *New Directions for Teaching and Learning,* (33), 47-561988.

Sheridan, Jean, Ann C. Byrne, and Kathryn Quina. "Collaborative Learning: Notes from the field." *College Teaching, 37* (2), 59-53, 1989.

Singer, B. A. "A practical annotated bibliography on college teaching and the teaching of psychology." *JSAS Catalog of Selected Documents in Psychology* (3) 1973: 34-35.

Toppins, Anne Davis "Teaching by testing: A Group Consensus Approach." *College Teaching,* 37 (3), 96-100, 1989.

Woods, P. (ed.). *Sourcebook on the Teaching of Psychology.* Association of Black Psychologists, 1989.

Young, R. E., & K. E. Eble (eds.). *New Directions for Teaching and Learning.* Jossey-Bass, 1988.

■ READERS

Banyard, P., & A. Grayson (ed.). *Introducing Psychological Research: Sixty Studies that Shape Psychology.* New York: Macmillan, 1996.

Chance, P., & T. G. Harris *The Best of Psychology Today.* New York: McGraw-Hill, 1990.

Duffy, K. G., (ed.). Dushkin Publishing Group. *Annual Editions: Psychology*. Guilford, CN: Dushkin/McGraw-Hill, 2002-2003.

Goleman, D., (ed.). *Psychology Updates* (articles from "The New York Times"). New York: HarperCollins, 1999.

Gross, R., (ed.). *Key Studies in Psychology.* New York: Hodder & Stoughton1994.

Hock, R. R., (ed.). *Forty Studies that Changed Psychology: Explorations into the History of Psychological Research,* 4th ed. New Jersey: Prentice-Hall, 2001.

Pettijohn, T. F. *Notable Selections in Psychology,* 3rd ed. Dushkin/McGraw-Hill, 2000.

Slife, B. D., (ed.). *Taking Sides: Clashing Views on Controversial Psychological Issues,* 12th ed.. Guilford, CN: Dushkin/McGraw-Hill, 2001.

Vitkus, J. *Casebook in Abnormal Psychology.* New York: McGraw-Hill, 1996.

■ FILM SOURCES

Annenberg/CPB
Corporation for Public Broadcasting
401 9th St. NW
Washington, DC 20004
1-800-532-7637
www.learner.org

Coast District Telecourses
11460 Warner Ave.
Fountain Valley, CA 92708
coastlearning@cccd.edu
(800) 547-4748
(714) 241-6109

CNN TODAY Introductory Psychology
Thomson Learning - Customer Service
PO Box 6904
Florence, KY 41022-6904
Tel: 800-354-9706
Fax: 800-487-8488
Email: esales@thomsonlearning.com

Films for the Humanities
P.O. Box 2053
Princeton, NJ 08540-2053
www.films.com
Email: costserv@films.com
(800) 257-5126
Fax: (609) 275-3767

Insight Media
2162 Broadway
New York, NY 10024-0621
(800) 233-9910

Magna Systems, Inc.
95 West County Line Road
Barrington, IL 60010
(800) 203-7060
Fax: (815) 459-4280

■ TRANSPARENCY ACETATES TO ACCOMPANY COON'S *ESSENTIALS OF PSYCHOLOGY, 9TH EDITION*

#	Figure/Table	Title
1	F I.1	The SQ4R study method
2	F I.2	Study skills checklist
3	T 1.1	The early development of psychology
4	F 1.3	Specialties in psychology; where psychologists work; what psychologists do
5	F 1.4	Operational definitions
6	F 1.5	Hypothesis testing
7	F 1.7	Correlation
8	F 1.8	Elements of a simple psychological experiment
9	T 1.6	Comparison of psychological research methods
10	F 2.1	Structure of a neuron
11	F 2.2	Action potential
12	F 2.3	Propagation of an action potential
13	F 2.4	Cross-sectional views of an axon
14	F 2.5	Structure of a synapse
15	F 2.6	The central and peripheral nervous systems
16	F 2.7	Subparts of the nervous system
17	F 2.8	Functions of the autonomic nervous system
18	F 2.9	A simple sensory-motor (reflex) arc
19	F 2.15	Relative size of the human cerebrum and cerebral cortex
20	F 2.19	Basic nerve pathways of vision
21	F 2.20	Hemispheric specialization
22	F 2.21	Information processing styles of brain hemispheres
23	F 2.22	Lobes of the cerebral cortex
24	F 2.23	Primary sensory, motor, and association areas of the cerebral cortex
25	F 2.25	The main structures of the human brain
26	F 2.26	Parts of the limbic system
27	F 2.28	Locations of the endocrine glands
28	T 3.1	Human growth sequence
29	F 3.2	DNA and the genetic code
30	F 3.3	Gene patterns for eye color
31	F 3.7	Typical patterns of motor development
32	F 3.9	Differentiation of emotion in infancy
33	F 3.13	Mother-infant and father-infant interactions
34	T 3.2	Piaget, a guide for parents

80	F 8.13	Forgetting after sleep and waking
81	F 8.14	The effects of interference on memory
82	F 8.15	Retroactive and proactive interference
83	F 9.1	Imagery in thinking
84	F 9.2	Storing and forming a visual image
85	F 9.8	The Stroop interference task
86	F 9.9	Animal phonemes from around the world
87	F 9.21	Culture-fair intelligence test
88	F 9.22	Distribution of Stanford-Binet IQ scores
89	F 9.23	Correlation of IQ scores among related people
90	F 9.26	Creative ideas combine originality with feasibility
91	F 10.1a,b	Needs, incentives, and drive strength
92	F 10.4	Hypothalamic areas associated with hunger and weight regulation
93	F 10.6	Body shapes as perceived by women with eating disorders
94	F 10.8	Arousal and performance
95	F 10.9	Maslow's hierarchy of needs
96	F 10.11	Primary and mixed emotions
97	T 10.3	Autonomic nervous system effects
98	F 10.17	Classic theories of emotion
99	F 10.19	Contemporary model of emotion
100	F 11.2	Eysenck's theory of personality
101	F 11.3	Source traits measured by Cattell's 16 PF
102	F 11.4	The "Big five" personality factors
103	F 11.6	Relationships between the id, ego, and superego
104	F 11.8	Congruence and incongruence
105	T 11.3	Four views of personality
106	F 11.10	MMPI-2 profile
107	F 11.11	Inkblot samples
108	F 12.1	Nine leading causes of death
109	T 12.2	Major health-promoting behaviors
110	F 12.3	Common reactions to frustration
111	F 12.5	Conflict diagrams
112	T 12.6	Social Readjustment Rating Scale
113	F 12.7	Biofeedback
114	F 12.8	The general adaptation syndrome
115	F 12.9	The stress game
116	F 13.1	Defining abnormality statistically
117	T 13.1	Selected psychological disorders
118	T 13.2	Major DSM-IV-TR categories
119	T 13.2	Major DSM-IV-TR categories
120	T 13.3	Personality disorders and typical degree of impairment
121	T 13.4	Anxiety disorders
122	F 13.4	Conversion reactions
123	F 13.7	Lifetime risk of developing schizophrenia
124	T 13.6	Classification of mood disorders